CAN RUSSIA CHANGE?

CAN RUSSIA CHANGE?

The USSR Confronts Global
Interdependence

WALTER C. CLEMENS, Jr.

Boston
UNWIN HYMAN
London   Sydney   Wellington

Unwin Hyman, Inc.
8 Winchester Place, Winchester, Mass. 01890, USA

Published by the Academic Division of
Unwin Hyman Ltd
15/17 Broadwick Street, London W1V 1FP, UK

Allen & Unwin (Australia) Ltd,
8 Napier Street, North Sydney, NSW 2060, Australia

Allen & Unwin (New Zealand) Ltd
in association with the Port Nicholson Press Ltd,
Compusales Building, 75 Ghuznee Street, Wellington 1, New Zealand

First published in 1990

Library of Congress Cataloging-in-Publication Data

Clemens, Walter C.
    Can Russia Change?: The USSR confronts global interdependence
by Walter C. Clemens, Jr.
    p. cm.
Includes index.
ISBN 0-04-445536-4.—ISBN 0-04-445537-2 (pbk.)
1. Soviet Union—Foreign relations—1985-   2. World
politics—1985-1995.   I. Title
DK289.C54   1989
327.47—dc20   89-33762 CIP

British Library Cataloguing in Publication Data

Clemens, Walter C.
    Can Russia change? the USSR confronts global independence.
    1. Soviet Union. Foreign relations. Policies of government
    I. Title
    327.47
ISBN 0-04-445536-4
ISBN 0-04-445537-2 Pbk

Typeset in 10 on 12 point Palatino by Fotographics (Bedford) Ltd
and printed in England by The University Press, Cambridge

Dedication

謹致愛妻

何麗蓮

Contents

[ix]

Tables and Figures

Acknowledgments

Many individuals and institutions have contributed to this study. I want to thank the following organizations for supporting portions of the research: Boston University; Harvard Center for Science and International Affairs; UCLA Center for Strategic and International Affairs; Rockefeller Foundation; U.S. Department of State; Harvard Russian Research Center; Kennan Institute for Advanced Russian Studies; Stanley Foundation; and American Enterprise Institute.

Many Fellows of the Kennan Institute and the Woodrow Wilson International Center for Scholars contributed to the surveys of Soviet and U.S. foreign policy discussed in chapter 1 and elsewhere in the book. Several Soviet scholars, some of them in internal or external emigration, as well as my friend from student days at Moscow University, Valerii N. Riabskii, have contributed to this study in many ways. Many individuals inspired or clarified much of the analysis: Andrei D. Sakharov, George F. Kennan, Howard Raiffa, Joseph S. Nye, Jr., and Jerome B. Wiesner. Conversations and correspondence with Kurt Campbell, José Garriga-Pico, B. Welling Hall, Sergei N. Khrushchev, Mark Kramer, Vojtech Mastny, Sergo Mikoyan, Stephen Meyer, Steven Rosefielde, and Stephen Shenfield have helped in understanding many of the issues studied here. Parts of the study were discussed by Richard Pipes, Gerhard Wettig, Robert V. Daniels, Alfred G. Meyer, Wladislaw Krasnow, and Robert Wesson at three meetings of the American Association for the Advancement of Slavic Studies.

Joe Nye, Kurt Campbell, and others at Harvard's Center for Science and International Affairs created a climate that nourished hard thinking and hard work, graced by a smile and comradery—just the right crucible for a study such as this to take shape. Hermann Fr. Eilts, Walter Connor, S. Frederick Starr, Roman Kolkowicz, and William Potter are among those who also helped to produce positive settings in which to work. An invitation from the Institute of World Economics and International Relations in Moscow in March 1989 permitted exploration of certain ideas in the manuscript with scholars there, the Institute for USA and Canadian Studies, and with scholars and political activists in Tallinn. My special thanks to Boris E. Messiia, Tiiu Pohl, Sergei E. Blagovolin, Aleksandr G. Saveleev, Raphael V. Vartanov, Viktor M. Sergeev, Rein Veidemann, Tiit Kabin, Aleksander Klauson, and Viacheslav V. Ivanov.

Boston University students Gerard Coyne, David Young, and Mark Jacobson assisted the research, Jacobson also doing the index. Students in Political Science courses 684 and 782 in 1988 and 1989 vetted the manuscript. Zhan Jun translated Chinese sources and provided calligraphy.

Lisa Freeman, Peggy McMahon, and Lauren M. Osborne at Unwin Hyman provided unfailing encouragement as well as solid professional judgment in bringing a bulky manuscript to print; Lois Smith carefully prepared it for publication. Shawn O'Neil found needed references.

In short, this study of interdependence has depended upon many persons who have shared their knowledge, energy, and resources and to whom I am very grateful.

Lai-Lin Ho Clemens asked the deepest questions and kept the home fires glowing, the rice steaming, the bills paid, the computers humming, did the graphics, and assisted with translations, while providing a global context far broader than the Soviet-U.S. perspective.

Introduction

Can Russia change? Can East-West relations be transformed so that they rest upon expectations of peaceful competition—even upon cooperation—rather than zero-sum struggle? For such a transformation to occur, what changes must first take place within the Soviet Union? In the West? In the realms of science, culture, and economics, which transcend but also include the two military superpowers? And if such a transformation commences, what are the factors that must be present to ensure that it becomes an enduring structure of peace and not merely a passing dream? These are the central questions explored in this book.

Soviet analysts ask whether their country can change in such a way that the first socialist state remains a great power. They worry that the USSR, in achieving military parity with the United States, has lost the ability to compete in the other domains that constitute the most relevant sources of influence in the modern world: economic and technological vitality founded in an "information society" where knowledge flows are not obstructed by bureaucracy; a capacity to protect the environment; moral strength and education. Completely reversing Marx, they contend that the USSR's political democratization is the precondition for its economic revival.[1]

Americans and Soviets, sobered by the fate of the rise and fall of other great powers,[2] are coming to understand that a wise security policy will endeavor to protect and enhance a country's values and way of life. Guarding society against armed violence and coercion, it will also be concerned for environmental, economic, health, and other dangers to society. It must balance immediate costs against more remote dangers. It may even have to look to outsiders' well-being for as the world shrinks, our neighbors' problems can quickly become our own.

As early as 1848 Karl Marx asserted that the "bourgeoisie has through its exploitation of the world-market given a cosmopolitan character to production and consumption in every country." Capitalism, said the *Communist Manifesto*, was destroying or had already destroyed the national basis for production and consumption: "In place of the old local and national seclusion and self-sufficiency, we have intercourse in every direction, universal interdependence of nations. And as in material, so also in intellectual production. . . . National one-sidedness and narrow-mindedness become more and more impossible."[3]

Herein lies a profound challenge for all countries: how to reconcile traditional views of "security" with the imperatives of a world exploding with escalating interdependencies? Confronting this challenge is especially difficult for the USSR. The Soviet regime, more than most other governments, has sought to advance its objectives without becoming economically, politically, or culturally dependent upon an international system that, even by 1848, was driven by the cosmopolitan imperatives of capitalism. How does one protect one's own system if survival requires integration, in whole or in part, with an alien system? What should security planners do if some values and parts of their country's life styles are anachronistic—not optimal even for survival? And what if the stakes include not only the security of the country but that of the ruling elite, the self-proclaimed "dictatorship of the proletariat" or, in softer phrasing, the "vanguard" of the working class? These are issues that have confronted Kremlin leaders with increasing force as the material and informational foundations of modern life change at an ever faster pace.

Security choices become increasingly complex as global forces shrink time and space and leap national borders. Does "best safety lie in fear" (as Laertes advised Ophelia) or in recognition of common problems and cooperation with others to minimize dangers and exploit opportunities that transcend national borders? Soviet Foreign Commissar Maxim Litvinov argued in the 1930s that "peace is indivisible."[4] But all countries are tempted, like the hunter in Rousseau's parable, to seize the hare at hand for private gain even though the resulting commotion drives off the stag that could have provided a common bounty.

Responding to these dilemmas, Mikhail S. Gorbachev, general secretary of the Soviet Communist party since March 1985, has contended that security between the superpowers can only be "mutual" security. If one side feels insecure, the other's safety is jeopardized. As regards the security of other nations, it can only be "universal." He affirms that all peoples are "interdependent"—with a potential to help or harm one

[xvi]

another. Nearly espousing John Donne's position—"No man is an island"—Gorbachev holds that no nation can live apart from the main.

Other views are also alive in the USSR. Thus some components of the Soviet Defense Ministry still indoctrinate their men to "hate the class enemy—imperialism."[5] Perhaps to sustain this hate, hazing of first-year recruits remains a brutal fact of Soviet army life, one that leads occasionally to murder and suicide.[6] Outsiders must wonder whether Gorbachev's statements are a smoke screen for militarism, whether the Politburo and Defense Ministry are at loggerheads, or whether political commissars have not yet been told to alter their standard operating routines.

Gorbachev's use of "interdependence" approximates the definition used in this book: Interdependence is a condition of *mutual vulnerability*. It may be symmetrical or asymmetrical—a long-term vulnerability (as to the Damocles sword of nuclear weapons) or a possibly short-lived sensitivity that can be countered by policy changes. When two or more countries interlock in specified ways, we may even talk of "complex interdependence"—a condition discussed in more detail in chapter 11.[7]

The Brezhnev regime in the 1970s affirmed that the USSR is interconnected with the West and that East and West are mutually vulnerable. However, it regarded the word "interdependence" as a mask for neocolonialism and rejected calls for North-South cooperation.[8] Under Gorbachev "interdependence" has acquired a positive connotation, and his regime talks of cooperation joining socialist, capitalist, and nonaligned developing countries—in brief, policies based on global interdependence.

Gorbachev pulled together several threads of his "new thinking" in a January 15, 1988 meeting with members of the International Fund for the Survival and Development of Humanity gathered in Moscow for their founding session.

> The developments in the present-day world where everything is interconnected and interdependent are undoubtedly making a strong impact on each country, on the processes there and, finally, on world politics as a whole. It is only by taking into consideration this interconnection and interdependence that one can plan his future, can draw up plans relying not only on the forces inside his own society, but also on cooperation with other nations. This is especially important [because] many problems have been accumulated that are of an international character. We usually call them all-human problems because they are facing the whole of civilization.

There is a growing awareness of the need for cooperation, said Gorbachev, even while "remaining committed to one's choice—social, ideological, and religious." Each nation has a "destiny" and "traditions of its own" which other nations must respect, including the largest. Indeed, "the bigger the country, the greater its responsibility before its own people and before other peoples."[9]

These and other aspects of what Gorbachev calls the "new political thinking" could provide key elements for a new paradigm for approaching statecraft and international relations. As Albert Einstein noted long ago, our social and political thinking lags the development of nuclear power and other scientific-technological revolutions of our era. To survive and prosper we may need a revolution in the way that governments approach policy and the ways that scholars study world affairs. Although the quality of life (at least by some measures) for many people is improving around the globe, potentially catastrophic perils—military, environmental, and other—loom like gigantic waves threatening to overwhelm and perhaps blot out human civilization.

But other, more immediate questions intrude. Leaving aside for a moment the truth and utility of Gorbachev's views, should they be taken at face value? Does he intend them as contributions to a long-term cooperative strategy in which the USSR will forgo unilateral for common advantage or—as in the 1918 Brest-Litovsk Treaty—are they meant only as tactics to gain "breathing space" in which to nurture Soviet power for a forward strategy? And assuming that Gorbachev *wants* to put Moscow on the track toward global cooperation, can he do so? Can he muster and sustain the necessary support within the USSR to pursue this course over time? And will he find the positive response and reciprocity in the outside world on which a cooperative strategy will ultimately depend?

Firm answers to these questions await the test of time, but past patterns shed light on the range of possible developments. Changes in the Kremlin's policy orientation have been propelled in part by outcomes—by successes and failures at home and abroad. There is an urgent need for change in Soviet foreign as well as domestic policy. As thoughtful persons begin to speak out freely in the USSR, they articulate many of the same criticisms long made by outsiders. In chapter 1 I attempt to outline the major achievements and failures of Soviet foreign policy since 1917 and to delineate the underlying reasons behind these patterns. Soviet leaders' main achievement has been to maintain their rule in the face of internal dissatisfaction and external threat, especially in the first years of the regime and during World War II. This accomplishment has been facilitated by the Kremlin's ability to marshal the human and material resources of a vast country, but this asset is Janus-faced. It is the flip side of a centralized system that has inhibited individual creativity and which breeds distrust and hostility among Russia's neighbors. The same system that helps the

Kremlin to impose its will at home and along the Soviet borderlands also raises the costs of protecting Soviet security from internal and external foes.

Lenin taught that the fundamental question of politics is *"Kto kovo"*—Who, whom? Which side will destroy the other? Armed with this view, he and his successors built a system that could seize and hold power but not one that interacts optimally with other states and systems or even with its own subjects. Fear and coercion have backfired at home and abroad. Gorbachev's campaigns for *glasnost'*, democratization, and mutual security seek to reduce these costs and to accelerate modernization of the USSR. Whether such campaigns can overcome the inertia of long-standing behavioral and cultural traditions remains to be seen.

Chapter 2 finds that the Soviet leaders pursued seven major approaches to foreign policy since 1917, from the forward strategy of War Communism to the trade *cum* arms control orientation of the 1970s. In the early 1980s, however, a defiant inversion came to dominate Soviet policy toward the West while in the Third World the Kremlin endeavored to prop up the left-wing governments its forward strategy had helped to install in the 1970s. Global interdependence was the abstract dream of a few technocrats and scholars while hard-line militancy dominated at home and in foreign policy.

Still, Gorbachev's predecessors rarely pursued any orientation in its purest form across the board; rather, they picked and chose, calibrating strategy and tactices to time and place. Thus Moscow has often sought détente with the West at the same time that it sought to support "anti-imperialist" activities in Asia and Africa. The Kremlin has hoped to have the best of both worlds: trade with the First World combined with enhanced Soviet influence in the Third World. Such pragmatism could have advantages, but it has often produced contradictory policies that garnered few gains in either sphere. Thus the combination of Soviet policies toward Washington and Cairo in the early 1970s undercut détente with the West *and* led to a sharp decline in Moscow's military and political ties with Egypt.

A new orientation has emerged under Gorbachev: espousal of mutual security in an interdependent world. This approach has roots in earlier policies, but it is in some ways unprecedented. Developments within and outside the USSR will help to determine whether the new orientation takes root and overcomes the *"kto kovo?"* attitudes shaping previous Soviet strategies. Even if Gorbachev wishes to pursue a consistent strategy oriented toward mutual security and interdependence, this plan could be vitiated by domestic turmoil, revolts in Eastern Europe or in the non-Russian republics, or the pressures and temptations to utilize other policy emphases—especially toward Third World targets of opportunity.

International relations proceed on many levels. This book examines major cases from "high" and "low" politics. High politics centers on nation-states and their struggle for power; low politics, by contrast, is concerned with the myriad ways that governments and nongovernmental actors interact on "functional," trade, scientific, and other interests without great manifest political or military import, from expediting the mail to halting epidemics. These interests, it turns out, are often of more immediate consequence to our daily lives and material well-being than the jostling of governments to enhance their power or to work their will on others. Soviet behavior on both levels has manifested tremendous continuity but also a capacity for significant change.

Our case studies illustrate the interaction of high and low politics in Soviet relations with the outside world. They also seek to shed light on the question: How does security cooperation arise in a world that is anarchic—without any central authority? Fear of nuclear arms is part of the answer but does not account for security cooperation in pre-nuclear times.[10]

In the realm of high politics chapters 3 and 4 trace the factors that have conditioned the quest of both tsar and commissar for security through arms control. History shows that ideological and propagandistic consider-ations have sometimes shaped the Kremlin's interest in arms accords but that strategic-military factors have—at least until the mid-1980s—been the most decisive considerations shaping Soviet arms control policies. To the extent that the USSR believes it has a credible deterrent and that further arms competition is unlikely to improve Moscow's relative power, economic and other incentives have pushed the Kremlin toward arms controls that could enhance mutual security. Domestic political struggles have sometimes narrowed Kremlin incentives to explore arms control seriously, but most Soviet leaders since Stalin have viewed détente and arms limitation as a dependable way to muster domestic support.

The Kremlin's security policies have long been driven by the realization that, as the Central Committee put it to Mao Zedong's regime in 1963: "The nuclear bomb does not adhere to the class principle." Moscow has been slower to recognize the degree to which environmental and other global problems threaten all humanity. Many of Russia's scientists and some of its statesmen have for centuries displayed a kind of cosmic consciousness, but it has often been drowned out by messianism—tsarist and then Communist. Returning from France in the early 1920s, geochemist Vladimir Vernadskii authored *The Biosphere* (1926), but even he expressed little alarm about the impact of "development" upon Russia's environmental health until the 1940s. Despite a Russian tradition of "cosmicism," Soviet political spokesmen long maintained that environmental, demographic, and other problems abroad arose from the contradictions of societies where socialism had not yet triumphed.

Beginning with chapters 5 and 6 this book investigates the responses of Soviet political figures and scientists to the "low politics" challenges of global interdependence. In the 1970s Soviet ideologists affirmed the "interconnected" and "interactive" nature of "global problems," but they generally condemned Western studies such as *The Limits to Growth* for lacking a Marxist class perspective. Despite the caveats of Soviet propagandists, some Soviet scientists in the 1970s took leading roles in inaugurating East-West-South studies of global linkages.

Even in the 1970s Soviet writings on global problems were not monolithic. Brezhnev threw his weight behind the dominant school— détente and trade with the West—but there were other voices and inflections: autarkic withdrawal to a Mother or "Fortress Russia" (Aleksandr Solzhenitsyn and some officials); a forward strategy in the Third World regardless of the consequences for East-West relations; a truly global interdependence (Andrei Sakharov and some officials). The complex reality of Soviet policy contained elements of all these approaches even though the dominant emphasis was on the "interconnection" between East and West.

After Afghanistan, U.S.-Soviet tensions rose and some Soviet spokesmen showed less enthusiasm for East-West cooperation.[11] By1980 Soviet ideologists claimed that a new discipline had been born in the USSR—*globalistika*—a Marxist approach to global problems. High priests of globalistics argued that global problems could not be fully resolved until the world triumph of socialism, when they would become part of "pre-history." This became the dominant line in Party publications in Brezhnev's last year and under Yuri Andropov. Some technocrats and scientists managed to continue their participation in global cooperation networks, sometimes defending their work as "systems analysis" trans-cendent of class and ideology. Bowing before the icon of the Scientific-Technological Revolution (STR), some Soviet officials and scholars continued and even intensified their contacts with international institutions which facilitated East-West-South studies of common problems.

Soviet parochialism intensified during the confrontationalist early 1980s. Andropov's brief tenure as general secretary witnessed a hardening of Soviet policies toward nearly every region and set of foreign policy problems. This orientation softened somewhat under Konstantin Chernenko, who even allowed that East-West cooperation might be useful in dealing with Third World hunger, as in Ethiopia.

This opening was broadened by Gorbachev, who became the first Soviet leader to speak consistently of interdependence as a potentially positive feature of modern life, one that should be used wisely to cultivate common interests of East, West, and South. The need for global co-operation has existed for years, but it has been perceived by the Gorbachev regime with greater clarity and urgency than under his predecessors. Economic necessity seems to have been the mother of such learning. In April 1985 Gorbachev told the Communist party that a "revolution" was needed in the way that science and technology are applied to the Soviet economy. The USSR, he declared later that year, is "interdependent" with the United States (not merely "interconnected"). He proceeded to enlarge on this theme, calling for an all-embracing system of international economic security as well as military security. Symptomatic of the new outlook (as noted in chapter 7), Gorbachev asked the president of the Club of Rome in late 1986 for advice on how the USSR could deal with its "pandemic problem of unemployment in a humane way."

Despite some opposition at all levels of Soviet society, Gorbachev was pushing through a veritable revolution in Soviet ideology. But was he serious? The Kremlin's public relations campaigns and Moscow's support for the total abolition of nuclear arms raised serious questions about Soviet intentions, for it is difficult to believe that Gorbachev genuinely wished to eliminate the nuclear guarantee that no rational foe will deliberately attack the USSR. Although total nuclear disarmanent may seem utopian to believers in *Realpolitik*, Gorbachev's deeds often harmonized with his words. The general secretary suspended nuclear testing for eighteen months while vainly challenging the White House to join a test mora-torium; he sacrificed more missiles than the United States and made many other concessions to bring Washington to conclude a treaty eliminating intermediate nuclear forces; the Kremlin accepted a system of on-site inspection of the INF Treaty so radical that the United States wished to reduce its scope; Moscow permitted American observers to look first hand at the Krasnoyarsk radar that Washington said was a violation of the ABM Treaty; and in a related sphere the USSR withdrew its military presence supporting a Marxist regime on its border.

Following up a September 1987 Gorbachev proposal for strengthen-ing the United Nations, Deputy Foreign Minister V. F. Petrovskii acknowledged that the USSR had been wrong not to pay for peacekeeping operations. We are paying up. We were wrong toward international civil servants. Now we accept permanent contracts. We consider that the whole UN Charter should be fulfilled, not just parts we like. We were wrong to oppose an active role for the Secretary General.

We want a new system for comprehensive security. We need a stable structure for international affairs and we see the UN as a major way of achieving it. We want an international verification agency of a new nature, not only to monitor arms control but also for crisis management. There will need to be staff, inspectors, equipment on a regular basis.

Decades earlier the Soviets opposed a standing UN military force. Since 1985, Petrovskii now says,

We see that interdependence matters; we no longer have a simple picture. We are working very hard to overcome this enemy image which was created on both sides.

Wars make no sense. Each system [capitalist and Communist] is evolving in terms of its domestic affairs. That's the only way to prove which system is better in the long run. You can't export revolution or counterrevolution [in a world of global dangers].[12]

All these words and deeds were virtually "unthinkable" a few years before; now they had become a part of the "restructuring" of Soviet foreign policy.

The major test of each side's intentions in the Reagan-Gorbachev years was the American-Soviet negotiations on intermediate nuclear forces. The 1987 INF Treaty invites a reexamination (attempted here in chapter 9) of the conditions that make arms agreements possible. The INF Treaty marked virtually the first instance of superpower disarmament under mutual inspection. The accord by itself eliminates only a small fraction of each side's missiles, but it could be a step toward larger arms reductions. Limited disarmament—not merely arms freezes—was proven feasible. The movement toward the treaty undermines many of the "conditions" that analysts have posited as necessary or sufficient for arms control. We must rethink such questions as these: What is the place in arms negotiations for unilateral concessions and for hard bargaining? What is the role of economic incentives? Which of the "old rules" may now be thrown overboard? Which of them still holds? What are the new lessons for the future?

The INF Treaty sets out a detailed system of on-site inspection. A more far-reaching accord on strategic arms, however, would probably require much more comprehensive verification measures. In chapter 10 I review the record and ask to what extent Moscow and Washington have lived up to their past arms control commitments. I also ask what could be the incentives tempting either side to evade arms control obligations.

Ultimately, perceived self-interest will shape Soviet and U.S. behavior, but enlightened self-interest should steer each side away from myopic dreams to gain strategic advantage and toward arrangements that contain the arms competition to mutual gain.

A new model for Soviet-U.S. relations may be emerging in the late 1980s, one that pushes the superpowers toward cooperation in areas of low and high politics. Each side confronts its weaknesses: the USSR is unable to feed its starving clients in Ethiopia, southern Africa, and Vietnam. America's vaunted space program is in need of a boost—indeed, of many boosters—to place its satellites into orbit. The USSR has the boosters; the United States has the high-tech equipment that needs boosting. Confronted by acid rain and a depleted ozone layer, the superpowers and most countries have perceived a need for pollution controls to conserve their common habitat.

High politics pulls Moscow and Washington in a similar direction: As Washington and Moscow become less concerned about military threats from each other, they can become more attuned to security and other threats from other sources. Each superpower is losing relative economic and political power. Among the reasons are the burdens of empire and the costs of arms competition. Both sides share some interest in minimizing chaos and the struggle for influence in the Persian Gulf, South Africa, the Middle East, and Central America. They certainly share an interest in curtailing proliferation of nuclear and other sophisticated arms.

How will Soviet-Western relations fare for the rest of this millennium? Can they escape the cyclic oscillation between limited détente and confrontation that has prevailed for decades? In chapter 11 I review this pattern and the factors that have driven the superpower roller coaster from euphoric peaks to rapid descents. Sources of change include the evolving structure of world politics, the permissive nature of international regimes, domestic factors, and the world beyond the superpowers. But most zigs and zags in Soviet-U.S. relations have been brought on by catalytic events foreseen by few analysts and seldom planned for by both sides—events such as the Hungarian revolution and the Cuban missile crisis. Analysts of world affairs must therefore be not only modest but cautious in projecting "alternative futures," and planners must think extremely broadly about how to contain the repercussions of wild cards in the deck.

Moscow and Washington stepped back from confrontation in the mid-1980s, and conditions arose that made it possible to create a détente along the lines of the early and mid-1970s. Chapter 11 considers the ways in which the new détente could be consolidated, how it could be deepened into a movement towards a model of "complex interdependence," and how it could revert to even more tense confrontation than existed in the early 1980s.

East-West relations are unlikely to plateau on détente. Either they will move toward consolidation of a structure of peace and cooperation or they will revert to confrontation triggered by competition in a still bipolar world. Transformation of the Soviet-U.S. relationship into a mutually beneficial complex interdependence may depend upon transformations of both countries' political cultures and acceptance of a new paradigm of global security and interdependence. Change of this depth and magnitude is difficult to conceive, but then most of the changes in the superpower relationship have been difficult to foresee.[13]

Moscow's "new thinking" has generated new ways of looking at security and interdependence. Here, as in the realm of arms control, opportunities probably abound for East, West, and South to move from confrontation toward mutually beneficial cooperation.

The United States as well as the Soviet Union faces severe challenges to its self-image and its relationship with the other superpower and with the rest of humanity. Suggested in chapter 12 is a way out of these dilemmas through the "mutual aid" doctrine espoused by Petr Kropotkin at the turn of the last century and the "value-creating" strategy proposed for negotiators by Howard Raiffa.[14] Treating others as adversaries in a zero-sum game, the record shows, is not the optimal way to enhance national interests; rather than claiming values from the other side, each political actor would gain more in the long run from a strategy in which each party sought to create values useful to all parties. This lesson fairly leaps from Soviet involvements abroad since 1917. It is reinforced by a comparison of U.S.-European successes with the Marshall plan (total cost to Washington: under $15 billion) with the short-lived gains of Soviet withdrawals from Eastern Europe after the war (worth perhaps $20 billion).

The title of this book focuses on Russia because Russian nationals and culture continue to dominate Soviet policies, even though (as we shall see) Georgians, Kirghiz, Estonians, and other national minorities have sometimes played key roles as policy innovators. For such innovations to bear fruit, however, they must enjoy at least the acquiescence of the Russian-dominated top leadership. A second reason for the focus on Russia is to underscore the impact of the past on the present and future of Soviet policy. The burden of Russian culture and traditions probably weighs heavier on the Kremlin's capacity for change than do the less deeply rooted influences of Marxism-Leninism-Stalinism. I shall therefore review aspects of tsarist as well as Soviet history that bear on the challenges of security with interdependence. A third reason is to acknowledge the

[xxv]

reality: some border republics seek autonomy or even independence from Russia. The USSR may not endure as we have known it.

Can Soviet foreign policy change without parallel development in the internal life of the USSR? This book focuses on foreign policy issues, but the domestic crucible cannot be ignored. In principle the Kremlin may use foreign policy for domestic purposes or vice versa. The respective weight of both domains and the ways they shape each other have changed over time. To judge by Gorbachev's words and deeds, his foreign policies have been calculated so as to facilitate perestroika—a broad restructuring of Soviet life. But the results of policies at home and abroad will surely affect each other, giving rise to new versions of "new thinking" and new policies. Policy initiatives will probably have to proceed largely from the top down, but to take hold they must receive support from the middle-level bureaucracy and ultimately from the mass of Soviet citizens—including non-Russians.[15] As Soviet society becomes more pluralistic and more open, resistance to change may become formidable by those whose interests are vested in "things as they are."[16]

Although this book focuses on Russia and the Soviet system, the key role of the other superpower is implicit on nearly every page. Often it is the American example or action that Moscow seeks to emulate or check; often it is the prospect of American acquiesence or countermove that inspires a Kremlin decision to act or to stay put. Whether Russia changes and how is mostly for Russians and other Soviet citizens to decide, but U.S. and other outside influences are important at every juncture.

Policy dilemmas for the United States as well as for the Soviet Union are considered in chapter 12. The root question for both societies is this: Shall we work with or against the other. Americans wonder, for example, if their interests are better served by a weak, unreformed Russia or by one that has been restructured and energized. Lawrence S. Eagleburger, for example, told the Senate Foreign Relations Committee in March 1989 that "the only purpose that explains [Gorbachev's] policy is to create a stronger, more efficient Soviet Union."[17] But this is a simplistic view, for virtually every government has such purposes, including the United States and its allies. The deeper question is whether a reformed and strengthened Russian state—remolded in the context of global interdependence—would be more likely to cooperate with or struggle against the West.

Both sides will no doubt choose to test the waters and the waves before discarding old security thinking. Still, what some Soviet scholars now say about a united Germany (not so impossible as Europe unites) may apply also to the USSR. They maintain that the Scientific-Technological Revolution (STR) makes territorial expansion outmoded: neither Germany

[xxvi]

nor Japan now feels any drive for *Lebensraum*. Were a united Germany to threaten its neighbors, it would lose its customers and incite them to unite against Germany. Prosperity as well as influence comes from nonmilitary factors, beginning with the information society.[18]

Perhaps the time has come for Washington as well as Moscow to remove the ideological sting from their confrontation. As Politburo adviser Georgii Shakhnazarov observes, capitalist and socialist *systems* do not deal with each other, but specific *governments* do. The very idea of a capitalist or social system is highly abstract and leads to a kind of ideological racism dividing everything and everyone into "ours" and "not ours"—from scientific achievements to the cut of trousers. Socialism, Shakhnazarov notes, was born from capitalism and in time has modified it. His point is that the two "systems" need not be perceived as in a zero-sum contest. "We are different but not opposites."[19]

My own reading is that a Soviet system that is more open, more democratic, and more affluent would present a smaller threat to the outside world—and offer a much better partner for addressing global problems—than one that is closed, dictatorial, totalitarian, and spartan. The utility of trade embargoes is limited; they are hard to maintain and easily punctured; they provide little incentive for the Kremlin to alter its behavior on matters of vital interest to Moscow because they can affect Soviet development only marginally; and they can hurt U.S. commercial interests while compelling the Soviets to become more self-reliant. Washington's main concern should be to put the United States at the leading edge of science and technology; meanwhile all Western countries should welcome a USSR attempting to restructure its life into the global web of complex interdependence in which military force plays a declining role.

Notes

Transliteration from Russian to English basically follows the Library of Congress system except with respect to names of some well-known figures, such as Trotsky.

1. Natal'ia A. Dolgopolova and Andrei A. Kokoshin, "Chemu uchat sud'by velikikh derzhav?" *Kommunist*, no. 17 (November 1988): 115–21. The tenor of this essay captures the sentiments found in many discussions in 1988–89 with Soviet specialists from the Institute of World Economics and International Relations (IMEMO) and the Institute for USA and Canadian Studies in Moscow and also at Harvard University.

2. The essay cited in note 1 is a commentary-review of Paul F. Kennedy, *The Rise and Fall of the Great Powers* (New York: Random House, 1987). The Soviet reviewers find fault in details but esteem the big picture, particularly its implications for the USSR. The Kennedy book gives rise to much commentary in the West, some of it cited in later notes.

3. Although this English translation of the *Communist Manifesto* was approved by Engels, the German reads "general [all-sided] dependence of nations upon each other" (An die Stelle der alten lokalen und nationalen Selbstgenuegsamkeit und Abgeschlossenheit tritt ein allseitiger Verkehr, eine allseitige Abhaengigkeit der Nationen voneinander). The Russian version of the *Manifesto* comes closer to the German: "Prikhodit . . . vsestoronnaia zavisimost' natsii drug ot druga." "Interdependence" in German would be "gegenseitige Abhaengigkeit": in Russian, "vzaimozavisimost'." "Dependence upon each other" or "mutual dependence" could imply a relationship less symmetrical and organic than theoretically perfect "interdependence."

4. See Z. S. Sheinis, *Maksim Maksimovich Litvinov: Revoliutsioner, diplomat, chelovek* (Moscow: Politizdat, 1989), chap. 7. For a study of the ways in which Soviet priorities shifted from international to domestic and then to defense concerns in the interwar years, see Sergius Yakobson and Harold D. Lasswell, "Trend: May Day Slogans in Soviet Russia, 1918–1943," in Harold D. Lasswell, Nathan Leites, et al., *Language of Politics* (Cambridge, MA: MIT Press, 1965), 233–97.

5. See General Major V. V. Volkov, *Ne stynet nenavist' k vragu* (Moscow: Voenizdat, 1987); also see R. Ia. Mirskii, *Patriotizm sovetskogo cheloveka* (Moscow: Mysl', 1988).

6. Complaints about hazing have been especially sharp from the republics, strengthening calls for local men to be stationed on their own turf. On a Ukrainian's suicide after prolonged hazing, see *Literaturnaia gazeta*, March 1, 1989, p. 11.

7. "Interdependence" and "complex interdependence" as used here are based on Robert O. Keohane and Joseph S. Nye, Jr., *Power and Interdependence: World Politics in Transition* (Boston: Little, Brown, 1977); for elaboration, see chapter 11 of this book.

8. For background on Soviet views in the 1970s, see Walter C. Clemens, Jr., *The U.S.S.R. and Global Interdependence: Alternative Futures* (Washington, DC: American Enterprise Institute, 1978).

9. TASS, January 18, 1988.

10. Security cooperation among rivals is highly context-dependent because it hinges upon the interplay of many variables. Complicating the picture, many different variables have led to similar outcomes—movement toward or away from arms control. The *Realpolitik* school cannot explain how cooperation arises from the anarchy of world politics. But transnationalists emphasizing the existence of strong common interests cannot explain why nations sometimes bite their nose to spite their face, why they myopically seek today's quick profit instead of optimizing long-term interests. See Alexander L. George, Philip J. Farley, and Alexander Dallin, eds., *U.S.-Soviet Security Cooperation: Achievements, Failures, Lessons* (New York: Oxford University Press, 1988), chap. 1.

11. Deputy Defense Minister V. I. Varrenikov asserted in 1989 that the Kremlin had sent troops into Afghanistan in 1979 over the objections of Marshals N. V. Ogarkov and S. F. Akhromeev and other members of the General Staff. The defense minister in 1979, Dmitrii F. Ustinov (a civilian), was "in over his head," and reports from Kabul told the Brezhnev Politburo what it wanted to hear. Interview with *Ogonek* summarized in *The New York Times*, March 19, 1989, p. 18.

12. Interview with Flora Lewis in *The New York Times*, July 6, 1988, p. A23. Many of the views Petrovskii expressed in his 1985 book *Iaderno-kosmicheskii vek* (The Nuclear Space Age) (Moscow: Mezhdunarodnye otnosheniia) have now become part of the Gorbachev line, with the difference that the new thinking is quite explicit in criticizing past Soviet mistakes. For a collection of relevant Party documents for 1986–87, see *Za novoe politicheskoe myshlenie v mezhdunarondnykh otnoshseniiakh* (Moscow: Politizdat, 1987); also *Sovremennaia ideologicheskaia bor'ba: slovar'* (Moscow: Politizdat, 1988).

13. Who would have foreseen that Marshal Akhromeev, then chief of the Soviet General Staff, would help to implement all three conditions for complex interdependence (as defined in chapter 11)? In July 1988 he looked at an ICBM-launch training site, observed Marine Corps exercises at Camp Lejeune, and was catapulted in a plane from an aircraft carrier. He also visited the Daughters of the Texas Revolution in Alamo, attended a rodeo and became an honorary Indian chief, and addressed the Council on Foreign Relations. The

previous December he had met historian Richard Pipes in Washington and offered to share with him a bibliography on Russian military history. Having helped to negotiate the INF Treaty, he also helped to defend it at the Supreme Soviet in 1988 (see chapter 10). Akhromeev's U.S. counterpart then visited the USSR. In December 1988, however, Akhromeev resigned his post, claiming old age but also hinting that he was displeased with Gorbachev's plan for a unilateral cut of Soviet forces.

14. Howard Raiffa, "Post-Settlement Settlements," *Negotiation Journal* 1, no. 1 (January 1985): 9–12; for elaboration see David A. Lax and James K. Sebenius, *The Manager as Negotiator: Bargaining for Cooperation and Competitive Gain* (New York: Free Press, 1986).

15. For anti-Soviet feelings in Estonia, see *Narodnyi kongress: sbornik materialov kongressa Narodnogo fronta Estonii 1–2 oct. 1988 g.* (Tallinn: Periodika, 1989); for a sample of the hostile Moscow commentary Estonians resent, see Iu. Zhukov, "Priezzhali gosti v Pribaltiku," *Pravda*, March 11, 1989. On March 9, 1989 some two thousand Estonians gathered by candlelight on the Tallinn main square to commemorate the bombing of their city by Soviet planes in 1944.

16. On the origins of Stalinism, still lingering in parts of Soviet society, see A. Tsipko, "Istoki stalinizma," *Nauka i zhizn'*, nos. 11, 12 (1988) and nos. 1, 2 (1989). After the monthly *Twentieth Century and Peace* published Aleksander Solzhenitsyn's 1974 essay, "Live Not By Lies!" in February 1989, it was again put under state censorship. For a study of the obstacles to economic reform, see Marshall I. Goldman, *Gorbachev's Challenge* (New York: W. W. Norton, 1987). For some of the questions facing any effort to democratize the USSR, see the series "Vote, but how?" on page 1 of *Literaturnaia gazeta* throughout much of 1987.

17. Confirmation hearings for deputy secretary of state quoted in *The New York Times*, March 20, 1989, p. A16.

18. Sergei E. Blagovolin and other members of the Military-Economic Sector of IMEMO, March 6, 1989. For elaboration, see Walter C. Clemens, Jr., "Inside Gorbachev's Think Tank," *World Monitor* 2, no. 8 (August 1989): 28–36.

19. The author may, however, go too far in minimizing the differences between East and West when he asserts: "The specifics of social structure have no more significance than those that flow from differences in the level of economic development or political regimes." All those differences—especially those arising from political regimes—could have great bearing on how governments relate to one another. See G. Shakhnazarov, "Vostok-Zapad. K voprosu o deideologizatsii mezhgosudarstvennykh otnosheii," *Kommunist*, no. 3 (February 1989); see also the enthusiastic commentary in *Novoe Vremiia*, no. 11 (March 10, 1989): 14–15.

I
Gorbachev's Inheritance:
Burdens of the Past

1
The Need for Change:
What Has the Kremlin Achieved
in Foreign Policy Since 1917?

What have been the successes and shortcomings of Soviet foreign policy since the October 1917 Revolution, given the objectives of Soviet leaders? And what have been the underlying reasons for achievement and failure? If the balance sheet shows that the basic objectives of successive Soviet leaders have been fulfilled, perhaps there is little reason to change Moscow's characteristic approaches to foreign policy. If the record suggests that failures have outweighed successes, or that assets have been wasted, this would offer cause to alter Soviet policy.

Official Soviet appraisals have been decidedly optimistic. The Party Central Committee asserted in 1977 that the world's first socialist state is "the main event of the twentieth century," leading the way to human liberation. Even Gorbachev, critical in so many ways of the Soviet past, declared in 1987 that "Great October" ushered in a "new dawn" for humanity. He even endorsed collectivization, affirmed the necessity of the 1939 pact with Germany, and praised Stalin's contributions to the war effort.[1]

To evaluate achievements we must know the ends for which policies were intended. Outsiders cannot read the minds of the Politburo, but Soviet external behavior has generally been consistent—at least until 1985—with an identifiable hierarchy of values. In rank order, these goals have been:

(1) Most important, to enhance the security of the top leaders and their followers and to legitimate their dominant position

[3]

(2)   To maintain and improve the security of the Soviet state, protect its
      borders, improve its position in the correlation of forces, and protect
      it from external (or internal) attack
(3)   To maintain and strengthen Soviet influence in borderlands—Eastern
      Europe, the Mongolian People's Republic, and Afghanistan
(4)   To mobilize Soviet economic resources, creating a material base for
      expansion of national power and, over time, improvement of Soviet
      living standards
(5)   Less tangible and less pressing than the first four goals, to maintain
      and strengthen Soviet influence in the international Communist
      movement and the Third World

Individual leaders may have had their own agendas as well. Lenin,
for example, probably was driven by the memory of his elder brother,
hanged for plotting assassination of the tsar; Stalin wanted to be treated
as another Lenin; both men probably wrestled with their ethnic minority
backgrounds. Every political leader—especially in countries such as
Russia—will have unique personal motives that keep him in the high-risk
business of politics.[2]

Despite individual agendas, the five priorities listed have probably
been shared by all Soviet leaders since 1917, though each used somewhat
different means to pursue these ends. Indeed, the deepest ambitions of
each leader has helped to keep the first goal at the top of the hierarchy.
Only if an individual leader retains power can he fulfill his personal goals
and those he has for the society. The second goal is also a *sine qua non*:
unless state security is protected, the other goals cannot be promoted. The
other three goals are instrumental to the first two.

Given these priorities, how does the Soviet balance sheet look to
outsiders?[3] We begin with a historical survey, provisionally identifying
successes and failures. We then explore systemic reasons for policy
outcomes—especially the role of military force and the "who, whom"
orientation of Communist doctrine. Then we relate these findings to
the hypothesis, stated in the introduction, that value-creating strategies
are more likely to enhance political interests than exploitative value-
claiming.

[4]

Successes

1917–21: Survival of the Bolshevik regime despite Civil War and foreign intervention. The Soviets quickly learned to maneuver and "exploit contradictions" among their enemies, all the while marshaling the human and material resources of the world's largest country. They also gained in self-confidence. Beginning with the 1918 Treaty of Brest-Litovsk the Bolsheviks learned how to use diplomacy as a way to buy time and regroup.[4] Lenin wrote off arguments about the need to await salvation from a German proletarian uprising or to embark on a revolutionary offensive as idle daydreams. Six months after the treaty, the kaiser fell and the Bolsheviks repudiated the treaty; indeed, as Lenin boasted, they had already violated it time and again. The success of Lenin's approach helped to generate a habit of hard-headed Realpolitik.

1922–34: Normalization of diplomatic relations with the West. Having survived its traumatic birth, the Soviet republic successfully broke from its isolation. It signed peace treaties with the Baltic republics, Finland, and Poland in 1920–21; concluded friendship treaties with Afghanistan, Iran, and Turkey in 1921; entered clandestine military collaboration with Germany; and attended the 1922 Genoa Economic Conference where, unable to reach a broad accord with the Entente powers, Soviet diplomats concluded a side deal with Germany. Europe's two pariah states retired to Rapallo to sign an agreement providing for the resumption of full diplomatic relations, cancellation of mutual claims, and establishment of most-favored-nations treatment.[5] The pact "drove an entering wedge, on terms favorable to Moscow, into the problem of diplomatic relations and resumption of trade relations between Russia and the West."[6]

In 1924 Britain and Italy vied for the distinction of being the next European countries to recognize the Soviet regime. Others followed. Washington finally recognized the USSR in 1933. The following year the USSR joined the League of Nations.

Creation of a new kind of actor in world affairs. The Soviet state practiced traditional power politics and diplomacy, but it also generated a new style and content in national and international politics. Lenin championed a form of open, egalitarian diplomacy and called for national self-determination even before Woodrow Wilson. The Bolsheviks in 1919 created the Comintern and, in time, a variety of other "nongovernmental" agencies to support their objectives abroad, permitting the Kremlin to promote revolution at the same time it preached "peaceful cohabitation" of opposing systems.

In 1922–23 the Bolsheviks also created a new basis for a multinational

[5]

state, the Union of Soviet Socialist Republics, which could and did expand later to include other bordering republics. Recognition of this entity by other states helped to legitimate Soviet imperium.

In the mid- and late-1930s the Kremlin used its foreign office and the Comintern in a coordinated campaign for collective security and a Popular Front against Fascism. Another innovation was sending "volunteers" to fight Franco. Ultimately these devices failed, but they marked creative adaptations to changing circumstances.

1939–41: Divide, conquer, and prepare. Having lost hope in the willingness of Britain and France to oppose German expansion, Stalin struck a sphere-of-influence deal with Hitler permitting the USSR to expand across Eastern Europe. The "nonaggression" treaty extended the time in which the USSR could prepare for an eventual war with Germany, though Stalin used this breathing space ineptly.

1930s–45: Policy toward Japan. The Kremlin helped to contain Japanese expansionism by an adroit combination of appeasement and military rebuffs in the 1930s. By concluding a nonaggression treaty with Japan in 1941 Stalin avoided a major two-front war and put off reckoning with Tokyo until August 1945, after victory in Europe.

By joining in the last days of war against Japan the USSR "earned" the territorial enlargements already approved by U.S. and British leaders. The Red Army's advance also helped Moscow to install a Communist regime in North Korea and to deal with Manchuria in a manner that aided the Soviet economy and left arms for the Chinese Communists.

1941–45. Military and diplomatic conduct of the Great Patriotic War. Regrouping after early losses, the USSR mobilized its vast resources and cost tolerance to rout the Wehrmacht. Soviet diplomacy secured a Grand Alliance with Britain and the United States that gained massive economic and military aid after Stalingrad and kept up pressure for a second front. Stalin maintained relative harmony with Washington and London while laying the groundwork for postwar settlements advantageous to the USSR.

After horrendous losses of life and property, the Kremlin achieved the greatest ever extension of Russian influence and control east and west. The war ended with Germany and Japan prostrate and with the USSR a leading member of the Big Three. If the Grand Alliance did not endure, the USSR had a veto in the Security Council and a broad glacis to buffer threats from any quarter.

1943–48. "Satellitization" of Eastern Europe. By diplomacy, coercion, and support for local Communists the USSR managed to establish a belt of compliant Communist regimes from the Baltic to the Black Sea and the Adriatic. This de facto expansion of Moscow's empire

[6]

fulfilled age-old Russian ambitions (though Greece and Turkey remained independent), added legitimacy to Communist global pretentions, facilitated economic extractions for a time, established a wide defense buffer, and helped Moscow threaten Western Europe, thereby compensating in part for the early U.S. lead in nuclear arms.

Maintenance of the "Socialist Commonwealth." Despite the challenges of aggrieved nationalism, the Kremlin has maintained its dominion over Eastern Europe except in Yugoslavia and Albania. Outer Mongolia has remained a loyal satrapy.

Expansion into the Third World. Soviet leaders since Stalin have courted Asia, Africa, and, to a lesser extent, Latin America. Moscow has championed anticolonial liberation movements and presented itself as the most dependable friend of peoples exploited by Western imperialism. It has generally succeed in tilting the "nonaligned movement" toward Moscow. Although Indonesia, Egypt, and other Third World countries have turned against the USSR, India and some Arab countries remain close partners.

Use of far-flung allies and proxies. Although the Korean War was probably instigated by Kim Il-Sung, North Korea, and, later China did the fighting with Soviet approval and support.[7] The armies of East Germany, Poland, Hungary, and Bulgaria joined Soviet forces to implement the Brezhnev Doctrine against Czechoslovakia in 1968. But Moscow's use of proxies was fine-tuned in the 1970s as Cuba became a partner and agent in joint expeditions throughout Africa. The cost of subsidizing Cuba has been staggering, but the Soviet leadership seems to have believed that the benefits justified the investment. The costs to Moscow of supporting Hanoi against France and later the United States were minimal compared with the damage done to those countries. Vietnam now provides strategic facilities that expand Moscow's global reach and threaten China's soft underbelly. As Vietnam's economy unravels, the cost of Soviet subvention rises, but the gains to Moscow from this relationship are weighty.

In the 1970s the USSR backed Hanoi's domination of Indochina. The Kremlin, joined often by Cuba, provided massive support to leftist (not merely "national bourgeois") movements that seized power in several African countries such as Angola and Ethiopia. Moscow and Havana also aided leftist Grenada and Sandinista Nicaragua. In 1978–79 Communists took power also in Kabul, supported after December 1979 by Soviet combat forces.

Many of the leftist regimes are tottering, weakened by intra-Party rivalries and challenged by other domestic rivals sometimes supported by the West. Still, by 1980 the Kremlin had demonstrated its capacity to help

[7]

such regimes come to power (for example, by airlifts of supplies and Cuban soldiers) and retain it (for example, by East German training of their security forces).

Gorbachev thus inherited a broad domain of Soviet influence in the Third World achieved partly through relatively businesslike, state-to-state relations with countries such as India; through active partnership with revolutionary Cuba and Vietnam; and through its support for weak but socialist-oriented regimes as in Angola.

Making the USSR a military superpower and a major industrial power. The Kremlin has sacrificed the living standards of most Soviet citizens to the gods of heavy industry and military force. The results of this sacrifice were negligible in the interwar years; since the end of World War II, however, the international arena has been heavily influenced by Western fears of Soviet military action, thus enhancing the leverage of Kremlin diplomacy. The forward deployment and periodic exercises of the Red Army across East Central Europe have been "permanently operating factors" for Western planners to consider. By the mid-1950s Soviet bombers and missiles permitted the Kremlin to threaten Western Europe and perhaps even the United States.[8]

By the early 1970s the USSR had acquired strategic nuclear parity with the United States. Each country led in some respects, but the permutations of these asymmetries produced an essential equivalence enshrined in U.S. acceptance of the Soviet right to "co-equal security" in arms control agreements. By the mid-1970s the USSR was demonstrating that its air- and sea-lift capabilities were also formidable, even if not equal to the American. The Kremlin also put to sea a blue-ocean navy able to show the flag and function far and wide, using facilities in Vietnam and other distant ports.

Although the USSR came nowhere close to overtaking the United States, it became the world's second industrial power in the 1950s–60s (unless one regarded the European Community as a whole), one that had cultivated its resources to make the USSR the most self-sufficient country in the world. The Kremlin had managed these achievements despite arms outlays at least twice as burdensome as those of the United States. In the 1980s Japan's GNP exceeded the Soviet, and the USSR's economic and technological development were falling behind world levels. Still, the USSR remained one of two military superpowers and was striving to restructure its flagging economy.

Failures

Many policy events wear a Janus face: they look both ways. Achievements in one domain may generate or permit failures elsewhere. Short-term successes often become long-run failures. Developments probably welcomed by Stalin, such as partition and, later, dominion of Poland, have been seen by later leaders as the sources of serious problems. Most Kremlin leaders have focused on enhancing personal and state power, neglecting general living standards and popular sentiment on which regime and state security would also depend.

1917–21: Failure of revolution beyond Soviet borders. The young Soviet regime failed to ignite enduring revolutions abroad despite its vigorous efforts in Central and Eastern Europe and in Asia. This failure resulted more from local conditions than from shortcomings of Soviet policy, but it undermined Communist assumptions that revolution would succeed first in the most industrialized lands. The Red Army's inability in 1920 to carry revolution to Warsaw signaled that nationalism still outweighed class consciousness in world affairs. The Babel of the Baku Conference later that year demonstrated how little Moscow could control liberation forces in the Middle East and Asia. The Kremlin's modest support for the March 1921 uprising in Germany showed that Moscow was already accepting the idea of "socialism in one country" affirmed three years later by Stalin.

1928–33: Misperceptions and misjudgments of Hitler. Soviet directives to the German Communists not to collaborate with the Social Democrats split the left and facilitated Hitler's rise to power in 1933. Soviet commentators had suggested that Hitler's rise would be a replay of Russia's "Kornilov affair"—a right-wing precursor to a leftist revolution. Although Stalin quickly perceived the folly of this diagnosis and labored to correct it, this was not the only occasion when he misjudged Hitler.

1934–38: Failure of collective security. Striving now to maintain the territorial status quo, Moscow endeavored to strengthen collective security at the League of Nations and through alliances with France and Czechoslovakia. The failure to contain Japanese, Italian, and German aggression lies mainly in London, Paris, and Washington; but Kremlin behavior and that of the Comintern—in the 1920s and even in the 1930s— did little to build Western confidence that the USSR could be trusted as a partner in collective security.

1939–41: Failures of expansionism and appeasement. Following shortly upon Stalin's purges, Soviet expansion under the Molotov-Ribbentrop accords alienated Communist sympathizers worldwide and

[9]

confirmed the darkest analyses of Soviet totalitarianism and imperialism. Moscow became embroiled in the Winter War with Finland, itself a setback for Soviet policies. Territorial gains elsewhere, as in Poland and the Baltic, created animosities that would simmer for generations afterward. The 1939–41 collaboration with Hitler also set Stalin up for a disastrous miscalculation. Despite loyal fulfillment of Soviet commitments under the Molotov-Ribbentrop agreements, Hitler's *Drang nach Osten* could not be indefinitely delayed. Almost any other course would have left the USSR more alert and ready to cope with Operation Barbarossa.

1944–47: Igniting the cold war. The wartime alliance collapsed for many reasons, but primarily because of Moscow's efforts to implant Communist regimes from Eastern Europe to northern Iran to Korea. Soviet policies in Poland, for example, steeled U.S. resistance to approving a set figure for German reparations to the USSR. Soviet policy to Germany—communizing the East, extracting heavy reparations, obstructing efforts to treat Germany as an economic whole—led to creation of what became West Germany. Washington lost hope in cooperation and commenced in 1946–47 to stress containment of the USSR, an inflection sharpened by the Kremlin's refusal to take part in the Marshall Plan for economic reconstruction.

The costs and risks from cold war competition have been substantial for both sides. The West, however, has gained from integration stimulated in part by fear of Russia; the USSR and Eastern Europe have lost much more than they have gained from the self-isolating Iron Curtain.

1945 and after: Lack of popular mandate for satellite regimes in Eastern Europe. The USSR has dominated Eastern Europe for two generations, but heavy-handed Soviet sponsorship has done much to alienate satellite governments from their own peoples. Soviet tyranny has triggered defections by Yugoslavia (1948) and Albania (1961); uprisings in East Germany (1953) and Hungary (1956), and serious challenges to Soviet-style communism in Poland (1956 and later) and Czechoslovakia (1968).

Stalinist exploitation gave way in the mid-1950s to Soviet subsidies to Eastern Europe. By the 1970s the Kremlin believed it should diminish these burdens of empire. By the 1980s neither Moscow nor anyone else pretended that the Soviet model offered any useful guidelines for purging Eastern Europe's malaise. By 1989 the Polish and Hungarian Communists sought participation of opposition movements in government—if only to spread responsibility for policy failures. The region's chronic instability constitutes one of the greatest failing of Soviet policy.

Eastern Europe has also created problems *within* the USSR, for it has often funneled in liberalizing breezes the Kremlin would prefer to keep out.

Alienation of China. Moscow's first major policy failure in China occurred in 1927, when the Kuomintang assaulted the Chinese Communists, urged to collaborate with the KMT by Soviet advisers. Stalin nonetheless continued to tilt toward the KMT and sometimes sought to intervene in internal CCP affairs. When the Communists finally seized power in 1949 and Mao Zedong came to Moscow to sign an alliance, the 1950 agreement contained unequal terms resented by Beijing.

Khrushchev mended fences with Mao and provided substantial economic/technological assistance during 1954–58, but this honeymoon ended in 1959–60.[9] After border clashes in 1969, the early 1970s even heard Soviet talk of a preventive war.

Not only did the Kremlin fail to make China a partner, but it generated a powerful enemy sometimes collaborating with the United States. Although Sino-Soviet rapprochement has occurred under Gorbachev, expectations for future cooperation are dampened by memories of past conflict and perfidy.[10]

1962: The Cuban missile crisis. Departing from the caution that has characterized Soviet foreign policy probes, Khrushchev's Cuban gambit could have produced a war, one the USSR would not win. If he sought to redress the balance of terror, as seems likely, he failed because the USSR had to pull back its missiles, planes, and even its torpedo boats, which the Americans classified as "offensive weapons." The retreat cost the Kremlin a considerable loss of face; it infuriated Castro and Ché Guevara, who preferred that the missiles be launched against the United States instead of being withdrawn; angry Cubans refused to permit international inspection to verify withdrawal of the weapons; and Havana turned toward Beijing for several years. Ultimately the Cuban venture was one of the "hare-brained, subjectivist" schemes that cost Khrushchev his job two years later.

In the longer run, however, the crisis netted several benefits for Moscow and even for Havana. First, Robert Kennedy pledged that U.S. missiles would be withdrawn from Turkey—a kind of quid pro quo even though Washington denied any connection with events in Cuba. Second, Khrushchev gained some stature as a statesman capable of sober action. Third, retreating from the brink, both sides shifted toward détente, arms control, and trade in 1963. Fourth, the USSR may have been strengthened in its determination "never again" to be dominated by American power. Fifth, Castro survived and with him the Soviet presence in what had been the sphere of the Monroe Doctrine. Indeed, some Soviets contend that

Khrushchev's major objective was to prevent a U.S. invasion to overthrow Castro. If so, the Kremlin suceeded in getting an American pledge not to intervene militarily in Cuba.[11]

The outcomes were mixed, but Beijing's critique seems basically correct: Khrushchev engaged in "adventurism" and then shifted to "capitulationism."

Third World boomerangs and rebuffs. Neither Lenin's two-stage theory of aiding the national bourgeoisie nor the more radical approach of supporting leftist radicals has provided a dependable way to enhance Soviet interests in the Third World. India has become a valuable partner for the USSR, but no bourgeois nationalist revolutions have gone on to yield a proletariat ripe for communism. Following Turkey's example in the 1920s and 1930s, Egypt and other developing countries have utilized Soviet aid for a time and then turned against the USSR. The list runs from Ghana to Indonesia to Somalia. Soviet military support for the Arab countries has been particularly dangerous, as the Kremlin found that it could neither control its clients nor ensure that they would use Soviet weapons to the best advantage.

Soviet support for radical regimes has netted the Kremlin a responsibility for the survival of some of the weakest and poorest countries in the world—from Vietnam to Ethiopia to Afghanistan. Although support for these clients underscored for a time Moscow's military might, the 1988–89 retreat from Afghanistan did not inspire confidence in Soviet willingness or ability to support leftist governments indefinitely. A comparable but less direct defeat for Moscow has been the growing disillusionment with Soviet development models for the Third or even the Second World.

Soviet forays in the Third World have also risked putting the superpowers on a collision course; they have done much to undermine détente and trade with the West.

Disintegration of the world Communist movement and loss of revolutionary élan. The Communist movement has been weakened by many factors: sectarianism and schism among its devotees; nationalism and other competing worldviews and religions; and the gradual disappearance of class consciousness in the West. Five features of Soviet practice have damaged international communism: Moscow's tendency to put Soviet interests over international; reliance upon command rather than democracy; the distortions and excesses of Soviet totalitarianism, especially under Stalin; the loss of élan within the USSR; and the shortcomings of the Soviet development model.

Almost from its inception the Comintern became more an instrument of Soviet foreign policy than of world revolution. Disciplined adherence to

[12]

Moscow's "line" became the essential quality for membership in the International. Many foreign Communists were alienated by Stalin's purges and collaboration with Hitler. The Chinese Communists had been alienated even earlier, since the 1920s. Despite such developments, many European Communists remained almost more devout than the pope. So it was a jolt to the Communist movement when the Yugoslavs split with Moscow in 1948. Other shocks followed: the use of Soviet tanks against East German workers; Khrushchev's exposé of Stalinism; the Hungarian uprising. For Beijing it was also a shock that Moscow would negotiate seriously with the West on arms control. The Chinese began to denounce the Soviets as "revisionists"—traitors to Marxism and revolution. The open rift between Moscow and Beijing destroyed the myth of solidarity and pressed other Communists to choose sides or go their own way. In 1961 Albania withdrew from the Warsaw Pact without serious reprisal. Rumania intensified its autonomous foreign policy. Czechoslovakia initiated a form of "socialism with a human face" but was stifled by Moscow and supplanted by Husak reaction. Many Communists of Western Europe attempted in the 1970s-early 1980s to adopt positions ostensibly independent of Moscow, but the trajectory of Eurocommunism was pulled ever lower by the dampened appeal of the USSR.

Failure to reach long-term accommodations with the West and Japan. The cold war and arms race have hurt the USSR even more than the West. Stalin soured the entente that developed during World War II; Khrushchev and Brezhnev tried to improve East-West relations but never secured more than a brief détente, often terminated by some Soviet action in the Third World or Eastern Europe. The arms control accords reached since the late 1950s have improved the overall climate but have not removed the nuclear sword of Damocles hanging over all humanity.

The USSR has failed also to come to terms with Japan—ostensibly because of the four islands claimed by both countries, but also for deeper historical, psychological, and cultural reasons.

Soviet alienation of Japan, China, Eastern Europe, and the West has recreated a many-front challenge that could probably have been avoided.

Analysis: Paradoxes of Power

Soviet leaders have sought "security" for their own rule and that of the Communist party and the integrity of the Soviet state against external challenges. By these criteria Soviet policy has been relatively effective.

Most top leaders have enjoyed a long if not unchallenged tenure; the Communist party has preserved its basic monoply of power; and the USSR has been invaded on a large scale only once since 1922.

A more demanding standard would judge a country's security policies successful to the extent that they protect and enhance its way of life and basic values. By this criterion Soviet policy has been a disaster. A series of catastrophes continued almost without interruption from 1917 to the late 1940s: civil war; deportations of peasants and national minorities; several major famines, some of them deliberately induced by Stalin; several sweeping purges striking down the country's intellectual, political, and military elites as well as countless ordinary citizens; and one world war and associated strife.[12] Tens of millions of Soviet citizens have perished unnaturally or emigrated since 1917; they have not reproduced themselves, and their talents (many above average) have been removed from the genetic and cultural pool. Their relatives and associates have been traumatized; some have walled themselves in to shut out others' sufferings.

Next to these miseries some of the other hardships imposed on the Soviet people seem minor: sacrifice of consumer goods to military might and heavy industry; sacrifice of industrial and agricultural efficiency to ideological dogmas; sacrifice of the arts to the Party line; sacrifice of environmental quality to material growth; sacrifice of political freedom to Party control.

A balance sheet must confront the question: does the government of any other major country feel itself so vulnerable to domestic dissent or foreign pressure as the Soviet? How has it happened that the world's largest country, with the world's third largest population, with a greater capacity for self-sufficiency than any other, has these problems: (1) It is surrounded on all sides by hostile neighbors, including its putative allies. (2) Its economy has been the second largest in the world, but it appears incapable of producing modernization or better living standards without injections of foreign goods and technology. (3) It is ruled by an elite that, at least until the mid-1980s, feared any sign of spontaneity by its subjects and depended heavily on police controls and armored security forces.

Problems of Analysis: Who and What Causes What?

What causes what? Some apparent "Soviet" successes were probably attributable more to other actors than to the USSR. Some examples follow.

[14]

—Churchill announced that Britain would side with Stalin against Hitler because it opposed Germany, not because it liked "supping with the devil."

—Mao Zedong signed an alliance with Stalin in 1950 not because he esteemed the USSR but because he had nowhere else to turn. He supported Soviet leadership of the international Communist movement in 1957 "because every snake must have a head."

—The Arab world thanked Moscow for its vocal intervention during the 1956 Suez crisis, though the outcome was affected more by Eisenhower's policies and by Anglo-French-Israeli ineptitude.

—Hanoi wore down France and then the United States with minimal aid from Moscow and in spite of the 1972 Nixon accords with Brezhnev. Still, the Kremlin gained from Hanoi's victories; it even acquired access to former U.S. bases in Vietnam.

It is less accurate to say that some Soviet "failures" were caused by actors or circumstances beyond Moscow's control. To be sure, Soviet collective security efforts in the 1930s got nowhere because Britain and France proved surprisingly flaccid in the face of Axis expansionism; later, however, the United States proved very resourceful against the Berlin blockade and the North Korean push southward. To say that Moscow was surprised by Western behavior in these cases, however, only means that Soviet intelligence and policy appraisals were incorrect. To put it another way, the Kremlin gambled but lost, even though the odds were favorable.

It is striking how important have been the roles of Germany and Eastern Europe in accounting for both achievements and shortfalls of Soviet policy— far more weighty than Britain, France, or even the United States and many times greater than any Third World area. Germany has probably been the single most important foreign actor for Soviet policymakers from Brest-Litovsk through the Euromissile negotiations of the 1980s. In between these dates our listings point to Rapallo, the rise of Hitler, the 1939–45 alignments and realignments, the issue of reparations, divided Germany, the Berlin blockade, rearmament, the Wall, Ostpolitik, and trade. Poland has played a less threatening but persistently important role: the 1920 Polish-Soviet war, the failure of collective security, the 1939 partition, Katyn, the Warsaw uprising, the legitimacy of the Lublin government, and the unrest of 1956 and the 1980s.

China has also played an important role since the 1920s as a potential partner and adversary, as a follower and then a challenger of ideological primacy. But China has remained a still sleeping giant without the geographic immediacy of East Central Europe for Soviet security interests.

[15]

India and Egypt have been important Third World actors for the USSR since the mid-1950s, but it is the Third World as a whole that has been weighty for Soviet interests. This is because Moscow has waged much of its struggle against the West through the Third World. And if one client, such as Egypt, fell away, others could be found and cultivated. Iran and Turkey have also been important because of their proximity to the USSR, making them likely targets for Soviet influence or potential threat.

Since 1945 the main threat to the USSR has come from the United States—its military forces, its position as leader of the non-Communist world, its awesome economic stature, against which Soviet leaders have measured their own progress. Because it would be so dangerous for the USSR and the United States to fight each other, their competition has taken place across a global chessboard on which Moscow has won and lost some key pieces. Although Moscow is often credited with long-term vision and strategic thinking, it is doubtful that the chess player is prevailing against the ever-changing hands of the American poker player. Perhaps both are losing.

Underlying Reasons for Success and Failure

The keys to policy outcomes lie in the interactions of deterministic and voluntaristic forces, the interplay between material power and human personality, the ways that leaders—their vision, skill, persistence (or lack thereof)—cope with luck, misfortune, and serendipity. Our analysis points to the great role of military force and the zero-sum outlook in shaping Soviet successes and failures. They arise from a context of structural, systemic, and cognitive factors shaping the formulation and implementation of policy.

Structural Restraints and Endowments

Geopolitics. Geopolitical and environmental factors create both problems and opportunities for every state. The USSR is more than twice the size of the United States with a raw materials endowment that makes the Soviet Union more self-sufficient than any other country. Russia's immense size has permitted defense in depth—useful against Napoleon and Hitler but of less value in the missile age. The flip side is that the Kremlin must stand guard over extensive borders and face directly many countries long antagonistic toward Russia. The continental climate, mountains, permafrost, and deserts make it extremely difficult to build dependable communications networks. The savage weather, combined with relatively poor soil in much of the country, puts agriculture at risk each season, making the entire economy hostage to favorable weather. Ice freezes many of Russia's ports for much of the year and has made the country's rulers anxious to establish warm-water ports. When the Soviet fleet goes out into the world's oceans, it must pass choke points controlled by potential foes—Turkey, Japan, and northern and Western European countries—all collaborating with the United States.

Moscow is locked into a rigid negotiating posture by its determination to uphold existing boundaries with all its neighbors. Having gathered whatever territories became available in the course of World War II, the Kremlin has found itself defending its boundaries and those of Eastern Europe on an all-or-nothing basis, from the southern Kuriles to Bessarabia and beyond.

Demography. Population factors also cut in two directions. The USSR has the world's third largest population, about half of which is Russian. In principle the heterogeneity of the country's many nationalities should contribute to a dynamic synergy drawing on the unique strengths of Slavic, Turkic, Caucasian, Baltic, and other cultures. But the country's ethnic diversity has generated more problems than assets for the Soviet leadership. Coercion more than persuasion impelled the various borderlands to join the Russian Republic in forming the USSR. Stalin used collectivization and famine to decimate the Kazakhs and Ukrainians. He judged whole peoples unreliable during World War II and had them uprooted. After the war he and his successors dispatched Russians by the millions into minority republics "to assist in reconstruction" and to Russify the provinces.

National memories of abuses under Moscow's rule run deep. The national problem is an Achilles' heel, ever more vulnerable as national and pan-religious feelings pulsate through nearby regions and as the USSR's economic model falls further behind those of its rivals. Ukrainians and Kazakhs, for example, will not soon forget collectivization and starvation that killed millions of their ancestors. Baltic peoples still struggle against the Russification that commenced in the 1940s and continued under Brezhnev. For a time the Soviet leaders hoped to exhibit Samarkand and Tashkent and win approval from the Islamic world; now Moscow sees Central Asia as a threat—demographically, ideologically, and in other ways—to Soviet security.

The global setting. Soviet fortunes in the Third World gained from anti-Western attitudes prevalent in many Third World countries; often these countries were disposed to welcome Soviet proposals promising to help them overcome dependence and backwardness. However, some Asian and Middle Eastern countries also had negative memories of tsarist imperialism. And Beijing in the 1960s and 1970s revived such memories saying that the USSR practiced a "great nation chauvinism" and "social imperialism" more rapacious than Western imperialism. Stoking these fires, "ugly Russians" abroad have offended many Third-Worlders, as have the racist attitudes of many Soviets toward Asians and Africans visiting the USSR. Most former Western colonies have retained strong cultural and even linguistic ties with the former metropoles. English and French are more popular than Russian; Hollywood more appealing than Eisenstein. Moscow has also had to carry the albatross of official atheism, a disadvantage in most Third World cultures.

Instability in the emerging nations has often created opportunities that Moscow could manipulate, as in Angola and Ethiopia. But ties with Moscow have seldom gone deep, and the Soviet diplomats have often watched as African or other Third World clients reversed their apparent alignment. Nationalism in the Third World has often worked to Soviet advantage, but when perceptions shift and the USSR is seen as a weak provider, the self-interest of Third World elites and nations drives them back to the West.

The Soviet System

Dictatorship of the Vanguard party. The Soviet system itself has been a double-edged sword. Centralization has harnessed the country's resources with less public accountability than would be needed in Western democracies: to act with more dispatch and greater secrecy, to adhere to a course with more persistence. Centralized decision making has also led to disastrous policies more readily avoided or corrected if subjected to public debate. If an energetic Lenin or Khrushchev is at the helm, centralization facilitates dynamism; if an aging Stalin or Brezhnev, plodding caution. Centralization permits high-priority targets such as *Sputnik* but also misallocation of resources in the face of the country's overall needs.

The Kremlin's security police and intelligence agencies have also been useful to Soviet foreign policy. They have defended Soviet secrets and acquired those of others. They have thwarted subversion of the Soviet system while helping to establish and maintain Soviet clients abroad. On balance, however, they have have injured Soviet interests by contributing

[18]

to paranoia and excessive secrecy within the USSR and by fanning anti-Soviet feelings abroad.

The command-and-coerce features of the Soviet system have undermined its appeal for many Soviet citizens and foreigners. How costly this could be in wartime was seen when Hitler's armies were welcomed in the Ukraine and other parts of the Soviet empire.

Power struggles at home and abroad. Kremlin power struggles have sometimes obstructed foreign policymaking. Thus Stalin's animus toward the German Social Democrats in the late 1920s probably reflected his fear that if they prospered, this might help the Right Opposition within the USSR. But he also feared Trotskyist tendencies within the German Communist party and in the Comintern *apparat*. Better perhaps to strengthen Hitler temporarily than the German political factions who might subvert Stalin's hold on the Kremlin. To cite another case from the mid-1950s: the thrust of Soviet arms control policy was vitiated as disarmament became a political football in the struggles among Molotov, Malenkov, and Khruschchev.

The pressures of Sino-Soviet competition have also shaped Kremlin behavior. Chinese carping added to Khrushchev's reasons to trumpet Moscow's commitment to aiding "just wars of national liberation," raising Washington's anxieties. The Sino-Soviet rivalry pushed both Moscow and Beijing to invest resources in arcane struggles to influence leftist and nationalist forces around the world. Thus because Cambodia's Prince Sihanouk was in Beijing, the Kremlin stood by Lon Nol until he was defeated, leading the Khmer Rouge to shell the Soviet embassy when they entered Phnom Penh. This event, in turn, pushed Moscow to support Hanoi's war against the Khmer Rouge.

Soviet leaders, in Kennan's phrase, have often proved themselves more interested in the dictatorial implications than the socialist essence of Marxist ideas.

Material power: economics and technology. The command economy is less subject to cyclical depression than free enterprise systems but much less innovative. Centralized powers have been used to nationalize and requisition, to drive the USSR into rapid industrialization and collectivization and to capture all resources for war and for postwar reconstruction. The system has produced space satellites and rockets and built dams and other showy projects in developing countries. By the 1970s, however, the economic promise of Soviet communism was badly compromised. It seemed incapable of building living standards or even public health standards comparable to those of the West; it seemed unable to compete in the world's high-technology revolutions. Critics wondered whether a

[19]

command economy presided over by a Communist *nomenklatura* could ever generate consumer abundance and technological leadership. As Gorbachev embarked on *perestroika,* some asked if socialism was not the longest possible route to capitalism.

The fruits of coercion. Many Soviet successes abroad have derived from the buildup of Soviet military power and its skillful management to pressure or bludgeon foreign adversaries. Though believing that history was on their side, Soviet leaders have also wanted the option to use force (in Mayakovsky's words) "to hustle old history's horse—left left, left."

Force and the diplomacy of power underlay many Soviet achievements: survival against domestic and foreign foes; containing and then assaulting Japan; repulsing Hitler and then advancing into East Central Europe; installing Communist governments in Outer Mongolia and, decades later, in North Korea; establishing and maintaining Soviet hegemony in Eastern Europe; influencing if not sucessfully bullying Western decision makers. Soviet export of threats, arms, and advisers—even of Cuba's foreign legions—has established outposts of Soviet influence in the Third World from the Middle East to India to Angola. The Kremlin's main claim to superpower status and "coequal security" has been its military prowess.

But the threat and use of force have been the leading source of failure in Soviet foreign policy, from the 1920 Polish defeat to the protracted bloodletting in Afghanistan. Even when the Red Army fulfilled its narrow mission, apparant victories have generated long-term headaches.[13] Violence at home—especially purges of the military command in the late 1930s—weakened the USSR objectively and in the minds of outsiders.

Sometimes the USSR has fought against long odds and lost, as in its intervention against Franco. Sometimes its putative allies gave way so there was no common stand, as at the 1938 Munich Conference. On occasion the Red Army fought poorly, as in the 1940 Winter War. More often it performed well and secured Moscow's immediate objectives: expanding Soviet borders or influence (as in 1939 and 1943–45) but at the cost of alienating potential or present partners. Whatever heroes' welcome greeted the Red Army as it entered Eastern Europe was soon forgotten as Moscow's heavy hand imposed regimes subservient to Stalin.

The greatest failure of Soviet military policy was Moscow's inability to dissuade Hitler from attacking the USSR and, once he invaded, to stop the invasion before it encircled Leningrad and approached Moscow. Here was the world's largest country engaged against only one major enemy after more than a decade of rapid industrialization, allied with Britain and the United States and profoundly threatened by the Wehrmacht for two years before it could turn the tide of battle. Although the USSR finally triumphed, more than a tenth of the Soviet population perished in this conflagration.

Moscow failed in 1945–46 to expand at the expense of Turkey or Iran. It did not win a meaningful role in the occupation of Italy or Japan. It rattled swords against Tito in 1948 to no avail. Stalin exercised a gradual squeeze on Berlin in 1948, one well calculated to succeed; but he demanded too much and was surprised by Western determination to supply Berlin by air bridge. He also made a reasonable assessment of U.S. weakness when he authorized Kim Il-Sung to attack South Korea but was again surprised by the resourcefulness of the United States, its allies, and South Korea.

The summary is bleak: Stalin helped to create Hitler's rise to power and then failed to stop his aggression until it was almost too late. Stalin then seized Eastern Europe after there was no active threat to the USSR and thereby provoked Western rearmament. His other probes—from Berlin to Korea—netted nothing for the USSR but generated an anti-Soviet alliance and Western rearmament.

Having used force to Sovietize most of Eastern Europe, the USSR has been forced to depend on force to keep its satellites in line. This dependency on force to intimidate nominal allies demonstrates a massive Soviet failure.

To aid China's nuclear weapons program in the mid-1950s was a blunder unless Moscow could be sure of Sino-Soviet harmony for ages to come. Although later alarmed by China's incipient atomic weapons capacity, Moscow did not remove it. For more than a decade the USSR deployed enormous forces along the Sino-Soviet border and otherwise provoked Beijing.

The Cuban missile gambit succeeded in some ways, but overall it was another failing of Soviet foreign and military policy.

Soviet arms shipments to the Middle East have gained some hard currency payments and superficial influence. But Moscow's clients there have gone their own ways, sometimes embroiling the Kremlin in dangerous confrontations. Their defeats by Israel have not enhanced the image of Soviet weapons or advice.

Moscow's ability to provide military supplies over long distances was demonstrated first in Vietnam and then in Africa. Soviet and Cuban aid has decisively aided the present governments of Angola and Ethiopia. These achievements, however, have led to Soviet alignments with some of the weakest governments in some of the poorest countries of the world.

The Afghan war hurt the USSR in the Islamic world, the Nonaligned movement, the United Nations generally, and in the West, where it

[21]

occasioned sanctions and nonratification of SALT II. The war also weakened Soviet society and lowered the morale of the Soviet armed forces, which were unable to destroy a resistance movement incomparably weaker than the Vietnamese Communists who finally flushed the last U.S. helicopters from Saigon.

Soviet military buildups have often sparked countermoves, thereby reducing USSR security. Kremlin sticks and carrots did not prevent West Germany's integration in NATO or, more recently, the deployment of Pershing II and ground-launched cruise missiles in Europe. Nor did they persuade the Reagan administration to renounce its Strategic Defense Initiative.

Plowing resources into military power has eroded the Kremlin's economic base. Becoming a military superpower has left the USSR a second-rate economic power except in the production of oil and a few other commodities. A similar syndrome overtook the United States in the 1980s—military might coupled with flagging economic power—but this malaise runs far deeper in the Soviet system.

Cognitive Factors

Political culture. The political culture inherited by the Bolsheviks in 1917 presented them with modes of operation and habits of thought that could be altered only slowly. Both the strengths and weaknesses of traditions (Russian and other nationalities') have provided the clay from which the Bolsheviks sought to shape a new man and new policies.

Despite many defections, the fortitude and stoicism of the Russian and other Soviet peoples were decisive in repulsing Hitler. In noncrisis times, however, these same traits yield a passive quietism that tolerates an elitist, exploitative regime and its foreign adventures, asking little else than less arbitrary repression and gradual improvement in living standards. A deadly circularity ensues and centralization stifles innovation and passivity permits more centralization. Accustomed to such order, much of the managerial class rejects reforms that might impart new life to the system, leading many of the freshest spirits to turn inward, revolt, or emigrate.

Leadership and skill. The top Soviet leaders have generally been adept in foreign affairs, skillfully using the means available—resources, opportunities, and constraints—to pursue far-reaching objectives. Lenin, Trotsky, Bukharin, and other Old Bolsheviks had wide experience with the languages and ways of Europe. Other top leaders—Stalin,

Khrushchev, Brezhnev—had limited experiences abroad, but they proved to be quick learners and were generally effective in summit and other negotiations.

Soviet policy has gained both from *fortuna* and from serendipity. On occasion these gains have been a matter of relatively pure luck; more often Soviet good fortune derived from incessant scanning of the globe for targets of opportunity.

Soviet diplomacy has usually demonstrated a high degree of professionalism, overcoming early problems of training and the difficulties of representing a dictatorship. The diplomatic service had to draw many of its cadres from other domains after each world war.[14] Many recruits in 1944-46, for example, had been trained as engineers. From Georgii Chicherin (who succeeded Trotsky as foreign commissar in 1918) to Andrei Gromyko, however, there has been considerable continuity in the leadership of the Foreign Ministry and its departments dealing with problems such as disarmament and regions such as North America. Though appointing a man not experienced in world affairs, Eduard Shevardnadze, to head the Foreign Ministry, Gorbachev has endeavored to strengthen the professionalism and enlightenment of Soviet foreign policy at all levels, including the International Department of the Party Central Committee.

The professional ways of Soviet diplomacy have been accentuated by the dilettantism of other governments. The standard components of Soviet diplomatic successes, according to George F. Kennan, have been "one part Soviet resourcefulness and single-mindedness of purpose; two parts amateurism, complacency, and disunity of the West."[15] Others have joined Kennan in criticizing Western diplomacy for its superficiality, smugness, national-emotional bias, and enslavement to the vagaries of domestic politics in the democratic setting. Western governments have often been cool toward Moscow when Soviet overtures should have been probed; at other times Westerners have been loath to face up to the dangers of Soviet expanionism.[16]

Kremlin operation code: "Kto kovo?" Ideology has given the Kremlin a long-range perspective conducive to perseverance, patience, and confidence in times of trouble.[17] It has also cloaked decisions with a veneer of wisdom and proffered to others a pseudo-scientific program for emulation. Dogmatic in some ways, Marxism-Leninism has also permitted great flexibility of tactics. At times it has draped blinders over Soviet eyes obstructing or distorting Moscow's perceptions of events at home and abroad. It has also interfered with free discussion and what to do about problems of the real world.

[23]

Why do the Soviet leaders choose a policy? And why does it succeed or fail? These are two different questions. Leaders choose a certain orientation because of their personal makeup and their internalized "operational code." That policy may succeed or fail, depending on how it suits the environment in which the USSR must function. The leaders' perceptions of policy outcomes and the evolving environment, in turn, will alter their operational beliefs.

Lenin's book *Imperialism* and other writings helped Soviet leaders to appreciate the importance of national liberation movements and the likelihood of intense competition among capitalist states. But Soviet perceptions and calculations about the external environment were frequently wide of the mark: Soviet leaders overestimated the "ripeness" of target proletariats in East Central Europe during 1917–21; Stalin underestimated Hitler; he and his successors underestimated the Chinese Communists for generations; Stalin probably undervalued the willingness of the West to collaborate with the USSR during and after World War II; then he underestimated the willingness of the West to resist Communist pressures from Iran to Berlin to Korea; Khrushchev, in turn, exaggerated Soviet dynamism and revolutionary trends in the Third World while underestimating Western ability and determination to hold fast in Europe and the Caribbean. At least until the mid-1980s Soviet leaders erred in assuming that history was deterministically on their side at home and abroad. This assumption helped them persevere in dark times, but it spawned a hubris and complacency that ill-served Soviet objectives.

A basic source of the successes as well as the failures of Soviet communism has been the *kto kovo?* ("who will do in whom?") premise of its political culture.[18] Far from assuming a natural harmony of interest among individuals, classes, and nations, Lenin and his colleagues posited that conflict pervades all life, including politics. They saw domestic as well as foreign policy in zero-sum terms: "Whatever the other side wins, we lose; and vice versa." This led the Bolsheviks to expect no quarter and give no quarter unless compelled by temporary weakness. To be sure, they would at times compromise with the adversary—even enter provisional coalitions—on the assumption that when conditions matured, the zero-sum struggle would resume.

This worldview put a premium on self-sufficiency. Expecting that they must ultimately rely on their own resources, the Soviet leaders held fast even when the European proletariat failed to come to their aid in 1918–21; they industrialized despite a worldwide depression; they dealt with Hitler by Realpolitik and, before massive Western aid arrived, by self-reliance; they later rebuilt their war-torn economy without Western credits.

[24]

Self-reliance can be a virtue for individuals and states, but it does not yield optimal results if it fails to tap the potential inherent in strategies of burden-sharing as rooted in comparative advantage and the division of labor. Thus the USSR and its satellites managed to raise their economic output after World War II, but they fell far short of the gains possible had they participated in the European Recovery Plan. Similarly, the Kremlin has achieved its security objectives primarily by building up its own military forces rather than by reaching mutually useful understandings with the United States. The result is that each superpower now has a rather dependable deterrent, sustained at levels far higher and more expensive than needed to hold the other at bay.

The *"kto kovo?"* outlook has helped Soviet Communists to nourish and count on their own strengths, but this Weltanschauung has also had another, basically counterproductive aspect. It has undermined the Kremlin's willingness and even its ability to pursue long-term strategies of mutual gain with other governments.

Projecting their own determination to overcome all rivals, the Soviets have tended to expect the worst from other political actors. This tendency has alienated potential partners from Prague to Paris to Peoria. Even when the Bolsheviks expected to find allies, as among European workers, they have often antagonized them by claims to omniscience and a concomitant right to dictate even when local circumstances diverge from Soviet conditions. Although the Kremlin protests that its motives are pure, it faces a credibility gap from Yerevan to Tallinn and from Beijing to Cairo.

"Kto kovo?" reinforced messianism and the insecurities that permeated Russian policymaking for centuries. They have contributed to a strong tendency to pursue policies oriented toward zero-sum exploitation rather than mutual gain. Many policy achievements have flowed from this approach, but profound shortfalls as well. This approach cannot yield optimal solutions to Soviet and global problems in a world of escalating interdependencies.

The Soviet track record supports the contention that exploitative policies based on zero-sum thinking may generate short-term successes but that they tend to produce counterproductive consequences harmful to the long-term interests of the initiating country. A similar conclusion emerges from a study of U.S. foreign policy since 1917, but the American record also includes much evidence of the utility of value-creating, as in the Marshall Plan and Fulbright exchanges. Moscow's most positive experience in the Third World has been with India, the partner with which the Kremlin has worked most consistently to create values. Despite propaganda claims about the Molotov Plan and the Council for Mutual

[25]

Economic Assistance, Soviet–Eastern European relations have often suffered from zero-sum thinking on one side or the other.[19]

Soviet leaders—at least until Gorbachev—have generally failed to learn history's lesson that enlightened self-interest requires long-term cooperation to create values with other actors. Though born of idealistic impulses, Soviet communism has gravitated toward cynical realism, rationalizing that all means are justified to achieve its lofty aims. This realism has boomeranged—if not devouring its children, then emaciating them. The Soviet leadership, at least until the mid-1980s, was hardly ready for constructive cooperation with its own subjects, not to speak of other peoples with whom they share planet earth.

Not just "new thinking" but "new acting" will be imperative if the Soviet system is to do more than survive and menace resentful subjects and neighbors.

Notes

1. See *Pravda*, February 1, 1977. On the seventieth anniversary of the revolution, Gorbachev declared: "In October 1917 we left an old world. . . . We are going to a new world—the world of communism." M. S. Gorbachev, "Oktiabr' i perestroika: Revoliutsiia prodolzhaetsia," *Kommunist*, no. 11 (November 1987): 3–40. Foreign affairs essayist Stanislav Kondrashov warned, however, that while not long ago "doing things for show [*pakazukha*]" dominated Soviet life, there was now a danger that people would take a superficial, mechanical follow-the-crowd approach to the challenges of perestroika. For his remarks and the sometimes critical reflections of other writers on the past seventy years, see *Literaturnaia gazeta*, October 28, 1987, pp. 2–3.

2. See Issac Deutscher, *Lenin's Childhood* (New York: Oxford University Press, 1970); Robert C. Tucker, *Stalin as a Revolutionary, 1879–1929* (New York: W. W. Norton, 1973).

3. This analysis builds upon surveys that I conducted at the Wilson Center's Kennan Institute for Advanced Russian Studies in 1976–77 and a follow-up survey in 1987 conducted among former Kennan fellows, all specialists on Soviet history and foreign policy. The survey instrument was quite open-ended. It asked respondents to list five to fifteen major successes and failures of Soviet foreign policy since 1917, given what they believed to have been the objectives of Soviet leaders, and to list several of the underlying reasons that account for these successes and failures. Considering the complexity of the task, it is gratifying that more than one in five addressees reponded to the 1987 survey. Most of the respondents are academics, but many have significant experience as government analysts or as diplomats. They include Anton Bebler, Cole Blasier, Henry Bradsher, Timothy J. Colton, Robert V. Daniels, Hon. R. T. Davies, Dennis J. Dunn, Hon. Robin Edmonds, Hon. Hans von Herwarth, Hak-Joon Kim, Jacob W. Kipp, Wladislaw Krasnow, Lyman Legters, S. Neil MacFarlane, Alfred G. Meyer, Roger Munting, Brig. Gen. William E. Odom, Walter M. Pintner, Thomas F. Remington, Yaacov Roi, Harriet F. Scott, Seth Singleton, Darrell Slider, Robert Wesson, and Robert C. Williams.

Most respondents are U.S. Citizens, but some are citizens of Canada, Great Britain, the Federal Republic of Germany, Israel, the Republic of Korea, and Yugoslavia. Soviet scholars who have worked at Kennan were also addressed, but they did not reply. A smaller but equally distinguished group of scholars responded to the 1976–77 survey. George F.

Kennan, Fred W. Neal, and Peter H. Vigor graciously offered their own evaluations in long, focused discussions at that time.

To help put the Soviet survey in a broader perspective, a parallel set of questions about U.S. foreign policy was put to Americanists at the Wilson Center—both in 1976–77 and in 1987—and long, analytical discussions held with Henry S. Commager and J. William Fulbright.

This chapter sketches the broad picture that emerges from the survey. It simplifies and omits many nuances in individual responses. It is one person's balance sheet, aided greatly by the generosity and wisdom of many colleagues. Tabulations of responses are available from the author.

Although this entire exercise endeavors to analyze policy outcomes in light of Kremlin objectives, Soviet analysts and leaders might well interpret history quite differently. A researcher at the Institute of USA and Canadian Studies told me in 1987 that in the age of *glasnost'* it might be feasible for Soviet scholars to take part in the survey of U.S. but not of Soviet foreign policy results. But nothing came of my efforts to obtain Soviet participation in either survey. In 1987–88, however, in the wake of Soviet withdrawal from Afghanistan, Soviet analysts began to publish candid assessments of Soviet achievements and failures at home and abroad.

The domestic achievements and failures of Soviet power are noted here only in passing. That record is a complicated problem in itself. Average life span and literacy rates, for example, rose dramatically (at least for the first sixty years). But they might have climbed even higher without the distortions imposed on Soviet life by Stalinism.

4. Most of the events referred to in this survey are treated in standard texts by Joseph L. Nogee, Alvin Z. Rubenstein, Adam Ulam, and other scholars. What is unique in this analysis is not documentation of specific turns in Soviet policy but rather the systematic attempt to rank successes, failures, and underlying factors, starting with the views of experts—many of them authors of basic works in the field. Still, note references are provided when an authority is quoted or when a little-known work may shed light on the issue.

For a set of structured case studies analyzing achievements, failures, and lessons, see Alexander L. George, Philip J. Farley, and Alexander Dallin, eds., *U.S.-Soviet Cooperation: Achievements, Failures, Lessons* (New York: Oxford University Press, 1988). The difficulties in knowing "what did they want" and "what did they get"—short- and long-term—are underscored in their chapters 2, 5, and 7.

5. For a Soviet study based on German as well as Soviet archives, see A. Akhtamzian, *Rapall'skaia politika* (Moscow: Mezhdunarodnye otnosheniia, 1974).

6. George F. Kennan, *Russia and the West under Lenin and Stalin* (New York: Mentor, 1961), 212.

7. N. S. Khrushchev, *Khrushchev Remembers*, 2 vols. (Boston: Little, Brown, 1970–74), I: 368–69.

8. For elaboration, see chapter 4 of this book.

9. On Khrushchev's double game, see Walter C. Clemens, Jr., *The Arms Race and Sino-Soviet Relations* (Stanford, Ca: Hoover Institution, 1968), 35–37. For a Chinese perspective, see *Memoirs of Marshal Nie Rong Zhen* [in Chinese], 3 vols. (Beijing: People's Liberation Army Publishing House, 1983–4), III: 800–9. See also Andrei A. Gromyko, *Pamiatnoe*, 2 vols. (Moscow: Politizdat, 1988), II: 129–37.

10. See, for example, Harry Harding, *China's Second Revolution* (Washington, DC: Brookings Institution, 1987), chaps. 6 and 9.

11. For new documentation, see Raymond L. Garthoff, *Reflections on the Cuban Missile Crisis* (Washington, DC: Brookings Institution, 1987); James G. Blight and David A. Welch, *On the Brink: Americans and Soviets Reexamine the Cuban Missile Crisis* (New York: Hill and Wang, 1989); also Soviet-Cuban-U.S. discussions held in Moscow in January 1989 and continued at Harvard in February (without the Cubans); see also Pierre Salinger in *The New York Times*, February 5 and follow-on letters published on February 22, 1989.

As indicated in the next chapter, Sergei N. Khrushchev and Sergo Mikoyan (who accompanied Anastas Mikoyan to Cuba in 1959 and 1962) expressed satisfaction with the

[27]

outcome of the Cuban confrontation. They also denied (February 15, 1989) that there was any post-Cuban decision in Moscow to accelerate the Soviet missile buildup.

12. This story has been told in many works by Aleksandr Solzhenitsyn and Robert Conquest. See the latter's *Harvest of Sorrow: Soviet Collectivization and the Terror-Famine* (New York: Oxford University Press, 1986) and corrections/additions by Peter Wiles, *The New York Review of Books*, March 26, 1897, pp. 43–45; also Iosif G. Dyadkin, *Unnatural Deaths in the USSR, 1928–1954* (New Brunswick, NJ: Transaction, 1983); and Roy Medvedev's estimates of Stalin's victims summarized in *The New York Times*, February 4, 1989, pp. 1, 4.

13. That paradox pervades military affairs is argued by Edward N. Luttwak, *Strategy* (Cambridge, MA: Harvard University Press, 1987).

14. Nikolai P. Zhukovskii, *Diplomatv novogo mira* (Moscow: Politizdat, 1986).

15. Kennan, *Russia and the West*, p. 212.

16. Almost none of the men appointed by former President Reagan to be national security adviser, secretary of state, or head of the CIA or U.S. Information Agency had institutional experience or professional training for his post.

17. See Nathan Leites, *The Operational Code of the Politburo* (New York: McGraw-Hill, 1951); Alexander L. George, "The 'Operational Code': A Neglected Approach to the Study of Political Leaders and Decision-Making," *International Studies Quarterly*, 13, no. 2 (June 1969): 190–222. On Soviet ideology compared with American "political beliefs," see Zbigniew Brzezinski and Samuel P. Huntington, *Political Power: USA/USSR* (New York: Viking, 1964).

18. For illustrations of the "who whom" concept from various Soviet writings, see Leites, *The Operational Code*, pp. 78–81. For the concept of *kto kovo* struggle in everyday Soviet life, see Chingis Aitamov, *Rannie zhuravli* [and other stories] (Leningrad: Lenizdat, 1982), 11.

19. The hypothesis regarding the utility of value-creating strategies over value-claiming exploitation seems to have been confirmed also by parallel surveys of U.S. foreign policy achievements and failures. See Walter C. Clemens, Jr., "America's Greatest Achievement in Foreign Affairs" and "The Fulbright Program: It's a Bargain," *Christian Science Monitor*, June 4, 1987 and November 18, 1981, respectively. Summary data are available from the author.

2

Models for Change:
Alternative Approaches, 1917–85

Can Russia change?[1] The country, its leaders, and their policies have often changed in the past.[2] Even under a single leader, such as Stalin or Khrushchev, there were significant zigs and zags in institutions, procedures, and priorities. The Soviet record does not uphold the facile slogan, *Plus ça change, plus c'est la même chose* (The more things change, the more they remain the same). This chapter points to major patterns in Soviet policy that continued for a time, only to be altered and even reversed. Later chapters inquire into what conditions led to change in the past and how they compare with conditions facing the USSR on the brink of the twenty-first century.

Between 1917 and 1941 the Kremlin developed five major approaches to the problems and opportunities it perceived in the West and in the Third World:[3]

(1) Direct advance/forward strategy (revolutionary agitation and/or Red Army coercion)
(2) Limited collaboration (diplomatic relations, trade, technology transfer, cooperation on arms and arms control)
(3) Indirect advance (fostering workers' parties, peace offensives, and other programs to promote Communist causes against bourgeois rule)
(4) Inversion: turning away from external involvements and withdrawal to "Fortress Russia" to cultivate and depend on its resources

(5) Support for the status quo *among* nations (though not within their societies)[4]

The Khrushchev and Brezhnev regimes later experimented with variations on the second approach, calling it "peaceful coexistence" or "détente," but their cooperative approaches to East-West relations differed little in basics from those worked out under Lenin and Stalin. Gorbachev, however, has explored a fundamentally different approach premised on global interdependence and the need for mutual security. Before considering the innovations worked out by Soviet leaders since Stalin's death, however, I will review briefly how the Kremlin moved among the five basic approaches during the first decades of Soviet rule. I shall also note cases in which Soviet policy blended elements from the various approaches in a "mixed model" suited to time and place or as a contradictory mélange reflecting internal inconsistencies.

Lenin the revolutionary focused on *kto kovo?*—"who will do in whom?"[5] Believing that a socialist regime and world capitalism could not long coexist, in 1917 Lenin launched a forward strategy aimed at promoting a revolution in Europe utilizing every means at Moscow's disposal, from agitation to the Red Army.

By 1920–21 Lenin became confident that the Soviet republic could stand alone, for a time, in a hostile environment.[6] He understood that it could pay to cooperate even with an arch rival when interests temporarily overlapped. He advocated that the Kremlin follow simultaneously the second and third policy approaches: limited collaboration with Weimar Germany and other bourgois governments *simultaneously* with efforts to promote an indirect advance of Communism—"peace offensives" and a United Front between Communist and non-Communist workers.[7]

Circumstances in the 1920s to early 1930s moved Stalin's Kremlin toward inversion. Partly to oppose Trotsky's line on "permanent revolution," Stalin declared in 1924 that the USSR was building "socialism in one country"—the "groundwork for the world revolution." But Moscow became even more inverted after 1927 when there were serious rebuffs abroad—in Japan, China, England, and Poland—at a time when Stalin wanted to mobilize all resources of the Soviet state for rapid industrialization and collectivization. Soviet media announced that foreign capitalists were preparing to strike the USSR and that great sacrifices would be needed to ensure its security. Autarky became a necessity as well as a predilection: when the Kremlin sought trade with the West to promote Russia's industrialization, it encountered a Great Depression in which Soviet exports earned little.

"Left" at home meant left abroad. Stalin ended the United Front line in 1928 and directed Germany's Communists not to cooperate with the German Social Democrats. This tactic backfired, dividing Hitler's opponents and helping him ascend to power.

Responding to new dangers, the USSR changed horses again and joined the League of Nations. From 1934 through mid-1939 Moscow supported the international status quo and collective security even as the Comitern again sought an indirect advance under the rubric of "Popular Front."[8]

Most of these policies flowed from a zero-sum conception of international relations. The "kto kovo?" policies that Lenin and Stalin practiced at home underlay Moscow's attempts at direct and indirect advance as well as its temporary retreats from foreign involvements. Even limited collaboration with bourgeois states and diplomatic support for the status quo were regarded by Stalin as expedient tactics in the power struggle with capitalism.[9]

Although many of these zigs and zags look as though they could have been coolly calculated by Stalin, some may have been a result of his tendency to let matters drift and to leave many foreign policy issues to competent subordinates, some of whom differed among themselves. Chicherin, for example, was cosmopolitan but anti-Western, whereas Litvinov was less polished but pro-English. Because Stalin often delayed decisions until situations had become clarified, this frequently left a vacuum that others could fill. Sometimes contradictory policies were pursued simultaneously. Decisions made below the pinnacle could be suddenly reversed by "unexpected intervention from above. This ensured that Soviet foreign policy was anything but monolithic."[10]

The USSR resumed a direct advance when the Red Army marched into the Baltic, Finland, Poland, and Rumania in 1939–40. After being surprised by Hitler's 1941 Blitzkrieg, however, Stalin usually performed as a relatively dependable partner in limited collaboration with Britain and the United States against the Axis.[11] It is not clear whether at Teheran, Yalta, or Potsdam Stalin expected to break with the West after the war or whether he hoped that the Grand Coalition might endure.[12] Still, the "kto kovo?" principles were ruthlessly applied as the Red Army and Soviet police forces endeavored to eliminate anti-Communist elements from Poland and the reoccupied Baltic countries.

In the last years of Stalin's rule Soviet behavior included a blend of "direct advance" (Turkey, Iran, Eastern Europe, Korea); "inversion" (after the Marshall Plan conference); and "indirect advance" (as in peace offensives toward France). It is unclear whether the 1948–49 Berlin Blockade was part of a "forward strategy" or an effort to "uphold the territorial status quo" as the Western allies unified their occupation zones.[13]

What produced these divergent emphases after World War II? Was this a "mixed model" shrewdly calibrated by a "rational actor"—a united leadership under Stalin adapting to changing conditions in different regions? Or was this a contradictory mélange brought on by indecision, "bureaucratic" politics, or infighting between rival political factions? This last interpretation is supported by a careful reconstruction concluding that while poor health kept Stalin on the sidelines, Andrei Zhdanov (joined until 1948 by Tito) pressed forward with a tough line at home seeking to "clear the decks" in anticipation of international conflict; this *Zhdanovchina* sought to extirpate "cosmopolitan" (i.e., non-Great Russian) forces and to promote Pan-Slav ties with Yugoslavia and Bulgaria. Opposing impulses were built into Soviet policy by an anti-Zhdanov clique led by Georgii Malenkov, who doubted that the "new democracies" in Eastern Europe could be detached from the West and welded to the USSR. The anti-Zhdanovites therefore backed the quick exploitation of Eastern European resources by "joint stock companies" while the going was good.[14] If this analysis is correct, the behaviors of both the Zhdanov and the Malenkov cliques bore many characteristics of the forward strategy model; both had defensive as well as offensive aspects.

Khrushchev's Innovations

Khrushchev sought to reform—one might even say "restructure"—Soviet policies at home and abroad. He declared in 1956 that war between socialism and capitalism was not fatalistically inevitable and that socialist transformations could take place without violent revolutions.[15] "Peaceful coexistence," he said, would be the main trend of Soviet foreign policy. It would paralyze the West while national liberation movements aided by the USSR destroyed capitalist empires. This kind of "peaceful co-existence" was just another "kto kovo?" operation against the West. Though Khrushchev said that arms agreements and trade with the West were *long-term* goals, he also asserted that Soviet communism would "bury" Western capitalism through economic competition.

Khrushchev initiated two policies that appeared to be elements in a forward strategy: the pressures on Berlin during 1958–61 and the Cuban missile gambit of 1962. Both cases show how mixed—even contradictory—policies can be in real life.[16] In the first case Khrushchev seemed intent upon demolishing a Western enclave within the German

Democratic Republic and compelling the West to recognize the GDR. He appeared to be "bargaining from strength" created by talk of a missile gap favoring Moscow. At his most "reasonable"—as at Camp David with former President Eisenhower—Khrushchev stressed that West Berlin was an anomaly and that it was wrong to have GDR borders unrecognized. A deeper look reveals, however, that Khrushchev proceeded from two growing weaknesses. First, the USSR was not turning out missiles "like sausages," as he claimed publicly, risking that his bluff might be called. Second, the East German regime was jeopardized not only by nonrecognition but by losses from emigration through West Berlin. The Wall was probably an East German proposal agreed to by Moscow. Thus Khrushchev's apparent forward strategy—somewhat like the 1948 Berlin Blockade—aimed at securing the status quo before it was lost.

The attempt to deploy Soviet nuclear arms in Cuba looked to Americans like a move to pierce the Monroe Doctrine and create a greater capacity to intimidate Washington. But this gambit also proceeded from fears of vulnerability. Moscow's experts believed (Sergo Mikoyan told Harvard audiences in 1987–89) that the United States was preparing a more serious intervention to unseat Castro; Khrushchev hoped that his nuclear deployment would prevent such a move. He also saw that President Kennedy was broadening the missile gap to U.S. advantage. A Soviet force in Cuba would offset this trend and maintain Moscow's bargaining leverage. Indeed, concern to redress the growing strategic imbalance may well have been the dominant objective—certainly it was in military circles.

"We had long lived with Western bases close of the USSR," said Dr. Sergei N. Khrushchev in 1989. "We thought that international law did not prohibit Soviet missiles in Cuba and that to put them there would be in our interest. We did not think about or expect the American response." Nor was the missile deployment planned because Nikita Khrushchev thought John Kennedy could be bullied. "My father wanted to test him at their Vienna Summit," Sergei said. "So he took an aggressive line—in general and on Berlin. But Kennedy held his own—unlike Eisenhower, who seemed weak to my father in 1955." Khrushchev aide Fyodor Burlatsky, however, disagrees on this point and thinks that Kennedy looked excessively "refined" to the elder Khrushchev, who concluded that he could be pushed around.

Whether Khrushchev wanted to protect Cuba or redress the nuclear balance, what appeared to be a forward strategy seems to have aimed at preserving the status quo. Whether these policies were well conceived and implemented was another matter. Burlatsky stresses that the first

[33]

secretary made important decisions with little input from other Soviet leaders. Khrushchev's son and the younger Mikoyan concur that Nikita's policies suffered because his advisers—Gromyko and others—were afraid to challenge his ideas. Nikita himself realized this and considered replacing Gromyko with ambassador Anatoly F. Dobrynin not long before he was deposed. Khrushchev's apparent emotionality, his son and Sergo Mikoyan agree, was sometimes for show; his important decisions were taken soberly even though he was a risk taker. (Despite his own concern to avoid nuclear brinks and his deep appreciation for the role of misunderstandings between Moscow and Washington, Sergo Mikoyan believes the Cuban gambit was a good policy and implies that were he in power under such circumstances, he would conduct a similar move. Sergei allows that he would undertake such a course only if he knew it would have a happy ending.)

Notwithstanding his penchant for risky adventures, Khrushchev also planted seeds of a "live and let live" policy that Brezhnev and, later, Gorbachev would carrymuch farther along the continuum from zero-sum conflict toward creating long-term values for each side.

Brezhnev's Variations

Brezhnev's regime paid obeisance to peaceful coexistence, wrapping it in the mantle of the Peace Program endorsed by the CPSU Congress in 1971. Actions taken under this program led to détente (rendered in Russian as *razriadka* or even as a transliteration from the French *détente*) with the West in the early 1970s.

Brezhnev's *razriadka* went further toward collaboration with bourgeois governments than Khrushchev's peaceful coexistence. Brezhnev's ideologists acknowledged an "interconnection" between East and West. Soviet spokesmen declared Moscow's desire to make détente "irreversible" and to expand political into militaty détente. The 1972 Antiballistic Missile (ABM) Treaty tacitly recognized the mutual vulnerability of both superpowers, and other accords Moscow signed with the West in the 1970s assumed the utility of cooperation with competition. The Soviet *Diplomatic Dictionary* (1973) duly noted the "visits" (*vizity*) of Brezhnev and lesser Kremlin personages to other countries.

Under Brezhnev the "who will do in whom" outlook was attenuated but not expunged. The *Soviet Military Encyclopedia* (1976) asserted that "eternal peace" will be possible only with the elimination of classes and the "transition of all countries and peoples to communism." Pacifism, the

[34]

Encyclopedia held, risked distracting the masses from "the true means of outlawing war" but could still be exploited to strengthen Soviet positions and "repel imperialist aggression."[17]

Even Brezhnev's détente shared important similarities with its dogmatically hard-line antecedents. The Brezhnev regime made clear that it did not believe in "convergence" of socialism and capitalism or "interdependence" between North and South. Brezhnev recognized "interconnectedness" between East and West, but not global (North-South) interdependence. Such views constrained Moscow's willingness to cooperate with the West; they also kept the USSR primed for advances in the Third World whatever their risk to East-West détente.

Still, Brezhnev's support for interconnectedness had a much larger potential to transform East-West relations than did Stalin's collective security *cum* Popular Front tactics of Khrushchev's blend of missile-rattling with summitry. Proceeding from Stalin to the present, we find that each major Soviet regime (omitting the brief Andropov-Chernenko interregnum) has moved further toward long-term accommodation with the West.

Approaches to the Third World

Russian policy has long focused on the West. But both tsar and commissar have increased their attention to the Third World when conditions in the West thwarted efforts to advance Russia's interests there by conciliation or coercion. Much of the vast and diverse area that Westerners now term the Third World or South was long termed the East by Russians, but Soviet leaders now talk of the Third World.

Soviet approaches to the Third World have followed diverse orientations analogous to those Moscow has pursued in the West, except that the Third World has not held the threat or the promise inherent in relationships with the West.[18] Not until the 1980s, for example, was there a developing country from which the USSR could import high technology.

The Bolsheviks began their Third World policies with a forward strategy: they appealed to the working peoples and peasants of the East to rise in a kind of *jihad* against Western colonial dominion.

Lenin was quite sensitive to the revolutionary potential of the East. But he disagreed with Indian Communist M. N. Roy at the 1920 Comintern Congress on the priority to be given to "national bourgeois" and Communist revolutionary movements. Lenin contended that in back-

[35]

ward countries Communists should be prepared to assist "a bourgeois-democratic movement of liberation" and support the peasantry against large landowners. He advocated a two-stage approach: first, to strengthen the nationalist bourgeoisie against foreign imperialism and local feudalism; and second, after an industrial proletariat had developed, to work with local Communists to overthrow capitalism. Roy, however, feared that supporting the national bourgeoisie could prove counterproductive; therefore he stressed the importance of creating Communist organizations of workers and peasants—"not through capitalist development, but through the development of class consciousness." Lenin granted that if the "victorious revolutionary proletariat" aided revolutionaries in an Eastern country, it might be able to avoid "the capitalist stage of development," but he emphasized the need to prepare for a long-term struggle. The Comintern endorsed both Lenin's theses and Roy's as supplementary, but in practice Lenin's became the accepted basis of Bolshevik theory and practice in the national and colonial question.[19]

The contradictions between Roy's and Lenin's theses were played out again at the First Congress of Peoples of the East held in Baku, September 1920, and in Soviet policy over the ensuing decades. Critics could charge that Turks, Persians, Koreans, Hindus, and Chinese were turning "not toward the communism of Moscow, but toward the political strength of Moscow," and that the Comintern was treating "the peoples of the East as pieces on the chessboard of the diplomatic war" with the West.[20] In this domain as in others the Kremlin has often been torn between principle and expediency.

Soviet policy conducted by the government as well as the Comintern supported a *forward strategy* against Western imperialism as part of an *indirect advance* to transform the societies of Eastern countries. Thus Moscow supplied arms as well as diplomatic and moral support for Kemal Ataturk's struggle against Greece, Britain, and France, but this aid was meant to prepare conditions over time for the emergence of communism within Turkey.[21] The same strategy led Moscow to support and train Chiang Kai-shek's Kuomintang and to encourge the Chinese Communists to work with the KMT. Closer to home, however, Moscow utilized the direct advance of the Red Army to subdue ethnic minorities on the periphery of the old Russian empire and compel their acceptance of Soviet rule; Stalin also attempted to establish by force a Soviet republic in northern Iran.[22] Still, Moscow's emphasis for most Eastern countries in the 1920s was on a two-stage, indirect advance.

A third approach emerged in 1927: withdrawal and isolationism. This was provoked by the KMT massacre of Chinese Communists, which,

Trotsky argued, showed the bankruptcy of Stalin's policies. Turkey also became a distant and ungrateful neighbor, eventually tilting toward Hitler.[23] These and other factors led Moscow to show little interest in the Third World from the late 1920s until after Stalin's death (although Moscow probed briefly in 1945–46 to expand its domain at the expense of Turkey and Iran and to request a UN trusteeship over Libya). Stalin's distrustful mind converted even Gandhi into a "lackey of imperialism."[24]

A fourth approach—limited cooperation to promote economic development—took shape in the mid-1950s as Khrushchev and Bulganin sought to lift the dead weight of Stalinism and curry the favor of the emerging nations.[25] This orientation resembled the indirect advance pursued earlier toward Kemal's Turkey and the KMT, but it was now backed by much greater technical and economic resources. The Khrushchev regime hoped for early gains in the anti-imperialist struggle, but it did not expect Egypt or India to move soon toward communism. Moscow grudgingly accepted that Nasser would persecute Egypt's Communists even as he received massive Soviet aid.[26]

On rare occasions Soviet and Western development efforts in the Third World overlapped in complementary ways, but usually they were competitive. From the mid-1950s until the mid- or late-1970s most USSR leaders and analysts seemed confident that the new nations would prefer Soviet to Western development models.[27] Moscow hoped that nationalist regimes with a "socialist orientation" could embark on planning, nationalization, and collectivization to put their countries on the road toward revolutionary transformation.[28]

The competitive development orientation promised enormous strategic advantages for the USSR as well as ideological gratification. It could help to displace Western colonialism; purchase Third World declaratory support for Soviet policies (e.g. through declarations by the Nonaligned Movement); facilitate Soviet penetration of local institutions—the military, the universities, and trade unions; and yield facilities to repair or station Soviet planes, ships, and tanks. Directed toward Turkey and Greece, it could undermine NATO.[29]

A development orientation might in certain cases also yield quick revolutionary gains. Thus Moscow probably hoped to expedite Communist rule in Indonesia through manipulation of Sukharno's regime;[30] Soviet representatives may also have backed a leftist coup in the Sudan in 1971.[31] In both cases, however, Moscow's clients were overwhelmed by a conservative counterrevolution.

Despite its theoretical devotion to the two-stage indirect advance and rebuffs in Indonesia and elsewhere, the Kremlin in the 1970s endorsed

[37]

direct advance in many parts of the Third World. Thus it backed Hanoi's conquest of Indochina; supported Communist takeovers of Mozambique and Angola; provided massive military assistance to the revolutionary regime in Ethiopia; and intervened militarily in an effort to keep Communists in power in Kabul.[32] Each of these moves flouted Lenin's warnings about left-wing, "infantile" adventurism. Each was a costly, potentially open-ended commitment with highly uncertain prospects despite Moscow's efforts to build "vanguard parties" and institutional stability amid seas of Third World flux.[33] In the region once dominated by the Monroe Doctrine, however, Moscow showed greater restraint, extending quite limited support to Allende's Chile, leftist Grenada, and Sandinista Nicaragua.[34]

A quite different orientation—one directed toward supporting the territorial status quo—has also emerged on occasion in Soviet policies toward developing countries. In the 1930s it was part of Moscow's collective security campaign at the League of Nations, where the Kremlin opposed Italy's invasion of Abyssinia. Using another technique Prime Minister Kosygin mediated Indian-Pakistani differences in a 1966 meeting at Tashkent. In the late 1970s Moscow tried unsuccessfully to mediate its two clients' conflict over the Ogaden, ultimately backing Ethiopia's drive to repel Somalia's invasion (an occasion when both superpowers urged clients to respect the territorial status quo).[35]

Moscow has often appeared anxious to keep the pot boiling in the Middle East—"the worse, the better." But another tendency has been Soviet support for a stabilizing accommodation, provided only that the USSR is partner to the settlement. The USSR has always held back on offensive arms deliveries to Egypt, one reason for Cairo's break with Moscow in 1972. Even after that slap, however, the USSR intervened to prevent Egypt's defeat in 1973. The Kremlin complains that Henry Kissinger and other U.S. leaders often reneged on promises to include the USSR in a Middle East accord.

Though not the dominant motif in Soviet policy, Moscow's efforts to uphold peace among developing countries could serve as a precedent for East-West policies devoted to stabilizing the Third World. It could also build upon East-West efforts since 1968 to halt the horizontal spread of nuclear weapons and upon East-West-South support for a comprehensive Law of the Sea Convention (jettisoned by the Reagan administration).[36]

In the 1970s and before 1985, however, the Kremlin shied away from policies connoting collaboration with the West in the Third World. Andrei D. Sakharov in 1968 proposed East-West collaboration on a global scale. And Dzherman Gvishiani, son-in-law of then Premier Aleksei

Kosygin, talked about spaceship earth.[37] But global interdependence (like East-West convergence) was anathema for Soviet ideology.[38] Brezhnev himself declared that underdevelopment is the result of Western colonialism and that Moscow bears no responsibility for alleviating its consequences.[39] Asserting that Western propaganda of interdependence cloaked aggressive designs on the Third World, Moscow pointed to its Council for Mutual Economic Assistance (CMEA) as an example of genuine rather than sham interdependence and cooperation.[40] The Kremlin was even quite slow in acknowledging the urgency of population and pollution controls, asserting that these problems too are a result of capitalism or colonialism.

In short, when Brezhnev signed SALT II in 1979, the Kremlin line welcomed far-reaching accommodation with the West, but not in North-South relations, where it expected and pursued zero-sum combat. The battle lines for Moscow became sharper in the early 1980s both in East-West and in Third World competition because of many factors: (1) the Soviet invasion of Afghanistan and U.S. countermeasures; (2) a more hostile attitude toward the USSR in the United States, one that elected and then followed President Reagan; (3) the fragile health of Party leaders Brezhnev, Andropov, and Chernenko, reducing their ability to run a tight ship and implement skillful policies at home and abroad; and (4) the arms control stalemate over SALT II, Euromissiles, and strategic missile defenses.

Rational Actor and Other Explanations

It must be stressed that the USSR (like most other nations) has seldom pursued any policy accent in its pure form across the board for long. Even when courting bourgeois moderates abroad, Moscow has often sought to exploit "contradictions" among and within Western countries and between the First and Third Worlds. As in the late Stalin years, the divergent emphases in Soviet policies have sometimes appeared to have been crafted as by a unified rational actor, wisely orchestrated to optimize overall objectives. But they have also reflected the push and pull of competing factors or persuasions, some going their own ways at odds with the main line.[41] Even when the Kremlin has operated on the basis of one-man rule or Politburo consensus, its decisions have not always been logically integrated.

The Kremlin has seldom functioned on the basis of a master strategy, but neither have its decisions been entirely ad hoc. Like the Kings of Serendip, Soviet leaders have been attuned to opportunities and, constantly looking, have often found them. As a consequence, Soviet policies have usually embodied one or more competing emphases.

When there is no trend line in Soviet policy, as happened after World War II until Stalin's death, summary analysis under one or two rubrics will be misleading. Falling back on the mixed model will explain very little if Soviet policy switches emphases rapidly or exhibits highly contradictory features. Alternatively, there may be times when a mixed model exists but a predominant trend can be discerned beneath the flux. Thus limited collaboration with the West was probably Moscow's *leitmotif* in the early 1970s, even though the Kremlin tried to keep its options open in the Middle East and elsewhere in the Third World. By the late 1970s, however, these emphases had been reversed, as Moscow became disenchanted with détente and more attuned to opportunities in Africa. Thus Moscow might prefer one approach in East-West relations and another in the Third World, sometimes failing to decide which sphere has priority. Honesty requires that we often posit mixed model as the overarching framework for Soviet policies, but it is possible at some times and places to identify a dominant priority pursued by the Kremlin leadership.

Dynamics of the Early 1980s

In the early 1980s the USSR pulled away from détente, trade, and arms control to a line that emphasized confrontation both in East-West and in North-South relations. Rather than East-West trade, the Kremlin leadership now stressed much more the need for autarky. Moscow permitted its hard line on Euromissiles to cloud Soviet relations with Europe and the United States. Soviet leaders endeavored to exploit contradictions within NATO but failed to prevent deployment in Europe of Pershing 2 and cruise missiles. The Kremlin continued to borrow money from the West and to tout the importance of the Soviet gas pipeline to Europe, but East-West transactions disappointed some Soviet leaders, who then called for self-reliance and less dependence on foreign whims, exports, and markets.[42]

In the early 1980s the United States appeared to be regaining its economic prowess. The Pentagon was accelerating the military buildup launched in the late 1970s and moving in new directions under the aegis of

Reagan's Strategic Defense Initiative. The Reagan doctrine promoted counterrevolution from Nicaragua to Afghanistan and augmented the U.S. Rapid Deployment Force. Reagan spurned the Nixon-Ford pledge to treat the USSR as a superpower entitled to "co-equal security." Instead he spoke of an "evil empire" and a "Mickey Mouse system" destined to end on the "ash heap of history."[43]

Washington's Japanese ally and Chinese partner remained hostile to Moscow. Japan, with less than half the Soviet population, was becoming the second largest economic force in the world. Its Self-Defense Forces were joining U.S. and Australian forces in large-scale maneuvers along Russia's Pacific coast.[44] China, gradually enlarging its nuclear arsenal and permitting U.S. intelligence facilities on its territory, added insult to injury by moving toward a market economy. Rather than placate Tokyo or Beijing, however, in the early 1980s Moscow proved unbending on its occupation of Japan's Northern Territories and its military deployments on the Sino-Soviet-Mongolian border.

Beyond Outer Mongolia the USSR's most dependable partner in Communist Asia was Vietnam, whose militarist imperialism and economic failures alienated other Asians. North Korea continued to stress "self-reliance" with occasional bows to Beijing (and with occasional terrorist acts against the Republic of Korea).[45] Meanwhile the other "Gang of Four"—Taiwan, Hong Kong, Singapore, and South Korea—mocked Communist development models.

The 1981 CPSU Congress was less ebullient on Soviet prospects in the Third World than party meetings of 1976 and 1971 had been, a pattern mirrored also in Soviet May Day slogans.[46] The widespread optimism of the late 1950s and the high expectations of the mid-1970s gave way by the early 1980s to cautious, often negative appraisals of the Third World. Many Soviet specialists admitted that the Soviet model had little appeal and little utility for most developing countries. Many acknowledged that although neocolonialism exerts a negative toll, the key to Third World development is really self-help.[47] Moscow's economic aid to the developing nations declined even as its military sales expanded.[48]

Some Soviet leaders and spokesmen continued to glory in Moscow's forward positions in the Third World. Even though Eurocommunism disintegrated, the creation in September 1984 of an Ethiopian Workers' party with its own "politburo" and "central committee" may have kept their dreams alive and legitimated the Soviet system.

Proponents of the classic two-stage, indirect advance had little to show for their case. There have been no instances in which a Soviet-backed liberation movement had passed through the national bourgeois

[41]

stage to a Communist transformation based on the growth of an industrial proletariat. Self-annointed Communists had seized power in some of the poorest Third World countries rather than in the most advanced. The only regimes claiming to be Communist or to have a socialist orientation preside over primitive agrarian economies. Even Cuba remained a monoculture despite the urbanization that preceded Castro. These anomalies helped to provoke a growing sophistication in the rationalizing powers of Soviet scholarship.[49]

An elaborate justification for doing little to help the Third World appeared in 1983. Why is it incorrect, the Soviet analyst asked, to divide countries into rich and poor? First of all, such distinctions based on per capita GNP reveal little about distributions of wealth. Second, this dichotomy ignores the fact that some economic systems are parasitic and exploitative, whereas others earn their wealth by work alone. Countries with a "socialist orientation" are more just and progressive than many other developing countries. Third, this approach mechanically lumps the socialist camp with the rich nations of the North—that is, with states that have long exploited the Third World.[50]

Continuing the hard line that became ascendant in the years before Gorbachev, I. Ivanov argued that it is illusory to call for a New International Economic Order based on voluntary concessions by the North to the South. The capitalist world should not be seen as the "rich North" but as an "alliance of imperialists of all countries, an alliance, natural and inevitable for the defense of capital not knowing any homeland." The "struggle against the cosmopolitanizing [*sic*] foe must not be national-state but international," concerned for the general interests of the oppressed. Sounding like Stalin's directives to the German Communists to avoid collaboration with Social Democrats, Ivanov declared that the anti-imperialist movement in the developing countries must be "democratic and mass, but cut away any accidental fellow-travelers, even if they pretend to leadership in the movement." Petty bourgeois-nationalist illusions about "equality of nations under capitalism" must be dispersed. The movement for economic decolonization must always remember the contradictions between social systems.[51]

Viewed in this way, of course, world politics is truly a zero-sum contest. Any appeal for North-South collaboration is at best naive; at worst, a trick to deceive the masses. On principle the CMEA nations should not join the capitalist countries in programs to ameliorate underdevelopment. This approach tilts towards Roy rather than Lenin in emphasizing the need for purging the liberation movement of fellow travelers not devoted to radical politics. Such arguments may have helped to justify the Soviet embrace of military dictators as in Addis Ababa, but they would imply a Communist defeat when governments such as Angola and Mozambique turned westward for assistance.

India remained the Soviet Union's most useful Third World partner for political, strategic, and commercial purposes. Thus a Soviet author expressed satisfaction that at its 1983 New Delhi summit the Nonaligned Movement remained progressive. Prime Minister Indira Gandhi fended off attacks on Soviet Afghan policies, declaring that if a legitimate government asks for foreign assistance, such aid is also legitimate. Americans were displeased with criticism of their policies at New Delhi, but Moscow was content with the outcome.[52]

The development orientation had paid off in that India could now help to supply Soviet industrial needs. Indeed, the value of Indian exports to the USSR far exceeded Soviet exports, leaving a huge debt that made a farce of Soviet offers to loan nearly a billion rubles to India.[53] A review of some of many Indian-Soviet transactions in early 1984 hinted at the extent to which both countries were involved in a complex commercial web:

—The Steel Authority of India planned to export 150,000 tons of steel to the USSR in 1984, including bars and rounds, angles, plates, and sheets.
—The Indian branch of Rank Xerox won a Soviet contract for 174 copying and multiplying machines in 1984. The USSR was expected to order an Indian version of the French-designed Alouette III helicopter; India planned to export to the USSR computer programs and electronic items in 1984 and 1985 valued at 40 million rupees while Soviet computers were to be imported and installed in India.
—Soviet teams would help India repair eighteen "sick" oil wells in Gujarat, aid seismic surveys there, and deliver seven complete drilling installations to India for 1.5 million rupees.
—USSR and Indian space experts would discuss Soviet launching of an Indian 900-kg remote-sensing satellite in 1986.[54]
—Despite India's plans to diversify sources of arms (e.g., by acquiring advanced Mirage jets from France), India signed with Moscow in 1983–84 for MiG production facilities.[55]

Notwithstanding these developments, the Kremlin was probably anxious that the United States replaced the USSR as India's largest trading partner in 1983, with bilateral volume at $4 billion compared with the Soviet-Indian volume of $3.1 billion.[56] Mrs. Gandhi and then her son Rajiv seemed intent upon improving and broadening sources of military and other technologies. Indians with means to do so preferred to visit, study, or live in Western countries rather than the USSR. But most Indians still saw the USSR as a dependable friend that had intervened very little in the country's internal affairs and had been a firm supporter against Pakistan.[57] Large U.S. economic and military commitments to Pakistan, meanwhile, helped to keep India within the Soviet embrace.

The upshot is that the relative "equality" or "partnership" characterizing Soviet-Indian relations appears to be unusual, if not unique, in Soviet-Third World relations.[58] Although the relationship is not an alliance, it is more than a mere treaty of peace and friendship. Still, Indian and Soviet leaders have usually discussed developments post facto so as to minimize deterioration of their relationship rather than cultivate a consensus-building system such as in NATO or ASEAN or in Japanese-U.S. relations.[59] For Moscow one danger was that New Delhi might switch its "tilt" if Soviet actions in Afghanistan seemed more threatening and if India's ties with the West became more meaningful.

Afghanistan in the early and mid-1980s remained a losing proposition for Moscow.[60] Soviet intervention there was costly at home and abroad, alienating much of the Third World and helping the United States to strengthen its presence from Suez to Malaysia. Routing the mujahideen could facilitate advanced Soviet bases from which to intimidate Pakistan, Iran, and regions to the south, but the prospects of such a victory were clouded. Indeed, Soviet military performance in Afghanistan was weaker that that of the United States in Indochina, considering Moscow's relative advantages: proximity, knowledge of the culture and geography, open terrain (compared with jungle), and lack of informed and articulate domestic opposition.

Nearby Iran remained a wild card beyond manipulation by any outside force. Although Moscow's relations with Khomeini's regime remained cool, however, the USSR and other CEMA nations purchased oil and other products from Iran and talked of broader commercial and technological collaboration.[61] From the early 1980s through 1987 there had also been reports of Soviet (as well as Israeli, U.S., and other) arms deliveries to Iran.[62]

The Kremlin seemed to gain influence in Syria, Iraq, and perhaps Libya and Morocco in the early 1980s, but Moscow was holding a series of tigers by the tail. Any one could lead the USSR into a dangerous confrontation; and any one could pull another "Sadat," ordering the Soviets to leave. Israel's 1982 invasion of southern Lebanon and rout of Syrian forces in the Bekaa Valley made the Kremlin again look like a shabby protector.[63]

In the Western Hemisphere Cuba remained a relatively faithful partner, especially as a collaborator in Africa. Grenada fell to the United States, but Sandinista Nicaragua held out, leading the Reagan administration to spend prodigious amounts of time and moral capital on the Contra cause.[64] But most Caribbean and Latin countries wanted economic development and knew that Soviet capacity for assistance was quite limited.

The Kremlin did not—perhaps could not—entirely discourage its clients from trading with the West. The USSR continued to support Angola, Mozambique, and Ethiopia, but they added to the string of basket cases among Soviet clients in the Third World. Moscow did not openly object to Mozambique's partial rapprochement with South Africa and its broader efforts to increase economic ties with the West.[65] France planned in 1984 to double its aid to Mozambique and establish a joint bilateral commission there.[66] Angola continued to derive revenues from oil operations by U.S. companies. Boeing, Arthur D. Little, and Utah International were also active there. Early in 1984 Geophysical Service of Dallas won an Angolan contract for an offshore oil survey, and Gulf Oil contracted with C-E Natco for a $1 million package to double oil production of the Takula field platform off Cabinda.[67]

Even though the USSR was embarrassed by famine in Ethiopia and its client's need to depend heavily on Western relief, Soviet propagandists had a field day with the tenth anniversary of the revolutionary regime in Addis Ababa. Treating the Worker's Party of Ethiopia with the respect due a fraternal party, Soviet Politburo member G. V. Romanov attended the celebrations in September 1984 along with comrades Todor Zhivkov and Erich Honecker (who found it easier to visit Africa than to accept a recent invitation to Bonn).[68]

Even Eastern Europe was becoming more dependent upon the West for credit and, at least in the case of Poland, for food. Moscow could no longer fulfill the region's need for oil and modern technology, but the Kremlin feared a wider opening by its CMEA partners to the West. Hungary with its limited market system and East Germany with its work ethic and ties to West Germany were the region's leading producers. Throughout most of Eastern Europe anti-Soviet sentiments were rising, coupled with antipathy or apathy toward local Communist regimes. It could not be known whether in a war Eastern European armies would fight with or against the USSR.[69]

Indeed, Moscow's emphasis on outward expansion through direct advance drew to a halt in the early 1980s. The Kremlin continued aid, particularly military assistance, to its clients such as Ethiopia and Vietnam. But the USSR seemed to have its hands full or to be sated and thus passed up possibilities for vigorous intervention in Iran, Guinea, Morocco, and Lebanon.[70] The Kremlin also appeared most reluctant to intervene militarily to impose discipline on wayward Eastern Europeans. Although in 1979–80 the Kremlin had dispatched over 100,000 troops to Afghanistan, for sixteen months (1980–81) Moscow watched the upsurge of antiregime activities in Poland without employing Soviet armed forces to reaffirm Communist rule. Finally, in December 1981 the Military Council of National Salvation led by General Wojciech Jaruzelski proclaimed martial law and repressed Solidarity, thereby removing any immediate need for Soviet military intervention.

The contrast with earlier cases of Eastern European unrest was striking. East Germany's 1953 uprising was crushed by Soviet tanks in days; Hungary's in 1956, in weeks. Czechoslovakia's 1968 experiment in "socialism with a human face" endured eight months before it was smothered—with little bloodshed—by Soviet and other Warsaw Treaty forces. The pattern seemed clear: each challenge from 1953 through 1981 endured longer than its antecedent, whereas active Soviet participation and blood-letting diminished after 1956. Both hegemonic and restive subjects had become more cautious. Soviet policy was becoming more sophisticated, but it also betrayed a loss of imperial will.[71]

Foreign troubles reflected and contributed to domestic weaknesses. The USSR was troubled by a stagnant economy and declining morale; increasing nationalism among the Soviet nationalities; a looming shortage of manpower for military, industrial, and farm needs; persistent agricultural shortfalls; entrenched interests resisting constructive change; falling standards of public health manifested in rising infant deaths and declining life spans; tensions between white-collar aspirations and the need for blue-collar skills and labor; and, until 1985, an experienced but ailing gerontocracy with no sure mechanisms for infusing younger energies and new ideas into leadership circles.[72]

Soviet policies in the early 1980s became as brittle and stiff as the bones of Kremlin leaders. In some respects Soviet behavior in the five years before Gorbachev's ascent resembled tsarist actions in the mid- and late-nineteenth century. Flirtation with Enlightenment ideas had long ceased at court; the Holy Alliance existed only on paper; Eastern Europeans gathered in Prague and spoke out against Russian dominion; France and Britain invaded the Crimea. From this humiliation nationalist and Pan-Slavic sentiments grew, driving a pendulum swing against the Caucasus, Central Asia, the Far East, and once again the Ottoman Empire. A latecomer to Africa, Russia became Ethiopia's patron against Italy at the end of the century, only to be defeated in the Far East a few years later by the up-and-coming Japan. Though the tsars and local government made some progress on perplexing domestic issues such as serfdom and educational reforms, social discord mounted, threatening the ancien régime even before the World War. Writers Ivan Turgenev and Lev Tolstoi won world approval, only to be seen as dissidents at court. Trade and other improvements in relations between St. Petersburg and Washington were undercut by Russian anti-Semitic outbursts and the American response. The United States stood aloof from Russia during World War I until the monarchy collapsed in the February Revolution.

Tsarist Russia did not cope well with the changing challenges and opportunities of the last century. The Soviet system in the 1970s and early 1980s seemed increasingly unable to cope with accumulating problems at home and abroad.

Table 2.1 summarises the dominant tendencies in Soviet policies toward the West and Third World in the early 1980s. Also outlined are the tendencies that appeared most likely to be useful in avoiding superpower confrontation and in resolving global problems.

A mixed approach characterized Soviet policy both in East-West affairs and in the Third World. The strongest motif in Moscow's stance toward the West, however, was inversion. Confronted with a tougher American posture and NATO's decision to proceed with INF deployment, the Bear withdrew to its corner in a mood of defiance, its growls more noticeable than any sweet overtures toward détente still resounding from the 1970s. The gerontocracies of the early 1980s may well have preferred to continue the détente politics of the previous decade, but they seemed unable to muster a creative response to the harder inflections in Western policy.[73] Their main success was carrying through the gas pipeline to Europe despite U.S. attempts to block the project. The Kremlin continued to make some effort to ensure the stability of the European territorial and political status quo through continuation of the "Helsinki process" and by backing East German representation in various forums. Moscow also did what it could to help the indirect advance of Soviet influence by giving qualified support to Eurocommunism and attempting to bribe European news media. The two polar alternatives—direct advance and global interdependence—had no apparent support within the Party leadership.

The most salient Soviet posture in the Third World was Moscow's continued support for leftist regimes in Afghanistan, Indochina, Africa, and the Caribbean. The Kremlin had to expand fresh and substantial resources to support the forward advances made since the mid-1970s. Soviet and Cuban troops were dying from engagements with anti-Communist forces backed by the United States. Less costly for Moscow

[47]

TABLE 2.1
Soviet Alternatives, Dominance Versus Utility*

Dominant Tendencies in Soviet Policy, 1981–85

	IN EAST-WEST RELATIONS	IN THE THIRD WORLD
Strongest and most likely ↑	1. Mixed model	1. Mixed model
	2. Inversion, defiance	2. Direct advance/forward strategy (holding pattern after 1980)
	3. Limited collaboration: détente, arms control, trade	3. Limited collaboration with developing countries: competitive development orientation
	. . .	4. Indirect advance
	4. Territorial status quo	5. Territorial status quo
	. . .	. . .
	5. Indirect advance	
	. . .	. . .
	. . .	6. Inversion, withdrawal
	6. Global interdependence	7. Global interdependence
	7. Direct advance/forward strategy	

Tendencies Most Useful to Resolution of Global Problems in 1980s–1990s

	IN EAST-WEST RELATIONS	IN THE THIRD WORLD
Hypothetically most useful ↑	1. Global interdependence	1. Global interdependence
	2. Limited collaboration: détente, arms control, trade	2. Limited collaboration: competitive development orientation
	3. Territorial status quo	3. Territorial status quo
	. . .	. . .
	4. Inversion, withdrawal	4. Inversion, withdrawal
	. . .	. . .
	. . .	. . .
	5. Mixed model	5. Mixed model
	. . .	. . .
	6. Indirect advance	6. Indirect advance
	. . .	. . .
	. . .	
	7. Direct advance/forward strategy	7. Direct advance/forward strategy

*Foreign policy tendencies here are analogous to "revealed preferences"; the ranking is basically along an ordinal scale, but ellipses indicate significant intervals between some choices.

and less attention-grabbing in the West was the continuation of limited Soviet collaboration with many developing countries not led by Marxist-Leninist regimes. In some Third World countries the USSR also paved the way for an indirect advance by cultivating young people and others likely to be alienated from the ruling circles, but this trend was checked by Soviet determination not to offend the non-Communist elites of countries such as India, Bangladesh, and Sri Lanka. Moscow continued also to uphold the territorial status quo of most established states in the Third World, except that Israel and South Africa were encouraged to give up some lands under their control. Despite rising challenges to Soviet clients, as in Kabul and Hanoi, and mounting costs of empire, Moscow showed little disposition in the early 1980s to withdraw from exposed salients in the Third World. Even less did it incline toward North-South cooperation.

On most counts the dominant tendencies in Soviet policy in the early 1980s were quite different from those that appeared most desirable from the standpoint of peacefully and constructively resolving global problems.[74] The inverted but defiant Bear confronted the talons of the Reagan counterrevolution, as Moscow and Washington "confirmed" each other's darkest expectations. Similarly, the dominant trend in Soviet policy toward the Third World—direct advance—was the one most likely to spur East-West conflicts and to obstruct cooperation to reduce hunger and reverse desiccation. The Kremlin took no account of the extent to which its behavior—especially the SS-20 deployment and Afghan expedition—was fueling this conflict spiral. With little empathy in either Moscow or Washington, there was also little hope for accommodation.

Would Gorbachev's regime continue the orientations of the early 1980s? If so, would it carry them out with greater tact and skill? Might it even introduce new priorities or at least new ways to pursue old goals? Later sections of this book argue that Gorbachev did in fact reorder Soviet priorities and change the means by which Moscow pursued its objectives. To underscore the differences and continuities between Gorbachev's "new thinking" and old Soviet thinking, we first review in more detail cases of "high" and "low" politics—Soviet policies toward arms control and "global problems"—before the Gorbachev revolutions.[75]

Notes

1. For an exemplary study, see Timothy J. Colton, *The Dilemma of Reform in the Soviet Union*, rev. ed. (New York: Council on Foreign Relations, 1986); for historical background, see S. Frederick Staar, "A Peculiar Pattern," *The Wilson Quarterly* 13, no. 2 (Spring 1989): 37–50.

2. On continuity and change, see Ivo J. Lederer, ed., *Russian Foreign Policy: Essays in Historical Perspective* (New Haven, CT: Yale University Press, 1962).

3. The approaches outlined here are simplified models abstracted from a more complex and contradictory reality. They will be of value if they provide tools for discourse and analysis. For example, "Has Moscow changed from the x to the y orientation?" or "Events show that conditions are not ripe for the y approach but will probably generate a z orientation." The analyst must resist reducing Soviet behavior to a dominant orientation when in fact it pulses with contradictions. State Department analyst Robert Baraz once cautioned that Soviet foreign policy resembles more the complexity of Bach counterpoint

than the allegro-andante patterns of a Beethoven symphony! This chapter suggests that leitmotifs often exist in Soviet policy despite much counterpoint. A dominant approach is more likely in Soviet than in U.S. policy because the former has usually been more centralized. In any event the analyst is bound to look for the forest and not just the trees. For further discussion, see Jack Snyder, "Science and Sovietology," *World Politics* 40, no. 2 (January 1988): 169–93.

4. These approaches are modifications of those developed in Walter C. Clemens, Jr., "Soviet Policy in the Third World in the 1970's: Five Alternative Futures," in W. Raymond Duncan, ed., *Soviet Policy in Developing Countries* (Walthan, MA: Ginn-Blaisdell, 1970), 313–43; idem, "Soviet Policy Toward Europe," in Roman Kolkowicz and others, *The Soviet Union and Arms Control: A Superpower Dilemma* (Baltimore, MD: Johns Hopkins University Press, 1970), 149–80; and idem, *The U.S.S.R. and Global Interdependence: Alternative Futures* (Washington, DC: American Enterprise Institute, 1978).

5. Lenin began with an "essentialist" image of capitalism similar to the "evil empire" view of the USSR held by the first Reagan administration. An essentialist outlook focuses on doctrine and system; a "mechanistic" lens on the mechanisms of geopolitics and the balance of power; and "interaction" model emphasizes interactive patterns and overlapping interests. See Alexander Dallin and Gail W. Lapidus, "Reagan and the Russians: United States Policy Toward the Soviet Union and Eastern Europe," in Kenneth A. Oye, Robert J. Lieber, and Donald Rothchild, eds. *Eagle Defiant* (Boston: Little, Brown, 1983) 206–10. In the early 1920s Lenin moved away from essentialism toward one or perhaps both of the other models. Gorbachev appeared in 1986–89 to be attuned to mechanistic and interaction models, but some of his speeches also showed dogmatic roots in essentialist thought.

6. For "peaceful coexistence" as used by Trotsky, Chicherin, and Lenin, see Walter C. Clemens, Jr., *The Superpowers and Arms Control* (Lexington, MA: Lexington Books, 1973) 41–42.

7. See Walter C. Clemens Jr., "Bolshevik Expectations of a German Revolution during War Communism," Russian Institute Certificate Essay, Columbia University, 1957; for a convenient translation of many key documents, see *The Bolsheviks and the October Revolution. Minutes of the Central Committee of the Russian Social-Democratic Labour Party (Bolsheviks) August 1917-February 1918* (London: Pluto Press, 1974).

8. For a Soviet exposition of this period, see A. A. Gromyko and V. N. Ponomarev, eds., *Istoriia vneshnei politiki SSSR*, 2 vols. (Moscow: Nauka, 1976), I: 283–389, which also gives a brief treatment of the Soviet-German nonaggression treaty of 1939, pp. 389–94. For a Baltic perspective on the treaty's secret protocol, see documents and analysis by E. Laasi and K. Ariakas in *Raduga* (Tallinn) 12 (1988): 78–94.

9. See also Vojtech Mastny, *Russia's Road to the Cold War* (New York: Columbia University Press, 1979); see also many of the essays in Brian D. Dailey and Patrick J. Parker, eds., *Soviet Strategic Deception* (Lexington, MA: Lexington Books, 1987).

10. See Jonathan Haslam, *Soviet Foreign Policy, 1930–33: The Impact of the Depression* (London: Macmillan, 1983), see 19–20.

11. On difficulties in the coalition, see Herbert Feis, *Churchill, Roosevelt, and Stalin: The War They Waged and the Peace They Sought* (Princeton: Princeton University Press, 1957); for a Soviet view, Viktor L. Israelian, *Diplomaticheskaia istoriia Velikoi otchestvennoi voiny, 1941–1945 gg.* (Moscow: Institut mezhdunarodnykh otnoshenii, 1959).

12. For ways in which Moscow and the West were out of phase, see Walter C. Clemens, Jr., "American Policy and the Origins of the Cold War in Central Europe, 1945–1947," in Peter J. Poltichnyj and Jane P. Shapiro, eds., *From the Cold War to Détente* (New York: Praeger, 1976), 3–25.

13. See Hannes Adomeit, *Soviet Risk–Taking and Crisis Behavior* (Boston: Unwin Hyman, 1982).

14. See Gavriel D. Ra'anan, *International Policy Formation in the USSR* (Hamden, CT: Archon Books, 1983). A former German Communist has described the conflicting emphases in Kremlin policy before and after Soviet forces began to administer East Germany: Wolfgang Leonhard, *Die Revolution entlaesst ihre Kinder* (Cologne: Kiepenheuer & Witsch, 1955).

15. For analysis, see Frederic S. Burin, "The Communist Doctrine of the Inevitability of War," *American Political Science Review* 57, no. 2 (June 1963): 334–54. See also Khrushchev on Lenin in *Pravda*, June 22, 1960.

16. Some of the following analysis is based on comments by Sergo Mikoyan, Sergei N. Khrushchev, and Fydor Burlatsky at meetings at Harvard University in 1988–89 and on reports of related discussions held in Moscow in January 1989 involving not only Soviet and U.S. but Cuban participants in the Cuban missile crisis. See also James G. Blight and David A. Welch, *On the Brink: Americans and Soviets Reexamine the Cuban Missile Crisis* (New York: Hill and Wang, 1989). On Berlin 1961, see also Adomeit, *Soviet Risk Taking*.

17. Volume VI quoted in Albert L. Weeks, comp., *Brassey's Soviet and Communist Quotations* (Washington: Pergamon-Brassey's International Defense Publishers, 1987), 115.

18. For collections of Lenin's writings on the East, see V. I. Lenin, *The National-Liberation Movement in the East* (Moscow: Foreign Languages Publishing House, 1957) and *Lenin o druzhbe s narodami Vostoka* (Moscow: Gospolitizdat, 1961). For background, see Elliot R. Goodman, *The Soviet Design for a World State* (New York: Columbia University Press, 1957), 375–77.

19. On the Lenin-Roy debate and its long-term significance, see Edward H. Carr, *A History of Soviet Russia: The Bolshevik Revolution, 1917–1923*, 3 vols. (London: Penguin, 1966), III: 254–58.

20. Criticisms by Western European socialists quoted in ibid., p. 268.

21. Mikhail Frunze, then commander-in-chief of Soviet forces in the Ukraine, arrived in Ankara on December 13, 1921 and signed a treaty between the Ukrainian Republic and Turkey on January 2, 1922. Frunze arranged for shipments of Soviet munitions to Turkey and mapped out a campaign against the Greeks in which, if need be, Soviet officers would participate. See Ministry of Foreign Affairs, *Dokumenty vneshnei politiki SSSR* (Moscow: Politizdat, 1961), V, Documents 1, 2, 3, 7, 8, 13, 22, and 76; also Louis Fischer, *The Soviets in World Affairs, 1917–1929*, 2 vols. (Princeton, NJ: Princeton University Press, 1951), I: 393–94.

22. On the Soviet conquest of the Caucasus, see Richard Pipes, *The Formation of the Soviet Union*, rev. ed. (New York: Atheneum, 1968), 214–41.

23. To impress both the Soviets and the British, Kemal Ataturk founded and staffed the Turkish Communist party in 1920; once firmly in control and enjoying good relations with Britain, he cracked down on the TCP and banned it in 1925. See Alvin Z. Rubenstein, *Soviet Policy toward Turkey, Iran, and Afghanistan* (New York: Praeger, 1982), 6–7. The two-stage approach did not work very well toward China or Turkey; Roy's approach, had it been followed, would at least have been more in tune with ideological principle.

24. For Soviet debates in the interwar years and after World War II, see Jerry Hough, *The Struggle for the Third World* (Washington, DC: Brookings Institution, 1986), chaps. 3 and 5.

25. The first sign of change came in May 1952 when the president of the USSR Chamber of Commerce told an International Economic Conference in Moscow that the Soviet Union wanted to expand trade with Southeast Asia and the Middle East. But little action was taken to do so until after Stalin's death. See Elizabeth Kridl Valkenier, *The Soviet Union and the Third World: An Economic Bind* (New York: Praeger, 1983), 2–3.

26. Military supplies have long played a major role in Soviet aid programs. For two case studies, see Uri Ra'anan, *The USSR Arms the Third World* (Cambridge, MA: MIT Press, 1969); also Bruce D. Porter, *The USSR in Third World Conflicts* (Cambridge: Cambridge University Press, 1984).

27. Valkenier, *The Soviet Union and the Third World*, chap. 3.

28. For a concise analysis, see Abraham S. Becker, "The Soviet Union and the Third World: The Economic Dimension," in Andrzej Korbonski and Francis Fukuyama, *The Soviet Union and the Third World: The Last Three Decades* (Ithaca, NY: Cornell University Press, 1987), chap. 4.

29. For an overview, see Stephen Sestanovich, "The Third World in Soviet Policy, 1955-1985," ibid., chap. 1.

30. See Stephen S. Kaplan et al., *Diplomacy of Power* (Washington, DC: Brookings Institution, 1981), 161–62.

31. See Alvin Z. Rubenstein, "Air Support in the Arab East," in Kaplan, *Diplomacy of Power*, pp. 468–518 at 490–99.

32. See Colin Legum, "Angola and the Horn of Africa," in ibid., pp. 570–637; of the many works on Afghanistan, see Henry S. Bradsher, *Afghanistan and the Soviet Union*, rev. ed. (Durham, NC: Duke University Press, 1985); on the connections between domestic and foreign policy in the 1970s, see Harry Gelman, *The Brezhnev Politburo and the Decline of Détente* (Ithaca, NY: Cornell University Press, 1984).

33. On vanguard parties, see Rajan Menon, *Soviet Power and the Third World* (New Haven, CT: Yale University Press, 1986, 50–54.

34. On U.S. as well as Soviet costs, see Walter C. Clemens, Jr., "The Superpowers and the Third World: Aborted Ideals and Wasted Assets," in Charles W. Kegley, Jr. and Pat McGowan, eds., *Foreign Policy USA/USSR* (Berverly Hills, CA: Sage, 1982), 111–35.

35. See Raymond L. Garthoff, *Détente and Confrontation* (Washington, DC: Brookings Institution, 1985), 630–53. For case studies of Soviet policy in Angola and the Ogaden war, see Porter, *USSR in Third World Conflicts*, chaps. 8 and 9.

36. See, for example, William C. Potter, "Nuclear Export Policy: A Soviet-American Comparison," in Kegley and McGowan, *Foreign Policy USA/USSR*, pp. 291–313.

37. See chapters 5 and 6 in this book.

38. A proponent of trade emphasized that the mutual influence of socialism and capitalism through economic ties "has nothing to do with the simple-minded *[ploskoi]* concept of 'convergence'. It is [rather] a living process of coexistence and struggle of two opposing systems." See V. Shemiatenkov, " 'Ekonomicheskaia voina' ili ekonomicheskoe sorevnovanie?" *Mirovaia ekonomika i mezhdunarodnye otnosheniia* (hereafter cited as *MEMO*), no. 3 (March 1983): 30–40 at 39–40.

39. See Brezhnev's replies to questions put by *Le Monde* as published in *Izvestiia*, June 16, 1977. Brezhnev and other Soviet spokesmen also made clear that their country had its own problems and that its capacities to aid others were limited. See *Pravda*, October 5, 1976.

40. Attacking interdependence as the ideology of neocolonialism, M. Valkov traced the concept to the European Economic Community, which provided for some economic integration despite distinct national political identities. He cited Lenin's insight, expressed during World War I, that the unity of nations under capitalism is a sophism in defense of opportunism. (Still other Soviets have traced "interdependence" to the 1950s when the United States used it to describe the nature of NATO.)

Though attacking Lester R. Brown's concept of a "world without borders" as an argument for hegemony by the strong, the author *endorsed* the use of the term "economic interdependence" in the Helsinki Final Act (para. 146). See M. Volkov, "Kontseptsiia 'vzaimozavisimosti natsii' i ideologiia neokolonializma," *MEMO*, no. 9 (September 1980): 64–76.

41. See Jiri Valenta and William C. Potter, eds., *Soviet Decisionmaking for National Security* (Boston: Unwin Hyman, 1984).

42. There were three broad stages: 1970–75, euphoric hopes for trade expansion; 1975–79, "sober reevaluation"; then, in the early 1980s, a shift toward autarky. An Taeg-Won, "Economic Debates within Soviet Leadership Circles from 1972–82: 'Interdependency versus Autarky'," *Sino-Soviet Affairs* (Seoul) 8, no. 2 (Summer 1984): 43–82. The article is a revised chapter of a Ph.D. dissertation at the University of Georgia, 1984.

43. For a summary of U.S. policies in Reagan's first term, see Oye et al., *Eagle Defiant*; on their assumptions, see Walter C. Clemens, Jr., "Intellectual Foundations of Reagan's Soviet Policy: The Threadbare Emperor," in Bernard Rubin, ed., *When Information Counts* (Lexington, MA: Lexington Books, 1985), 155–72, 227–31.

44. On multinational maneuvers off the Soviet coast, see *Far Eastern Economic Review*, June 16, 1983, p. 53.

45. Hanoi's greater dependency upon Moscow was manifested in 1986–87 through its relatively positive response to Gorbachev's campaigns for greater openness and democracy in the USSR; Vietnam even held some multicandidate elections. Kim Il-sung, by comparison, went no further than to praise revolutionary changes taking place in the USSR, not

committing himself to any of the specifics of the Gorbachev program. Source: Research paper by Michael Jackman, Boston University Graduate School, spring 1987. For studies of Soviet policies toward Korea and Indochina, see Richard H. Solomon and Masataka Kosaka, eds., *The Soviet Far East Military Buildup* (Dover, MA: Auburn House, 1986), esp. chaps. 10 and 11.

46. For comparative comments on all Party congresses, 1956 through 1981, see the index to Valkenier, *Soviet Union and the Third World*, p. 178.

47. See ibid., p. 117 and Hough, *Struggle for the Third World*, esp. chap. 8.

48. See Menon, *Soviet Power*, chap. 4.

49. Nodari Simoniia argued that there is a differentiation in the internal structure of the developing countries and in their external orientation. Some developing countries take a revolutionary-democratic route, whereas others follow a capitalist path. Those of "socialist orientation" are in a presocialist stage. There will be inconsistencies between their domestic and foreign policies. He noted also that local conflicts, as between Arabs and non-Arabs, can push countries from left to right or from right to left. Further, countries with significant internal markets and in which the share of the economy inherited from the colonial regime is small, such as India, usually favor nonalignment. When raw material production predominates, this may lead local governments to keep ties with colonial regimes and side with imperialism, as in the African states associated with the EEC. See N. A. Simoniia, "Natsional'no-gosudarstvennaia konsolidatsiia i politecheskaia differentsiatsiia razvivaiushchikhsia stran vostoka," *MEMO*, no. 1 (January 1983): 84–96. Reference to presocialist stage is at p. 94. For elaboration, see L. I. Reisner and N. A. Simoniia, eds., *Evoliutsiia vostochnykh obshchestv: sintez traditsionnogo i sovremennogo mira* (Moscow: Nauka, 1984).

50. I. Ivanov, "Kontseptsiia 'bednykh' i 'bogatikh' stran: Itoki, suchshnost', napravlennost'," *MEMO*, no. 1 (January 1983): 22–31.

51. Ibid., esp. pp. 30–31.

52. Iu. Alimov, "Dvizhenie neprisoedineniia na vazhnom rubezhe," *Kommunist*, no. 7 (May 1983): 99–110; see also K. Brutents, "Dvizhenie neprisoedineniia v sovremennom mire," *MEMO*, no. 5 (April 1984): 26–41. There were other indications in the Soviet press, however, that Moscow was displeased that Mrs. Gandhi had not kept the Nonaligned movement on a more pro-Soviet inclination. See Joseph G. Whelan, *The Soviet Union in the Third World, 1980–1982: An Imperial Burden or Political Asset? The Soviets in Asia, an Expanding Presence* (Washington, DC: Congressional Research Service, 1984), 150–51. For an evaluation of the movement's pre-1983 tilt, see Walter C. Clemens, Jr., "Nonalignment and/or Interdependence?" in U. S. Bajpai, ed., *Non-Alignment: Perspectives and Prospects* (New Delhi: Lancers, 1983), 39–50 (and Atlantic Highlands, NJ: Humanities Press, 1983).

53. See Leo E. Rose, "United States and Soviet Policy toward South Asia," *Current History* 85, no. 509 (March 1986): 135.

54. See *Interflo: An East-West Trade News Monitor* (Maplewood, NJ) 3, no. 4 (February 1984): 28; ibid., 3, no. 5 (March 1984): 24. A Soviet economist told an Indian audience at the Soviet cultural center in New Delhi in September 1983 that the current Soviet Five-Year Plan counted on trade with India. Between the two countries there had emerged, he said, a relationship of mutual dependence (author's observation).

55. For background, see *Financial Times* (London), October 19, 1983, p. 6; Menon, *Soviet Power*, p. 202.

56. In 1985 the USSR was India's second largest trading partner and would have been number one if India had found products other than oil and arms to import from the Soviet Union. See Rose, "United States and Soviet Policy," p. 135. In 1983 the USSR claimed to be India's largest trading partner. See the Soviet claim and an Indian analysis cited in Whelan, *Soviet Union in the Third World*, p. 143.

57. Author's observations and interviews during three visits to different parts of India in 1982–83. Surveys conducted by the Indian Institute of Public Opinion during 1971–81 revealed that the USSR "has almost always led the United States in popularity." See Whelan, *Soviet Union in the Third World*, p. 132. There were also many occasions in 1982–83, however, when Soviet cultural and trade representatives could be seen as "ugly Russians," haughty and aloof from India's people and their problems.

[53]

58. Whelan, ibid., pp. 130–31.

59. Rose, "United States and Soviet Policy," p. 134.

60. See also chapter 1 in this book.

61. See e.g., *Interflo* 3, no. 4 (February 1984): 28, and no. 5 (March 1984): 4, 18. For a broader picture, see Michael J. Dixon, *The Soviet Union in the Third World, 1980–1982: An Imperial Burden or Political Asset? The Soviet Union and the Middle East* (Washington, DC: Congressional Research Service, 1983), 12–25.

62. Ibid., p. 23. See also Leslie Gelb, "Iran Said to Get Large-Scale Arms from Israel, Soviets and Europeans," *The New York Times*, March 8, 1982, p. A10.

63. See Cynthia Roberts, "Soviet Arms Transfer Policy and the Decision to Upgrade Syrian Air Defences," *Survival* (July-August 1983): 155.

64. See, John Tower et al., *The Tower Commission Report* (New York: Bantam Books and Times Books, 1987).

65. For many reports on Mozambique negotiations with South Africa and various Western countries, see *Interflo* 3, no. 4 (February 1984): 22.

66. Ibid., no. 5 (March 1984): 20. After his predecessor's fatal flight on a Soviet aircraft, Mozambique's new president, Joaquim Chissano, reportedly decided to fly on a Boeing jet piloted by Mozambican or Portuguese crews. See William M. Carley in *The Wall Street Journal*, July 1, 1987, pp. 1, 13.

67. *Interflo* 3, no. 4 (February 1984): 4; no. 5 (March 1984): 4.

68. See many items in Foreign Broadcast Information Service (FBIS), *Daily Report: Soviet Union*, September 1984.

69. See Valerie Bunce, "The Empire Strikes Back: The Transformation of the Eastern Bloc from a Soviet Asset to a Soviet Liability," *International Organization* 39, no. 1 (Winter 1985): 1–46; also Ivan Volgyes, "Guns or Butter? The Impact of Military Spending upon the Social Sectors in Eastern Europe," paper presented at the Annual Meeting of the American Association for the Advancement of Slavic Studies, New York, 1985.

70. Andy Bennet, "Soviet Military Intervention and Retrenchment: Alternative Explanations," seminar at Harvard Center for Science and International Affairs, November 25, 1987.

71. See Walter C. Clemens, Jr., *National Security and US-Soviet Relations*, rev. ed. (Muscatine, IA: Stanley Foundation, 1982), 33–37. Soviet passivity continued in 1986 as Moscow sat tight during South Yemen's intra-Communist war and the chaos that ended the ancien régime of the Philippines, where the Soviet ambassador presented himself to "President" Marcos when even Washington was distancing itself from its former client.

72. See Seweryn Bialer, *The Soviet Paradox* (New York: Knopf, 1986). Some aspects of this malaise, however, derive from social progress. Thus higher infant mortality results in part from the fact that more frail babies are now delivered in hospitals who might otherwise have died of asphyxia and been counted as stillbirths. See Colton, *Dilemma of Reform*, pp. 240–41, notes 6 and 13.

73. In late 1984–early 1985 the Kremlin became more conciliatory at the Stockholm security conference and on possible collaboration on global problems. It is not known whether this change resulted from Chernenko's setting or from Gorbachev's rising star. See chapter 5 of this book.

74. This perspective assumes that resolution of global problems would be easier if Moscow cooperates with the West in value-creating than if the Kremlin persists in one or more of its zero-sum orientations.

75. Gorbachev's interest in learning from history is mentioned repeatedly in his book *Perestroika* (New York: Harper & Row, 1987). His willingness to draw radical lessons was, however, quite muted in his speech on November 2, 1987 appraising seventy years of Soviet power.

II
Pressures for Change, 1917–85

3
Driving Forces in the Soviet Crucible:
Arms Control Imperatives

The Eagle and the Bear: Talons and Hugs

Leading sometimes from strength but more often from weakness, Russia's rulers have championed arms limitations to bolster their strengths and lessen those of their adversaries. No other country has campaigned so often and so urgently to curb arms and ban force. These campaigns have emanated not from a small, weak state but from the world's largest geopolitical entity possessing a huge military force that intimidates others.[1]

Second to Russia in such advocacy has been the United States—strong supporter at the turn of the century of compulsory arbitration, leading proponent of the League of Nations and the United Nations, and initiator of many moves to curb the engines of war, from the Washington Naval Limitations of 1922 through the "zero option" on intermediate-range missiles of the 1980s.

Why should any country propose, accept, or implement arms control? The Eagle may seek to destroy the Tiger's fangs or the Lion's claws while keeping its own talons; the Bear, as Salvador de Madariaga suggested during the League of Nations disarmament talks, might seek to prohibit every weapon except the all-encompassing embrace![2]

Adversaries could agree to seek common objectives such as strategic stability through arms control, but one or both sides might also try to exploit arms negotiations and agreements for one-sided gains. The weaker

[57]

or more aggressive side might try to pull down the enemy's forces or neutralize its advantages and then conduct an end-run sweep while it naps.[3]

The experience analyzed in this book, however, suggests that state interests can best be advanced by negotiations that seek to *create* values for both sides, not *claim* or extract them for unilateral advantage. If one or both sides approaches arms control as a zero-sum struggle, it is unlikely that either will achieve any accord. Like diffident players in game theory's "Prisoner's Dilemma," they will continue to punish themselves because they cannot coordinate their efforts to gain freedom. If rivals do somehow reach an accord enshrining a significant *unilateral* advantage, the deal may fall apart and the climate for follow-on accords will be harsher. Arms control accords, if they are to prove durable, should not give either party asymmetrical gains that the other will strive to overthrow—as Germany did the "unequal" obligations of the Versailles Treaty.

In the nuclear era Americans have generally viewed arms control as a technical exercise: as a way to ease the costs of defense, reduce the likelihood of war, and contain war's devastation should it occur. Their ultimate standard for evaluating arms control has been this question: Do these measures contribute to crisis stability—to reducing incentives to strike first?

A far broader range of interests and concerns has shaped arms and arms control planning in St. Petersburg and Moscow than in Washington and Santa Monica. It has included the following.

Ideology: Far more concerned about political doctrine than Americans, Russian leaders before and after 1917 have sought policies that seemed to flow logically from their official worldview and to confirm or justify its basic suppositions.

Propaganda: The Kremlin has been deeply conscious of the political uses to which campaigns for peace and disarmament can be made at home and abroad. They have used "peace offensives" to strengthen their own regime and to justify its policies to foreign as well as domestic audiences while dividing Russia's opponents.

Economics: Like American arms controllers, tsar and commissar have considered the ways in which arms control might contain the costs of defense, but Russians have also valued its role in promoting trade and technology transfer and in economic modernization.

Domestic politics: The Soviet political system, especially since Stalin's death, has often made disarmament a political football, a tool by which one faction can justify its own line, muster support, and weaken its rivals.

Alliances: Tsarist as well as Soviet governments have been alert to ways in which arms control could jeopardize or strengthen ties with governments or transnational movements.

Adversary relations: The Kremlin has assigned arms control a leading role in reducing international tensions. But Moscow has also used arms control as a wedge to divide the Western alliance and to support factions and tendencies abroad deemed useful to Soviet interests.

Strategic-military: Like other governments, tsarist and Soviet Russia have supported arms control policies that enhance their military assets.

All of these factors, as will be argued in the following chapters, have stamped Soviet behavior in different ways. Ideology and propaganda have functioned mainly to rationalize arms control postures deemed useful for "reasons of state." Material weaknesses have generated strong pressures to economize on defense and seek trade, sometimes leading the Kremlin to forgo military outlays if external threats could be managed by diplomacy. Domestic political considerations have sometimes provided incentives for arms accords but could also shut the door on negotiations. Concerns for the feelings of allies or Third World clients have rarely elicited more than lip service from Soviet policymakers. Concern to play upon Western "contradictions," however, has been a near constant in Soviet policies. Moscow has also studied the West to try to understand when political conditions there opened or closed the gate on arms accords.

But the factor that most consistently explains the zigs and zags of Kremlin policy has been military-strategic. When weak, the Bear has wanted to eliminate all weapons except the all-encompassing embrace. When equipped with modern weapons, however, the Bear has often campaigned to preserve not only its brute strength but also its teeth and claws while outlawing talons and other weapons it lacked. As the Bear and the Eagle developed comparable arsenals, agreements to mutual advantage proved feasible. As both sides find themselves with redundant weapons, major reductions are thinkable.

The military balance and other considerations do not affect Soviet thinking in some mechanical way but rather through the perceptions of top Kremlin leaders. A Khrushchev or Brezhnev, for example, would probably perceive the present climate for arms control quite differently from Gorbachev, even though all drank from the wells of Marxist ideology and Russian tradition. Even members of the Gorbachev Politburo differ about the proper course at home and abroad. Differences in body chemistry, in education, and in life experiences as well as changes in the material and spiritual environments of each generation lead individuals and groups to perceive challenges and opportunities through different lenses.

[59]

Still, imposing continuities persist despite changes in top leaders and regimes. Some continuities are rooted in Russia's material realities: the insecurities inherent in its long borders and open plains; its economic and technological underdevelopment relative to the West. Continuities also derive from Russian "cosmicism"—a penchant for the abstract phrase and grandiose plan to save the world—linked with ambivalence about whether to fear or follow the West. Finally, there are the influences of upbringing— not merely in the sacred scriptures of Marxism-Leninism but in observing how to get ahead in a milieu dominated by "kto kovo?" and one's standing in the nomenklatura.

This is the framework in which we will assess the major influences on Russia's policies on arms and arms control. A brief review of the pre-1917 period underscores that major changes as well as continuities have characterized Russia's policies over the centuries.

Imperial Traditions: Messianism and Realpolitik

To put Soviet policies in perspective we go back at least to the sixteenth century when Moscow first claimed it was the Third Rome, the seat of right doctrine inherited from a degenerate West and Byzantium. Here began the combination of self-righteous Messianism mixed with imperial Realpolitik that has permeated tsarist and Soviet arms control policies.[4]

The drive to overcome Russia's material and cultural backwardness became official when Peter the Great went to the workshops of the West to master and acquire the means to make Russia a modern power— Khrushchev, in a similar manner, toured American cornfields in 1959 to bring back seeds and techniques to enrich his country's diet. Peter, like later tsars and commissars, imported men, machinery, and ideas from the West. Whereas Peter forced his nobles to shave their beards and dance, recent Soviet leaders—also groping for the optimum cultural setting to accelerate economic development—have permitted their elites to grow long hair and to rock "red and hot."

Catherine the Great went even further than Peter toward Westernizing Russia's culture. Flirting with the Enlightenment, she was also intent on maximizing power. She was not beyond bribing Western intellectuals to write in positive terms on the liberalizing trends sweeping her domain. And whereas Peter established Russia's window on the West, Catherine's armies drove successfully to the Black Sea. She also greeted the American Revolution because it weakened England.

Alexander I, Catherine's grandson, put forward policy initiatives influenced by Enlightenment humanism and by Christianity. His espousal of Anglo-Russian condominium in 1804 and a Holy Alliance in 1815 provoked questions about the tsar's deeper motives. But Alexander probably believed that his task was to save not only Russia but the entire Christian world.[5]

His Messianic message, however, was interlaced with demonstrations of raw power, not unlike the air shows and H-bomb tests favored later by Khrushchev. Arriving in France later than the other European leaders who defeated Napoleon, Alexander summoned his allies to the Plaine de Vertus, where the Romans had checked Attila the Hun in A.D. 451. There Alexander paraded 180,000 Russian troops with six hundred big guns in a show of might followed by an immense prayer of thanksgiving led by priests and choristers of the Russian Army intoned during the Orthodox service. Following these ceremonies Alexander announced his plan for a Holy Alliance—a plan that he later wrote was inspired by God.[6]

A sort of "monarchical Woodrow Wilson," Alexander I also yearned for a "constitutional" harmony between subjects and rulers.[7] He postulated that every government—whether the monarchies of Austria and Prussia or the republics of Switzerland and the United States—should base its actions on rules of Justice, Christian Charity, and Peace.[8]

Although London and Vienna were skeptical, the Massachusetts Peace Society took Alexander quite seriously. It wrote to him in April 1816 recalling "to the attention of His Imperial Majesty that the Society was founded in the very week in which the Holy League of the three sovereigns was announced in Russia." The Massachusetts group informed the tsar that the Society had as its object "to disseminate the very principles avowed in the wonderful Alliance."[9] Thus the peace plans of imperial as well as Soviet Russia sometimes won the support of the "pacifist bourgeoisie."

Despite reservations, Austria and Prussia joined the tsar in a Three-Emperors' League that helped the support of Europe's status quo. Indeed, the Holy Alliance evolved into the congress system that helped to regulate the balance of power until 1914.

Russia emerged from the Napoleonic Wars militarily and politically triumphant but economically shattered. Like Soviet leaders in peacetime, Alexander sought a way to put military might to productive use. He approved a plan to set up colonies in which discharged veterans could maintain their military skills while cultivating their lands. All peasants in such areas were made subject to military service for life. The colonies were

[61]

unpopular with the soldier-peasants and their families but neat and orderly, benefiting from government subsidies.[10] Disbanded in 1857, they provided a precedent for the "territorial" army on which Soviet Russia depended from 1922 to 1935 and for similar schemes considered in 1960 and again in 1989.[11]

For several decades after Alexander, Russia's large armies permitted St. Petersburg to act as the gendarme of Europe. At midcentury, however, Russia was humiliated by France and Britain in the Crimean War. In the last decades of the century St. Petersburg could do well enough against the ailing Ottoman Empire and China; against industrial Europe war could only be a desperate last resort. The tsars did not yet know the power of the Rising Sun.

Most of the incentives and restraints that later shaped Soviet policies on arms control were found in late nineteenth century St. Petersburg. The words and deeds of Nicholas II and his ministers provide a benchmark against which to measure continuity and change in the Soviet period.

In the late 1890s Russia learned that Austria-Hungary was acquiring rapid-fire cannon that Russia could not develop or purchase except at great expense. Finance Minister Serge Witte urged that the government economize on arms so as to invest more in Russia's infrastructure and productive resources. Thus economic and military motives combined to motivate Nicholas II to issue a circular letter in 1898 inviting other governments to a peace conference to be held at The Hague.[12]

Bowing to practical considerations, the tsar also paid a nod to pacifist sentiment in Russia and in Europe.[13] He moved on a path already paved by the multi-volume study of a Polish railway magnate (published in Polish, Russian, German, and French) "demonstrating" that the likely costs of war in an interdependent Europe made it unthinkable as an instrument of policy.[14]

But the French government, now Russia's cordial ally against Germanic expansionism, told St. Petersburg that it opposed arms limitation. (Expressing its own continuities, Paris generally opposed disarmament when proposed by Soviet Russia in 1922, by other nations at the League of Nations, and by the superpowers from 1960 through the 1980s.) After much deliberation, St. Petersburg assured Paris—even before the Hague convocation—that no disarmament measures would be adopted there.

A consideration more weighty than alliance solidarity accounted for this change of heart. The war minister had persuaded the tsar that Russia had foreign policy objectives in the Far East and the Ottoman Empire that could not be achieved except by force of arms. Therefore the Russian state would need more, not fewer, arms. Wishful thinking—not for the first time in history—overrode sober calculation.[15]

Despite these unpublicized restraints and broad skepticism among governments about the Hague conference, it convened in 1899 on the tsar's birthday. Russia proposed a freeze on the number of land and sea forces and their budgets; a ban on the use of "new firearms of every description and of new explosives, as well as powder more powerful than the kinds used at present"; a ban on the use of powerful explosives "such as are now in use" and the "discharge of any kind of projectile or explosive from balloons"; a ban on the use of submarines or diving torpedo boats; an agreement not to build warships armed with rams; and acceptance in principle of the use of good offices and voluntary arbitration.[16] Russia also proposed that the number of troops in the home country (but not in the colonies) be fixed for a five-year term and that military budgets be frozen for five years.[17]

Many of the 1980s disputes about what is a new or a merely modernized weapon were prefigured in 1899 discussions about Russia's proposal to ban "the use in armies and fleets of *any new kinds* [emphasis added] of firearms whatever, and of new explosives, or any powders more powerful than those now in use, either for muskets or cannon." Challenged to define "new kinds of firearms," the Russian delegate replied that the term meant "an entirely new type, and should not include transformations and improvements." But France objected that "a new type of cannon was merely an old type gradually modified and improved," while a no less skeptical Japanese delegate asked if a "new type" referred to a weapon already invented but not yet adopted.[18]

The distinction offered by the Russian delegate in 1899 is the same used by the USSR to justify one of its missiles radically improved since the 1979 SALT accord, and also by the United States for upgrading two overseas radars since the 1972 ABM treaty, as noted in chapter 10.

In 1899 as in the 1970s and 1980s there was a resort to temporary restrictions. The Russian delegate proposed a ban on new weapons for three or four years, saying that governments could use the opportunity (he could have said "moratorium") to investigate and decide on appropriate action.

Speaking in 1899 for the United States, Captain Alfred T. Mahan (author of two studies on the *The Influence of Sea Power* in history, 1890 and 1892) declared that his delegation approached "limitation of invention with much doubt." It was postulated that technological invention has generally served to diminish rather than to increase "the frequency and indeed the exhausting character of war."[19]

The 1899 discussions also illustrated the connection between offense

[63]

and defense. Russia wanted to limit the caliber of naval guns. In that case, Mahan countered, armor should also be limited. Russia then proposed that armor thicknesses be limited to fourteen inches (355 mm), the latest Krupp pattern. Although he brought up the idea in the first place, Mahan replied that the United States would not be inclined to restrain inventions, especially the perfecting of armor plate. Washington, joined by London, also held out against most other delegations and refused a ban on the use of projectiles whose purpose is to release asphyxiating gases because such weapons had not yet been produced and their effect could not be assessed.[20] Even Siam opposed the Russian proposal to ban new types of weapons, saying that technology could help smaller states to deal with threats from larger ones.[21]

Russia's diplomats at The Hague were rebuffed politely but no less decisively than were Soviet representatives to the League of Nations three decades later. The other delegations said the tsarist proposals were well meaning but not feasible; hence they should be studied. All governments agreed to a five-year ban on the launching of projectiles and explosives from balloons—the same length accord as the "interim" agreement on strategic missiles reached in 1972.[22]

Despite its early reservations regarding arms limitation, the United States as well as Russia has played a leading role throughout the twentieth century—though not always at the same time—in calling for disarmament. Thus Washington and St. Petersburg engaged in competitive collaboration to call the second Hague Conference. President Theodore Roosevelt summoned the meeting in 1904, responding to an appeal from the Interparliamentary Union meeting at the world's fair held in St. Louis, Missouri; but as Russia was still engaged in fighting Japan, the United States delayed until 1905 any further action to propose the conference that finally met at The Hague in 1907.[23] Russia's delegation to the 1907 conference offered more modest targets than those rebuffed in 1899. Whereas other delegations talked about another five-year ban on dirigibles at the 1907 Hague Conference, however, Russia and Italy proposed a permanent ban.[24]

The Russian-U.S. interaction in 1899 and 1907 reflected basic continuities: America has usually been confident about its technological capabilities; Russia, uncertain. This insecurity has led both tsar and commissar to advocate arms reductions and technology freezes that would bring their foes to Russia's level and keep them there. Whereas tsarist Russia was never more than one of five or more great powers, however, the USSR has become a military superpower relatively confident in its ability to deter outside attack.

Turning now to the years since 1917, we analyze the considerations that have shaped Soviet arms policies under Lenin and his successors, looking for clues to what factors have proved most weighty.

Ideology and Propaganda: Servants of Policy

An Evolving Worldview

The beliefs and values of Russia's rulers have been heavily shaped by Western perspectives as well as by Russia's traditions, material problems, and assets. Western ideas on social progress stamped Communist as well as imperial court ideology, but through different channels and with quite different emphases. Whereas Alexander I learned from the West that there should be a natural harmony between ruler and subject, Russia's Communists have been schooled—until the late 1980s—to believe that class conflict is an inevitable and necessary prelude to socialism. Indeed, though Friedrich Engels sometimes called for disarmament, he also affirmed that the more militarism, the better, for this would hasten the day of revolution.[25]

From Marx and Engels the Bolsheviks learned to be suspicious of any talk of peace and disarmament among capitalists. How can there be peace, Lenin asked, when capitalism pulses with internal contradictions and seeks foreign markets for its surplus capital? Starting from such premises, Lenin argued from 1905 until after the Bolshevik Revolution that disarmament is an "ideal" of socialism but that it cannot be achieved until capitalism is overthrown. Communists, he said, should therefore oppose the slogan of disarmament, for it can only create illusions harmful to revolutionary activity. The task of Communists, Lenin argued, is not to preach "disarmament" (*razoruzhenie*) but take arms and then "disarm" (*obezoruzhit*) the bourgeoisie. So long as private property remains, ruling classes will use arms against their subject peoples; one set of capitalists will fight another; and the first socialist republic will confront hostile forces at home and abroad seeking to destroy it by force. Only with the triumph of socialism on a wide scale can the dream of disarmament be realized.[26]

Once the Bolsheviks had achieved state power, however, Lenin urged that they negotiate pragmatically with foreign adversaries until such time as revolution expanded beyond Russia's frontiers. The Soviet Republic in 1918–21 signed many accords with neighboring states

[65]

establishing demilitarized zones and other measures that could be regarded as arms control.[27]

In mid-1921 Foreign Commissar G. V. Chicherin announced that his government, while remaining skeptical that "guarantees" would be found to ensure any disarmament measures agreed to at the Washington Naval Conference, asserted interest in "disarmament of any kind."[28] Although the United States spurned Moscow's bid to attend the Washington conference, Soviet diplomats attended three other international conferences in 1922–23 (held in Genoa, Moscow, and Lausanne), in each case championing radical measures of arms limitation. The rationale guiding Moscow's diplomacy was set forth by Lenin in instructions to the Soviet delegation to the Genoa Economic Conference: the Soviet republic should seek to divide its foreign adversaries, setting France against Britain and the Versailles victors against Germany. Soviet diplomats should also strive to strengthen the "pacifist" wing of the European bourgeoisie, particularly in England, "as one of the few chances for a peaceful evolution of capitalism to a new structure. . . ."[29]

Lenin had taken his regime through three stages of thinking about arms limitation: first, that talk of negotiated disarmament could be counterrevolutionary; second, that arms accords on such measures as demilitarized zones could be useful, at least until they were overridden by the spread of revolution; and third, that disarmament negotiations could be used to divide Soviet Russia's enemies, pitting class against class and nation against nation. Disarmament negotiations became for Lenin the continuation of revolution by other means.

But toward the end of Lenin's life still another—a fourth— perspective emerged. Lenin speculated that advances in military technology might some day make war unsuitable as an instrument of policy.[30] Although Lenin was too ill to carry this line of thought very far, his vision implied that negotiated arms limitations with the class foe could promote the survival of communism. Soviet decision makers did not act on this idea until after the mid-1950s when mutual destruction appeared the likely outcome of any war with the West.[31]

Even after the Kremlin began to advocate negotiated disarmament in the early 1920s, Soviet spokesmen continued to cast doubt on the ability or willingness of capitalist regimes to disarm. They stressed Moscow's interest in real—not feigned or token—measures of arms reduction. The Washington conference ceilings on capital ships, for example, were criticized for failing to curb the weapons of the future: aircraft carriers and submarines. Like good Marxists, Soviet diplomats stressed that they wanted "material" disarmament—not demands for "moral" disarmament (which France sought to curb Comintern agitation and Soviet subversion).[32]

Similar problems arose in 1946 when Washington offered to abolish its nuclear monopoly once a system of international controls had been established. Stalin's diplomats wanted instead to reverse this sequence.

So long as Moscow's leaders remained skeptical about East-West accords, Soviet diplomats scorned Western proposals for arms *control* as proof that capitalism did not seek genuine measures of arms reduction but only wished to legitimize espionage on Soviet territory or to deceive their own people. Distrust was exacerbated because Russia has no equivalent for the English word "control" in the sense of "regulate" or "manage." The Russian *kontrol'* derives from the French *controler* ("to count, audit or inspect"). Soviet-U.S. negotiations for much of the postwar era were troubled by the suspicion that U.S. support for "arms control" implied "inspection without disarmament."[33]

Under Khrushchev and then Brezhnev the Kremlin endorsed not merely negotiations but agreements on arms control as part of a broad approach to secure limited collaboration with the capitalist world. Arms control and trade were pursued under the rubrics "peaceful coexistence" and, in the 1970s, "détente." The emphasis, however, was on *limited* collaboration because Moscow hoped merely to avoid war while advancing its influence and the "liberation struggle." The Kremlin portrayed peaceful coexistence as a continuation of class warfare.

Departing from slogans to "ban the bomb," Khrushchev's diplomats began to advocate specific arms control measures, such as denuclearized zones, referring to them as "partial measures of disarmament." By the 1970s, as understanding between East and West improved, the Soviet political vocabulary came to accept as legitimate the goal of "control over armaments" (*kontrol nad vooruzheniiami*). But although Moscow had tended since the 1960s to downgrade comprehensive utopias in favor of attainable limited measures, there remains in Soviet diplomacy—even under Gorbachev—a tendency to advocate all-out, sweeping measures.[34]

Thus ideology has been a permanently operating factor in the shaping and rationalization of Soviet arms control policy, but its content has changed radically over the years. From Lenin's initial principled rejection of disarmament negotiations Soviet policy has evolved to accept arms control as a feasible goal of diplomacy that is useful tactically and perhaps even strategically.

The extent to which the "kto kovo?" qualifiers of earlier times have been put aside under Gorbachev is considered in part III. But their ideological heritage has presented Soviet Communists with contradictory thoughts about arms accords. Despite its pragmatic evolution, Communist ideology continues to exert a negative as well as a positive influence on prospects of East-West arms control. Can arms control be more than a palliative if capitalism and socialism are locked in a struggle to the death? Why should Moscow make any concessions except for tactical reasons? And why should it trust the class foe? Why permit it access to Soviet territory and facilities to verify arms controls that are bound to collapse some day? Why risk staying the tide of revolution? Such questions readily leap to the minds of those responsible for military preparedness or ideological purity. They occur also to so-called progressives in other countries who worry that Soviet support for their causes may wither under East-West détente.

Against this line of thought is the ideological premise that communism rides the wave of history and that its victory depends upon evolving material and spiritual conditions—not on war. How deeply this premise has entered the operational code of specific Soviet leaders is difficult to know. For those who believe history is on their side, arms controls and other steps to prevent war can only aid the long-term goal of revolution. For those who do not care about revolution, arms control promises survival and less economic hardship.

Propaganda for Hawks and Doves

Ideological shifts have been reflected in propaganda directed to diverse audiences within and outside the USSR. Like Peter the Great and Catherine, the Soviet leadership has gone to great lengths to shape foreign opinion about Russia. Less frequently than the tsars the Soviet leadership at times has appealed to "fellow Slavs"; it has occasionally played up ties between Russian Orthodoxy and Western Christianity and between Soviet Muslims and the broader world of Islam.[35] The Kremlin's first priority has been to promote the image of a Soviet Union successfully leading the way to socialism and communism. But Moscow's most consistent propaganda themes have included peace and disarmament.[36]

Moscow has confronted a perennial dilemma: how to please both pacifist and revolutionary audiences. If Soviet diplomats propose arms limitation in a style reassuring to pacifists (especially among the moderate elites), this can erode revolutionary élan. But if the Kremlin strongly supports revolution, this undercuts the credibility of Soviet peace campaigns. Moscow worked out a kind of one-two punch to deal with this dilemma in the 1920s and early 1930s. Soviet diplomacy would propose disarmament—preferably general disarmament, and if rebuffed, then partial measures—in ways that appealed to many non-Communists; the Comintern would later explain to its faithful that capitalist rejection of Soviet proposals "unmasked" bourgeois hypocrisy and demonstrated the impossibility of disarmament until capitalism is overthrown.[37]

This coordinated approach worked well enough in the interwar years when few arms controls were negotiated except poison gas and naval limitations. Moscow could then appeal to both its peace and its revolution constituencies, though it scored no breakthroughs in either domain. In the late 1950s and early 1960s, however, when the Kremlin began to enter a number of arms controls with the West, Mao Zedong and other Communists charged that Moscow was betraying Lenin and ideological principle. The Khrushchev regime retorted that arms limits and peaceful coexistence would raise the tide of revolution, but this argument got nowhere in Beijing.[38]

The Kremlin has had fewer problems with its own citizens. Given the regime's near monopoly on communication media, propaganda shifts have been easy to explain to a population anxious about its security and not inclined to challenge its governors. When East-West accords seem undesirable or distant, Soviet media have underscored the need for vigilance against Western machinations; when arms limitation seems feasible and useful, Kremlin propaganda glorifies the leadership for its farsighted struggle for peace. Justification for nearly any policy switch can be found in Lenin's collected works (fifty-five volumes plus index), and if this is impossible, Moscow can announce, as Khrushchev did in 1960, that Vladimir Il'ich could not foresee all changes in the world now facing the USSR.[39]

Soviet propaganda faces a second problem. If it paints Western leaders either as would-be aggressors or as whimpish milquetoasts, will Western elites accept protestations that the Kremlin wants serious negotiations? Moscow's response to this dilemma has been skillful. When Moscow wants an accord, Soviet media distinguish between "madmen" and "sober, realistic" forces in the bourgeois camp. Some Western leaders, *Pravda* may assert, favor aggression while others understand the need for East-West accommodations.

Bolstering Khrushchev's case for negotiating with the West, *Pravda* and *New Times* published for the first time in 1959–64 documents showing Lenin's determination (in 1922) to exploit divisions among the bourgeoisie by playing the pacifist card.[40] The Soviet media then pointed to moderate forces in the West—in the early 1960s and again in the early 1970s—as if to show that the Kremlin leadership was applying guidelines set down long before by the prescient Lenin.[41] Not surprisingly, such differentiated images of America's ruling circles receded in the early 1980s, but traces of such nuance reappeared as Gorbachev prepared for summitry in 1985–88. Former President Reagan, earlier cast among the goats of America's military-industrial complex, was moved out from this shadow and portrayed as a man of goodwill if not of good sense, unlike the Pentagon civilians attempting to prevent détente. And *Kommunist* published an essay comparing Lenin's approach to East-West accords at the 1922 Genoa Conference with Gorbachev's in the 1980s. Lenin urged coexistence and cooperation—trade and disarmament—between socialism and capitalism; Gorbachev, the article implied, was continuing Lenin's visionary strategy.[42]

What has been the effect of Soviet propaganda upon the worldview of Kremlin leaders? Have they laughed it off as good public relations, or have they come to believe it as a real picture of a reality in which the USSR virtuously campaigns for peace while others plot aggression? Statements meant to impress others can also limit one's own vision and options. Perhaps foreign policy professionals, East and West, could discount the hypocrisy behind the annual public relations bombshell presented by Soviet diplomats at the United Nations.[43] Perhaps some could accept it as a cost of doing business, even if the business is peace. But sophistry—from any quarter—also widens the credibility gaps between East and West.

Soviet propaganda efforts abroad have achieved some successes but have generally fallen short of their goals. They probably helped to torpedo plans for a Western European supranational army in 1954 but failed to prevent West Germany's integration into NATO and subsequent rearmament after 1955. Moscow's overtures might have contributed something to France's independent posture within the Western alliance but have not derailed the development of a powerful French *force de dissuasion*. In 1963 Khrushchev failed to persuade Beijing of the merits of arms limitations, but his tactics helped to deepen divisions between Washington and London on one hand and the governments of Konrad Adenauer and General de Gaulle on the other.[44]

The Kremlin has abetted antinuclear movements in Europe, but it has failed to stop deployment of several generations of nuclear arms from the 1950s through the 1980s. Although Moscow intensified its drumbeat to exacerbate differences within NATO in the early 1980s, the alliance's solidarity became stronger.[45] Still, the resistance to INF deployment in 1983 made NATO governments extremely cautious about attempting to modernize their arsenals after the 1987 INF treaty. The sources of this resistance were mainly native and could be bolstered by Soviet propaganda. The sweet notes in Soviet propaganda have probably been more useful to the Kremlin than the harsh, for example, in persuading Western elites that their interests would gain from arms accords and more trade.

Propaganda considerations have run like a red thread in Russian policies on arms and arms control from tsarist times through the 1980s, but they have ultimately carried little weight when difficult choices had to be made among competing policies. Propaganda themes have simply been revised to fit changing conceptions of *raison d'état*. One day capitalism or even its Nazi variant is threatening; the next day it is a promising partner. Roosevelt's America was a friend; Truman's a foe. Similar transformations have overtaken Soviet images of Communist China and other countries once allied with the USSR.[46]

Despite the Soviet regime's concern to court Third World opinion, Moscow launched a new series of nuclear tests in 1961 exploding the largest warhead ever tested—even as nonaligned nations were convening in Belgrade. In short, the Kremlin has been willing to take a few lumps for letting down its supporters if this were the price for advancing military or other weighty objectives.

Neither ideology nor propaganda, the record shows, have been decisive factors in Soviet policies toward arms and arms control, for both can be reoriented to justify practically any orientation. Ideology has been an important conditioning factor, but, like propaganda, its official expression has been a flexible instrument in support of changing and sometimes contradictory ends.

The Material Base: Economic Determinism?

Economic considerations have shaped Russian policies toward arms and arms control in several ways, creating both incentives and restraints. To begin, the material base of any society—its production and social relations—strongly influences (but does not determine) the consciousness of its people and the policies it pursues. Second, the material base also conditions military power. As Engels noted, "nothing so depends upon economic conditions as the army and navy. The arms, staff, organization, tactics and strategy at a given time depend first of all on the attained stage of production and on the means of communications."[47] In October 1917 Lenin put this view in still more extreme terms, implying that even morale required an economic foundation:

[71]

> To make Russia capable of defense [*oboronosposobnoi*] and to realize in her the "wonder" of mass heroism, it is necessary, with "Jacobin" mercilessness, to sweep away everything old, renovate and regenerate Russia *economically*. . . . War is implacable; it puts the question with merciless acuteness: either perish or catch up with the advanced countries and surpass them *economically* as well.[48]

Russia's rulers have been driven, at least since Peter, to modernize and economize. At times they have ordered the country to pull in its collective belt and do whatever seems necessary for security. When foreign threats or opportunities abated, however, the Kremlin has used the breathing space to build productive resources. At times the leadership has stressed self-sufficiency; at other times the Kremlin has placed its hopes on foreign trade and technology transfers.

Like Finance Minister Witte at the turn of the century, Soviet leaders have wanted to overcome Russia's backwardness. They have wanted to limit defense costs without undue risk to Soviet security interests. Self-restraint is one way to curb arms spending but may not be feasible if Moscow's foes have armed far beyond Russia's level.

Peace, Lenin said in 1918, is a "breathing space for war . . . a means for the building-up of forces."[49] Lenin asserted that wars would be won by the side having the "greatest technology, organization, discipline, and the best machines."[50] At other times he stressed the importance to the front and the rear of a stable system of food supplies, oil, warm clothes, and shoes.[51] Lenin, like Stalin after him, emphasized that modern wars are won not by relatively small, professional armies of the traditional type but by the overall mobilization of the material and moral forces of the nation.[52]

Lenin's logic was implemented in 1920–22 when the immediate prospect of war receded. It was not feasible or desirable to maintain an army of over five million (the approximate size of Soviet forces in the 1980s), but it was not simple to move and demobilize troops in the midst of a fuel and transportation crisis or to find civilian jobs for them. The solution: first, reduce forces as quickly and drastically as possible, retaining demobilized soldiers in a territorial militia located at farm and factory; second: try to persuade other states to match Soviet reductions.[53] Thus at the Moscow Disarmament Conference in 1922 Maxim Litvinov called on Soviet Russia's neighbors to join Moscow in cutting their armies by 75 percent or, if that were unacceptable, at least by 25 percent. When Poland and the Baltic states refused, the Kremlin announced a move that it had already planned for its own reasons: a massive reduction in the Red Army.

TABLE 3.1
Size of Regular Soviet Armed Forces, 1920–90

DATE	TOTAL*	ANNOUNCED REDUCTIONS
December 1920	5,300,000	
April 1921	4,495,000	
September 1921	1,744,000	
March 1922	1,615,000	
September 1922	896,000	
December 1922	610,000	200,000
February 1923	600,000	
1923/1933	586,000	
1934	940,000	
1935	1,300,000	
1937	1,433,000	
1941	4,207,000	
1945	11,365,000	
1948	2,874,000	
1955	5,763,000	640,000
1956/1957		1,200,000
1958	3,623,000	300,000
January 1960	3,623,000	1,200,000
July 1961	3,023,000	
1962 (1960 Khrushchev projection)	2,423,000	
1962 (actual)	3,600,000	
1963	3,300,000	
1965	3,150,000	
1970	4,000,000	
1975	4,434,000	
1980	4,378,000	
1981	4,837,000	
1985	5,300,000	
1988	5,096,000	500,000
1990 (target)	4,596,000	

* Totals exclude border and internal security forces, which numbered 250,000 in 1936, 300,000 in 1963, 575,000 in late 1970s–1980s. They exclude militia units, which were over twice as numerous as regular forces in the late 1920s; they also exclude all reserve forces, which in 1988 numbered 6,217,000 with conscript service within five years. The totals for years since 1975 include command and support forces (railroad, construction, and civil defense), which in 1988 numbered some 1,476,000. Large increases in the early 1970s resulted from increased deployments along the Chinese border and in the early 1980s, from Afghan operations, but some jumps in totals result from revised Western methods for estimating Soviet forces. In January 1989 Soviet estimates placed Soviet forces at less than 5 million.

SOURCES: Most figures through 1960 are from N. S. Khrushchev's report to the Supreme Soviet, in *Pravda*, January 15, 1960; on early 1920s: Walter C. Clemens, Jr., "Soviet Disarmament Proposals and the Cadre-Territorial Army," *Orbis* 7, no. 4 (Winter 1964): 779 and 789; on the 1950s–1960s: Lincoln P. Bloomfield, Walter C. Clemens, Jr., and Franklyn Griffiths, *Khrushchev and the Arms Race* (Cambridge: MIT Press, 1966), 100–1; also *Documents on Disarmament, 1945–1959* (2 vols. Washington, DC: U.S. Department of State, 1960), I: Docs. 126, 127, 164, 165; II: Doc. 1132. On 1970–84: John M. Collins, *U.S.-Soviet Military Balance 1980–1985* (Washington, DC: Pergamon-Brassey's, 1985), 167; on 1985–88, International Institute for Strategic Studies, *Military Balance* (London, annual). In 1983 the IISS began to include nearly 1.5 million command and support troops not previously listed. "Civilians" employed by the U.S. Defense Department have numbered more than a million for many years. For a Soviet view of the "present danger," see *Whence the Threat to Peace*, 3d ed. (Moscow: Military Publishing House, 1984).

The 1922 cut in Soviet regular forces was the first of many unilateral reductions keyed to threat perception and economic need and orchestrated with Soviet disarmament diplomacy. The shifting numbers of Soviet armed forces over the years are summarized in Table 3.1. The context of these shifts is presented later in this and in following chapters.

All Soviet leaders have been driven to close the economic and technological gaps between the USSR and the West. Soviet planners, at least until 1985, have perceived their choices not as between butter and guns but among light industry, weapons, and heavy industry. From 1928 until 1985 Kremlin dogma posited that over time heavy industry would be the source for more and better weapons as well as more and better consumer goods.

Following this approach Stalin took draconic measures in the late 1920s and 1930s to accelerate the industrialization of the USSR, sacrificing living standards and even immediate military power to the gods of steel and machines.[54] Stalin abetted war scare propaganda in 1927–28 and later partly to justify the stepped-up pace of industrial development and collectivization. This propaganda campaign dovetailed with agitation by Litvinov at Geneva for disarmament and with a leftist shift in Comintern activity.

Stalin emphasized that heavy industry was the prerequisite for a modern military machine, but the economic Five-Year Plan was accompanied by a similar plan for development of the Red Army drawn up by military authorities and approved by the Party and government in 1928. In July 1929 the Politburo called for an even faster drive to reequip the Red Army and revised targets in the military plan upward. During the First Five-Year Plan (1928–32) the production of arms and equipment rose rapidly; it remained more stable in the second plan (1933–37) but rose again in the late 1930s. Thus average production of military aircraft was 860 per year in 1930–31; 2,595 in 1932–34; 3,758 in 1935–37; and 8,805 in 1938–40. Production of artillery pieces rose from 1,911 in 1930–31 to 3,778 in 1932–34; to 5,020 in 1935–37; and to 14,996 in 1938–40. Stalin kept an ear cocked for wonder weapons and materials as well as miraculous medicines (to prolong his own life).[55]

Still, it appears that Stalin tried to curtail military outlays as long as possible while giving priority to heavy industry. He articulated and perpetuated theories that downgraded the importance of modern arms and punished their critics severely. The theory of the Red Army's "special maneuverability" (favored by Stalin's crony, War Commissar Klementi Voroshilov) was ridiculed by Marshal Mikhail Tukhachevskii in 1937. Writing in *Red Star* on May 6, Tukhachevskii called the theory a "heroic" sentiment based on Russia's Civil War experiences and not on analysis of modern arms possessed by Soviet enemies but potentially available to the large-scale industry developed by the socialist state. The following month Tukhachevskii was convicted of high treason and shot.[56]

Stalin may have choked on any hint of open rebellion rather than on the content of Tukhachevskii's article, for serious modernization of the Red Army and Navy was already under way by 1937. But Stalin seems to have hoped for some years that symbols of power, such as aviation distance records, would cow Russia's foes and help substitute for a real fighting force. Only when Stalin saw that the Axis powers were becoming strong and went unchecked by their foes, and that German planes prevailed over Soviet in the Spanish "Civil" War, did he steeply raise the share of military allocations in the national plan and shift from a cadre-territorial system to a regular army. Indeed, veterans of the Spanish conflict were put at the head of some weapons design bureaus.[57]

Economic considerations also played a role in the onset of the cold war. At Yalta Stalin had claimed the right to collect massive reparations from Germany. President Franklin Roosevelt accepted a total reparations bill of $20 billion (half to go to the USSR) as a basis for later discussion, whereas Winston Churchill refused to set any fixed sum. At Potsdam, however, President Harry Truman also backed away from any precise figure for reparations partly because Washington hoped still to influence events in Poland and elsewhere in Eastern Europe. Indeed, Washington suspended most aid shipments to Russia, even some already on the high seas.[58]

Stalin again announced the priority of heavy industry. In his February 9, 1946 preelection speech he called for a threefold increase in heavy industrial production over the next fifteen years. "Only then will our country be safeguarded against all kinds of eventualities," he warned. This speech shocked some American leaders, some of whom saw it as a "declaration of World War III."[59]

A week before Stalin's speech the Central Committee reminded Soviet society that "there are still reactionary forces in the world, and that these forces are trying to sow dissension and hostility among nations." This preelection appeal, a Soviet military history reports, "contained the principal tenets of the party's military policy during the first postwar years." They focused on strengthening the country's logistical base, using science and technology for this end, and reducing and reorganizing the armed forces while increasing their vigilance and readiness. This was also a time when work accelerated to produce a nuclear bomb.[60]

Stalin, according to Khrushchev, "trembled with fear" at the end of World War II because he knew that the USSR lagged behind the West in the ability to manufacture the latest weaponry. "He ordered the whole country to be put on military alert" and surrounded Moscow with 100-mm antiaircraft guns. "We remained in a state of constant alert right up to the time Stalin died and afterwards as well." Despite Russia's need to rebuild its shattered economy, Stalin committed substantial resources not only to crash programs in nuclear and thermonuclear weapons and to a broad net of antiaircraft defenses but also to building cruisers and destroyers for the Soviet navy. He did not invest in aircraft carriers, however, perhaps because he saw that the USSR could not afford their huge expense.[61]

These developments shaped Moscow's response to a U.S. proposal in 1946–47 for a four-power pact to keep the former aggressors disarmed. The Kremlin gave no formal reply to this proposal until March 1947, when Molotov countered that the USSR wanted Germany disarmed industrially as well as militarily so that its war machine could not be restarted. The Kremlin probably hoped too that "industrial disarmament" might supplement the machinery and current production it was already taking from East Germany as reparations. The Soviet proposal was unacceptable to the West, which was already deeply concerned with creating a viable German economy.[62]

The Kremlin considered but then refused participation in the Marshall Plan for European reconstruction, contending that the plan would intrude in the internal affairs of the USSR and its Eastern European allies. Alarmed by the impending fusion of the three Western occupation zones of Germany and their plan for a united currency, Stalin responded with the Berlin Blockade—broken after many months by the Air Bridge— a demonstration of Western technical, economic, and moral strength.

Stalin's successors inherited what Khrushchev termed a "plateful" of military and other problems. "It wasn't as though we could afford to concentrate all our attention on military matters," Khrushchev recalled. "We had to increase our economic potential"—above all, to provide "more bread, more butter, and other agricultural products for our people. On top of that, we understood that without the restoration and modernization of our industry we were doomed to remain a backward country both economically and politically."[63]

Khrushchev's memoirs underscore the sense of technological backwardness underlying many of his regime's decisions on arms and arms control.[64] Khrushchev believed that a surface navy without aircraft carriers was no navy at all. He envied the U.S. aircraft carriers but decided that "they were simply beyond our means." Regretfully he even ordered the melting down of many large surface ships built in Stalin's time— proceeding, however, to construct four new "expensive showpiece" cruisers as beautiful "concessions" to the Navy and to "show them off to foreigners." He also built up the Soviet submarine fleet for both defense and counterattack.[65]

In the mid-1950s Khrushchev cut Soviet land forces by a large fraction;[66] he refused to build troop transports "since we do not aspire to occupy other countries";[67] but Khrushchev deeply wanted to negate American superiority in the air. The Mya-4 (Bison) bomber could hit the United States only on a one-way mission, terminating perhaps in Mexico. Khrushchev asked its designer, "What do you think Mexico is—our mother-in-law? You think we can simply go calling whenever we want?"[68]

Khrushchev's regime wanted a means more reliable than airplanes to deter the enemy; it sought the answer in guided missiles. Khrushchev's anxieties turned to bluster after the USSR tested the world's first artificial satellite and ICBM in 1957. "We were satisfied," he recalled, "to be able to deter the hostile forces of the world by means of our ICBMs."[69] It became the turn of "our enemies to tremble in *their* boots. Thanks to our missiles, we could deliver a nuclear bomb to a target any place in the world."[70] Still, visiting President Eisenhower in 1959, the Party leader felt compelled to beg Ike to sell him two U.S. helicopters because those made in the USSR were unsafe. Illustrating still another material result of summitry, Khrushchev opined that after Soviet scientists had studied these craft, they were able to produce world-class helicopters.[71]

Khrushchev sought to "economize" through a combination of bluff and selective development of nuclear rocketry. He used the *Sputnik* and ICBM tests to heighten the image of Soviet power, press for change in divided Germany and elsewhere, and hold down defense expenditures. Had the first generation of ICBMs been of better quality, perhaps the Kremlin would have accelerated its production schedule. Instead, Soviet factories turned out relatively few of these weapons while Khrushchev boasted publicly that they were being produced "like sausages."[72] This tack earned him mileage for a time, though Eisenhower did not panic. Khrushchev told his own people that the Strategic Rocket Forces he had created would make it possible to economize on military manpower and on other armaments—in effect, to get more rubble for the ruble. In January 1960 he announced that Soviet military personnel would be cut by one-third and the demobilized forces transferred to productive employment.[73]

Ultimately Khrushchev's bluster cost the USSR dearly. The Kennedy administration elected in 1960, having cried "missile gap," raced far ahead of the Soviet Union in deployments of strategic arms on land and at sea while maintaining America's near monopoly in intercontinental bombers.

By October 1962 the gap ran quite the other way: 5,000 deliverable warheads for the United States; 300 for the USSR—perhaps as few as 20 on Soviet ICBMs.[74]

Before and after the Cuban missile crisis one of Khrushchev's concerns was to master the logic of minimum deterrence. According to his son, Sergei, the first secretary was carrying a translation of William W. Kaufmann's *McNamara Strategy* when he was summoned back to Moscow and ousted in October 1964. Khrushchev's son and Sergo Mikoyan deny that the Kremlin decided in the aftermath of Cuba to step up Soviet missile procurement. Nikita Khrushchev, they agreed (February 1989 discussions at Harvard), believed that a few nuclear weapons sufficed for deterrence. He distrusted reports from Soviet spies and regarded the military as insatiable in its demands—a sentiment reinforced when he heard Eisenhower say the same thing in 1959. Contrary to this interpretation, Khrushchev's memoirs and the bold Cuban emplacement suggested that he was not satisfied with the Kremlin's infant arsenal.

Not by Bread Alone?

The Kremlin has also seen arms control and détente as means to open up East-West trade and technology transfer. Even before Stalin's death Soviet spokesmen affirmed Moscow's interest in broader ties with other countries.[75] Stalin's successors have sensed that trade would depend on détente and that the best way to relax tensions would be through serious arms control talks. Former U.S. Ambassador Chip Bohlen concluded that the Soviet leaders, as Marxists, believed that a material base impregnated with weapons would someday explode, whereas a base rich in East-West trade would be conducive to peace.[76]

The Western and Soviet heads of state instructed their foreign ministers in 1955 to negotiate three interrelated problems: European security and Germany, disarmament, and development of contacts (freer communications and trade) among peoples.[77] The "Helsinki process" since the mid-1970s has devoted its energies to similar "baskets" of distinct but related issues. But the U.S. government has been less interested in trade than have the Soviet or European. Although Washington has sometimes had high hopes for East-West trade—for example, in 1933 and at some moments since 1972—the White House has usually seen trade as a reward to Moscow for progress on strategic and political issues. Western Europe, more dependent on foreign trade than the United States, has put far less emphasis on such linkage. Many U.S. leaders have assumed that the American economy could withstand and even profit from an arms race while bankrupting the USSR.

With the onset of each détente—1955 and later—Soviet representatives have tried to persuade the West that Russia had something to sell (not only furs) as well as to buy (chemical and auto plants) abroad. But these explorations were usually cut short by the early demise of détente— for example, in the 1956 Suez War and Hungarian "events."

The lagging fortunes of Soviet agriculture may well have played a more decisive and catalytic role in Moscow's arms control initiatives than the Kremlin's amorphous desire for a general broadening of East-West trade. Russia has often suffered famine, both before and after 1917. The tsarist regime exported grain and did not store surpluses for lean years. American food aid saved millions of Soviets from starvation in the early 1920s, as the Council of People's Commissars acknowledged in 1923. But Stalin hid the 1932–33 famines (induced by collectivization and Soviet grain *exports*) from world scrutiny. With the most fertile Soviet lands—the Ukraine and northern Caucasus—occupied by Germans, the USSR again depended heavily on U.S. food aid during World War II. "Without Spam we wouldn't have been able to feed our army," Khrushchev recalled. His memoirs also noted that Stalin again allowed massive starvation in the Ukraine after the war.

Khrushchev, for his part, showed his willingness to learn from U.S. agricultural practices. Returning from Iowa with hybrid corn in 1959, he urged his compatriots to eat a variety of corn products. A Soviet publisher then reprinted a *fin de siècle* account of how Russian agronomists learned about agriculture and collected seed from "patriarchs of the East" (Egypt, India, China, and especially Ceylon).[78]

The first large Soviet purchase of American wheat came in 1963 after the signing of the Nuclear Test Ban Treaty, which coincided with a poor Soviet harvest. This marked the beginning of a pattern. Since 1963 the Soviets have proved willing and even anxious to import Western grain to avoid forced slaughter of livestock and to keep bread prices stable. Nearly every significant advance in arms negotiations—1963–64, 1972–73, 1978–79—came at a time when the Kremlin wanted to import much grain from the United States.[79] Such a desire could never be a sufficient condition for arms accords, and it is probably not necessary. The record suggests, however, that poor harvests in the USSR have often both reinforced and focused the Kremlin's other reasons for pursuing détente and arms control. It is also noteworthy that Moscow's forward strategy in the Third World began in the mid-1970s when the USSR had three unusually good grain harvests.[80]

The connections among poor harvests, grain imports, and arms control are more difficult to trace in the 1980s. The Soviet-U.S. confrontation was so tense during 1980–85 that Moscow's marginal need for grain imports could carry little weight in arms control negotiations, especially because the Kremlin managed to buy from other suppliers after President Carter imposed limits on U.S. shipments. When a *nouvelle détente* came in sight after 1985, the recurrent Soviet need to import grain rekindled both sides' interest in trade and reinforced the Kremlin's other incentives for arms limitation. Soviet grain imports from the United States reached a new high in 1984–85, tapered off in 1985–87, and in 1988 approached the previous highs of 1973, 1976, and 1978–79. There were surges of U.S. grain sales to Russia even in 1981–82 and 1983–84—years of confrontation, but also times when demand jumped, reducing U.S. shipment to only one-third of total Soviet grain imports.[81]

There have been continued shortfalls in Soviet agriculture in the late 1980s. From Gorbachev's accession through 1989 complaints about the "food question" became sharper throughout the USSR. Each year Soviet citizens said, "There is no meat, no vegetables" in the stores; and each year they declared the situation worse than before. Although starvation was not at issue, public support for Gorbachev and his reforms was in doubt. The situation impelled the Kremlin to pursue a positive climate for trade of all kinds and for a shift of human and other resources to agriculture. Arms limitation could help to foster such moves.

The Kremlin's drive to acquire Western technology and to promote trade intensified in 1971 under the Peace Program adopted by the Communist party and reaffirmed throughout the decade. The Politburo urged that the USSR become associated with Western nations in a long-term program of economic collaboration to master the many challenges of the STR. On one hand, the Brezhnev Kremlin rejected autarky and acknowledged East-West "interconnectedness"; on the other, however, it spurned the notion of North-South interdependence.

What was more important to the Brezhnev regime: "peace"/arms control or technology/trade? Moscow was prepared to go a long way to make progress in both domains. The Kremlin bent some practices—even its treatment of Jews—to promote trade with the West. Shortly after announcing its Peace Program in 1971 the Kremlin commuted the death sentences imposed on two hijackers who had attempted the previous year to fly a plane of Soviet Jews to the West.[82] Now began a veritable exodus that continued in bursts throughout the 1970s. Indeed, movement on arms control was usually bracketed by imports of grain and the release of Jews and other minorities. In 1970 the Kremlin dropped its previous opposition to U.S. participation in an all-European security conference—the beginning of the Helsinki process that would later ratify the postwar territorial arrangements and foster both trade and human rights.[83] Each side now made concessions that resulted in SALT I and other accords signed in 1972.

The U.S. Congress, however, was not mollified. It wanted more explicit commitments on Jewish immigration before it would approve extensive long-term credits to the USSR or most-favored-nations treatment. Moscow refused to bo beyond private assurances on immigration, and this torpedoed hopes for a major expansion of Soviet-U.S. trade.

The Kremlin was also frustrated on arms control by the shifts of fortune and mood in Washington. The Nixon presidency collapsed and gave way to that of Gerald Ford. Ford worked out general principles for a SALT II agreement at Vladivostok in 1974 but then turned against even détente during the 1976 presidential elections. The Carter White House, in turn, scrapped Vladivostok and proposed instead "deep cuts."

Lack of progress on trade and arms control lessened the inhibitions on Soviet expansion into unfolding vacuums in the Third World.[84] The ensuing Soviet forward strategy deepened the reluctance of the U.S. Congress to go along even with negotiated limits on underground nuclear tests, not to speak of SALT II.

What happened to Soviet defense spending and weapons procurement in the 1970s? The evidence suggests that well before Gorbachev the Kremlin wanted to reduce the economic burden of military spending and to modernize its economy overall. Soviet outlays and production slowed in some areas by 1980–81, but the previous patterns and momentum continued unchecked in many areas.

Military outlays in the USSR have consumed a much higher share of gross national product than they have in the United States. For many decades the American economy has been roughly twice as large as the Soviet; the USSR has fielded a comparable military force, making up in size what it lacked in quality. As Soviet economic growth slowed from about 5.0 percent per year in the 1960s to 1.5 to 2.0 percent in 1984–85, the economic and social burdens of Soviet defense spending grew heavier. In the last decade of the Brezhnev era the USSR probably spent about 13–14 percent of GNP on military expenditures, rising to as much as 15–17 percent in the mid-1980s—over twice their share in the United States.[85] In the years following the Vietnam War U.S. defense spending declined but rose again starting in the late 1970s and continuing into the mid-1980s. Did the Kremlin act to take advantage of American complacency? Did it follow or lead the American example? None of these simple explanations seems to fit.

[81]

From 1965 until 1975, at a time when the USSR was establishing its claim to be the strategic equal of the United States, Soviet military outlays increased annually at between 3 and 5 percent. The annual rate of increase (measured in 1970 prices) then declined to about 2 percent from 1976 until at least 1982, with virtually a zero growth rate in weapons procurement, no matter whether measured in rubles or dollars.[86] Of course the absolute amount of these outlays was increasing, for it was only their growth rate that declined.[87] Indeed, measured in 1982 prices, growth in defense spending averaged over 5 percent annually during 1971–84.[88]

Whatever the budgetary restraints, Soviet military assets broadly expanded:[89]

	1970	*1975*	*1980*	*1985*
ICBM warheads	1,220	1,537	5,140	6,420
SLBM warheads	41	196	874	2,412
Tanks		40,000	50,000	52,600
Attack submarines		265	257	371

Soviet warhead accuracy increased; submarines became quieter; missiles became more mobile; troops and officers became better educated. Some military personnel contributed to dual-purpose functions, such as the Railroad Troops of the Rear Services, who played an important role in building the Baikal-Amur-Magistral (BAM) line initiated in 1974.[90] But the military branches of the Soviet economy are no more efficient than the civilian; therefore, every increase in military output costs dearly.[91]

From 1978 through 1987 the USSR outproduced the United States in most types of weapons by better than two to one: tanks, armored vehicles, long-range and intermediate-range bombers, fighter aircraft, ICBMs, and SLBMs. Since 1981, however, numbers of SLBMs, warships, submarines, and tactical aircraft produced in the USSR have decreased while quality, sophistication, and total capability have increased.

Still, the USSR did not mount a crash program in the late 1970s to outspend the other superpower wrapped in its post-Vietnam syndrome. Total outlays for the Strategic Rocket Forces and Air Defense declined in absolute terms from 1977 until at least 1983.[92] Complaints by Marshal Nikolai Ogarkov indicate that some uniformed officers believed the Kremlin was investing too little in modernizing its conventional weaponry.[93] The rising tide of Soviet espionage and third-party buying also implied that the Kremlin feared it could not compete effectively with its foreign rivals in mastering the scientific-technological revolution.[94] Soviet diplomats lamented that the ongoing arms race kept the best brains and research institutes in the USSR engrossed with military applications instead of conducting broad-based research. Last but not least, the decline in Soviet life expectancy and other indicators of public heath and morale manifested a social malaise to which militarism was probably a large contributor.[95]

The Brezhnev team appeared reluctant to increase the rate of defense spending in the early 1980s even in the face of a rapid U.S. military buildup. Brezhnev pledged that the USSR would never surrender strategic parity with the United States, but he also insisted that the Soviet Armed Forces already had "everything necessary to fulfill their current mission." Instead he pushed for continued heavy investment in domestic programs, especially the 1982 Food Program. Faced with criticism from the military and from other Party leaders, in October 1982 Brezhnev said in a meeting with the military high command that the USSR would speed up the pace of its military research and development, but he also reaffirmed the Food Program and argued its importance to national security and social welfare.[96]

Brezhnev's economic priorities persisted under Andropov and Chernenko and were supported by several commentaries in Party and military journals arguing that economic growth was more important to long-term military power than the size of existing forces. Some authors stressed that high-technology Western weapons posed a great threat to the USSR but that they could be matched only if resources were channeled into Soviet economic and technological development.

The Kremlin may also have had an eye cocked toward Poland, where consumer unrest threatened Communist rule in 1956, 1970, 1976, and the early 1980s.[97] Perhaps the Soviet Politburo reasoned that consumer satisfaction was also a prerequisite for stability in the USSR and that domestic consumption could not be turned off or lowered arbitrarily. "In short," according to one authority, "it appears that both growth and consumption are becoming part of the Soviet leadership's national security calculus."[98]

Soviet military spending may have picked up again in the mid-1980s, spurred in part by the Afghan campaign and by the bills for supporting beleaguered Third World clients. On September 27, 1984, Finance Minister Vasily Barbuzov announced an 11.8 percent increase in official defense spending for 1985 to some 19 billion rubles (just over $22 billion at the official exchange rate). The reported figured was surely a mere fraction of the actual total but it may have signaled the direction of real outlays. The announced increase was the largest reported in twenty-five years and was portrayed as a measured response to recent increases in U.S. defense expenditures. The pace of Soviet defense spending could accelerate with new product cycles or with a decision to respond actively to improving arsenals of the West, Japan, and China.

Enhanced national security does not necessarily require increased defense spending.[99] It could be made through reducing external threats and/or through domestic reform. These alternatives were perceived and acted on by Gorbachev's predecessors. From the mid-1950s through the early 1980s successive Soviet regimes attempted to reduce external threats by upgrading the USSR's alliances, diminishing East-West tensions, undermining Western alliances and defense programs, and reaching arms controls. Moscow sought also to improve intelligence gathering, stimulate Soviet R&D, broaden arms sales abroad, and increase the efficiency of Soviet military and other industries. By 1985, however, the security threats facing the Kremlin were probably greater than they had been a decade earlier. Moscow had achieved little on either front—arms control or economic reform. The burden of defense was a major component in the "plateful" of problems inherited by Gorbachev just as it had been for Khrushchev three decades before.

Russia's economic backwardness could modify the "kto kovo?" outlook. True, Soviet commentators in the Brezhnev era continued to argue that "rivalry" and "struggle" (*sopernichestvo, sorevnovanie, bor'ba*, even *protivoborstvo*) would still be needed to resolve the "historical dispute" (*istoricheskii spor*) between Soviet Russia and the West in the long run.[100] In the interim, however, it would be in Moscow's interest to secure a long breathing space in which to build Soviet economic and other strengths, if possible, aided by East-West trade and infusions of Western technology.[101]

By 1985 there had been almost no arms control dividend for the flagging Soviet economy. Stalin, Khrushchev, and Brezhnev had all seized on opportunities to slight defense preparations to the extent that international conditions permitted. Khrushchev had unilaterally cut the Soviet armed forces in 1955 and again in 1960. Despite decades of negotiations, there had been no major arms accords permitting a significant reduction in defense spending. Nor had there been any breakthrough in the barriers impeding trade between the USSR and Cocom, the U.S.-led "Coordinating Committee" of Western nations plus Japan committed to limiting sales of strategically useful goods to the Eastern countries.

Domestic Political Competition: The Gating Factor

Even within a highly centralized political system there may be disputes and competition not visible to outsiders—especially on sensitive issues of security and resource allocation. The ministers of Nicholas II disagreed on what priorities should dominate Russian policy at The Hague. Lenin debated with Trotsky and Bukharin over peace and security arrangements with Germany in late 1917–early 1918. Lenin and Trotsky disputed whether and when to dismantle the Soviet coast guard in 1921.[102] Some Soviet political and military leaders argued about the pace and scope of the transition to a cadre-territorial army in the 1920s.[103]

Probably Soviet leaders disagreed about arms and arms control issues in the 1930s and 1940s, but direct evidence of such disputes has been in short supply except for Litvinov's dissent on the unraveling of the anti-Hitler coalition.[104]

The political contest that followed Stalin's death and Khrushchev's ouster eleven years later showed how peace and disarmament issues can be used in domestic infighting. Georgii M. Malenkov's 1954 pronouncement on the general destruction that would result from a nuclear exchange was used against him by Viacheslav M. Molotov and Khrushchev. But by spring 1955 Khrushchev was in a position to urge flexibility on most foreign policy issues across the board, from Yugoslavia and Austria to arms control. Molotov fought a rearguard action as foreign minister trying, as had John Foster Dulles, to pursue a tougher line than directed by his superior. In 1956 Khrushchev strengthened his bid for supremacy by revising Communist doctrine on war, peace, and revolution. He came to stake his own political career on the feasibility and desirability of reaching arms and other accords with the West.[105] Molotov and other hard-liners were retired when they challenged Khrushchev. In 1957 Andrei A. Gromyko became foreign minister and presided for nearly three decades over a policy that displayed considerable continuity in its admixture of expansionist and accommodationist features.

There was grumbling over Khrushchev's 1960 unilateral force cut, his heavy reliance on the Strategic Rocket Forces, his confidence in Eisenhower, and his Cuban missile gambit. But he was finally sacked for his subjectivist style, not for the content of his policies on arms and arms control. Khrushchev's successors, to be sure, in mid-1965 initiated a broad "all-services" increase in defense allocations. They put new life into the manned bomber programs and blue water navy downgraded under Khrushchev; they vastly increased Soviet ground forces. Some of these changes probably would have occurred, however, even if Khrushchev had stayed at the helm. Failure of talks with China in November 1964–February 1965 prompted a long-term military buildup on the Sino-Soviet frontier. Escalated U.S. involvement in Vietnam at the same time gave another fillip to Soviet military outlays. That Moscow's third-generation ICBM seemed worthy of serial production was another factor that would likely have generated heightened spending even had Khrushchev remained.[106] As for arms control, the Kremlin swallowed its self-respect and negotiated the 1967 outer space treaty and 1968 nonproliferation treaty despite U.S. bombing of a "sister socialist state." Indeed, in 1968 the Kremlin invited Lyndon Johnson to Moscow and stood ready to initiate strategic arms limitation talks. In many respects the Brezhnev and Kosygin team was continuing what Beijing termed "Khrushchevism without Khrushchev."

Brezhnev's decision to tilt toward heightened defense spending, coupled with massive investments in agriculture, helped to neutralize two contending factions. At one pole Nikolai Podgorny made himself vulnerable by his extreme support for consumer allocations over defense; at the other, Aleksandr Shelepin threatened Brezhnev by his all-out commitment to military outlays, popular among some Party ideologues. Brezhnev's right-of-center position enabled him to win the support of Mikhail Suslov (the "kingmaker") and the military while he manipulated personnel within the Party Secretariat to put allies in key places.[107]

The record since 1953 suggests that within the Kremlin it has been more dangerous politically to oppose détente than to support it. Apart from Malenkov's case, there is no evidence that any top Soviet leader has suffered because he was soft on the dangers of nuclear war or too zealous for arms control. Shevchenko reports that Shelepin, Dmitrii Polyansky, and Petr Shelest doubted the wisdom of Brezhnev's receiving Nixon in 1972 and that this contributed to their downfalls.[108] Kissinger himself observed a dispute among Brezhnev, Kosygin, and Podgorny at one meeting on the relative importance of economic versus security issues.[109] Because of the tendency toward rule by consensus after 1964, any Politburo faction can do much to obstruct if not veto moves toward East-West accords. When foot-draggers are dismissed or fade away, the way is opened wider to whatever arms controls the dominant Politburo faction wishes. In Moscow as in Washington, of course, any step toward accommodation with the other superpower must be protected from charges of selling out.

Opposition to arms control and to détente can brake movement in that direction, whether in the Kremlin or the White House. Internal political competition is thus a "gating" factor that opens or closes the door to policies that the leadership prefers but may fear to pursue if the domestic

[86]

costs are excessive. Once the opposition has been neutralized, however, the regime may go on to champion arms limitation in order to demonstrate its wisdom and skill in strategy and tactics. Both Khrushchev and Brezhnev attempted to use arms control treaties and moves toward détente to win additional support at home, providing models that Gorbachev has also sought to emulate.

Compared with the United States, the role played by arms control oppositionists has been minimal in the USSR. President Podgorny, some reports hold, may have been relieved in 1977 for opposing détente; Marshal Ogarkov seems to have been put down, at least for a time, because he campaigned too insistently for heightened allocations to some military purposes. Even when the U.S. Congress pulled the rug from under Brezhnev's vaunted Peace Program by refusing to liberalize trade with Moscow and approve some arms accords, Brezhnev was not displaced. Ill health rather than concessions to the West brought on his eclipse. Andropov, had he been in better health, might have injected a much more energetic note into Soviet diplomacy; Konstantin Chernenko, for his part, seems to have given Gromyko a loose rein in foreign policy.

Do components of the Soviet bureaucracy sometimes undermine détente or arms control deliberately by conducting their responsibilities with excessive zeal or by blind devotion to standard operating routines? Some disagreements and frictions are likely if only because of personal or institutional preferences and responsibilities. Thus military publications probably warn more often about the dangers of accommodations with the West than, say, *Pravda* or *Izvestiia*. The KGB may have wanted to spike détente, or it may only have been conducting business as usual when it attacked a German diplomat and arrested Professor Frederick C. Barghoorn in 1963 not long after the limited test ban was signed in Moscow and before Khrushchev's planned visit to Bonn. Another possible explanation of sweet-and-sour notes in Soviet policy is that the top leaders, even at moments of détente, may wish to demonstrate that they are ever vigilant.

But the Soviet system has no analogue to the profound bureaucratic infighting that often pits the U.S. National Security Council, the intelligence community, the State, Defense, and Commerce Departments, and the U.S. Arms Control and Disarmament Agency at cross-purposes. Nor is there any Soviet parallel to the domination of the House or Senate by one party, the White House by another, each party asserting that the other is either too soft or too lenient toward the USSR. If the top Soviet leaders sign a treaty, it will be endorsed by the Supreme Soviet; if they direct the Ministry of Defense or other agencies to implement the treaty, the order will be carried out, if reluctantly. Despite signs that many officers disagreed with the asymmetrical or unilateral force cuts championed by Gorbachev after 1985, the military machine dutifully implemented the orders received from the Party leadership. And Marshal Akhromeev, though he resigned just as Gorbachev announced a unilateral force cut in 1988, continued to serve as a Kremlin adviser. Though Westerners look for other motives, old age can overtake even Soviet officers.

The American public frequently hears from the RAND Corporation or the Livermore, or Los Alamos laboratory that a new technology is available that makes existing or planned nuclear accords obsolete or contrary to U.S. interests. Thus U.S. seismologists reported in 1958–59 on new techniques for conducting underground nuclear tests so that they could not be identified by a verification system just endorsed by U.S. and Soviet specialists in Geneva.[110] In the mid-1980s other U.S. government-supported scientists contended that impending breakthroughs rendered the premises of the ABM Treaty passé.[111] Probably analogous voices have existed in the USSR, but they have not had ready access to the media. Hence they have played a smaller role than in the United States in raising public doubts about the utility of specific arms controls.

Not until Gorbachev's *glasnost'* campaigns opened the doors to expression of many viewpoints was there a way for Soviet peace activists to make themselves heard unless they merely parroted the Party line. Thus before 1985 Soviet scientists echoed their Western counterparts on the dangers of Strontium 90 and the dangers of "nuclear winter" only when it suited the Politburo. To be sure, some Soviet scientists privately expressed reservations to Party leaders about arms developments. Thus Andrei Sakharov's private views were weighed by Khrushchev as he considered the pros and cons of renewed nuclear testing.[112] When Sakharov began issuing his broadsides in public, however, he became almost a nonperson in the USSR. Even his 1968 manifesto, it should be noted, depended heavily on Western sources such as *Scientific American* for its policy inferences.[113] Working groups have been set up within the USSR Academy of Sciences on accidental nuclear war and other dangers of arms competition. But the independence and influence of such groups are in question, for they have been overshadowed by what John R. Thomas has called the "militarization" of the academy.[114] The few Soviet papers in recent years endorsing the nuclear winter thesis have derived from data and models developed in the United States sometimes handed over or mailed to Moscow by U.S. scientists wishing to interest Soviet colleagues in their conclusions.[115]

The Soviet military and the military-industrial complex, for their parts, cannot lobby so openly for their narrow objectives as in the United States. The military press can delete paeans to arms limitation and détente when it reprints speeches by Party leaders. It can underscore the hazards of complacency in the face of aggressive imperialism. But there are severe limits to self-serving words or deeds by military officials. Upstarts such as Marshals Mikhail Frunze, Mikhail Tukhachevskii, and (less brutally) Georgii Zhukov were cast aside; more recently, Marshal Nikolai Ogarkov was merely demoted. Military professionals were passed over when Dmitrii Ustinov became defense minister; some potentially more influential marshals were slighted again when Sergei Sokolov was named to succeed Ustinov and when Dmitrii Yazov replaced Sokolov following the Cessna landing in Red Square in 1987. Yazov, like Sokolov before him, was made only a candidate (nonvoting) member of the Politburo. His modest position in the Party hierarchy may be seen in Table 3.2.

How, then, has domestic political competition within the USSR affected the prospects for arms control? The absence of well-organized opposition within the ruling circles or the broader public can both facilitate and obstruct arms control. The CPSU general secretary can pursue arms accords and order their implementation with much less risk of internal opposition than an American president. The other side of this coin is that Soviet leaders are also much freer to build whatever weapons they choose and to use them, as in Afghanistan, with little public outcry. Their license to use force in Eastern Europe or the Third World, in turn, makes Western governments chary of arms accords with an unscrupulous foe.

Domestic politics thus serves as a gating factor, opening or closing the path to arms controls. A minimum but not sufficient condition for high-level endorsement of arms control is that it not hurt and may help in the domestic struggle for power. Economic considerations may add to and reinforce other motives for arms control but cannot be a necessary or sufficient condition to embrace arms limitations. Whatever the regime decides, propaganda organs will devise a plausible rationale. The Kremlin's operational code is heavily influenced by ideological suppositions coloring perceptions and responses of Soviet leaders to their environment. But Lenin himself counseled flexibility, and his successors have chosen and revised ideological postulates as they deemed useful to legitimate policies geared to present-day challenges and opportunities.

The picture has been in flux since 1985—not only because of glasnost' and democratization campaigns but because of *perestroika*. Gorbachev's drive to reform the Soviet economy will at best require years of sacrifice and experiment before it results in higher living standards. In the meantime, he has used arms control and the *nouvelle détente* to win

[89]

support for his regime and its domestic program. He has shown that peace—more than alleged external bogeys—can elicit popular backing. Whether foreign policy successes of this kind can override the effects of prolonged shortages of consumer goods remains to be seen.[116]

To evaluate the broader context in which Soviet arms control policy has taken shape, we turn in the next chapter to the global arena.

TABLE 3.2
Party-Government Overlap (as of March 1989)

PARTY OFFICIALS	CONCURRENT GOVERNMENT POSITIONS
Politburo Full Members	
Mikhail Gorbachev	Chairman, USSR Supreme Soviet Presidium ("president")[1]
Viktor Chebrikov	(Former Chairman, KGB[2]; replaced by Vladimir A. Kriuchkov in October 1988)
Egor Ligachev	
Vadim Medvedev	
Viktor Nikonov	
Nikolai Ryzhkov	Chairman, USSR Council of Ministers ("premier" or "prime minister")[2]
Vladimir Shcherbitskii	
Eduard Shevardnadze	Minister of Foreign Affairs[2]
Nikolai Sliun'kov	
Vitalii Vorotnikov	Chairman, RSFSR Supreme Soviet[3]
Aleksandr Yakovlev	
Lev Zaikov	
Politburo Candidate Members	
Aleksandra Biriukova	Deputy Chairman, USSR Council of Ministers for Light Industry and Social Affairs[2]
Anatolii Luk'ianov	First Deputy Chairman, USSR Supreme Soviet Presidium[1]
Yuri Masliukov	First Deputy Chairman, USSR Council of Ministers; Chairman, State Planning Committee[2]
Georgii Razumovskii	
Yurii Solov'iev	
Nakolai Talizin	Deputy Chairman, USSR Council of Ministers[2]; Permanent Representative to Council of Mutual Economic Assistance (CMEA)
Aleksandr Vlasov	Chairman, RSFSR Council of Ministers[3]
Dmitrii Yazov	Minister of Defense[2]

[1] Legislative
[2] Administrative
[3] Republic-level

Notes

1. For surveys of Soviet military power, see *50 let vooruzhennykh sil SSSR* [*50 Years of USSR Armed Forces*] (Moscow: Voennoe izdatel'stvo Ministerstva Oborony SSSR, 1968) and *Sovetskie vooruzhennye sily: istoriia stroitel'stva* (Moscow: Voennoe izdatel'stvo MO SSSR, 1978). Also see Raymond L. Garthoff, "Military Influences and Instruments," in Ivo J. Lederer, ed., *Russian Foreign Policy: Essays in Historical Perspective* (New Haven, CT: Yale University Press, 1962), 243–77.

2. For the ambience of the League talks, see Salvador de Madariaga, *Disarmament* (New York: Coward-McCann, 1929). Boris E. Shtein, Litvinov's assistant at the League, remembered de Madariaga warmly in talks at Moscow University in 1958. In an era before glasnost', however, passages in de Madariaga's book on the USSR as an "obstacle" to disarmament were either pasted over with opaque paper or excised at the Lenin Library and the Fundamental Library, Academy of Social Sciences.

3. Arms control could entail a freeze, a decrease, or even an increase in the quantity or quality of military forces. Disarmament, by contrast, means the reduction or elimination of such forces. Some radical pacifists view any disarmament as progressive; arms controllers, by contrast, worry lest any change in military deployments—up, down, or sidewise—increase the risk of war.

Arms controls goals such as stability, economy, and military advantage could be promoted even though no treaty is ever signed—for example, by raising or decreasing military spending, by deploying or using arms aggressively or defensively, or by propaganda campaigns and protracted negotiations that immobilize or deceive the other side. Some goals can also be achieved by "understandings" pledging joint or parallel actions. Either or both sides may contribute to arms control by restraint in the kinds of weapons acquired or supplied to others, in the direction and level of defense spending, and by means of command and control exercised over forces deployed.

In short, the arms control process and its outcomes can be "good" or "bad" for one or all sides in its short- and long-term impact.

4. For background on the "Third Rome," see James H. Billington, *The Icon and the Axe* (New York: Vintage, 1970), 70, 84, 659; on propaganda, see Frederick C. Barghoorn, "Propaganda: Tsarist and Soviet," in Lederer, *Russian Foreign Policy*, pp. 279–309 at 280–81; on mass movements, Alexander Dallin, "The Use of International Movements," in ibid., pp. 311–49; on ideology, Walter C. Clemens, Jr., "Ideology in Soviet Disarmament Policy," *Journal of Conflict Resolution* 8, no. 1 (March 1964): 7–22.

5. Alexander I wrote that he was enabled by "the Most High" to write out his plan for a Holy Alliance based on justice, Christian charity, and peace. See W. P. Cresson, *The Holy Alliance: The European Background to the Monroe Doctrine* (New York: Oxford University Press, 1922), 29–30. See also the many observations on Alexander's idealism throughout *Mémoires du Prince Adam Czartoryski et correspondance avec l'Empereur Alexander Ier*, 2 vols. (Paris: E. Plon, Nourrit et Cie, 1887). For analysis, see Patricia Kennedy Grimsted, *The Foreign Ministers of Alexander I* (Berkeley: University of California Press, 1969), chaps. 1 and 4.

6. Maurice Paleologue, *The Enigmatic Czar: The Life of Alexander I of Russia* (New York: Harper & Brothers, 1938), 248–49; see also Cresson, *The Holy Alliance*, p. 30; Pierre Rain, *Alexandre Ier (1777–1825)* (Paris: Perrin et Cie., 1913), 280–81.

7. Robert V. Daniels, *Russia* (Cambridge, MA: Harvard University Press, 1985), 59.

8. Alexander's grand designs were probably influenced, at least superficially, by V. F. Malinovskii, a diplomat who spent some years in England and wrote much of his *Discourse on War and Peace* [*Rassuzhenie o mire i voine*, written 1790 to 1798]—a treatise that arose from the same intellectual ferment that stimulated Rousseau, Kant, and others to write on ways to end war. Malinovskii, however, was nearly unique among his peers in insisting upon the need for a system of laws as a condition for eliminating war. The thrust of Malinovskii's book resembled more *World Peace through World Law*, 2d ed. (Cambridge, MA; Harvard University Press, 1960), written by lawyers Grenville Clark and Louis B. Sohn.

Malinovskii's grounding in law and reason was completely absent from Alexander's mystical appeals and, one might add, from later Soviet proposals for radical disarmament without preconditions.

Whatever Alexander thought of Malinovskii's *Discourse*, he made him director of the *lycee* at Tsarskoe Selo, a school where Pushkin imbibed the liberal attitudes for which he was later banished to the provinces.

9. Cresson, *The Holy Alliance*, p. 48.

10. A French observer in 1824 estimated that the colonies could mobilize 300,000 soldiers in time of war and that when the entire army was "colonized," it would include four to six million men. The colonies provided both men and supplies for Russia's military involvements in the late 1820s but were disbanded after 1857 partly because of their unpopularity. See Rain, *Alexander Ier*, pp. 355–59.

11. Walter C. Clemens, Jr., "Soviet Disarmament Proposals and the Cadre-Territorial Army," *Orbis* 7, no. 4 (Winter 1964): 778–99; and "The Soviet Militia in the Missile Age," *Orbis* 7, no. 1 (Spring 1964): 81–105. On 1989, see chapter 8 of this book.

12. See Count S. Y. Witte, *Vospominaniia: Tsarstvovanie Nikolaia II*, 2 vols. (Berlin: "Slovo," 1922), I: 143–46. For documentation on tsarist policy in 1899, see L. Teleshevskoi, ed., "K istorii pervoi Gaagakoi konferentsii 1899 g.," *Krasnyi arkhiv* 50–51 (Moscow, 1932): 64–96, and "Novye materialy o Gaagskoi mirnoi konferentsii 1899 g.," *Krasnyi arkhiv* 54–55 (Moscow, 1932): 49–70. For a Soviet analysis, see F. A. Rotshtein, *Mezhdunarodnye otnosheniia v kontse XIX veka* (Moscow-Leningrad: Izdatel'stvo Akademii Nauk SSSR, 1960), chaps. 16 and 17. For documentation on the conferences, see *Actes et documents relatifs au programme de la paix publies d'ordre du gouvernement par Jhr. van Dachne van Varick* (The Hague: Martinus Nijhoff, 1899); *The Proceedings of the Hague Peace Conferences: The Conference of 1899*, translated and edited under the direction of James B. Scott (New York: Oxford University Press, 1920); *The Proceedings of the Hague Peace Conferences: The Conference of 1907*, translated and edited under the direction of James B. Scott (New York: Oxford University Press, 1921–22), vols. I and II.

13. See Nikolai Notovitch, *La Pacification de l'Europe et Nicholas II* (Paris: P. Ollendorf, 1899).

14. Jean de Bloch [Ivan Bliokh], *La guerre: Traduction de l'ouvrage Russe. La guerre future, aux points de vue technique, économique et politique*, 6 vols. (Paris, 1898–1900).

15. See for example, the arguments as Athens debated whether to accept Sparta's proposal to end the impasse at Pylos: Thucydides, *History of the Peloponnesian War* (Baltimore, MD: Penguin, 1974), 274–78.

16. *Reports to the Hague Conferences of 1899 and 1907*, ed. James Brown Scott (Oxford: Clarendon Press, 1917), p. 3.

17. Ibid., pp. 175–77.

18. See William I. Hull, *The Two Hague Conferences and Their Contributions to International Law* (Boston: For the International School of Peace, Ginn & Co., 1908), 83–85. Publisher Edwin Ginn established the International School of Peace in 1910; within five months it was renamed the World Peace Foundation. See *75th Anniversary Report* (Boston: World Peace Foundation, 1985).

19. Hull, *Two Hague Conferences*, pp. 84–85.

20. Ibid., pp. 87–89. Ambassador Andrew D. White, formally head of the U.S. delegation, recorded that he was not satisfied with his government's position on asphyxiating bombs but asked, "What can a layman do when he has against him the foremost contemporary military and naval experts?" Quoted in ibid., p. 90.

21. Ibid., p. 91.

22. Scott, *Reports to the Hague Conferences of 1899 and 1907*, pp. 172–77.

23. *The Hague Conventions and Declarations of 1898 and 1907*, ed. James Brown Scott, 2d ed. (New York: Oxford University Press, 1915), xv–xxxi.

24. Scott, *Reports to the Hague Conferences of 1899 and 1907*, p. 899.

25. Friedrich Engels, *Anti-Dühring: Herr Eugen Dühring's Revolution in Science*, 3d ed. (Moscow: Foreign Languages Publishing House, 1962), 233–34; Engels advocated

disarmament in *Kann Europa abrüsten?* (Nüremburg, 1893), but in 1894 he issued a third edition of *Anti-Dühring*, originally published in 1878.

26. See Walter C. Clemens, Jr., "Lenin on Disarmament," *Slavic Review* 23, no. 3 (September 1964): 504–25.

27. For a summary of these measures and documentary sources, see ibid., p. 507.

28. *Sovetskii Soiuz v bor'be za mir: Sobranie dokumentov i vstupitel'naia stat'ia* (Moscow: Gosizdat, 1929), 131–32.

29. First published in *Pravda*, April 12, 1964; see also Lenin documents first published in *Pravda*, April 22, 1964.

30. See Clemens, "Lenin on Disarmament," p. 518.

31. Georgii Malenkov, the first Soviet leader to warn that nuclear war could destroy all civilization (1954), was forced out of public life in 1957. From retirement he could observe other Soviet leaders endorsing his basic thesis. He outlasted other rivals—Andrei Zhdanov and N. S. Khrushchev by many years, and V. M. Molotov by one and a half years. For a review of the decade after Stalin, see Lincoln P. Bloomfield, Walter C. Clemens, Jr., and Franklyn Griffiths, *Khrushchev and the Arms Race: Soviet Interests in Arms Control and Disarmament, 1954–1964* (Cambridge: MIT Press, 1966); for a survey of zigs and zags in Soviet military doctrine, see for example, James M. McDonnell, "Shifts in Soviet Views on the Proper Focus of Military Development," *World Politics* 37, no. 3 (April 1985): 317–43.

32. A Soviet writer in 1922 condemned tsarist policy for proposing to freeze the arms race instead of calling for complete disarmament. He also condemned British policy (1906) and former President Harding (1921) for seeking merely to limit arms spending until such time as conditions again favored investing heavily in armaments. M. Pavlovich writing in *Ot Vashingtona do Genui* (Moscow: Vysshii voennyi redaktsionyi sovet, 1922), 5–11.

33. See Clemens, "Ideology in Soviet Disarmament Policy," pp. 12–13.

34. For Khrushchev's views on general disarmament versus partial measures, see Arkady N. Shevchenko, *Breaking with Moscow* (New York: Alfred A. Knopf, 1985), 161; see also Bloomfield et al., *Khrushchev*. For Gorbachev's appeal for total nuclear disarmament, see *Pravda*, January 16, 1986, pp. 1, 2.

35. See *Conference de Toutes les Eglises et Associations Religieuses de l'U.R.S.S. Pour la defense de la paix dans le monde, Zagorsk . . . 9–12 mai 1952. Documents* (Moscow: Editions du Patriarcat de Moscou, 1955). Proceedings of a conference attended by representatives of many religious sects in the USSR: Russian, Georgian, and Armenian Orthodox; Catholic; Lutheran; Baptist; Old Believers; Methodist; Baku and Tifilis Molokane; Seventh Day Adventists; Muslim; Buddhists; Moscow and Kiev Jewish. The speeches praised Stalin's policies in behalf of peace and attacked positions of the United States, West Germany, and Japan. This volume—published three years after the conference—was seen in East Berlin; no record of a Russian edition has been found.

36. For a chronology with extensive bibliographic notes on the "movement of the supporters of peace in the Soviet Union," see Iu. A. Zhukov et al., *Letopis' bor'by za mir, 1949–1984: Dvizhenie storonnikov mira v Sovetskom Soiuze* (Moscow: Mezhdunarodnye otnosheniia, 1984); see also the documents of various peace movements cited in Walter C. Clemens, Jr., comp., *Soviet Disarmament Policy, 1917–1963: An Annotated Bibliography of Soviet and Western Sources* (Stanford, CA: Hoover Institution, 1965), items 185–99.

37. See, however, the *Pravda* cartoon showing Chicherin's frustration arising from the passionate speeches of Comintern Chairman Zinoviev. Reprinted in Louis Fischer, *The Soviets in World Affairs, 1917–1929*, 2 vols., 2d ed. (Princeton, NJ: Princeton University Press, 1951), II: 471.

38. See Walter C. Clemens, Jr., *The Arms Race and Sino-Soviet Relations* (Stanford, CA: Hoover Institution, 1968), 65–81.

39. "We must not repeat mechanically what . . . Lenin said about imperialism many decades back," *Pravda*, June 22, 1960.

40. See Clemens, "Lenin on Disarmament."

41. Walter C. Clemens, Jr., *The Superpowers and Arms Control* (Lexington, MA: Lexington Books, 1973), 69, 85–86; also Franklyn Griffiths, *Genoa plus 51: Changing Soviet*

Objectives in Europe, Wellesley Paper no. 4 (Toronto: Canadian Institute of International Affairs, 1973). Griffiths' analysis is continued in his article "The Sources of American Conduct: Soviet Perspectives and Their Policy Implications," *International Security* 9, no. 2 (Fall 1984): 3–50. Although Griffiths and I have interpreted "Genoa" materials as a code word for "opportune moment for serious negotiations," several international relations specialists in Moscow told me (Marcy 1989) that "Genoa" meant nothing special to them. Still, the recurrence of Genoa materials during crucial negotiating periods implies an intent to signal even though the message might not register.

42. S. Dangulov, "Lenin. Genuia. Novaia diplomatiia," *Kommunist*, no. 17 November 1987): 81–91. This article, dedicated to the seventieth anniversary of the Soviet diplomatic service, appears in the same issue as Gorbachev's November 2 address on the eve of the anniversary of the Bolshevik Revolution.

43. Shevchenko, *Breaking with Moscow*, p. 161.

44. See Blomfield et al., *Khrushchev*, pp. 130–35.

45. For background, see F. Stephen Larrabee, "Westeuropaeische Interessen im amerikanisch-sowetischen Dialog ueber Kernwaffen und Waffen zur strategischen Verteidigung," *Europa-Archiv* 6 (1985): 165–74; on Soviet propaganda, see Gerhard Wettig, "Security Diplomacy and Propaganda in Soviet Foreign Policy: The INF Controversy," paper presented at the Kennan Institute for Advanced Russian Studies, Washington, DC, April 25, 1985.

46. Western governments have also been ready to change their tune to promote serious objectives. Former President Roosevelt urged Charlie Chaplin and others in Hollywood to create a positive image of America's brave Russian allies and Uncle Joe. During the 1963 Spirit of Moscow, *Life* magazine brought out a special issue showing Soviet leaders as lovable Santa Claus figures—smiling faces wrapped in soft furs. Western propaganda, however, is not so coordinated as in Moscow, where dramatic reverses have been well orchestrated.

47. Quoted in Christopher Davis, "Military and Civilian Economic Activities of the Soviet Armed Forces, 1975–85" (Birmingham: Centre for Russian and East European Studies, University of Birmingham, England, 1986), 1. That military power depends on economic is a central thesis of the "force theory" in Engels, *Anti-Dühring*, pp. 219–54.

48. V. I. Lenin, *Sochineniia*, 2d ed., 30 vols. (Moscow: Gosizdat, 1926–32), 31: 189–90.

49. Ia. L. Berman, ed., *Vsesoiuznaia Kommunisticheskaia Partiia (bol'shevikov) i voennoe delo*, 2d ed. (Moscow: Izdatel'stvo Voennogo Vestnika, 1928), 204.

50. Lenin, *Sochineniia*, 22: 405.

51. Ibid., 22: 14, 25: 203, 407.

52. In 1921 and 1922 Stalin stressed the importance of mastering all forms of warfare and organization, the development of which (he said in 1923) changes with the development of production. See I. V. Stalin, *Sochineniia*, 13 vols. (Moscow: Gosudarstvennoe Izdatel'stvo Politicheskoi Literatury, 1946–1951), 5: 77–79, 164–65. For a collection of articles quoting Lenin in a manner that implies that he originated the "permanently operating factors" doctrine later articulated by Stalin, see *Marksizm-Leninizm o voine i armii: sbornik statei* (Moscow: Voennoe Izdatel'stvo Ministerstva Oborony Soiuza SSR, 1956).

53. See *Sovetskie voennye sily* (cited in note 1), pp. 126–127; also Walter C. Clemens, Jr., "Origins of the Soviet Campaign for Disarmament: The Soviet Position on Peace, Security, and Revolution at the Genoa, Moscow, and Lausanne Conferences" (Ph.D. diss., Columbia University, New York, 1961), pt. III.

54. Military spending as a percentage of the overall Soviet budget amounted to 33.4 percent in 1922; it fluctuated between 14.0 and 17.0 percent in 1923–26; dropped to 12.0 percent in 1927–28; rose to 14.6 percent in 1928–29, and then *declined* to 8.5 percent in 1929–30. The military budget (in millions of rubles) fell from 627 in 1922 to 230 in 1923; rose from 402 in 1924 to 774 in 1927 and 1,207 in 1929, falling to 1,046 in 1929–30 even though the overall budget rose sharply. See the official budgets available at the Hoover Institution and cited in Clemens, "Origins of the Soviet Campaign for Disarmament," pp. 53–54. See also J. Cooper, "Defence Production and the Soviet Economy, 1929–1941," CREES Discussion

Papers, Series SIPS, no. 3 (Birmingham: Centre for Russian and East European Studies, University of Birmingham, 1976), questioning official statistics.

55. On the growth in military inventories, see David Holloway, *The Soviet Union and the Arms Race* (New Haven, CT: Yale University Press), 6–8. On Stalin's role in decision making, see Vernon V. Aspaturian, "The Stalinist Legacy in Soviet National Security Decisionmaking," in Jiri Valenta and William C. Potter, eds., *Soviet Decisionmaking for National Security* (Boston: Unwin Hyman, 1984), 23–73 at 47 ff. The professional military is credited with a far greater voice in the companion article by Jerry Hough, "The Historical Legacy in Soviet Weapons Development," in ibid., pp. 87–115. Stalin's role in wartime decision making is minimized in the uncensored version of Marshal Zhukov's memoirs, forthcoming.

56. On Tukhachevskii, see Albert Nenarokov, "Armour and Horses," *Moscow News*, no. 14 (April 10–17, 1988), pp. 8–9. Nenarokov recounts also that in 1936–37 Ivan Kozhanov, commander of the Black Sea Fleet, insisted that the navy should not be limited to large ships (as Stalin then wanted) and suggested building submarines, a naval air force, and smaller ships. Nenarokov's essay implicitly accepts Aspaturian's thesis (see note 55) that to challenge Stalin was to risk death. If Hough's thesis were true, Kozhanov was only playing his role in a rational bureaucracy. In any case, Tukhachevskii's execution was part of a far-reaching purge of military, foreign affairs, and Party leaders.

57. See Kendall E. Bailes, *Technology and Society under Lenin and Stalin* (Princeton, NJ: Princeton University Press, 1978), 381–406. The cadre of the Red Army numbered 885,000 men in 1933, nearly doubling in 1938 to 1,513,400. Production of rifles, tanks, and planes was many times higher in 1938 than in 1931. (*50 let vooruzhennykh sil*, pp. 193–98). In 1936 the Soviet defense budget jumped by 80 percent and defense industries were taken away from the Commissariat of Heavy Industry and placed under a newly formed Commissariat of the Defense Industry under the Commissariat of Defense. See Bailes, *Technology and Society*, pp. 398–99. Soviet expenditures on research and development (not exclusively military) rose from 120 million rubles in 1927 to 700 million in 1932; 1,100 million in 1935; 1,651 million in 1941. Soviet expenditures on R&D have been higher than in the United States since at least the mid-1930s. See Walter A. McDougall, *The Heavens and the Earth: A Political History of the Space Age* (New York: Basic Books, 1985), 462–64.

58. At Potsdam Philip E. Mosley advised his government that if Washington continued its position on reparations, Moscow might gain the impression that the United States sympathized more with the German than the Soviet people. See *Foreign Relations of the United States: The Conference of Berlin, 1945*, 2 vols. (Washington, DC: U.S. Government Printing Office, 1960), II: 850. Khrushchev later recalled that the Soviets were "bitterly offended" when the United States took back transport ships conveyed to the USSR under Lend-Lease "and sank them before our eyes." See *Khrushchev Remembers*, 2 vols. (Boston: Little, Brown, 1970, 1974), II: 19.

59. Stalin, *Sochineniia*, 3 vols. (Stanford, CA: Hoover Institution, 1967), III: 1–22 at 20.

60. *The Soviet Armed Forces*, pp. 370–71, 378–79.

61. *Khrushchev Remembers*, II: 11–12, 20. Khrushchev was probably on less certain ground when he said that Stalin "failed to realize the crucial role which aircraft carriers and submarines had played in World War II." See ibid., II: 20, 39. On Stalin's personal participation and oversight of programs during World War II aimed at improving Soviet technology in ways that would overtake the West (e.g., in range of fighter planes), see the memoirs of a leading Soviet engineer and designer: A. Iakovlev, *Tsel' zhizni (sapiski aviakonstruktora)*, 2d and enlarged ed. (Moscow: Politizdat, 1969), esp. 336–51.

62. See Walter C. Clemens, Jr., "American Policy and the Origins of the Cold War in Central Europe, 1945–1947," in Peter J. Potichnyj and Jane P. Shapiro, eds., *From the Cold War to Détente* (New York: Praeger, 1976), 3–25. For a broad picture, see Robert A. Pollard, *Economic Security and the Origins of the Cold War* (New York: Columbia University Press, 1985).

63. *Khrushchev Remembers*, II: 12.

64. In the mid-1950s Admiral N. G. Kuznetsov proposed that the USSR build up its

fleet of destroyers and cruisers. Khrushchev asked him, "If we had all the ships you've proposed we build . . . would we be able to withstand the full force of a sea attack by the British and American navies?" When the admiral replied *nyet*, Khrushchev asked, "Then what sense does it make to invest these colossal sums of money? Even if we approved your recommendations, it would take ten years for us to build all the ships you want, and by then the United States would probably be even further ahead." Quoted in ibid., II: 26.

65. Ibid., II: 30–33.

66. Ibid., II: 13.

67. Ibid., II: 31.

68. Besides its limited range, the Mya-4 did not perform well in flight tests and may not have been able to fly through dense antiaircraft fire. Ibid., II: 39.

69. Ibid., II: 31, 43.

70. Ibid., II: 53.

71. Ibid., II: 37.

72. See Arnold L. Horelick and Myron Rush, *Strategic Power and Soviet Foreign Policy* (Chicago: University of Chicago Press, 1966), esp. pt. 2.

73. Clemens, "The Soviet Militia in the Missile Age," pp. 81–105.

74. The consensus estimate of a panel reviewing the Cuban missile crisis at the Harvard Center for Science and International Affairs in October 1987 was 5,000 versus 300. Participants included Robert S. McNamara, McGeorge Bundy, Raymond L. Garthoff, Fyodor M. Burlatsky, and Sergo Mikoyan. But Soviet archivist General Dmitrii Volkogonov told a follow-on conference that the USSR had only twenty ICBMs aimed at the United States in late 1962. See *The New York Times*, January 29, 1989, p. 10.

75. See the speech of the president of the USSR Chamber of Commerce at the International Economic Conference held in Moscow in 1952, cited in Elizabeth Kridl Valkenier, *The Soviet Union and the Third World: An Economic Bind* (New York: Praeger, 1983), 1.

76. Speech to the Russian Institute, Columbia University, 1957.

77. *Documents on Disarmament, 1945–1959*, 2 vols. (Washington, DC: U.S. Department of State, 1960), I: 492–94.

78. L. N. Klingen, *Sredi patriarkhov zemledeliia narodov blizhnego i dal'nego vostoka: Egipet. Indiia. Tseilon. Kitai* (Moscow: Gosudarstvennoe izdatel'stvo sel'sko-khoziaistvennoi literatury, 1960). Klingen lived 1851–1922. His journey appears to have been subsidized by the Russian government. He brought back over two tons of seeds and seedlings, including thousands of tea plants and orange trees.

79. The broad picture is that Soviet grain output had several good years in the mid-1970s, only to decline and stagnate for most of the 1980s. Grain imports occurred on a small scale in the mid-1960s and then stopped until the early 1970s, after which it became a massive feature of Soviet trade for the rest of the 1970s and all the 1980s. See *The New York Times*, March 19, 1989, p. E3. For background, see Marshall I. Goldman, *U.S.S.R. in Crisis: The Failure of an Economic System* (New York: W. W. Norton, 1983), 65. For the conditions that led to the poor harvest in 1963, see *Production of Grain in the USSR* (Washington, DC: Central Intelligence Agency, October 1964). See also D. Gale Johnson and Karen McConnell Brooks, *Prospects for Soviet Agriculture in the 1980s* (Bloomington: Indiana University Press, 1983), esp. chap. 2 ("Agricultural Performance since 1950"); see also Harry Gelman, *The Brezhnev Politburo and the Decline of Détente* (Ithaca, NY: Cornell University Press, 1984), 124 ff.

80. Roy D. Laird cautions (letter dated May 28, 1987) that a time lag of one or even two years might be needed before a bad harvest could lead to conciliatory moves in foreign policy. Crop dimensions are not known until late summer. Time would be needed to assess the need for imports and then to change Soviet behavior. Any major impact on behavior might require the cumulative effect of repeated shortfalls, as in the early 1980s.

81. See "USSR Grain Situation and Outlook," *Foreign Agricultural Service Circular Series* (Washington, DC: U.S. Department of Agriculture, February 9, 1987) and similar reports dated January 17 and March 12, 1984. See also the department statistics published in *The New York Times*, August 25, 1988, p. D2. These and other materials are insightfully

analyzed in Roy D. Laird, "U.S.-Soviet Food Relations in the Age of Interdependence," unpublished manuscript, Lawrence, KS, 1987; also M. Mastanduno, "Strategies for Economic Containment: U.S. Trade Policies with the Soviet Union," *World Politics* 37, no. 4 (July 1985): 503–31.

82. One of the hijackers, Edward Kuznetsov, told the author (interviews in San Francisco, 1981) that he and some colleagues decided to risk the hijacking attempt in part because they had advance information that the 1971 Party Congress would endorse a policy aimed at vast expansion of Soviet trade and technical ties with the West. They calculated— correctly, it turned out—that the authorities would not execute them if they were apprehended. Still, Kuznetsov had to serve a second long term in prison; he had previously been sentenced for public poetry readings and *samizdat* activities. See his *Prison Diaries* (New York: Stein and Day 1975).

83. See Walter C. Clemens, Jr., "Shifts in Soviet Arms Control Posture," *Military Review* 51, no. 7 (July 1971): 28–36.

84. See Raymond L. Garthoff, *Détente and Confrontation* (Washington, DC: Brookings Institution, 1985), chaps. 13, 15, 16, 19; also see several essays in W. Raymond Duncan, ed., *Soviet Policy in the Third World* (New York: Pergamon, 1980), 295–311; and *The Soviet Union in the Third World, 1980–85: An Imperial Burden or Political Asset?* Report by the Congressional Research Service Committee on Foreign Affairs, U.S. House of Representatives (Washington, DC: U.S. Government Printing Office, 1985).

85. See *Soviet Military Power 1987* (Washington, DC: U.S. Department of Defense, 1987), 10, 146; and "The Soviet Economy under a New Leader," Report to the Subcommittee on Economic Resources, Competitiveness, and Security Economics of the Joint Economic Committee by the Central Intelligence Agency and the Defense Intelligence Agency, March 19, 1986, in *Allocation of Resources in the Soviet Union and China—1985*, pt. 11, March 19, 1986 (Washington, DC: U.S. Government Printing Office, 1986), 64–66.

86. Richard F. Kaufman, "Causes of the Slowdown in Soviet Defense," *Soviet Economy*, no. 1 (January-March 1985): 9–31, with comments by John Steinbruner and David Holloway, pp. 32–41. Not by accident the next article is "The Slowdown in Soviet Industry, 1976–1982" by Gertrude E. Schroeder, ibid., pp. 42–74.

87. The U.S. Defense Intelligence Agency saw evidence of an upturn in Soviet weapons procurement beginning in 1983, but the Central Intelligence Agency qualified its appraisal in January 1985 hearings. See *Allocation of Resources in the Soviet Union and China—1984*, pt. 10, Hearings before the Subcommittee on International Trade, Finance, and Security Economics of the Joint Economic Committee (Washington, DC: U.S. Government Printing Office, 1985), 56, 135.

88. Measured in 1982 prices, total defense spending for the period 1966–84 increased on average almost 3 percent annually—somewhat less rapidly than the series in 1970 prices. See "The Soviet Economy under a New Leader," p. 37.

89. See summary data in Christopher Davis, "Military and Civilian Economic Activities of the Soviet Armed Forces, 1975–85" (Birmingham: Centre for Russian and East European Studies, University of Birmingham, November 1986), 22, 33.

90. Ibid., pp. 28–29, 48; also see Kaufman, "Cause of the Slowdown."

91. *Soviet Military Power: An Assessment of the Threat, 1988* (Washington, DC: U.S. Government Printing Office, 1988), 32–40. The Department of Defense estimated (p. 149) that U.S. technology was superior to Soviet in fifteen deployed military systems, such as SLBMs; equal in ten, such as cruise missiles, an area where trends favored the United States; and behind in six, such as SAMs. In at least four of the alleged six areas of Soviet leadership (for example, antisatellite weapons) many outside experts regarded the Soviet weapons as comparatively primitive.

92. Statement by Robert Gates, deputy director for Intelligence, Central Intelligence Agency, in *Allocation of Resources in the Soviet Union and China—1984*, p. 54. For an argument that the CIA has tended to underestimate the Soviet arms buildup, see Steven Rosefielde, *False Science*, 2d ed. (New Brunswick, NJ: Transaction Books, 1987).

93. For the context of Marshal Nikolai Ogarkov's dismissal as chief of the General

Staff, see William Odom, "Soviet Force Posture," *Problems of Communism* 34, no. 4 (July–August 1985): 1–14 at 8–9.

94. See *Soviet Military Power 1987*, p. 120; P. Hanson, "New Light on Soviet Industrial Espionage," *Radio Liberty Research Bulletin*, RL 36/86, January 20, 1986; and other sources, many of them in French, cited in Davis, *Military and Civilian Economic Activities*, p. 52.

95. See for example, Mark G. Field, "Soviet Urban Health Services: Some Problems and Their Sources," in Henry W. Morton and Robert C. Stuart, eds., *The Contemporary Soviet City* (Armonk, NY: M. E. Sharpe, 1984), 129–55 at 151. "Poverty is a reality, our national tragedy," reported *Komsomolskaia Pravda*, while Soviet officials acknowledged that at least one-fifth of the population enjoyed less than "minimal material security," See Esther B. Fein in *The New York Times*, January 29, 1989, pp. 1, 9.

96. Bruce Parrot, "The Politics of Soviet Defense Spending," Meeting report, (Washington, DC: Kennan Institute for Advanced Russian Studies, October 23, 1985).

97. For an appraisal of Polish-Soviet relations since 1920, see Wojciech Jaruzelski, "K novym gorizontam," *Kommunist* (Moscow), no. 11 (July 1987): 59–73.

98. Parrot, "Politics of Soviet Defense Spending."

99. Christopher Davis, "Economic and Political Aspects of the Military-Industrial Complex in the USSR," in Hans-Hermann Homann, Alec Nove, and Heinrich Vogel, eds., *Economics and Politics in USSR* (Boulder, CO: Westview, 1986), 92–123 at 93, 99.

100. Many Soviet statements spoke of this conflict in increasingly antagonistic terms after the mid-1970s. See Walter C. Clemens, Jr., *The U.S.S.R. and Global Interdependence: Alternative Futures* (Washington, DC: American Enterprise Institute, 1978), 48–49.

101. Although this was the dominant line during most of the 1970s, there were also Soviet Party and government leaders who seemed to worry about excessive dependence on outside connections and who favored autarky. See ibid., pp. 15–39.

102. See Trotsky Archive, Houghton Library, Harvard University, T-688, T-689.

103. Clemens, "Soviet Disarmament Proposals and the Cadre-Territorial Army."

104. Vojtech Mastny, "The Cassandra in the Foreign Commissariat: Maxim Litvinov and the Cold War," *Foreign Affairs* 54 (1975–76): 366–76.

105. Bloomfield et al., *Khrushchev*, esp. pp. 73–74.

106. See Harry Gelman, *The Brezhnev Politburo and the Decline of Détente* (Ithaca, NY: Cornell University Press, 1984), pp. 79–80.

107. Ibid., p. 83.

108. Shevchenko, *Breaking with Moscow*, p. 178.

109. Henry Kissinger, *The White House Years* (Boston: Little, Brown, 1979), p. 1213.

110. Statement by President's Science Advisory Committee regarding detection of underground nuclear tests, January 5, 1959, in *Documents on Disarmament*, II, 1335–36; also *Hearings before the Joint Committee on Atomic Energy, Congress of the United States, on Developments in Technical Capabilities for Detecting and Identifying Nuclear Weapons Tests* (Washington, DC: U.S. Government Printing Office, 1963), esp. 18–19. One analyst concluded that Soviet leaders had cause to infer that the reversal of U.S. policy was not because a test ban was "unenforceable but that the United States in the interest of its security should resume tests." Bernhard G. Bechhoefer, *Postwar Negotiations for Arms Control* (Washington, DC: Brookings Institution, 1961), 510–11.

111. Dr. Edward Teller played a key role in the conception of the 1983 "Star Wars" initiative as he did in 1959 and at many other decisive moments in the history of U.S. weapons development. According to the former director of weapons research at the Lawrence Livermore National Laboratory, former President Reagan and other high officials had been receiving "overly optimistic, technically incorrect" information concerning the development of a nuclear-powered X-ray laser. Robert D. Woodruff, who until 1985 was associate director for nuclear weapons at Livermore, stated that "for us to be potentially basing national policy on the speculations of Dr. Wood, advanced through Dr. Teller, is totally inappropriate." See *Science News* 132, no. 18 (October 31, 1987): 276.

112. *Khrushchev Remembers*, II: 68–71.

113. Andrei D. Sakharov, *Peace, Coexistence and Intellectual Freedom* (New York:

W. W. Norton, 1968). Sakharov's views on Afghanistan may have precipitated his exile to Gorky. See Julia Wishnevsky, "Afghanistan and Soviet Dissidents," in Vojtech Mastny, ed., *Soviet/East European Survey, 1983–1984: Selected Research and Analysis from Radio Free Europe/Radio Liberty* (Durham, NC: Duke University Press, 1985), 152–55 at 153.

114. Address at the Kennan Institute for Advanced Russian Studies, Washington, DC, May 15, 1985.

115. Author's interviews with U.S. scientists involved in the nuclear winter studies. For a statement by the U.S. Department of Defense on the potential effects of nuclear war on the climate, see *Survival* 27, no. 3 (May/June 1985): 130–34.

116. On Gorbachev's use of arms control issues to gain support for *perestroika*, see Alan B. Sherr, *The Other Side of Arms Control: Soviet Objectives in the Gorbachev Era* (Boston: Unwin Hyman, 1988), 65–71.

4
Arms Control Imperatives in the Global Arena

The global arena—sometimes in tandem, sometimes at odds with the Soviet domestic context—has also generated both incentives and restraints for the Kremlin's interests in arms control and other accommodations with the West. These will be discussed in ascending order of importance.

Friends, Allies, and Comrades

The United States has sometimes been charged with formulating its arms policies first and consulting its allies second. What of Russia? The Soviet regime has had to consider the arms control preferences of a bewildering array of potential partners: anti-Communist, Communist, and nonaligned. Although Moscow has preferred not to offend its friends, allies, and comrades, it has done so whenever this was necessary for Soviet security objectives. The Kremlin has often subordinated the sentiments of Communists and Third World backers to Soviet interests of striking a deal with the West. Power has counted far more than ideology.

No Soviet government ever paid the deference on arms control issues that St. Petersburg did to France in 1899. Even then the tsar seemed to listen more to his own war minister than to the viewpoints of a cordial ally.[1]

Soviet Russia's first collaborators and clients were non-Communist

Germany, Turkey, and China. From the early 1920s until the mid-1930s the Kremlin permitted Germany to conduct clandestine military activities on Soviet territory, thus evading some arms restrictions of the Versailles Treaty. In the early 1920s Moscow aligned with Ankara to support Turkey's right to govern the Straits and to keep foreign warships from the Black Sea. Reluctantly the Soviet Delegation signed the 1923 Lausanne Straits Convention, but the Kremlin did not ratify it.[2]

Soviet leaders spoke of the world proletariat as their own true ally. Moscow did what it could to promote a direct or indirect advance of the Communist cause. Thus Litvinov's disarmament campaigns at the League of Nations helped to "demonstrate" that disarmament was impossible until the overthrow of capitalism. But the Comintern became much more the servant of Soviet Realpolitik than a tool of class struggle.

Joining the League in 1934, the Soviet Union argued that "peace is indivisible" (a stronger formulation than Gorbachev's "mutual security"). The USSR took the lead in attempting to help Abyssinia and Republican Spain against fascism. The Soviet Union took no part in the Munich betrayal of Czechoslovakia in 1938. (Moscow's mutual defense pact with Czechoslovakia was contingent upon French support of Prague.[3]) With China, however, the Kremlin played one of its double games: Soviet diplomats encouraged China to resist Japan, keeping alive the prospect of USSR entry into the war, even though the Kremlin endeavored to avoid hostilities with Tokyo.[4]

Having decided in 1939 to collaborate with Nazi Germany, Stalin became a dependable supplier to Hitler's war machine. The Kremlin's pacts with the Baltic countries, however, served only as legal pretexts for their 1940 incorporation as Soviet republics.

Caught by Hitler's surprise attack in 1941, Stalin switched and became a reasonably faithful ally to Britain and the United States for most of the war. His subsequent policies in Eastern Europe, however, violated wartime agreements as they were understood in the West. Rapid buildup of East Germany's Volkspolizei (People's Police) violated East-West pledges to keep Germany disarmed.[5]

The Kremlin may have been willing to sell out its East German puppet for a broad security understanding in eastern Central Europe, but the West never probed these offers in depth. Responding to growing Western military strength—the formation of NATO, West German rearmament, tactical nuclear weapons—Soviet diplomats from 1952 through the mid-1950s asserted that Moscow would agree to a Germany unified on the basis of free elections, provided that it joined no alliance and remained disarmed. Soviet and Polish proposals from 1956 to 1958 for nuclear-free zones and reduction of foreign troops in Central Europe, had they been accepted, could also have undermined Communist rule in the region.[6]

Far more than any other Soviet ally, Mao Zedong sought to influence Moscow's policies on arms and arms control. Mao wanted Soviet support for China's advanced military technology programs and opposed Soviet attempts to conclude arms controls with the West. After the USSR successfully tested the world's first ICBM and space satellite in 1957, Mao urged Khrushchev to press his bargaining advantages forcefully against the West and to support Chinese efforts to take Quemoi and Matsu.

In 1956 the Kremlin refused to provide advanced military technology to China, but after the Hungarian and Polish events that year the Kremlin was more responsive to Chinese aid requests. According to Chinese sources, the USSR entered an agreement on October 15, 1957, to supply China with advanced military technology for missiles and nuclear weapons. The man who negotiated this agreement and supervised its implementation reported that Soviet aid proceeded smoothly for more than half a year: "Although the Soviet Union provided us only with a few outdated missiles, airplanes, and prototypes of other military equipment, and with relevant technical data, technicians, and experts, these things helped us to improve our research. Thus, we saved some time and narrowed the gap between our weapons technology and that of advanced countries." Relations between Moscow and Beijing deteriorated in 1958, however, due in part to repeated Soviet proposals for a joint fleet and long-wave radio communications center on China's coast, which the Chinese interpreted as the scheme to dominate China.[7]

The Soviets, for their part, were increasingly upset by Chinese words and deeds. Mao and Stalin, even when they signed an alliance in 1950, were cool to each other. In Gromyko's account—called sheer fiction by Beijing in 1988—when Khrushchev sat with Mao as his dinner guest in 1958, the Chinese leader said only a few protocol words. When Foreign Minister Gromyko visited Mao in August 1958, the Chinese leader laid out a scenario alarming even to Soviets accustomed to hearing that America is a "paper tiger." Mao proposed that the USSR stand by while the United States hit China with nuclear weapons. Chinese forces would then withdraw to the interior, sucking the Americans into a vice, whereupon the USSR could unleash its full force upon them. Instead of the diplomatic "maybe," even Gromyko said *"nyet."*[8]

Chinese officials provide details not mentioned in Soviet accounts. On June 20, 1959, according to Marshal Nie Rongzhen, the CPSU Central Committee wrote the Chinese Central Committee

[103]

with the pretext that the Soviet Union, the United States and other Western countries were holding talks in Geneva on the prohibition of nuclear tests, and feared that if the Western countries knew the Soviet Union was providing China with aid in the area of new technology, "the socialist countries' efforts for world peace and the relaxation of international tensions would probably be seriously damaged." So the letter requested a halt to certain important aid projects and a wait to see how the situation developed within the next two years. Thus, the Soviet regime led by Khrushchev unilaterally abrogated the October 15 [1957] agreement.[9]

This Chinese account, published in 1984, confirms the general picture that emerged from the Sino-Soviet polemics in the early 1960s. It appears that Khrushchev attempted to play a double game: he promised China advanced military technology to secure Beijing's backing for Soviet domination of Eastern Europe and the international Communist movement at the November 1957 Moscow meeting of Communist Parties. At the same time, he intensified arms negotiations with the West hoping to conclude a nuclear test ban that could serve as a pretext for breaking off aid to Beijing before China acquired a nuclear bomb. Although all Soviet aid technicians were withdrawn in 1959–60, China proudly "walked on its own feet" to continue its own nuclear and missile research. Fearing external pressures to halt China's nuclear development, in September and October 1962 and again in June 1963 Beijing gave Moscow "earnest counsel" not to sign a nuclear test ban. Khrushchev ignored Beijing's warnings and went on to sign the 1963 limited test ban and other accords that the Chinese saw as Soviet collusion with capitalism. Khrushchev's double game failed resoundingly in mid-October 1964: he was deposed and China tested its first nuclear bomb—five years after Moscow (in Beijing's phrasing) "refused to provide China with a sample of an atomic bomb and technical data concerning its manufacture."[10]

Many factors contributed to the break between Moscow and Beijing, but arms issues provided the last straw. The intra-Communist feud paralleled that between Washington and Paris, but France remained within NATO even after withdrawing from its military organization in 1966.[11]

Moscow's Cuban ally also had cause to complain when, without Havana's approval, Khrushchev capitulated to Washington and withdrew Soviet nuclear delivery systems from Cuba. Indeed, according to Sergei Khrushchev addressing a Moscow conference in January 1989, in October 1962 Fidel Castro wanted Russia to launch its missiles against the United States. Whether or not there is truth in this report, it is clear that Castro refused to permit international inspectors to observe the withdrawal, even though Moscow had extracted a U.S. pledge not to invade Cuba as part of the deal. For a time Castro tilted toward Beijing. Profoundly dependent upon Soviet assistance, however, he later returned to Moscow's fold.

Burned once in China, the Kremlin opposed any programs that might promote the spread of nuclear weaponry to other countries. Unlike the United States, the USSR has refused to share its nuclear arms with its European allies in any form. For many years the Soviet Union was reluctant even to station its own nuclear warheads in Eastern Europe, though Soviet launchers were available there. With the demise of the multilateral force (MLF) proposal within NATO in 1966, Moscow felt the conditions were ripe for a treaty to halt nuclear proliferation, which was concluded in 1968. Romania, like India, sniped at the treaty's discriminatory features protecting nuclear haves and restraining have-nots.[12] But all Warsaw Pact members eventually signed the treaty, though Albania (withdrawn from the pact in 1961), China, France, and India were among the countries that refused. Although Moscow has long courted New Delhi, the USSR has cooperated with the United States to curtail nuclear proliferation on the subcontinent and elsewhere.

In the 1960s and early 1970s the Kremlin often hinted it would welcome U.S. collaboration in curbing or even removing China's capacity for nuclear war.[13] As Washington and Beijing grew closer, the Kremlin railed against transfers of advanced technology to China. The USSR often extended an olive branch to Beijing in the late 1970s and early 1980s, but Moscow refused until after 1985 to address Beijing's three conditions for improved relations: Soviet military activities in Afghanistan, Indochina, and along the Sino-Soviet border.[14]

There is little evidence that Eastern European views have shaped Soviet decisions on theater weapons or other arms issues affecting other Warsaw Pact countries. If other pact members had reservations about the wide-scale deployment of SS-20s or the Kremlin's subsequent walkout from arms negotiations, these views were ignored. To be sure, some Warsaw Pact communiqués lacked the threatening language often found in Soviet statements about U.S. Euromissiles. And some Soviet carrots— for example, offers to curtail SS-20 deployment—were probably aimed at Eastern as well as Western European audiences. But the naked fact of a significant SS-20 deployment remained, one likely to trigger counter-measures. When they came, Moscow then deployed new short-range missiles in some Eastern European countries even though their govern-ments showed some reluctance to accept or pay for them.[15]

The United States has usually consulted its allies more than has Moscow and taken account of the often diverse views within NATO. The difference between the two alliances is seen in the fact that parliamentary approval was needed for U.S. Euromissiles to be stationed in any NATO country—a situation completely absent in Warsaw Pact affairs. On the other hand, the Reagan administration embarked on two radical changes of policy—SDI and support for nuclear disarmament—with little consultation at home or abroad.

For the 1980s the USSR remained the hegemon able to make decisions on arms and arms control without consulting its allies. But imperial will seemed to be flagging. The Kremlin took longer and used less decisive means to put down each challenge to Soviet dominion: in 1953 instant use of tanks against East Germans; in 1956 military force in Hungary only after negotiations and other stratagems failed; in Czechoslovakia 1968 a nearly bloodless occupation after eight months of delay; in the early 1980s sixteen months of Solidarity unrest until a local leader imposed martial law.

Centralized decision making within an alliance, as at home, generates both advantages and liabilities for arms control. If the Kremlin wants an accord, it will not be restrained by Communists elsewhere who warn against supping with the devil. But neither will Soviet military buildups or intransigence in arms talks be curtailed to please moderates in the socialist camp.

Adversary Relations: The Global Thermostat

Calculations about the viewpoints of comrades, allies, and Third World clients have influenced Soviet propaganda on arms and arms control, but they have shaped only marginally the substance of Kremlin policies. Soviet perceptions of adversaries, on the other hand, have exerted a decisive weight on Soviet decision making. Politburo leaders have asked: Are our adversaries united among themselves and internally? What are their strengths, their weaknesses? What factions favor accommodation with the USSR? Which are unshakably hostile? Answers to these questions helped to determine whether Soviet diplomacy sought to expose capitalist aggressiveness or strike a deal with the other side.

Projecting Moscow's own "kto kovo?" outlook onto the West, Soviet disarmament policy in the 1920s became the pursuit of revolution by other means—another tool for indirect advance. Paradoxically, Litvinov's assaults on Anglo-French "hypocrisy" at the League of Nations helped to legitimate Berlin's argument that if Paris and London did not disarm, Germany should rearm.[16] Stalin initially perceived Hitler as a welcome

[106]

prelude to a leftist revolution, a misperception with heavy consequences. The net result of Soviet policies toward Germany throughout the 1920s and 1930s was to promote German militarism.

Exposure tactics receded after Stalin's death. The Kremlin seemed to perceive openings for deals with Western moderates such as Eisenhower, provided the influence of John Foster Dulles and other hard-liners could be countered. Moscow often saw and acted upon differences between France and other NATO allies and welcomed any show of Gaullist independence from Anglo-U.S. domination.[17] If an opportunity for a Soviet-U.S. deal came along, however, the Kremlin sometimes rubbed the image of superpower condominium in the faces of America's NATO partners.[18]

In the late 1960s Soviet campaigns for an all-European security conference sought to split Europe and the United States. When Western Europeans balked at losing their major ally, Moscow reluctantly invited the United States to such gatherings. Washington, though skeptical, joined to placate its détente-minded allies.[19]

To the extent that Moscow has sought to promote revolution or disunity in the West or Japan, the results have been minimal—sometimes even counterproductive. Even France, beneficiary of an imputed special relationship with Russia, has built and expanded a powerful *force de frappe*.

Aware that a heavy-handed approach can stimulate Western solidarity, the Kremlin has sometimes combined a soft touch with intermittent displays of power to shape Western attitudes toward the USSR. An apparent willingness to negotiate seriously has become a major instrument of this approach. It helped to bring Eisenhower to the Geneva Summit in 1955; it became the main ingredient in shaping the brief détentes of the 1960s and 1970s; it helped to set the stage for Reagan-Gorbachev summitry in the 1980s.[20]

Apart from specific accords, Soviet diplomacy has used the arms control process to regulate the international climate, usually pushing toward détente and liberalization of East-West trade. The imperatives of modernization and some domestic political considerations have contributed to this orientation. Ideology and propaganda have then attributed each success as a victory for farsighted Leninism and each setback to malevolent capitalists.

The Kremlin has often labored to create a political climate that shrinks the prospects of a major war and emasculates hard-liners in the West pressing for militancy toward the USSR. Even if no arms accords are reached or implemented, the appearance of a "sincere" negotiating posture can shape East-West relations. A mood change can lead the West to slacken its military preparations, thus permitting the Kremlin to do the same or, if it wishes to alter the balance of power, intensify its buildup while the West stands still. Indeed, détente without arms accords might foster Soviet goals better than would actual agreements because the Pentagon often secures more funding as the price for its blessing of arms treaties.

Building upon Lenin's 1922 advice, Soviet diplomacy since the mid-1950s has sought to cultivate "sober realists" in the West and to isolate "mad" supporters of confrontation and aggression. Soviet specialists in *amerikanistika* have read the tea leaves and *U.S. News & World Report* to determine which party and which candidates in U.S. elections are most likely to take a moderate approach to the USSR.[21] When an East-West accord appears on the horizon, as in the early 1960s and early 1970s, the Soviet media remind Communists that Lenin too urged a differentiated approach to the class enemy.[22] Diplomatic campaigns are then reinforced by red carpets rolled out for the farsighted representatives of Chase Manhattan, Pepsi Cola, Control Data Corporation, and other firms whose leaders not by accident lobby energetically to reduce barriers to Soviet-American commerce.

In the early 1980s, however, the Kremlin seemed nearly to give up hope that it could strike an accord to mutual advantage with the Reagan White House. In January 1984 Foreign Minister Gromyko told an international meeting in Stockholm that the Reagan administration was planning a new war and exporting "militarism, enmity and war hysteria" to Europe.

Party leader Chernenko declared on September 27, 1984, that "the capitalist countries should know that provided there is reciprocity, they will always have in the Soviet Union an honest and well-wishing partner ready to promote cooperation on the basis of equality and mutual benefit." He called on Soviet citizens to be vigilant and work to lessen the war threat and to safeguard peace.[23]

On the same day, however, Gromyko told the United Nations that Washington had "spared no effort to wreck all the gains" the USSR and United States had achieved in the past. "What is more," he said, the U.S. side "virtually flaunts" its indifference to its reputation as a partner in international relations. Gromyko criticized the United States for basing its policies on the slogan "Peace through strength." What this means, he said, is "weapons, weapons, weapons." He called for deeds—not words—from Washington. Gromyko noted that the USSR had cultivated positive relations with the countries of Western Europe, but he condemned those that had permitted deployment of U.S. "first-strike weapons" on their territories. He warned also that "revanchism" had arisen in some quarters "fueled by statements which seek to question commitments assumed by members of the anti-Hitlerite coalition." He cautioned against "yielding to this dangerous psychosis" and appealed instead for "sobermindedness."

Still, in meetings with Secretary of State Shultz and Democratic presidential candidate Walter Mondale at the same time as his UN speech, Gromyko kept open the possibility of improved Soviet-U.S. relations. A State Department official noted that statesmen often speak in one voice publicly and in another privately.[24]

Do periodic Soviet assertions that the West is dominated by hotheads and warmongers represent the Kremlin's real assessments? Or are such statements nothing but signs that the USSR is not currently prepared to bargain? We cannot read the minds of the Politburo, but we can take Soviet statements about the propensities of Western elites as good indicators of what negotiation strategies the Kremlin considers feasible and useful. Thus if Moscow says there are "sober forces" as well as "madmen" in Washington, as it did in 1963 and in 1972, this means the Kremlin thinks it may be possible and desirable to strike a deal with the West. The pessimistic tone in most Soviet appraisals of the Reagan White House in the early 1980s pointed in the opposite direction.

Moscow's readiness to shift from inversion toward a serious attempt at limited collaboration with the adversary was signaled, for example, when in 1987 *Kommunist* again recalled the lessons of Genoa, 1922.[25] Gorbachev put the case even more forcefully in his February 18, 1988 speech to the CPSU Central Committee. Changes in the international situation, he said, are favoring the "party of peace" over the "party of war" in the West, "between, in Lenin's words, the 'crude-bourgeois, the aggressive bourgeois, the reactionary bourgeois' and the 'pacifist camp' in the West's ruling class."[26]

As in domestic affairs, so in the global arena: perceived conditions may open or close the door to serious attempts at arms control. If the door appears to be shut, Soviet diplomacy may pursue other approaches, or it may try to pry open the door and see what opportunities lie beyond.

The Balance of Power: Strategic-Military Determinism?

Many factors have shaped Soviet policies on arms and arms control, but the zigs and zags in Kremlin words and deeds are most consistently explained as a response to strategic-military factors: perceived threats to Soviet interests, Soviet capacity to threaten others, and the evolving balance of power as seen in the West and in Moscow.

Soviet negotiators have often bargained so as to give the USSR time to match or overtake its rivals. And when the USSR achieved parity or superiority in some respects, Soviet diplomats labored to protect these advantages. From 1922 through the 1980s, however, the USSR has cut its forces unilaterally when they were deemed redundant (as summarized in Table 3.1). But the asymmetrical obligations accepted by Moscow in the 1987 INF Treaty broke precedent in many ways, as will be discussed in chapters 8 and 9.

A model for keying disarmament diplomacy to military plans was established at the 1922 Moscow Conference for the Limitation of Armaments. Litvinov proposed to Russia's neighbors force reductions of 75 percent, whereupon Poland and the Baltic states balked, saying—much like NATO later on—that smaller states cannot afford to match larger ones in percentage cuts. Moscow then urged 25 percent reductions, but its neighbors still refused, stressing the need for nonaggression and arbitration agreements before "material" disarmament could be considered.[27] After the conference ended amid mutual recriminations, the Kremlin announced a 25 percent cut in the Red Army. If Litvinov could not persuade Russia's neighbors to match a move already planned in Moscow for its own reasons, the Kremlin could still make propaganda hay. Had the other conferees agreed to a 75 percent cut, Moscow might have been caught bluffing. Could Russia reduce its forces so drastically while those of major rivals were unrestricted?

In fact Moscow objected to any proposals that permitted the Eagle to keep its talons or the Lion its claws. Soviet commentators complained that the 1922 Washington Naval Treaty placed no constraints on submarines or other arms likely to be significant in future wars.[28] Later in 1922–23, given that the Red Navy was extremely weak, Soviet diplomats proved to be more Turkish than the Turks in seeking to close the Dardanelles to military ship traffic.

From the 1920s through the 1960s Soviet spokesmen scorned Western proposals that would limit but not end the arms race.[29] Soviet diplomats denounced Western calls for "inspection first, arms control second" as an espionage trick. In 1959–62 Khrushchev championed general disarmament that would leave only the Bear's universal embrace. When China became more menacing, however, Moscow altered its disarmament plan so the superpowers could retain a "nuclear umbrella" until the end of staged reductions.[30]

[110]

Senior civilian as well as military leaders conveyed to a senior Soviet diplomat in the early 1970s that they would oppose radical measures of nuclear disarmament, for the USSR would then cease to be a superpower and would lose its capacity to exert influence on world affairs. Defense Minister Andrei Grechko objected even to a procedural move to invite all five nuclear powers to a conference, arguing that the only real guarantee of peace was Soviet nuclear and strategic power.[31]

Moscow has usually rejected Western efforts to set the condition of arms limitation on security assurances.[32] In the 1920s Soviet diplomats scoffed at French and Polish demands for "security first" before "material disarmament." In the 1970s Moscow protested U.S. "linkage" between arms control and Soviet behavior in the Third World.

Stalin would not accept the 1946 Baruch Plan to eliminate nuclear arms because it allowed the United States to retain an atomic weapon monopoly until Washington decided that an adequate control system was in place. Therefore he countered with "ban the bomb" propaganda and an urgent program to develop a Soviet nuclear and H-bomb arsenal. He also deprecated the utility of the atomic bomb, just as he earlier did the German Blitzkrieg and as Beijing later ridiculed Khrushchev's "nuclear fetishism."[33]

When only the USSR possessed large ground forces and America monopolized atomic weapons, disparities in the needs and assets made it hard to find common ground for arms limitation. As Western conventional strength grew and as the USSR acquired a nuclear deterrent, mutual interests were easier to identify.

The conditions for achieving arms agreements are examined more closely in chapter 9, but the Soviet-U.S. record shows that there need not be precise parity to reach an accord because trade-offs can sometimes be created from asymmetrical assets. If forces are constrained or eliminated, however, each party must feel it has "sufficiency" with those that remain. There is little chance of banning an emerging weapons technology unless it is seen as redundant, not cost-effective or suicidal. If Moscow or Washington sees a potential accord as stacked to favor the other side, neither will accept it.

Not until the Kremlin possessed a minimum deterrent and the beginnings of strategic parity with the United States was there serious movement toward arms control. This happened in the mid- and late-1950s as the USSR acquired aircraft and missiles that might deliver nuclear warheads to U.S. targets. For the first time in history Russia had the means to deter any rational aggressor.

Conditions emerged in which Soviet leaders could act upon Lenin's

[111]

vision that weaponry would make war too dangerous to serve as an instrument of policy. Malenkov warned as early as 1954 that nuclear war could mark the end of all civilization. He lost in the immediate power struggle, but his view resurfaced as Khrushchev defended his arms control policies against Chinese criticism. In 1963 the CPSU Central Committee declared the brutal reality: "The atomic bomb does not respect the class principle—it destroys everyone with the range of its devastating force." A few Soviet commentators have continued to find relevance in the writings of Karl Von Clausewitz, but top Party organs have often downgraded the value of war—any war—as an "extension of policy" in the nuclear age. They did this more than a generation before Gorbachev's "new thinking."[34]

Once both sides had a relatively persuasive deterrent, Moscow and Washington had reason to avoid inadvertent war and to limit dangerous or costly aspects of their competition. With deterrence assured, other motives could come into play: economic, domestic political, even ideological. Soviet policy was virtually transformed in spring and summer 1955, leading a hesitant Washington in September to place a "reservation" on its earlier disarmament positions.

Having taken another look, the United States joined the USSR in 1958 to explore ways to prevent surprise attack and to halt nuclear testing. Khrushchev even agreed to accept limited inspection systems on Soviet territory. The Kremlin and White House observed a nuclear test moratorium (off and on again) in 1958–61, signed a multilateral treaty to demilitarize Antarctica in 1959; accepted the 1962 Cuban missile understanding and set up a "hot line," concluded the 1963 tripartite nuclear test ban and opened it to others, recorded a 1963 "gentleman's agreement" and a 1967 treaty on outer space weapons, and pledged restraint (in military spending, 1963, and in production rates of fissionable materials, 1964). With cause Khrushchev spoke of momentum through "disarmament by mutual example"; some Western social scientists saw it as "graduated and reciprocal initiatives in tension-reduction."[35]

But Moscow showed less interest than the West in exploring ways to prevent a small-scale nuclear exchange from escalating into an all-out conflagration. When NATO began to deploy tactical nuclear weapons in the 1950s, Soviet spokesmen derided the idea of a "limited" nuclear war. Even after the USSR acquired its own "battlefield" nuclear weapons, Moscow's representatives tended to argue that any form of "controlled" nuclear war was impossible.[36] Perhaps this attitude is realistic, but Moscow's position also meant to underscore Soviet conventional prowess and to discourage any Western resort to tactical nuclear arms, "clean" (neutron) bombs, or limited counterforce attacks. The position also reflected relative Soviet weaknesses in smaller, more accurate nuclear weapons and in command-control-communications systems.

Still far behind the U.S. nuclear arsenal in 1964, Moscow then spurned Lyndon Johnson's January call for exploration of "a verified freeze on the number and characteristics of strategic nuclear offensive and defensive vehicles." As the USSR approached parity, the Kremlin agreed in 1968 to negotiate limits on strategic missiles. After Congress provided funds for an ABM deployment, in 1971 Moscow agreed to negotiate limits on defensive and offensive weapons concurrently. In 1972 SALT I put ceilings on strategic missile forces and severely limited ABM capacity for each side. The mutual hostage relationship (mutual vulnerability) became official.[37]

Both sides welcomed accords to reduce the dangers of incidents at sea involving Soviet and U.S. warships.[38] But Moscow showed more enthusiasm than Washington for declarations outlawing aggression or first use of nuclear arms.[39]

Asymmetries and tunnel vision thwarted any accords in 1972 on multiple warheads, cruise missiles, or even intercontinental and forward-based bombers. But Soviet and U.S. leaders wanted to enlarge the scope of strategic arms control and finally signed a more comprehensive SALT II in 1979, which Washington never ratified because of alleged imbalances and Soviet aggression in Afghanistan.[40]

Brezhnev and his entourage claimed to want "military détente" as well as political. The 1971 CPSU Peace Program anticipated a long-term collaboration between the CPSU and the capitalist world. Authoritative statements acknowledged "global problems so complex that no one nation can solve them alone, no matter how powerful it may be." The first of these global problems was said to be preventing nuclear war and capping the arms race.[41] In 1977—a high point in the USSR's overall military buildup—Brezhnev and other Soviet spokesmen declared that the USSR did not seek military superiority but wanted only to ensure that parity existed with the United States. Well before Gorbachev, Brezhnev asserted at Tula (*Pravda*, January 19, 1977) that Soviet defense policy was doing only what was "sufficient for defense"; he denied that the USSR was developing forces for a first strike. On November 7 he denied that Moscow sought superiority for any purpose. Soviet civilian and military commentators echoed the view that arms control could buttress parity. In June 1982 Brezhnev pledged that the USSR would never be the first country to use nuclear arms. Well before Gorbachev, booklets issued by the Ministry of Defense stressed the "defensive" character of Soviet military doctrine.[42]

The Bear proved menacing as well as conciliatory in the decade before

[113]

1985. Echoes of the 1972–74 détente continued, but East-West relations were strained not only by Soviet, Vietnamese, and Cuban expansion in the Third World but by the buildup of Soviet power. The Brezhnev regime, like Khrushchev's, seemed to think it could expand in the Third World while the West sat mesmerized by détente or intimidated by Soviet power. To be sure, their line made clear Moscow's determination to assist "national liberation" struggles, and their analysts noted that détente did not stop U.S. military activities in the Middle East and elsewhere.

The Kremlin used arms and arms control to stake its claim to "co-equal security" with the other superpower. When Soviet power seemed not only equal but superior, the USSR often used this edge to intimidate, exploiting a leverage multiplied by inflated Western appraisals of Soviet power.[43]

Even as Brezhnev spoke, however, Warsaw Pact forces continued to practice maneuvers that looked like rehearsals for a quick march to the Atlantic. Furthermore, in the mid-1970s the USSR began replacing its older missiles targeted on Europe with the SS-20. For decades the Kremlin had held Europe hostage with a combination of large conventional forces and nuclear arms. Sometimes Soviet diplomacy has tried to remove the sting from Moscow's threatening force posture; at other times it has reminded Westerners of Soviet power. When NATO threatened to respond to the SS-20s by deploying its own intermediate-range missiles, Moscow produced a kind of "protection racket diplomacy." Having created a vivid threat to its neighbors' security, the Kremlin offered to protect them from the threat if they made certain concessions. When the Western European countries took compensatory measures instead, Moscow evoked the specter of nuclear war.[44] The USSR may have seen the SS-20 only as a force "modernization," but Soviet analysts later conceded that Moscow had failed to consider how such modernization would look to Europe.

As Gorbachev's "new thinkers" later explained, the USSR aimed at overcoming military inferiority but overshot the mark. The Brezhnev regime then underestimated political opportunities for accommodation and depended excessively upon military power.[45]

What Factors Were Most Weighty in Soviet Arms Control Policy, 1917–85?

Contrary to Edward Gibbon, history is not simply the record of "man's inhumanity to man," people's crimes and follies. It is also a relatively open book from which individuals, governments, and peoples can learn how to enrich their lives alone and together. Learning, however, is ultimately done by individuals. Each Soviet leader has interpreted experience and present opportunities through different lenses. There is no "Bolshevik operational code" binding upon each generation since Lenin. Each of his successors has placed a personalized stamp on Soviet policies, including arms control. Indeed, the style and content of Soviet policy under Stalin, Khrushchev, and Brezhnev may well have been more diverse than those of U.S. presidents over the same generations even though the Americans did not come from a single, monolithic party.

The Kremlin, no less than the White House, has faced competing considerations in formulating arms and arms control policies. But the learning of successive Soviet leaders has moved them toward acceptance of arms control as a way to prevent war and to promote other objectives. How have the various factors, pro and con, contributed to this movement?

Ideology has set limits on Soviet thinking and expectations, but it has also justified a wide range of foreign policy approaches, from forward strategy to limited collaboration with rivals. Propaganda considerations have pushed and pulled in different directions. But both ideology and propaganda have proved to be flexible instruments capable of rationalizing whatever course the Politburo prefers, from revolution to temporary accords with "sober forces" in the capitalist camp. Some Soviet leaders may have believed that in the long run, peace depends upon eliminating private property and class struggle. In practice, however, since the mid-1950s Soviet ideology and propaganda have upheld some form of peaceful coexistence with capitalism as both feasible and desirable.

Economic concerns have pressed both ideology and propaganda toward support for arms control. Lenin, Stalin, Khrushchev, and Brezhnev all recognized the importance of constraining military outlays and building up the USSR's industrial base. At times even Stalin and Khrushchev stinted on military investments in order to devote maximum resources to industry; at times they curtailed military manpower to aid the civilian economy.

Russian leaders since Peter have wanted to import technology and other goods from the West; Brezhnev went all out in 1971 to modernize the Soviet economy through East-West interconnectedness. Pressures to import grain have, at least since 1963, also added to the incentives to create a positive climate for trade.

The Communist party has generally had sufficient control over Soviet society to impose whatever belt-tightening it judges necessary. From this standpoint economic incentives could *reinforce* other motives for arms control but could never bring the USSR to its collective knees.

[115]

Despite technological backwardness, the USSR has usually been able to concentrate the necessary energies to produce world-class weapons. But even before Gorbachev thoughtful Soviets feared that Soviet ability to compete in a high-tech arms competition was quickly eroding. These anxieties added to Moscow's motives to halt U.S. development of SDI, antisatellite weapons, and other military systems difficult for the USSR to emulate.

Domestic political struggle has seldom imposed a serious drag on movement toward arms control. Most Soviet leaders since the mid-1950s have championed East-West accords. If criticized by hard-line skeptics, Khrushchev and Brezhnev could have replied that their negotiating positions (apart from an occasional bluff) would benefit Soviet security if accepted by the West.

Still, a lack of Politburo consensus or threat of a serious internal challenge may have closed the door to initiatives favored by top Kremlin leaders. Such problems probably contributed to the slow pace and few initiatives displayed by Soviet arms negotiators before 1985.

The making and implementation of Soviet arms control policies have been less affected than American by the conflicting interests and work habits of rival bureaucracies, political factions, and interest groups. There has also been less job turnover in Moscow than in Washington (except during the Stalin purges), resulting in an experienced if sluggish bureaucracy.

The Kremlin has been little constrained by allies, friends, or clients who object to negotiations with Western imperialists. The USSR has generally shaped its arms and arms control policies as it saw fit, even when this meant alienating China.

The USSR has aimed more at manipulating its foreign foes than at rallying its allies. Moscow has sought to "exploit contradictions" in the capitalist world—either to promote revolution or, more often, to cultivate conditions for limited collaboration in arms control and other matters.

From 1898 through the mid-1980s the most decisive influences shaping Russia's policies on arms control have been strategic-military. The last Romanov's advisers calculated that the continuation of Russia's policies abroad sooner or later would depend on war. Soviet leaders beginning with Lenin have shown an abiding respect for the political uses of military power, but they have tended to count more on history and a wide range of measures short of war to promote their foreign objectives.

Whether the broad correlation of forces seems to favor socialism, as Khrushchev thought in the 1950s, or seems to be tipping away from it, as many Soviet observers feared in the 1980s, the Soviet leadership has been inclined to use war only as a last resort and not as a major means for advancing the domain of socialism.[46] Moscow has sought to avoid Soviet participation in war even if it could serve as a midwife to "progress." It has been more willing to assist clients to fight, provided there was little risk of a major East-West confrontation.

Soviet policy has gradually departed from that of the Bear seeking to ban talons and claws while upgrading the universal embrace. To be sure, "value-claiming" has remained a major theme of both superpowers' policies. But in Moscow as well as Washington there has also been a trend away from zero-sum conceptions of security issues toward realization that unilateral advantages can be destabilizing.

Arms control experiences have been dialectical. Seeking arms controls that would nullify Western advantages and enhance Soviet strengths, with SALT I Moscow achieved a virtual freeze in U.S. levels of strategic nuclear submarines while permitting Soviet forces to climb to higher levels than those of the United States. Conversely, in the 1970s–1980s the USSR has agreed to arms control packages ignoring America's forward-based aircraft and the nuclear forces of other powers. Soviet as well as U.S. leaders have come to understand that balanced arms controls may depend upon permutations of asymmetries. Each side has redundant weapons, so trade-offs can be useful to each side. If arms controls can be fashioned that promote the narrow objectives of the Kremlin and Washington, the result can be value-creating for both sides.

That Soviet arms control policies have been heavily driven by material reality is no trivial conclusion. It implies that there can be a rational basis rooted in self-interest on which Moscow and its adversaries can reach accords to mutual advantage. This would not be the case if the USSR (or its rivals) were driven inexorably by ideological or propaganda imperatives hostile to negotiated arms controls, if the warrior class or military-industrial complex threatened to overthrow any leader favoring a deal with the enemy, if the regime were paralyzed by its allies' objections to arms accords, or if the regime were blind to divisions in the other camp that could make arms control both useful and feasible as an instrument of policy.

The zigs and zags of high politics, as will be seen in the next chapters, were often followed—occasionally preceded—by changes in Soviet approaches to the domains of low politics.

Notes

1. In addition to the *Krasnyi arkhiv* documentation cited in the preceding chapter, see F. A. Rotshtein, *Mezhdunarodnye otnosheniia v kontse XIX veka* (Moscow-Leningrad: Izdatel'stvo Akademii Nauk SSR, 1960), chaps. 16 and 17.

2. A. Ia. Vyshinskii, ed., *Diplomaticheskii slovar'*, 2 vols. (Moscow: Gospolizdat, 1950), II: col. 954. The Soviet commissariat for foreign affairs, however, supplied information on Soviet naval strength in the Black Sea to the International Straits Commission.

3. Soviet documents on Munich are presented in *Vestnik Ministersva inostrannykh del SSSR*, no. 18 (October 1, 1988): 37–47.

4. See John W. Garver, "Chiang Kai-shek's Quest for Soviet Entry into the Sino-Japanese War," *Political Science Quarterly* 102, no. 2 (Summer 1987): 295–316.

5. Thomas M. Forster, *NVA—Die Armee der Sowjetzone* (Cologne: Markus-Verlagsgesellschaft m.b.H., 1966).

6. Lincoln P. Bloomfield, Walter C. Clemens, Jr., and Franklyn Griffiths, *Khrushchev and the Arms Race: Soviet Interests in Arms Control and Disarmament, 1954–1964* (Cambridge: MIT Press, 1966), 147–51. By 1970 things had changed. When Willy Brandt visited Moscow in August to discuss the FRG-Soviet Treaty, the Politburo—after lengthy debate—decided that any negotiations on German reunification might take place only if West Germany withdrew from NATO *and* became a "socialist state." See Arkady N. Shevchenko, *Breaking with Moscow* (New York: Alfred A. Knopf, 1985), 179.

7. *Memoirs of Nie Rongzhen*, 3 vols. (Beijing: People's Liberation Army Press, 1983–4), III, 804–6; translated from Chinese by Zhan Jun and Ali Ho Clemens. See also John Wilson Lewis and Xue Litai, *China Builds the Bomb* (Stanford, CA: Stanford University Press, 1988).

8. Andrei A. Gromyko, *Pamiatnoe*, 2 vols. (Moscow: Politizdat, 1988), II: 128–34.

9. *Memoirs of Nie Rongzhen*, p. 805.

10. Walter C. Clemens, Jr., *The Arms Race and Sino-Soviet Relations* (Stanford, CA: Hoover Institution, 1968), 35–42.

11. In the late 1950s President Eisenhower turned down General de Gaulle's request for French participation in a Western nuclear directorate. Spurned, France tested its first atomic bomb in 1960 and later refused, like China, to sign the 1963 nuclear test ban.

12. ENDC/199, October 19, 1967; ENDC/223/Rev. 1.

13. See Henry Kissinger, *White House Years* (Boston: Little, Brown, 1979), 1226–27, 1251.

14. For changes since 1985, see Thomas W. Robinson, "The New Era in Sino-Soviet Relations," *Current History* 86, no. 521 (September 1987): 241–44, 303–4. Despite Chinese criticisms of Soviet policies, many Chinese publications meant for internal use have stressed positive aspects of the USSR. See Gilbert Rozman, "China's Soviet Watchers in the 1980s: A New Era in Scholarship," *World Politics* 47 no. 4 (July 1985): 435–74. Some U.S. China watchers, in turn, believe the evidence cited by Rozman to be misleading.

15. At the 1984 Stockholm Conference on Confidence- and Security-Building Measures in Europe, some Eastern European diplomats told Westerners that they had been instructed to do nothing but reinforce Soviet diplomacy. Romania, however, introduced a plan different from Moscow's basic package. See Kenneth Hunt et al., "New Soviet Missiles for Eastern Europe," in Vojtech Mastny, ed., *Soviet/East European Survey, 1983–1984: Selected Research and Analysis from Radio Free Europe/Radio Liberty* (Durham, NC: Duke University Press, 1985), 93–97; also Ronald Eggleston et al., "The Stockholm Conference," in ibid., pp. 97–109 at 100; and Robert English, "Eastern Europe's Doves," *Foreign Policy*, no. 56 (Fall 1984): 44–60.

16. For background, see Franklyn Griffiths, "Proposals of Total Disarmament in Soviet Foreign Policy, 1927–1932 and 1959–1960," Columbia University Russian Certificate Essay, 1962.

17. On early years of the Soviet peace movement, see Marshall D. Shulman, *Stalin's Foreign Policy Reappraised* (Cambridge, MA: Harvard University Press, 1963).

18. See Walter C. Clemens, Jr., "Shifts in Soviet Arms Control Posture," *Military Review* 51, no. 7 (July 1971): 28–36; idem, "Mutual Balanced Force Reductions," ibid., no. 10 (October 1971): 3–11.

19. Gorbachev visited President François Mitterrand in 1985 before his first summit with Reagan, but the Mitterrand government altered none of its key positions.

20. See Gordon R. Weihmiller, *U.S.-Soviet Summits: An Account of East-West Diplomacy at the Top, 1955–1985* (Lanham, MD: University Press of America, 1986).

21. For a collection of essays by Moscow University specialists, see N. V. Sivachev, ed., *Problemy Amerikanistiki 3* (Moscow: Izdatel'stvo Moskovskogo Universiteta, 1985); for a bibliography, see pp. 317–19.

22. For documentation on the early 1960s and early 1970s, see the previous chapter, notes 40, 41, 42.

23. *The New York Times*, September 28, 1984, pp. A1, 12, 13.

24. Ibid.

25. On *Kommunist*, see the previous chapter, note 42.

26. Text in *Vestnik Ministerstva inostrannykh del SSSR*, no. 5 (March 15, 1988): 1–4 at 3.

27. *Conférence de Moscou pour la limitation des armements* (Moscow: NKID, 1923).

28. M. Pavlovich, *Ot Vashingtona do Genui* (Moscow: Vysshii voennyi redaktsiionyi sovet, 1922); similar appraisals were made by Comintern representatives.

29. See E. A. Korovin and V. V. Egor'ev, *Razoruzhenie: Problema razoruzheniia v mezhdunarodnom prave: Liga Natsii v faktakh i dokumentakh, 1920–1929* (Moscow: Gosizdat, 1930).

30. Gromyko to General Assembly on September 21, 1962 in *Documents on Disarmament 1962*, 2 vols. (Washington, DC: U.S. Arms Control and Disarmament Agency, 1963), II: 896–909 at 904–5.

31. Urged on by Brezhnev and Gromyko, the Politburo endorsed a proposal for a five-power meeting, but the top-level resistance to real disarmament reportedly shocked even the experienced diplomat Shevchenko. See his *Breaking with Moscow*, pp. 162–63.

32. They ignored the argument of a tsarist diplomat that arms limitation can occur only if agreed-upon procedures exist to resolve disputes by peaceful means. See V. F. Malinovskii, "Rassuzhenie o mire i voine," reprinted with some deletions in I. S. Andreeva and A. V. Gulyga, eds., *Traktaty o vechnom mire* (Moscow: Sotzekgiz, 1963), 213–54.

33. See George H. Quester, "On the Identification of Real and Pretended Communist Military Doctrine," *Journal of Conflict Resolution* 10, no. 2 (June 1966): 172–79.

34. See "Open Letter of the CPSU Central Committee," *Pravda*, July 14, 1963. That "the Soviet Union thinks it could fight and win a nuclear war" was one of the myths rationalizing U.S. policy in the early 1980s. See Walter C. Clemens, Jr., "Intellectual Foundations of Reagan's Soviet Policies: The Threadbare Emperor," in Bernard Rubin, ed., *When Information Counts* (Lexington, MA: Lexington Books, 1985), 155–72, 227–31.

35. See Bloomfield et al., *Khrushchev*, also Amitai Etzioni, "The Kennedy Experiment," *Western Political Quarterly* 20, no. 2 (June 1967): 361–80.

36. For some contrary inferences drawn from the Soviet military press, see Albert Wohlstetter, "Between an Unfree World and None: Increasing Our Choices," *Foreign Affairs* 63, no. 5 (Summer 1985): 962–94 and 983–86.

37. For reviews of issues and agreements, see Coit D. Blacker and Gloria Duffy, eds., *International Arms Control*, 2d ed. (Stanford, CA: Stanford University Press, 1984); also Committee on International Security and Arms Control, National Academy of Sciences, *Nuclear Arms Control* (Washington, DC: National Academy Press, 1985).

38. Soviet ships, however, harassed U.S. vessels attempting to recover parts of the Korean airliner shot down in 1983. Letter of Rear Admiral William A. Cocknell, Jr., commander of the U.S. task force in that operation, to the Harriman Institute, Columbia University.

39. Three writers in *Izvestiia* (June 24, 1973) wrote of the U.S.-Soviet agreement on the prevention of war: "A Historic Day and a Historic Document." For further analysis, see Raymond L. Garthoff, *Détente and Confrontation* (Washington, DC: Brookings Institution, 1985), 334–44.

40. See Strobe Talbott, *Endgame: The Inside Story of SALT II* (New York: Harper & Row, 1979).

41. See, for example, V. V. Zagladin and I. T. Frolov, "Global'nye problemy sovremennosti," *Kommunist*, no. 16 (November 1976): 93–104.

42. See Garthoff, *Détente and Confrontation*, pp. 771–77.

43. See also Clemens, "Intellectual Foundations."

44. See Bruce Porter, "The Tactics of Soviet Policy," in Mastny, *Soviet-East European Survey*, pp. 77–81 at 81.

45. See chapters 7 and 8; for highly analytical studies, see Jiri Valenta and William C. Potter, eds., *Soviet Decisionmaking for National Security* (Boston: Unwin Hyman, 1984).

46. For a critique of the narrow conception of power allegedly favored in the United States, see V. M. Kulish et al., *Voennaia sila i mezhdunarodnye otnosheniia: Voennye aspekty vneshnepoliticheskikh kontseptsii SShA* (Moscow: Mezhdunarodnye otnosheiia, 1972), 5–6. For an argument that America's economic hegemony has collapsed, never to return, see G. Skorov, "Amerikanskii 'sentr sily' sovremmenogo kapitalizma," *Kommunist*, no. 8 (May 1987): 112–23.

5

The Third Rome Confronts
the Club of Rome: "Globalistika"

The USSR and Global Interdependence

The "high politics" of Soviet security policy evolved in tandem with "low politics" issues of trade, environmental protection, and scientific and cultural exchange. High politics led the way toward limited collaboration with the West; when détente stalled and shifted toward renewed confrontation, low politics shriveled but did not expire. Instead, East-West contacts continued in a subdued way, creating a framework on which security cooperation and other exchanges could build in the last half of the 1980s.

Khrushchev's and Brezhnev's policies on arms control triggered and paralleled a broader change in Soviet thinking: a secular trend toward acceptance in the 1970s of East-West interconnectedness. Some Soviet lawyers and scientists moved in this direction ahead of the Party line; others waited for the Party to endorse this movement and then jumped on the bandwagon. Party ideologues tried at times to restrain and channel this enthusiasm, only to find that the ground was already shifting beneath their feet.

Many of the same pressing concerns shaping Soviet arms control policies—the dangers and costs of arms competition coupled with Russia's technological lag—elicited a new approach toward global problems generally. But the Kremlin also responded to many of the same issues heightening ecological consciousness throughout the world, leading to the

[121]

1972 Stockholm Environmental Conferences (boycotted by the Soviet bloc because East Germany was not invited) and then to the creation of the UN Environmental Program. Moscow, reviving its ancient Third Rome mentality, tried to create its own science of "globalistics" (*globalistika*) to rebut the "limits to growth" views endorsed by the Club of Rome, founded in 1968 by Italian industrialist Aurelio Peccei and other internationalists.[1]

The Brezhnev regime conceded that there exist "global problems [*global 'nye problemy*]—problems so vast and complex that they cannot be resolved by any one country no matter how large or powerful." These problems, for Moscow, began with the danger of nuclear war but also included pollution, resource shortages, and other issues in the "world problematique" addressed by the Club of Rome.

Recognition that the "socialist fatherland" is part of the world problematique did not come easily for a regime claiming to be the leading force in historical progress. Not until Mikhail Gorbachev's ascendancy did Soviet ideology admit that "interdependence" [*vzaimozavisimost'*] links not only East and West but also developed and less developed countries. "Interdependence" implies a mutual sensitivity or vulnerability that can be manipulated for gain or loss, joint or one-sided.[2] Viewed in this way, interdependence is a condition—a fact of life to which policymakers can respond in a cooperative or in a zero-sum spirit. The Kremlin approved the principle of East-West economic interdependence in the 1975 Helsinki Declaration. But the idea that the USSR is part of an industrialized tier of northern nations sharing vulnerabilities with one another and with the South was anathema to Party thinking until the mid-1980s.

Unlike CPSU ideologists, Western theorists of "functionalism" have welcomed interdependence as a fact of life, hoping that economic and technological imperatives will strengthen cooperation and trust among nations and individuals. Functionalists hold that cooperation in relatively apolitical domains such as delivering the mail and eradicating disease will transform the nature of high politics. Habits of cooperation in nonpolitical endeavors should lessen—perhaps even transcend—ideological hostility and the struggle for power.[3] Supporters of UNESCO and similar movements add that cultural exchanges could lessen misunderstanding and raise mutual esteem among nations.

Against this vision Realpolitik asserts that power politics reflects deep drives in human nature that can be shaped only marginally by functional cooperation and deeper empathy. Still, even the unsentimental Henry Kissinger of the early 1970s hoped that détente would spill over to enmesh the USSR in a seamless web of ties with the West inhibiting to Soviet expansionism. For him the starting point would be high politics, but low politics would make peace more secure. The functionalist logic would be reversed, but with a similar result.

Taken to their logical extremes, the visions of both functionalists and Kissinger looked toward an ideal world of complex interdependence in which governments and societies are linked on many levels and the role of military power sharply reduced.[4]

Moscow's response to the strategic and environmental challenges of the 1970s–80s did not vindicate the hopes of either camp—the functionalists or the modified Realpolitik of Dr. Kissinger. As often happens, Russian behavior did not meet Western expectations. Instead, the Kremlin produced a unique response in keeping with the Russian-Marxist penchant for messianic, visionary thinking. Soviet commentators announced in the early 1980s that a new branch of knowledge had been developed in the USSR—"globalistics"—to understand and resolve "global problems of our time." Interdisciplinary *globalistika*, they said, stands at the interface between natural and social sciences and between science and ethics. Unlike environmental studies sponsored by the Club of Rome and other "bourgeois" groups, globalistics combined up-to-date science with the perennial insights and principles of Marxism-Leninism.[5]

Western functionalists and many Soviet scientists wanted to depoliticize the common problems facing humanity; Kremlin ideologists underscored their "class" essence. Globalistika became an instrument in the inward-looking, hostile worldview dominating the Kremlin in the five or six years before Gorbachev. As we shall also see, however, Soviet praxis often moved beyond the Party line. Ecologists, systems analysts, and other Soviet scientists continued to look and act globally even as the Party line narrowed.

Origins of Globalistika

The connections between environmental quality and national security appear tenuous. But a deeper look reveals significant overlaps. First, a wise security policy aims at preserving and enhancing the country's way of life. Environmental quality is both a material and a spiritual asset to virtually any way of life. But it can be directly imperiled by military approaches to "security"—arms buildups, weapons testing and pollution, maneuvers, diversion of resources from productive ends, and the ultimate environmental killer: war. Second, international cooperation to protect and enhance the common habitat is not simply another way to reduce

[123]

tensions but a sine qua non for national and global security. "The most elemental values of all are those associated with biological existence: level of health and length of life. In more specifically ecological terms, but still in the context of a world community, or ecosystem, these values can be summed up as the need *to make the earth a reasonably safe and salubrious place to live, not only for ourselves but also for our descendants, and not only for one or a few nations but for all.*"[6]

Thus the ecological challenge to international studies and enlightened foreign policymaking is to understand and cope effectively with the global problems resulting from the interaction between the world of politics and the biosphere.[7]

Karl Marx and Friedrich Engels had insight into such matters; most Soviet leaders before Gorbachev, however, took a much more narrowly dogmatic and parochial perspective. Marx perceived that the dynamo of capitalism was overcoming the barriers of national frontiers.[8] Engels, however, cautioned about material development: each apparent "victory" over nature exacts a toll—its second- and third-order consequences often canceling immediate gains.[9]

Lenin, caught up in revolution and civil war, had little time to reflect on ecology, but he usually opposed any leaning toward chauvinism. By 1920 he also saw that "peaceful cohabitation" had become a fact and he looked for ways to make the most of this situation. The League of Nations, however, he denounced as a plague of nations, a bourgeois consortium. Instead, Foreign Commissar Chicherin at the Genoa Conference in April 1922 called for a "real League of peoples" based on complete equality of all nations and "official participation of worker's organizations. . . ."

But mutual vulnerability had already overtaken Party dogma. Famine led the Kremlin to welcome food relief organized by Herbert Hoover. And the first international meeting attended by Soviet government officials was a league-sponsored All-European Sanitary Conference held in Warsaw in March 1922—weeks before Chicherin agitated Genoa. It met to plan action against typhus epidemics in the Ukraine and their spread westward. Soviet representatives insisted, however, on stripping conference halls and committees of any reference to the League of Nations. Even after the crises of 1922 had passed, Soviet medical personnel requested and accepted league assistance despite official hostility to the "bourgeois consortium." In 1924 the USSR asked the League Health Organization to collaborate with Russian scientists in experiments with cholera vaccine. In 1925 Soviets asked the same body to help investigate endemic plague in Siberia. Soviet doctors used league fellowships to study public health programs in Europe.[10] All this anticipated the zeal of Soviet

[124]

scientists to take part in international studies in the early 1980s (as noted in the next chapter)—even as Moscow denounced the very idea of interdependence. It also resembled the willingness of the Gorbachev regime to accept foreign assistance in coping with the Chernobyl nuclear disaster and the 1988 Armenian earthquake.

Where Stalin's Kremlin thought it had nothing to gain, however, it roundly condemned low politics activities in Geneva: Moscow rejected league efforts to curtail traffic in narcotics as being dominated by commercial motives, adding that Soviet power had already suppressed drug traffic within the USSR. The Kremlin was even more hostile to the International Labor Organization, terming it an "abominable masquerade to trick the proletariat."[11]

In the 1930s Stalin grudgingly accepted the necessity of collaboration with others—the League of Nations, Hitler, the West—for survival purposes, but he usually maintained a profound distrust of other political actors, both domestic and foreign. And his artisans of industrialization basically ignored the second- and third-order perils of which Engels warned.

Stalin's worldview continued to influence Soviet policies for decades after his death. Although Khrushchev and Brezhnev favored trade and other exchanges with the West, their regimes were reluctant to admit a shared destiny with the rival camp. Instead Moscow has blamed virtually all social ills on the absence of socialism. War and hunger, for example, were said to be the result of unjust, ineffective social systems. Soviet ideologues have contended that the socialist system neither causes nor suffers from the ordinary ills of nonsocialist humanity. It exploits no one—neither at home nor abroad.

Whether all humanity is interdependent and, if so, in what ways, are questions that go to the heart of Russian communism's messianic role. If humanity is interdependent but needs a savior to point the way, the USSR could be called upon to bring enlightenment and redemption. But if all states and social systems are vulnerable to global challenges threatening to overwhelm them, Russian communism's unique role is diminished, opening the way to ideological relativism and eclectic pragmatism.

Beginning gingerly in the 1960s and continuing forcefully into the early 1980s, Soviet ideologists endeavored to meet and master issues of dependency and interdependence in ways that would preserve and enhance the USSR's role as the leader of progressive humanity.

Under Brezhnev the USSR and United States tacitly recognized their mutual vulnerability to nuclear attack, for SALT I and II posited the absence of broad ABM defenses. In the early 1980s Soviet scientists joined those in the West warning that even a limited nuclear exchange could bring on a pervasive nuclear winter.[12]

The Brezhnev regime's affirmation of "global problems" arose from fears of Armageddon and economic-technological lag, but it was also heavily conditioned by other factors—environmental, ideological, and propagandistic. In the 1960s if not before, it was clear that environmental degradation in the USSR was undermining the quality of Soviet life and impeding economic expansion. Looking for ways to check this trend, the Politburo looked to foreign as well as indigenous wisdom and technical solutions. By placing the USSR's environmental problems in a global context, the Kremlin probably sought to spread responsibility for the country's ecological malaise.[13] Only later would Party spokesmen put the blame squarely on Soviet shoulders.

Talk of global problems and interdisciplinary analysis harmonized with the Party's claim to base its policies on "scientific Communism" and the Scientific-Technological Revolution (STR). This revolution, ideologists now granted, had spawned environmental and other problems in the USSR and globally. But, they continued, it can also generate the needed answers—when guided by Marxism-Leninism.

Brezhnev's Kremlin also wanted to rebuff Western environmental studies casting doubt on the USSR's claim to a unique and superior social system. The very process of industrialization, whether capitalist or socialist, the Club of Rome implied, generated pollution and other aspects of the world problematique. The irony and tragedy of Moscow's response was that the CPSU chose to turn such apolitical reports into grist for polemics, even though many Soviet scientists had reached similar conclusions and a few had even contributed to the same Western studies![14]

Brezhnev posited the need for East-West cooperation, but his Party line also set limits to such cooperation: collaboration with the class enemy could not extend to North-South relations. Moscow refused to be considered part of the North, for this would league the USSR with capitalist imperialism and neoimperialism. Brezhnev denied any Soviet responsibility for underdevelopment of the South—a consequence of capitalist exploitation.[15]

Soviet ideologues were condescending toward the problems of other countries. Tinkering and reformism could not get to the bottom of the world's ills: the World Bank, birth control, the Green Revolution, smoke filters—all of these gimmicks would fail so long as private property and the class struggle continued. Hostile to any intimation of limits to growth, the dominant Soviet line held that if development conflicted with environmental protection, growth should prevail.

[126]

Soviet ideologists elaborated three kinds of global problems: (1) those that flow from political realities, particularly the contradictions between socialism and capitalism and the insidious impact of capitalism on the emerging nations; (2) those generated by interactions between society and nature; and (3) those arising from the spiritual world of the individual. Seen in this way, global problems would naturally affect the USSR despite its advanced social system.

The Party line placed primary responsibility for global problems on the continued existence of the private property system in the First and Third Worlds. If the Second World occasions any global pollution, this is for superficial or temporary reasons not associated with the essence of socialism. Thus Soviet analysts acknowledged that "governments" have sometimes been slow to reevaluate past methods of utilizing natural resources. Narrow bureaucratic thinking, lack of discipline, and passivity within governments also played a role. Individuals, they allowed, are often slow to react to scientific-technological progress including its negative affects on demography, morbidity, food supplies, and ecological ethics.

One might think that such shortcomings would not occur in a system that is at once omniscient and prescient. But these problems were traced to rapid changes in the economic base of society and its evolving technology. Although socialism may not immediately respond in the optimal way to such challenges, it is the system best able to solve global problems because only socialism is capable of defending the common interests of all citizens and of planning the overall development of society.

The Kremlin recognized interconnectedness and complexity in world affairs, but Brezhnev's spokesmen insisted that the USSR and its allies had a superior system that would lead the world toward resolution of global problems. Thus the Third Rome could assert its world historical mission even as it multiplied cooperative accords with capitalist countries. Soviet spokesmen averred that the only true model of genuine inter-dependence is the Moscow-led Council for Mutual Economic Assistance (CMEA). Western advocacy of zero growth and warnings of overpopula-tion were treated as neo-Malthusianism—false science inimical to social progress.

Moscow consistently praised "internationalism" while condemning rootless "cosmopolitanism." It assailed the idea of "convergence" between socialism and capitalism and any forecast or prescription of movement in that direction. Urging expanded trade with the West, the Kremlin also hinted that such intercourse would yield the rope by which to hang the other side.

The inward-looking approach to global issues was illustrated by a Soviet naval officer well versed in Western thought, who over lunch at the Smithsonian Castle in 1976 told me, "You feed your allies and we'll feed ours."

Operational Levels of Globalistika

There was no single Soviet approach to global problems, in either theory or praxis. There were many domains of word and deed other than the Party's ideological assertions and propaganda campaigns. There were also actions by the Soviet government within the USSR and abroad—not merely in government-to-government relations but in international organizations, nongovernmental forums, and transnational movements; the policies and practices of Soviet economic, scientific, and military enterprises registering a global impact—even when none was intended; also official and unofficial educational campaigns to instill an "ecological culture" in Soviet citizens and to "ecologize" production.[16]

Many Soviets were more concerned with truth or environmental conservation than with safeguarding Party dogma. The imperatives of East-West trade also pushed to break down inversion. Thus a Soviet technocrat affirmed for the San Francisco Chamber of Commerce in 1973: "All of us . . . are aboard the same spaceship which, by the way, does not have any exhaust valves."[17]

Side by side with ideological polemics there were at least three other major streams of Soviet writings on global problems: legal pragmatic, holistic ecological, and technocratic systems analysis. While ideology blamed capitalism for environmental disruption, the other three streams looked beyond ideology. Some jurists wanted tighter laws; environmentalists wanted limits to growth and greater ecological literacy; technocrats wanted greater rationality in planning. The ecological approach has been dominated by natural scientists joined by a few philosophers; the technocratic school, by systems analysts and economists. When ideology acknowledged that global approaches to global problems need to be considered, ecologists and systems analysts rushed into the breach. When ideology later tried to narrow or shut the portal, the streams of ecological and systems analysis were narrowed but did not stop.[18]

Soviet international law doctrine since the 1920s championed "national sovereignty" against the incursions of hostile majorities at the League of Nations and United Nations. Soviet jurists (much like senators from the American South) opposed international or supranational laws that could interfere in domestic affairs. Against this tendency, however, Soviet law also admitted that national law could be extended beyond the borders in a *force majeure* situation when failure to act in a timely way could result in irreparable damage to a natural resource. This argument accompanied the USSR's unilateral imposition in 1956 of stringent quotas (aimed especially against Japanese) on the catch of salmon and other fish off Soviet Far Eastern shores.[19]

Over time Soviet lawyers helped to articulate the doctrine of *res naturae internationalis*. Contrary to the "first come, first take" philosophy, this doctrine is based on the principle of equitable access to and use by the entire family of nations of an object possessed of international dimensions—for example, atmospheric purity, marine resources, or migratory species. Soviet lawyers favored rational use of such objects through coordinated action.[20] This attitude contributed to the 1959 Antarctica Treaty, the 1967 Space Treaty, and the 1981 Law of the Sea Convention.

The increasing attention given by Party ideologues to global problems in the late Brezhnev years created new forums for expression of legal, ecological, and technocratic viewpoints. The early 1980s saw a proliferation of conferences and publications on global problems in the USSR and Eastern Europe—for example, a symposium at the Soviet Diplomatic Academy in 1980 sponsored by the Ministry of Foreign Affairs and the State Committee on Science and Technology (GKNT) in cooperation with the Institute for World Economics and International Relations (IMEMO), the Institute of the USA and Canada, the Institute of the Far East, and the All-Union Scientific Research Institute on Systems Studies (VNIISI).[21] Deputy Foreign Minister V. F. Mal'tsev set the stage by recalling Soviet support for disarmament, the Law of the Sea, peaceful uses of outer space, UNCTAD, the International Atomic Energy Agency, and the International Institute for Applied Systems Analysis (IIASA). He cited a Brezhnev speech defining "peaceful coexistence" as a way to solve the great problems facing humanity through international collaboration.

Nearly forty papers were presented at the conference. A few implied that all relevant knowledge could be found in Marxist classics; others looked to experiments with new forms of science and technology. Some stressed the need for self-help and more indigenous agricultural research in less developed countries; a few took potshots at Mao Zedong or at U.S. imperialism. Topics ran from futures modeling to class struggle; from protein deficits and health care to the ways of transnational pharmaceutical conglomerates; from loss of land to exploration of outer space.

One of the most free-thinking approaches presented at the academy was a statement by N. F. Reimers on "Ecological Crisis and Horizons of the Future." He called for the most rapid resolution to the fundamental problems of what he called "econology" (ecology *cum* economics).[22] Our usual standards of permissible concentrations of pollutants are not adequate guides to constrain dynamic systems of pollution. To save nature from the blight of narrow economism we must accept the principle "the polluter pays." To deal with the complexities of econological interactions we must construct a noosphere, not by a basic transformation of nature but through a deep change in our production and social institutions and a rebuilding of international relations.[23]

None of the speakers at the Diplomatic Academy came out for East-West cooperation to aid the South, but B. B. Runov put the onus for food shortages in the Third World on the governments of the developing countries. "European" experience, he said, is not helpful to African agronomy. Nor did he make any claims for the Soviet model. Instead he blamed Africans for not building larger cadres of scientific-research workers and for spending a great deal on arms. This situation, he said, can be changed "only in conditions of détente . . . and shifting of military expenditures in science to civilian goals," as the USSR has proposed.[24] In short, many (probably most) speakers at the Diplomatic Academy took a positive approach to international cooperation on global problems.

A relatively liberal globalistika displayed a healthy ferment in 1980–81. Young scholars met in Jurmala (near Riga) in 1981 and in Pushkino (near Moscow) in 1982 to discuss and draft theses on global problems. Economists, mathematicians, geographers, and biologists also published essays on the same theme touching on its links with their respective disciplines. Eastern European scholars also took part in some of these symposia.[25] Essays in *Kommunist* and *Problems of Philosophy* tried to establish or test the allowable parameters of global cooperation.

Soviet scholars and Party officials generally agreed that global studies should be interdisciplinary. Many also displayed an eclecticism little different from that for which some Soviets criticized the Club of Rome. But are there no limits to the intermingling of methods and ideas? Philosopher I. T. Frolov wrote in 1981 that a new synthesis must be created embracing science, values, and humanism. But he drew a line to keep theologians at a distance. Marxism and theology, he declared, have nothing in common, even though some theologians welcome science as an instrument to supplement morality. This "scientism" is alien to Marxism, though it sees science as a vital source of moral knowledge and values. Frolov quoted Chekov to the effect that earlier civilizations have perished because they lacked good critics. And Frolov granted that his own vision of science and humanism is so remote that it is not a goal but an ideal. He ended one essay by quoting the symbolist poet Guillaume Apollinaire (1880–1918): "We wage an unending battle on the frontiers of the future and the unlimited."[26]

Early 1980s: East-West Differences Emphasized

In the early 1980s many Soviet authors kept up the contradictory posture of the 1970s: they traced many global problems to capitalism but welcomed serious cooperation to deal with East-West if not North-South problems. In 1982–83 the senior Party globalist, Vadim V. Zagladin, injected a new inflection: Not only do global problems derive primarily from capitalism; there is little prospect of resolving them until capitalism is liquidated.

Zagladin, deputy director of the International Department, CPSU Secretariat, had for almost three decades published pamphlets and books on many international topics, from the Algerian independence struggle to "scientific communism."[27] Frolov had written some of the first essays on global problems published in the mid-1970s. They became in the early 1980s a gang of two dominating Soviet ideological analysis of global problems. Sometimes they collaborated in editing books, writing articles, and giving interviews to *Literaturnaia gazeta*; at times they quoted each other, each strengthening the other's authority—the Party propagandist and the Party pundit—who usually took a less rigid stand than his partner, the tougher cop. Their sayings, in turn, were almost ritualistically cited by others, even those who seemed to strive toward a more liberal worldview. Frolov often served as the chief *retsenzent* (reviewer, censor) for others' writings on globalistika. He served as chairman of the Scientific Council on Philosophical Problems of Science and Technology under the Presidium of the USSR Academy of Sciences. In 1983 Frolov's Scientific Council sponsored a meeting of Party leaders and scholars to review global problems in light of decisions made at the Twenty-Sixth CPSU Congress; Zagladin then wrote the main article reviewing the meeting.[28]

Writing in *Problems of Philosophy* (April 1983), Zagladin asserted that globalistika deals with the sharpening economic crisis on a global scale, falling levels of development in the former colonies and in the industrialized capitalist economies, demographic and food problems, the energy crisis, and the possibility of a nuclear crisis brought on by

[131]

imperialism. All these problems arise because private property continues to exist. Only if capitalism is replaced by the rule of the working class can these problems be resolved. To do so is the "world-historical mission" of the working class. When this class triumphs, these problems will be regarded as having belonged to the "prehistory" of mankind![29]

Many schools of thought have arisen in the West to discuss global problems. But, said Zagladin, they tend to be metaphysical and idealistic, too eclectic, or too hostile to socialism and to social progress in general. "A typical example of this is the work of the so-called 'Club of Rome', which contains significant and highly interesting empirical material but which nonetheless suffers first of all from its class limitation." Not by accident, Zagladin wrote, recent reports of the club have returned to the highly gloomy and pessimistic flavor of its early studies.

Only Marxist-Leninist theory is able to penetrate global problems and identify the road to their resolution. It is time, Zagladin said, for researchers in Communist countries to make a comprehensive study of the works of Marx, Engels, and Lenin on global problems.

The only class capable of finding a resolution to the sharpening social problems of our times is the proletariat, according to Zagladin. The ability of the working class to fulfill its historical mission will not be realized through "class collaboration" or in some kind of "third way" between class struggle and the bourgeois dream of class compromise. No, it requires instead "class victory"—the liquidation of capitalism. In the building of socialism and later of communism will be found the complete solution to global and other general human problems.[30]

Zagladin's expression of the Party line was more rigid and polarizing than the more neutral definition favored in the mid-1970s that global problems are too complex for one nation to resolve. That view opened the door to East-West cooperation; Zagladin's early 1980s position tended to close it. His hard line resembled Lenin's approach to disarmament. Both held that the solution to the problem depends on the triumph of the working class. Zagladin came close to asserting, as Lenin did before October 1917, that efforts at negotiation or meaningful cooperation with the capitalist world are not only futile but dangerous because they could nurture reformist illusions.[31]

In 1982 a Soviet scholar, Grigorii S. Khozin, devoted an entire book to criticizing bourgeois conceptions of global problems.[32] Khozin attacked (1) technological optimists Herman Kahn et al.; (2) "existential-cultural globalists" such as Saul H. Mendlovitz and the World Order Models Project; (3) social optimists such as Richard A. Falk and Johan Galtung; (4) liberal internationalists such as George Ball, Lincoln P. Bloomfield, and

[132]

Robert Wesson; (5) champions of "convergence," and (6) champions of functionalism. Most of these viewpoints, he said, tend to deny or "ignore" socialist contributions to civilization, from agriculture to health care.[33] Each of them tends to overplay or underestimate a key element in world affairs. Thus Kahn was right to be optimistic but wrong to assume that raw materials are inexhaustible. One American who got high marks from Khozin is ecologist-activist Barry Commoner. Khozin said Commoner is correct that capitalism has raised productive efficiency while also increasing the demand for capital, energy, and other resources, thereby limiting the number of jobs and ravaging the environment.[34]

The fundamental weakness of bourgeois scholarship on global issues, according to Zagladin, Khozin, and other Soviet commentators, is that it lacks the class perspective of Marxism-Leninism. As a consequence, studies such as those sponsored by the Club of Rome tend at best to be naive and, at worst, conscious instruments of Western imperialism.[35] The supraclass or nonclass perspective spawns at least ten derivative shortcomings in bourgeois scholarship, as follows:

(1) *Superficiality*. Blinded to the deepest factors shaping global problems, Western writers respond to symptoms. Smugly confident about material progress in the 1950s and 1960s, they suddenly became alarmist in the 1970s.

(2) *Philosophical pessimism*. Allegedly influenced by Arthur Schopenhauer, Friedrich Nietzsche and Oswald Spengler (a somewhat unlikely set of readings for systems engineers at MIT or Case Western!), bourgeois scholars are programmed to expect environmental decay.

(3) *Reformist illusions*. Although some Westerners have been trained to expect the worst, others naively trust that "social dynamics" will provide solutions to global issues even though private property remains.

(4) *Abstract humanism*. Incorrectly assuming that global problems arise everywhere from the human condition, bourgeois writers fail to see the ultimate source and remedy for such problems: the creation of a society not dominated by private property.

(5) *Anti-Sovietism*. Some Western writers go out of their way to denigrate the unique capabilities of the Soviet system for coping with global problems. Thus according to Khozin's skewed analysis, Garrett Hardin's parable, "The Tragedy of the Commons," aims to show that socialism is not capable of protecting the environment![36]

(6) *Loose methodology*. Some Club of Rome studies extrapolate from U.S. patterns of resource consumption and pollution to generalize about the entire world.

(7) *Eclecticism*. The multidisciplinary outpourings of the club have

[133]

no anchor. They gather from many directions without the guiding insights of Marxism-Leninism.

(8) *Wishful thinking.* Akin to reformist illusions, this weakness presumes too much for the human condition. Thus *No Limits to Learning* is naively optimistic about human capacities. This flows from a kind of "anthropocentrism" now popular in the West. As yet there is no social basis for such optimism.

(9) *The ideology of "interdependence."* This doctrine generates a propaganda figleaf to mask continued Western domination of the former colonies.[37] It teaches that Western technology—especially American—leads the world and that all nations must bow to the material superiority of the United States or its trilateral partners in Japan and Western Europe. Such concepts are at the bottom of bourgeois globalistics. Appearing to be reformist, they are in essence reactionary. Like Western futurologists, bourgeois champions of interdependence refuse to recognize the inevitability of revolutionary transformation as the magisterial route leading to a bright future for all humanity.[38] Ideologists of interdependence seek to create an alarm about the state of the world so as to perpetuate bourgeois hegemony even as they demand (unjustly) universal sacrifices by asserting the duty of all states to contribute equally to the underdevelopment caused by Western imperialism.

(10) *Cosmopolitanism.* This ideology is both reactionary and utopian. Part of the arsenal of American imperialism, it would deprive other peoples of their patriotic roots and subject them to U.S. dominion, all the while prating about "common interests of one world." Deliberately or not, when Aurelio Peccei called for a merging of nations, he objectively supported aggressive world imperialism.

Cosmopolitanism runs contrary to "patriotism" and to "proletarian internationalism." Communists understand that the "merging of nations" is not feasible now but must be preceded by a "coming together of nations" and a long development proceeding on the basis of objective regularities.[39]

The harder inflection in the Party line occurred as the tenuous détente of the 1970s gave way to a new round of cold war, for which Moscow and Washington blamed each other. Although the tougher stance began while Brezhnev still lived, it intensified during Yuri Andropov's brief tenure (late 1982–early 1984). The Party line on global problems evolved within a wider syndrome: more discipline and self-reliance at home; walkouts, rebuffs and threats abroad against adversaries ranging from Japan to America. Andropov wanted more discipline not only in the workplace but in intellectual life. Judging from book reviews in *Kommunist* throughout 1983, the Party perceived a near anarchy in Soviet social science and philosophy as works published in the early 1980s deviated broadly from ideological orthodoxy. Given that many scholars were jumping onto the global problems bandwagon, the Party probably wanted to establish clearer guidelines. The topics included under global problems were interesting and important of themselves, but they also offered an excuse to read Western publications and to make closer contact with the ideological foe.

Kosygin's poor health toward the end of the 1970s and his death in 1980 removed some of the support for pursuing East-West ties. The imposition of trade sanctions by the United States and its allies in 1980 added to the incentives for Moscow to move toward self-sufficiency.[40] At the same time that Zagladin dimmed the prospects for East-West collaboration to resolve global problems, he also affirmed that U.S. sanctions would be of minor importance to Soviet development and that the USSR would "produce everything that is necessary for us unaided and by the development of relations and cooperation with the socialist countries."[41]

Some Soviet specialists hewed closely to the Zagladin line, but others seemed to pay it only lip service. In a new and growing field such as globalistika a scholar could cite Marx, the current general secretary, and Zagladin in the first and last footnotes and do something creative between this ideological sandwich. A few Soviet writers followed precisely this practice.[42]

Researchers at IMEMO continued to produce books and articles on global problems, often in a nondogmatic vein. In June 1983 Iu. Feodorov analyzed U.S. policy and found much to recommend the *Global 2000 Report* prepared in the last years of the Carter administration. The report, Feodorov said, conveys "anxiety" about the state of the world in the twenty-first century but without the hopeless pessimism characteristic of Club of Rome studies. It attempts a more balanced appraisal and calls for a "just" approach by the United States in collaboration with other countries. Feodorov even found some common ground between the U.S. study and a 1981 book by Zagladin and Frolov which also called for "extraordinary measures" to save civilization from catastrophe.[43]

Feodorov also used the vehicle of his essay on the *Global 2000 Report* to address internal needs of the USSR. True, he said, socialism is the system best equipped to resolve global problems. But this does not happen automatically. Rather, it must come about as a result of conscious and goal-oriented activity.

Feodorov made other points relevant to the USSR. He charged that some Western theoreticians wanted to constrain East-West collaboration within narrow limits lest it undermine capitalism and place it in a vulnerable position that could yield one-sided advantages to the other side.[44] One wonders if he was not also addressing Soviet proponents of autarky worried about destabilizing foreign influences. He also took note, regretfully, of Reagan administration efforts to pressure and blackmail the USSR by trade and other sanctions. Feodorov quoted Andropov and other Soviet authorities to prove that the Soviet government stood ready for extensive collaboration with the West. Unfortunately, he declared, the Reagan administration rejected Carter's *Global 2000 Report* and embarked instead upon a quest for superiority and expansion.

Toward the end of 1984, as Chernenko's star set and Gorbachev's rose, there was some movement away from inversion toward limited collaboration with the West.[45] How much of the shift should be attributed to Gorbachev's influence is impossible to say, but on September 27, 1984, Chernenko called for a radical solution to arms problems and "constructive development in Soviet-American relations." Such a relationship, he said, would open "broad potential" for Soviet-U.S. cooperation in solving global problems such as famine and environmental pollution—a position much more outgoing than previous Kremlin stances.[46]

Replying to a question from journalist Marvin Kalb, Chernenko said: "All of us live on one planet or, as they say, in one common home. One must take care that there should be the least possible amount of explosives in our home" (*Pravda*, November 18, 1984). Between September and December 1984 Soviet diplomats showed a new flexibility at the Stockholm Conference on Confidence- and Security-Building Measures and Disarmament in Europe. In January-March 1985 the "deep freeze" was over and Soviet diplomats "turned up the heat," developing patterns that led to agreements in 1986.[47]

Chernenko's offer to work with the United States on global problems was accompanied by some deeds. Soviet trucks, helicopters, and planes helped to distribute Western food to starving Ethiopians, sometimes using fuel paid for by Western donors. "Life itself" had dragged the USSR into this posture. Soviet advisers knew about starvation in Ethiopia even before news media brought the country's plight to Western viewers and ignited Western relief campaigns. The Soviet naval officer was wrong: the USSR could not feed its allies, but it could hardly refuse to distribute food from the West. Indeed, Moscow's greater flexibility on arms control was again coinciding with food deficits in the USSR as well as in Ethiopia and Mozambique.

Perhaps hunger brought Moscow down to earth. The famine ravaging Africa was surely a problem "too complex to be solved by any one country no matter how powerful." Quite to the point, a Soviet diplomat joined others at Ambassador Arthur Hartman's 1984 Thanksgiving dinner in Moscow in singing "We are all in one boat." As Americans were to learn just a few years later, the quirks of nature—combined with those of people—can suddenly transform abundance into shortfall.

The challenges of feeding, housing, and educating the globe's billions demanded a synthesis of the best insights from Novosibirsk to Palo Alto to Ibadan to Hyderabad. Even as Party ideologues branded the Western studies of the world problematique as a Trojan horse of imperialism, many Soviet scientists and some officials continued their participation in East-West-South studies of global problems in ways that subordinated dogma to scientific imperatives. Soviet praxis—at least in low politics—often differed sharply from Communist prescription.

Notes

1. For background, see Eric P. Hoffmann and Robbin F. Laird, *Technocratic Socialism: The Soviet Union in the Advanced Industrial Era* (Durham, NC: Duke University Press, 1985); Walter C. Clemens, Jr., *The U.S.S.R. and Global Interdependence: Alternative Futures* (Washington, DC: American Enterprise Institute, 1978). One of the first publications sponsored by the Club of Rome was Donnella H. Meadows et al., *The Limits to Growth* (New York: Universe Books, 1972). For a critique of the methodology and assumptions underlying this book and eight other reports to the Club, see Nicholas Greenwood Onuf, "Reports to the Club of Rome," *World Politics* 36, no. 1 (October 1983): 121–46. Onuf argues that *Limits to Growth* resembles the thesis of Trotskyite Ernest Mandel, *Late Capitalism* (London: Verso, 1978), that capitalism displays a tendency—driven by many factors—toward periodic overproduction and consequent crisis. For a broader perspective, see Barry B. Hughes, *World Futures: A Critical Analysis of Alternatives* (Baltimore, MD: Johns Hopkins University Press, 1985).

2. See Robert O. Keohane and Joseph S. Nye, Jr., *Power and Interdependence* (Boston: Little, Brown, 1977). For the authors' reflections on the achievements and shortcomings of that book's approach, see *International Organization* 41, no. 4 (Autumn 1987): 725–53.

3. David Mitrany, *A Working Peace System* (Chicago: Quadrangle Books, 1966). One of Mitrany's first functionalist expositions, written in 1943, is included in this collection.

4. "Complex interdependence" is presented as a "thought experiment" in Keohane and Nye, *Power and Independence*, chap. 2. The concept is applied to Soviet-U.S. relations in chapter 11 of this volume.

5. "Global" (*global'nyi*) seems to have entered the Russian language only after Stalin's death. Dictionaries published before that time have only a cognate adjective from *globus*, the global sphere found in map rooms.

By the 1960s the USSR claimed to have a "global rocket" that could fractionally orbit the globe before making impact. A Soviet book published in 1967 spoke of "global pollution" produced by nuclear explosions. By the 1970s the term was widely used in a value-free manner: "global balance in the biosphere," "global water exchange," and, of course, "global problems of our times." See, for example, S. G. Malakhov and A. F. Iakovlev, eds., *Global'noe zagriaznenie vneshnei sredy radkioaktivnymi produktami iadernkh vzryvov: Sbornyk statei* (Moscow: Gidrometeoizdat, 1967); D. D. Venedik et al., *Global'nye problemy zravookhra-*

[137]

neiia i puti ikh resheniia (Moscow, 1978, a brochure published in only 100 copies); A. N. Marei et al. *Global'nye vypadeniia produktov iadernykh vzryvov kak faktor oblucheniia cheloveka* (Moscow: Atomizdat, 1980); V. M. Konontai and Iu. S. Berma, eds., *Global'nye problemy i mezhdunarodnyeekonomicheskieotnoshenniia* (Moscow: VKIISI, 1981, 500 copies printed). For an anthology of Soviet writings demonstrating the wide range of disciplines contributing to globalistika, see V. V. Zagladin and I. T. Frolov, eds., *Marksistsko-Leninskaia kontseptsiia global'nykh problem sovremennosti* (Moscow: Nauka, 1985).

6. Harold Sprout and Margaret Sprout, *Toward a Politics of the Planet Earth* (New York: Van Nostrand Reinhold, 1971), 28. Three years earlier the man who would become the USSR's leading dissident issued in samizdat his proposal for Soviet-U.S. cooperation to make the globe a more salubrious place. See Andrei D. Sakharov, *Progress, Coexistence and Intellectual Freedom* (New York: W. W. Norton, 1968). From a more nationalistic perspective, another dissident, Aleksandr Solzhenitsyn, called for preservation of Russia's resources in his September 5, 1973 *Letter to the Leaders of the Soviet Union*. See Clemens, *U.S.S.R. and Global Interdependence*, p. 35.

7. See Walter C. Clemens, Jr., "Ecology and International Relations," *International Journal* 28, no. 1 (Winter 1972–73): 1–27 and other essays in this special issue on "Earth Politics," especially George Ginzburgs, "The Soviet Union and the Biosphere," in ibid., pp. 50–68. See also Clemens, "The Ecology of Weaponry," *Bulletin of the Atomic Scientists* 26 (September 1970): 27–31.

8. Marx in the *Communist Manifesto* (1848), chap. 1.

9. Friedrich Engels, *The Dialectics of Nature* (Moscow: Progress Publishers, 1974), 180.

10. See Kathryn W. Davis, *The Soviets at Geneva: The U.S.S.R. and the League of Nations, 1919–1933* (Geneva: Libairie Kundig, 1934), 44–52. Similarly, some of Beijing's first associations with the United Nations—while Taipei still held China's seat there—were with UN health agencies.

11. Ibid., pp. 52–70.

12. Soviet scholars V. V. Aleksandrov and G. L. Stenchikov shared authorship with S. L. Thompson and three other Americans of the article entitled "Global Climatic Consequences of Nuclear War: Simulations with Three Dimensional Models," *Ambio* 13, no. 4 (1984): 236–43. One of the other Americans told the author that the Soviets contributed almost nothing to this and other ostensibly collaborative efforts except their names. The data and models were sent from the United States to Moscow, where Aleksandrov was chief of the Climate Modeling section of the Computing Center of the USSR Academy of Sciences. Aleksandrov later disappeared under mysterious circumstances while attending a scholarly conference in Spain, prompting his mother to beg Presidents Reagan and Bush to secure his release if he were held by the CIA. For more on the USSR and nuclear winter theory, see *Bulletin of the Atomic Scientists* 40, no. 4 (April 1984): 10S–13S. For subsequent research, see Starley L. Thompson and Stephen H. Schneider, "Nuclear Winter Reappraised," *Foreign Affairs* 64, no. 5 (Summer 1986): 981–1005, esp. 992, 1003.

13. Brezhnev's report to the Twenty-Fifth CPSU Congress in 1976 announced that 11 billion rubles would be allocated for environmental protection in the Tenth Five-Year Plan. Text in *Current Digest of the Soviet Press* 28, no. 8 (March 24, 1976): 17–18. For a review of Soviet policy and the literature, see Charles E. Ziegler, *Environmental Policy in the USSR* (Amherst: University of Massachusetts Press, 1987); see also Karl Schloegel, "Oekologiediskussion in der Sowjetunion," *Berichte des Bundesinstituts fuer ostwissenschaftliche und internationale Studien* (Cologne), no. 49 (1984); and in the same series, Wolf Oschlies, "Aus Sorge um 'Mutter Erde': Umweltschutz und Oekologiediskussion in Bulgarien," in ibid., no. 8 (1985).

14. Indeed, five Politburo members turned out for a Club of Rome computer demonstration in Moscow in 1977. Interview with Dr. Alexander King, Washington, D.C., February 4, 1987.

15. See Brezhnev's reply to questions posed by *Le Monde* and published in *Izvestiia*, June 16, 1977.

16. See *Literaturnaia gazeta*, no. 42 (1981); ibid., no. 7 (1985). For a review of the Soviet globalist literature, see V. A. Los', "Issledovaniia v oblasti global'nykh problem; itogi i perspektivy," *Voprosy filosofii*, no. 12 (1983); 143–50; also citations in Zagladin and Frolov, *Marksistsko-Leninskaia* and other citations that follow in this chapter. References to early ideological as well as legal literature are in Ginzburgs, "Soviet Union and the Biosphere."

17. D. M. Gvishiani quoted at greater length in Clemens, *U.S.S.R. and Global Interdependence*, p. 24.

18. Research by B. Welling Hall, Ohio State University and Earlham College, identifies three Soviet perspectives on global environmental problems: the polemical, the ecological, and the technological. See her "Soviet Views of Global Environmental Problems," presented at the International Studies Association Annual Meeting, Washington, DC, April 1987.

19. Ginsburgs, "Soviet Union and the Biosphere," p. 62.

20. The doctrine of *res naturae internationalis* was considered more progressive than *res naturae nullius* (an object any government could claim) or *res naturae communis* (connoting exclusive control of a resource by the first countries to exploit it). Ibid., pp. 60–61. As of 1966 the USSR had joined twenty international organizations studying the protection of nature and the rational utilization of natural resources (out of an estimated sixty-eight such agencies then functioning) and had signed forty agreements regulating aspects of the question (from a cumulative total of one hundred fifteen). See ibid., pp. 52–53. By 1970 a Soviet lawyer affirmed that "in the biosphere everything is interdependent." See Vladimir A. Chichvarin, *Okhrana prirody i mezhdunarodnye otnosheniia* (Moscow: Mezhdunarodnye otnosheniia, 1970), p. 21, cited in B. Welling Hall, "Soviet Perceptions of Global Ecological Interdependence: Some Implications of 'New Political Thinking,' " presented to the Midwest Slavic Association, Indiana University, March 25–26, 1988, p. 5.

21. *Global'nye problemy i mezhdunarodnye otnosheniia: materialy nauchnoi konferentsii*, ed. S. L. Tikhvinskii and others (Moscow: Diplomaticheskaia Akademiia MID SSSR, 1981). *Retsenzenty* (reviewers, censors) were I. G. Usachev and G. S. Khozin, whose book is discussed later. The printing was limited to 500 copies; price: 2 rubles for 416 pages; sent to press in January 1981.

22. Reimers looked back and said that "for a certain period it was possible to consider the biosphere for man as an unlimited metasystem [*nadsistema*] not placing any limits on his economic development." Of course there were limits, but they were regional rather than global in character. Only in the second half of the nineteenth century did scholars perceive the global impact of interaction between man and nature. "But it took an entire century to understand the reciprocal impact of a nature changed by humans." This impact is understood only superficially even now, said Reimers, because the price of a finished good is still the main factor in human consciousness. We use gross economic criteria to evaluate a ship leaking oil without factoring in the damage to the fish population and its importance to people who depend on fish for protein. N. F. Reimers, "Ecological Crisis and Horizons of the Future," *Global'nye Problemy*, p. 307.

23. Reimers called for radically new approaches to "econological" problems in many countries—including the USSR. Although Reimers specifically blamed the capitalist world for polluting the South, some of his remarks implied a grave critique of the USSR. "In a series of countries," he said, overpopulation had caused an increase in birth defects, an increase in illness, and "a reduction in the average life expectancy relative to levels recently attained." In addition, "mechanical resettling" of people to marginal areas (such as Siberia?) causes illness and other negative effects. Instead of depending on economic stimulation to encourage migration to marginal areas rich in resources, governments should try to create in such regions ecological conditions similar to those the workers left behind. These and many other suggestions made by Reimers could have appeared in *The Futurist*.

He also recommended the following: (1) concentrate industry and agriculture in certain areas to free other lands for ecological balance and for recreation, (2) stop pollution of the less developed countries by the "capitalist" world, and (3) close the circle of production and use—both regionally and globally—to minimize pollution and maximize econological values.

[139]

24. Ibid., p. 388.

25. A review of the conferences and literature on global problems from the late 1970s through 1983 is in Los', "Issledovaniia v oblasti."

26. I. T. Frolov, "Nauka—tsennosti—gumanizm" (Science—values—humanism), *Voprosy filosofii*, no. 3 (March 1981): 27–41 at pp. 40–41.

27. Vadim Valentinovich Zagladin, *Alzhirskaia problema* (Moscow: Znanie, 1957); idem, *Istoricheskaia missiia rabochego klassa i sovremennoe rabochee dvizhenie* (Moscow: Znanie, 1979). He also edited works on scientific communism, the revolutionary movement and nationalism, and relationships between the Western bourgeoisie and proletariat. Vadim Valentinovich should not be confused with Vladimir Viktorovich Zagladin, who also writes on international themes.

28. V. V. Zagladin, "Global'nye problemy i sotsial'nyi progress chelovechestva," *Voprosy filosofii*, no. 4 (April 1983): 87–101.

29. Ibid., p. 100.

30. Ibid., pp. 100–1; see also p. 89.

31. See chapter 3 of this book.

32. G. S. Khozin, *Global'nye problemy sovremennosti: kritika burzhuaznykh kontseptsii* (Moscow: Mysl', 1982), 279 pp., 20,000 printing.

33. Khozin made high claims for Soviet public health achievements, including the reduction of infant mortality. See ibid., p. 191.

34. Although Khozin and other Soviet commentators sometimes distort American writings, their footnotes show a deep curiosity and wide familiarity with the "other side"—qualities that are relatively rare in the other superpower. Of course Jerry Hough and many other Sovietologists diligently read Soviet writings; environmentalists such as Dennis Meadows work with Soviet colleagues; but most mainstream foreign policy specialists in the United States rarely footnote Soviet authors. The problem extends wider; many Soviets read American novels (at least in translation), but few Americans can name even one Soviet novelist except those condemned by the Kremlin for their deviations. Asked what *Soviet* writers they have read, many American college students reply, "Dostoevsky and Tolstoi."

35. The reports to the Club of Rome have been widely criticized also in the West from a variety of perspectives. Onuf, for example, asserts that the aims of founder Aurelio Peccei were to "alert the cosmopolitan '*haut-bourgeois*' class, whose concerns define contemporary liberalism, to the dangers facing the world in its present course, and to encourage corrective measures." See his "Reports to the Club of Rome"; for a discussion of hubris and utopianism in early Club work, see Clemens, "Ecology and International Relations." For a news report on successful implementation of some ideas in *No Limits to Learning* (issued by the Club in 1979), see "Governor's Schools Catching On," *The New York Times*, August 18, 1985, sec. 12.

36. Western evaluations of the 1986 Chernobyl disaster, Soviet commentators complained, exaggerated initial Soviet casualties and overstated structural differences between Soviet and Western reactors.

37. For a sharp critique published two years before Khozin's book, see, M. Volkov, "Kontseptsiia 'vzaimo-zavisimosti natsii i ideologiia neokolonializma," *MEMO*, no. 9 (1980): 71–72.

38. As I. Frolov makes clear, of course, not all "futurology" is bourgeois. To hold that view would be to hand over to the enemy many terms that could be filled with Marxist content. See *Literaturnaia gazeta*, no. 7 (1985): 14.

39. Some of these points are touched on in Khozin's book and in Zagladin's writings, but they are amplified in many entries in a "dictionary for Communist upbringing" published in 1984 but reflecting the Party's ideological concerns of 1982–83: *Kommunisticheskoe vospitanie: Slovar'*, eds. L. N. Ponomarev and Zh. T. Toshchenko (Moscow: Politizdat, 1984), initial printing: 300,000. On Peccei, see p. 104.

40. An Taeg-Won, "Economic Debates within Soviet Leadership Circles from 1972–82: 'Interdependency versus Autarky,' " *Sino-Soviet Affairs* (Seoul) 8, no. 2 (Summer 1984): 43–82. The article is a revised chapter of a Ph.D. dissertation at the University of Georgia, 1984.

41. Zagladin speaking on Hungarian radio, January 23, 1982, cited in ibid., p. 75.

42. See, for example, M. M. Maksimova, *Global'nye problemy i mir mezhdu narodami* (Moscow: 1982); and the collection *Marksizm-leninizm i global'nye problemy sovremmenosti* (Moscow, 1983), where Maksimova also has an article.

43. Iu. Feodorov, "SShA pered litsom global'nykh problem: rekomendatsii uchenykh i real'nosti politiki," *MEMO*, no. 6 (June 1983): 38–47. Despite the "communications revolution," it required three years for the State Department study to be printed by Penguin Books (2 vols., Harmondsworth, 1982) and to reach Feodorov in Moscow, and one more year for his review to appear in *MEMO*, by which time the Reagan administration had already passed the midpoint of its first term.

44. Ibid., p. 46.

45. Yuri Andropov replaced Brezhnev in November 1982; Chernenko succeeded Andropov in February 1984; Gorbachev took over formally in March 1985.

46. Chernenko added: "The capitalist countries should know that provided here is reciprocity, they will always have in the Soviet Union an honest and well-wishing partner ready to promote cooperation on the basis of equality and mutual benefit." Quoted in *The New York Times*, September 28, 1984, p. A13. On the same day, however, Foreign Minister Gromyko expressed skepticism about U.S. good intentions and called on Washington to translate its "verbal assurances" into "concrete deeds."

47. See James E. Goodby, "The Stockholm Conference: Negotiating a Cooperative Security System for Europe," in Alexander George, Philip J. Farley, and Alexander Dallin, eds., *U.S.-Soviet Security Cooperation: Achievements, Failures, Lessons* (New York: Oxford University Press, 1988), 144–72 at 161.

6
"Life Itself" versus the Party Line on Global Issues

The Soviet response to global problems has been multifaceted and often contradictory as narrow dogmatism encounters the demands of life itself. On each level of globalistic theory and practice there has been a tug-of-war between forces seeking international solutions to global problems and those militating for a Fortress Russia inversion. These forces arise from a crucible of Russian history and the legacy of communism fired by the challenges and opportunities of the environment at home and abroad. On balance, narrow dogmatism in recent decades has fought a losing battle against internationalizing praxis.

Chauvinism versus Cosmopolitanism in Russian Culture

Despite massive purges severely depleting the genetic and cultural pool of Soviet talent, courageous and gifted streams of Soviet scientists and scholars have sustained one another, survived, and produced a renaissance of critical thinking erupting in stages since Stalin's demise.[1]

Russia's leading globalist has been the "father of the Soviet H-bomb" and its leading dissident—Andrei D. Sakharov, whose 1968 "manifesto" called on the USSR and United States to take the lead in a program to redeem the planet.[2] Sakharov and other Soviet scientists stand on the shoulders of many generations who have strived to implement a global, even cosmic consciousness.

Globalism and environmentalism have a mixed heritage both in Marxism and in Russian tradition. In each domain there have been currents favoring both chauvinism and cosmopolitanism; also an exploitative as well as a nurturing attitude toward the biosphere. Russians have long been noted for their proclivity for grandiose visions and far-reaching solutions, as with the Third Rome or the Third International marching at the head of a regenerated humanity. Various factors may have contributed to this tendency: the endless steppe; the extremes of the Continental climate; the mystic tradition of the Orthodox Church unchecked by Renaissance or Reformation; a culture in which society is taught to look for guidance to a benevolent and all-knowing despot. Here is a society where radical reforms have long been imposed from the top down, where a capital city was built on swamplands, where huge canals have linked distant waterways, and where "constructive geologists" have proposed reversing directions of the largest rivers and raising the temperature of Siberian cities—a culture of two-volume novels, five-hour operas, and four-hour movies; a war machine that has tested by far the largest thermo-nuclear warhead ever (1961) and the largest rockets and nuclear sub-marines.

Many Russian scientists have espoused a holistic vision of man, matter, spirit, and knowledge. Mikhail Lomonosov (1711–65), for whom Moscow University is named, displayed an almost Da Vinci-like capacity to excel in many fields of knowledge. He was a grammarian, poet, chemist, metallurgist, geographer, historian, and tireless inventor. He taught the first course of physical chemistry in the world. The poet Aleksander Pushkin later referred to Lomonosov as the first Russian university.[3]

Pushkin himself benefited from rigorous training in the lycée established for children of the nobility under Alexander I and organized by V. F. Malinovskii (1765–1814), a diplomat who, while sojourning in England, wrote a visionary treatise on war and peace.[4] Although Pushkin was only a fair student in most subjects at the lycée, his poetry sparkles not only with a cosmopolitan knowledge of classical and European literature but with a sharp eye for the physical world. Himself trained to look outward, nevertheless Pushkin once warned: "But in foreign ways Russian grain does not grow."[5]

Another poet—Russia's Byron—Mikhail Lermontov (1814–41), mourned Pushkin's death by dueling only to meet the same fate. Like Pushkin, he was exiled to far-away places for his writings. One of the characters in Lermontov's *Hero of Our Time* notes some of the nuances of Russian globalism:

I was impressed against my will by the ability of the Russian to adapt to the customs of those peoples among whom he happens to live; I don't know whether this quality of mind warrants reproach or praise, only that it shows incredibly the Russian's flexibility and the presence of that clear common sense which forgives evil wherever it seems necessary or impossible to destroy.[6]

Despite the country's deep ambivalence about alien influences, tsarist Russia's scientific and educational establishments were long dominated by foreigners. Peter the Great had launched the Imperial Academy of Sciences as a way to cultivate native Russian science from imported seeds. The top layers of the academy would be foreign and the lowest tiers partly Russian. But only the top layer prospered, and the academy became an organization largely of foreigners, most of them German-speaking. The first Russian academician was not elected until twenty years after the birth of the society, and ethnic Russians did not gain control of the academy until the late nineteenth century.[7]

Even when some tsars and cultural magistrates sought to repress free thinking and practical subjects in education, Russia's science and arts kept important ties with the outer world. Although philosophy languished under Nicholas I, history and oriental studies flourished. In the second quarter of the nineteenth century St. Petersburg University offered courses on magnetism and electricity unmatched outside Russia. The Academy of Sciences established the Pulkovo observatory in 1839 with the largest telescope in the world, training American as well as European astronomers. Pulkovo later played an important part in the Soviet space program. Before the Crimean War a St. Petersburg chemist experimented with nitroglycerine in ways that aided Alfred Nobel to develop dynamite. Russians laid the world's first electrical telegraph—the St. Petersburg–Kronstadt link in 1835 (which, like the Petersburg-Warsaw line of 1839, was for military purposes). Russian mathematicians were very advanced in the theory of probability and by mid-century were building mechanical computers.[8] Russian explorers such as Bellingshausen (1778–1852), who circumnavigated Antarctica in 1819–21, and Mendeleyev (1834–1907), who published over five hundred works on chemistry, physics, aeronautics, meteorology, and agriculture, helped to advance the frontiers of knowledge in many fields.

Well before October 1917 there were in Russian science strong currents of revolutionary titanism and determination to transform the world.[9] Thus at the turn of the century Ivan Klingen led a three-year expedition to Egypt, India, Ceylon, and China to collect data, insights, and plants to nourish Russian agronomy. He felt himself much at home among English tea planters in Kandy and reflected on the ways that they had recovered from a coffee blight analogous to the catastrophe that overcame Russia's sunflower harvest some decades earlier.[10]

Also at the turn of the century the "gentile anarchist," Prince Petr Kropotkin, was developing an early version of sociobiology. Having studied the geography and wildlife of Siberia, and having been repressed in Russia and France for his radical political views, Kropotkin settled in London and took on the Social Darwinists, arguing that cooperation—"mutual aid"—is more important than individual struggle in raising life to higher forms.[11]

Some giants of Russian science who made major contributions before and after the Soviet Revolution were known for their strong spiritual beliefs as well as their studies of the material world. They included psychologist Ivan Pavlov (1849–1936) and Konstantin Tsiolkovsky (1857–1935), innovator in aerodynamics, rocketry, and airship theory, who was inspired to expand human consciousness through the universe.

Vladimir I. Vernadskii (1863–1945) adapted the concept of the noosphere from Teilhard de Chardin. Rather than a layer of thought over and above nature, Vernadskii saw the noosphere as a stratum of thought and work *immanent* in the biosphere, with humans becoming the most powerful geologic force. His worldview joined chemistry, physics, geology, and other sciences. His paeans to free thought are cited even by writers who otherwise defend Party dogma. Vernadskii has become the patron of the Soviet environmental movement.[12]

Other trends in Russian education and science have pushed for parochialism, especially the subjugation of knowledge to the whims of the Orthodox Church or Communist Politburo. The fact that Russian scientists had often scored firsts—often unknown or unrecognized in the West—strengthened scientific chauvinism under Stalin. Stalin also endeavored to purify Soviet science from external influences such as Einsteinian relativity, Freudian psychology, and Toynbeesque relativism. He launched campaigns against "cosmopolitanism"—campaigns that still echoed in the early 1980s. One of Stalin's targets was the physicist Petr Kapitsa, who returned to Russia in 1934 after a stint at Cambridge University. He was not allowed to leave the country again until the Khrushchev era, when he became a leading figure in the Pugwash movement with Western scientists.

Some Soviet champions of environmental protection have an internationalist, even cosmopolitan mindset; others are nativistic nation-alists. Some still believe in the Communist party and want only that it modify certain practices; others blame the Party for having raped and polluted the land, its culture, its churches and historic monuments. Their anger is joined by Ukrainians who blame Moscow for Chernobyl, by Armenians and Tadzhiks who castigate central authorities for careless construction in earthquake zones, by other nationalists who claim that local republics have lost control over their own borders and environmental destinies, and by a whole school of village writers who lament the destruction of village life (*mir* means not only "commune" but "world").[13] Whether these diverse concerns look inward toward greater self-reliance or outward toward international cooperation, they all contribute to an ecological awareness submerged during most of the Stalin and Khrushchev decades.[14]

Praxis

No matter whether détente or cold war dominated high politics, some Soviet officials and scholars pushed for East-West cooperation on global issues. If need be they would cover themselves by appropriate references to Marx, Lenin, and even Zagladin, but they persisted in seeking transnational modes to study and alleviate global problems. Their story illustrates the role that determined, creative individuals can play in forging constructive relationships among diffident societies.

Sometimes wearing a nongovernmental hat and other times that of a state official, Dzhermen M. Gvishiani helped to generate a number of East-West-South investigations of global problems in the 1970s and 1980s. Sometimes he acted as deputy director of the USSR State Committee on Science and Technology (GKNT), an agency of the Council of Ministers (headed by his father-in-law, Aleksei Kosygin). At other moments he could act in a nongovernmental capacity as director of the All-Union Research Institute for Systems Studies of the Academy of Sciences (VNIISI). Donning one or the other of these hats, Gvishiani helped to spark formation of the Club of Rome and took part in many of its meetings. He threw Soviet support behind an effort to create a joint Soviet-U.S. study (ECOMIN) based on a Club of Rome computer model and played a leading role in the successful establishment of the International Institute for Applied Systems Analysis (IIASA).

The Club of Rome

The Club of Rome was founded in 1968 by Italian industrialist Aurio Peccei in collaboration with Alexander King, whose meeting was sparked by Gvishiani.[15] Dedicated to sponsoring creative research on the predicament of mankind, the club has ranged in size from about seventy to one hundred members drawn from twenty to thirty nationalities. Their main premise has been that many components of the "world problematique" are interrelated and that long-term planning is needed to cope with global challenges. Gvishiani did not at first become a member, but he attended some planning meetings as well as conferences after the club was established.[16] In the 1970s he took an active role in club activities, but in the early 1980s he had to meet club members elsewhere—for example, at IIASA.

The club's first major project was *The Limits to Growth*, written by a team of scholars at MIT. Before the book's publication in 1972, King and other club members were invited to Moscow. They were invited again for a three-day meeting after the book appeared. Soviet scientists, King recalls, were polite but extremely skeptical about the report's findings.

Gvishiani's Institute for Systems Studies helped to organize a number of symposia to explore applications of systems analysis to global problems. Thus VIISI invited a number of club members to Moscow from August 30 to September 1, 1977, to review the World Integrated Model (WIM) developed by Mihajlo D. Mesarovic and Eduard Pestel for research that led to the second report to the Club of Rome: *Mankind at the Turning Point* (1974). There was an on-line demonstration of WIM over a telephone satellite link between Cleveland, where Mesarovic teaches at Case Western Reserve University, and Moscow. King recalls that pollution of Lake Baikal and other environmental issues were then quite salient in the USSR and that five Politburo members took part in the three-hour demonstration, some of them putting questions to the computer program. "Fortunately, the system did not break down."

ECOMIN, 1977–80

At the conclusion of the 1977 Moscow meeting, Gvishiani proposed development of a joint Soviet-U.S. effort employing WIM and its associated Assessment of Policies Tool (APT) to analyze some aspect of the world problematique. Both sides agreed that this joint effort should focus on the ways in which human activities and developmental processes

[148]

influence the global environment. The project was termed ECOMIN, from Ecology-Man-Interaction. Gvishiani pledged all necessary Soviet support through VNIISI, assuming that corresponding funds could be found in the United States. Several other leading Soviet scientists in climatology and environmental assessment expressed their personal interest in participating in this venture. Upon returning to the United States Mesarovic, with assistance from the U.S. Association for the Club of Rome (USA/COR), organized a working group to develop the project.[17]

While the search for ECOMIN funding continued in the United States, Gvishiani—now as deputy director of GKNT—called an international symposium on "Trends and Perspectives in Development of Science and Technology and Their Impact on the Solution of Contemporary Global Problems," to meet in Tallinn, Estonia, January 8–12, 1979.[18] The Tallinn meeting was one of four symposia around the world linked to preparations for the UN Conference on Science and Technology for Development later that year. It was sponsored jointly by the USSR State Committee on Science and Technology, the UN Advisory Committee on the Application of Science and Technology to Development, and—in fact, if not in the official papers—the Club of Rome.[19] Of the more than fifty foreigners invited, many were associated either with IIASA or the Club of Rome; others included officials from the UN Environmental Program, UNESCO, and other UN agencies. Gvishiani's invitation letter contained a provisional list of some thirty Soviet participants including G. Arbatov (USA and Canadian Institute), N. Inozemstev (Institute for World Economics and International Relations), E. Primakov (Far East Institute), and E. Velikhov (Academy of Sciences).

Addressing this symposium in January 1979, Gvishiani declared that "a number of qualitatively new problems—global problems—[call for] action on the entire world scale." The broad, comprehensive, multidisciplinary nature of these problems necessitated a systems approach and global modeling.

> Each national economy should not deal with its "own" natural environment only (as has been the case so far) but in some very important respects must also consider the entire ecosystem of the Earth. . . . We are confronted with the task of elaborating a scientific concept that would provide an understanding of not only the meaning and contents of modern economic, technological, and other problems, their cause-and-effect relationship, but also cover their external links, their interactions with societal and international processes.[20]

Other Soviet specialists reported on the global situation in energy, population, food, and natural resources. The USA/COR found that these papers were prepared "with a high degree of conscientiousness and

[149]

concern, and with a minimum of ideological discussion." Soviet representatives continued at Tallinn to plug for ECOMIN with their U.S.
counterparts.[21]

A few days following Tallinn, the Joint U.S.-USSR Commission on
Scientific and Technological Cooperation met in Moscow. The U.S. team
was headed by Dr. Frank Press, science and technology adviser to former
President Carter, and the Soviet delegation by V. A. Kirillin, deputy
chairman of the Council of Ministers and chairman of the USSR State
Committee for Science and Technology and Gvishiani's immediate
superior. Press, Kirillin, and U.S. Ambassador Malcolm Toon also met
with Chairman of the Council of Ministers A. N. Kosygin. The commission
reviewed cooperation carried out since the Soviet-U.S. agreement on
Cooperation in the Fields of Science and Technology signed May 24, 1972,
and the new agreement dated July 8, 1977. Both sides noted progress in
many fields of scientific cooperation and affirmed "their intention to
continue to further broaden and deepen existing scientific and technical
contracts." The commission planned its next session for the United States
in early 1980—a meeting not held owing to the Soviet actions in
Afghanistan in December 1979.[22]

Discussion of ECOMIN among the Americans and with the Soviets,
both in the United States and the USSR, continued from late 1977 into 1980.
The Americans became ever more convinced that Gvishiani and his
colleagues were committed to the project and could make substantive
contributions to it. Indeed, they prepared to downgrade the key role
originally expected for the WIM and APT to allow a broader gauged
approach making use also of Soviet simulations.[23] ECOMIN was aborted,
however, for lack of funding—governmental or private—to support the
U.S. share of the project.[24]

Many agencies were approached, but only the Department of
Agriculture showed much interest in the project.[25] Even before the Soviet
Afghan expedition, ECOMIN was dead in the Potomac. As with SALT II,
the invasion gave the quietus to bilateral cooperation of this kind.[26] The
Carter administration sponsored a major study of the dire prospects for
the environment by the year 2000, but it was unwilling to support a U.S.-
Soviet project to study aspects of the problem in more detail.[27] The director
of the Soviet office in the State Department advised USA/COR, however,
to "keep the initiative in proposing specific ideas for the research and
implementation steps" in his negotiations with Gvishiani![28]

Did Soviet actions in Afghanistan mean that the USSR had written
off bilateral cooperation with the West? A syndicated article by Daniel
Greenberg, "Cold War Cold Shoulder," appearing in the *Washington Post*

on January 29, 1980, said "yes." Greenberg pointed to Afghanistan, the recent exile of Andrei Sakharov to Gorki on January 22, and the resignation "without explanation" of Gvishiani's sixty-seven-year-old boss, Vladimir Kirillin, from the chairmanship of the State Committee for Science and Technology. These events, said Greenberg, have led "some of our leading proponents of technological collaboration with the Soviets" to conclude reluctantly "that the brutes are on top in Moscow" and that "the xenophobic old guard has won out over the new class of Western-oriented technocrats" such as the "Western tailored, jet-setting technocrat" Gvishiani. There was an "admirable kind of innocence in the notion that Soviet society, seeking the benefits of modern science and technology, would inevitably be softened by contacts with Western-style scholarship. Against the background of Afghanistan, Sakharov, and Kirillin, that congenial expectation now looks quite silly."

The silliness of this instant analysis was underscored by a more thorough study by Radio Liberty. It concluded that "Gurii Marchuk, the Soviet mathematician recently named to replace Vladimir Kirillin as deputy chairman of the USSR Council of Ministers and chairman of the State Committee for Science and Technology, is a man who evidently favors scientific and technological cooperation with the West as much as his predecessor." Officials at the State Department, the National Science Foundation, and the National Academy of Sciences all welcomed Marchuk's appointment and inferred that his promotion meant the USSR was still interested in scientific and technological ties with the West. American officials also noted that Gvishiani, far from falling out of favor, appeared in a favorable light on Soviet television six days after Kirillin relinquished his posts.[29] Marchuk, born in the Ukraine, retained both these hats until 1986, when he became president of the USSR Academy of Sciences. (In early 1989, however, thousands of Soviet scientists demonstrated and demanded Marchuk's resignation because the academy had refused to include Sakharov and Roald Sagdeev among its twenty-five delegates to the Congress of People's Deputies. Sakharov, visiting Boston in February 1989, was reluctant to discuss Marchuk's role, emphasizing instead institutional factors. By late spring another vote was held and the academy included Sakharov and Sagdeev among its delegates.)

Even though Gvishiani's father-in-law died in 1980 and he himself remarried, Gvishiani held onto his positions of influence. (Under Gorbachev he rose to become deputy chairman of Gosplan, only to lose this job in 1986–87 apparently for reasons of personality and perhaps ill health—not ideology.) Gvishiani's star was tied to the Party's enduring enthusiasm for the "Scientific-Technological Revolution." Who could oppose international cooperation to bring the best science and technology to the USSR? Gvishiani treated systems analysis as an apolitical problem-solving tool—just the thing for approaching global problems, even while socialism and capitalism contended. At times, however, Gvishiani looked like a medieval schoolman apologizing for his pursuit of objective knowledge gained by value-free methodologies.

An appeal for a truly scientific and humanistic approach to global challenges by Gvishiani appeared in *Problems of Philosophy* in March 1981. While other Soviet writers were coming to extol "Communist transformation" as the necessary and sufficient condition for the resolution of global problems, Gvishiani looked to a systematic synthesis of humanistic and natural science guided, of course, by the insights of dialectical materialism. What we need for such science to work, he said, is détente, arms limitations, and peace—not necessarily a Communist transformation. Indeed, he recognized that scientists of different countries were likely to perceive global challenges differently depending on the problems most pressing in their regions. He made a clear appeal for scientific modeling of alternative scenarios, utilizing huge quantities of statistical data as well as calculations about the human factor, to construct and test alternative hypotheses. He praised the principle of *systemnost'*—"system-ness," one might say in English. For an imprimatur Gvishiani quoted Brezhnev's report at the Twenty-Sixth Party Congress the previous month: "Life demands the fruitful collaboration of all states for the resolution of the peaceful, constructive tasks standing before each people and all humanity." Though Gvishiani had published before in *Problems of Philosophy*, he felt it necessary to defend in a footnote his use of "systematic analysis" from those who say that this approach ignores synthetic knowledge.[30]

IIASA

The International Institute for Applied Systems Analysis provides another case of East-West cooperation in global studies. Conceived in 1966 on former President Lyndon Johnson's initiative and finally established in 1972, IIASA was the product of long and delicate negotiations.[31] McGeorge Bundy, then president of the Ford Foundation, and National Academy of Sciences President Philip Handler represented the United States; Gvishiani was the principal Soviet representative. Both Bundy and Gvishiani wanted the institute to be multilateral to shield it from bilateral U.S.-Soviet tensions. Compromise bridged many differences. To facilitate participation by West and East Germany (the latter not then recognized by Washington), it was agreed that IIASA would be international but not intergovernmental. Representation would be through nationally recognized scientific organizations. The USSR and United States agreed jointly and equally to take leading roles in financing and managing the institute. Unique among international organizations, in IIASA both superpowers have equal assessments while the other fifteen national organizations pay smaller equal amounts. Practice has been that the IIASA Council chairman has been a Soviet (until 1987, Gvishiani); the director operationally in charge has been a North American. Early on it was agreed that English would be IIASA's official language and that the institute would be located in London. After Britain expelled many Soviet diplomats for spying, however, a site in France was considered. Finally, after five years of alternating polemics and negotiations, this outpost of modern science settled in a Hapsburg hunting lodge in Laxenburg near Vienna.

At first the Soviets wanted the institute to emphasize methodology—mathematical modeling—whereas the Americans wanted substance as well. Gradually the Soviets also opted for policy relevance. Initially leery of population studies, within two years they were criticizing IIASA for not doing demography. The institute then backed its way into the problem beginning with food and agriculture. By the early 1980s U.S. and Soviet scholars were collaborating in significant demographic inquiries.[32] First the Soviets sent "dismal" participants; the United States sent world-class scholars. To obviate selection problems in the USSR Gvishiani suggested that the Soviets send many scholars for two-month stints and that the director select those to be invited for longer periods. Initially the Soviet bureaucracy displayed anxiety about Soviet scholars working closely with Westerners, but the quality and number of Soviet participants in Laxenburg has steadily increased.[33]

Soviet participation in IIASA projects expanded from Gvishiani's systems research institute to include a large number of scientific institutions spread across the entire USSR. A sampling in 1983—a year of political inversion—is given on the next page in Table 6.1.

The number of IIASA projects in which Soviet institutions have collaborated is quite large, though it has lagged participation by U.S. organizations:

IIASA Projects	Cases of Soviet Collaboration	U.S. Collaboration
1979	21	32
1981	27	54
1983	48	75

[153]

TABLE 6.1

Examples of Soviet Participation in IIASA Projects, 1983

IIASA PROJECT	SOVIET INSTITUTION
Economic Structural Change and Industrial Adjustment	Central Economic-Mathematical Institute, Moscow
Mineral Trade	Mining Institute, Kola Branch of the USSR Academy of Sciences
Structural Change in the Forest Sector	Lithuanian Science Research Institute of Forestry, Lithuanian SSR Academy of Sciences, Vilnius
Integrated Regional and Urban Development	Faculty of Economics, Cybernetics and Finance, Vilnius State University
Energy Development	Siberian Power Institute, USSR Academy of Sciences, Siberian Branch, Irkutsk
Institutions and Environmental Policies	Laboratory for Climatic Monitoring, Moscow
Human Impacts on Environmental Systems	Institute of Water Problems, USSR Academy of Sciences, Moscow
National Agricultural Policies	Research Laboratory of Protein Substances and Food Analysis, Tbilisi State University, Georgian SSR
Population: Aging and Changing Lifestyles	Institute of Gerontology, Kiev
Systems and Decision Sciences	Institute of Control Sciences, Moscow
Adaptation and Optimization	Institute of Mathematics, University of Leningrad
Interactive Decision Analysis	Institute of Cybernetics, Ukrainian Academy of Sciences, Kiev
Information Dissemination	Institute of Economics and Industrial Engineering, USSR Academy of Sciences, Siberian Branch, Novosibirsk

SOURCE: *IIASA Annual Report, 1983* (Laxenburg): Appendix B, pp. 52–60.

In some fields a particular country collaborates extensively; in others, not at all. Thus in 1983 six Soviet institutions collaborated in studies of Adaptation and Optimization and nine in Information Dissemination; eleven U.S. institutions collaborated in System and Decision Sciences. However, neither superpower collaborated in studies of Institutional Settings and Environmental Policies, in which three Hungarian institutes took part. Indeed, collaboration by institutions from smaller countries such as Bulgaria, Canada, Hungary, Sweden, and—above all—Austria has exceeded that of the USSR and United States on a per capita basis.[34]

In March 1985 there were fifteen U.S. research scholars at IIASA, fourteen from the USSR, nine from Austria, and seven Australians providing scientific support staff. The other fourteen member countries had from one (France, Italy, Poland) to six (Federal Republic of Germany) research scholars at Laxenburg. Japan (with three scholars) is the only

[154]

non-Western country with membership in IIASA, but scholars from several Third World countries (e.g., Bangladesh, Kenya) have worked at IIASA for as long as two years.[35] Although some Westerners find it hard to believe that Soviet and Eastern European scholars would contribute meaningfully to IIASA, many Americans with experience there have commented on the importance of Soviet inputs to joint research projects— difficult-to-obtain data about the USSR as well as mathematical sophistication.[36] Some U.S. participants in IIASA projects, however, have regarded their Soviet colleagues as parasites. Some deny that good science can be produced in this setting but admit some gains for East-West understanding. Judgments may differ, of course, depending on individual experiences.

By the mid-1980s Soviet scholars were working with Raiffa to establish through IIASA a program on Processes of International Negotiations (PIN), an inquiry into "how to engage jointly in mutual problem-solving activities." Just how far IIASA was moving toward policy relevance could be seen in the fact that PIN proposed to study all phases of the negotiating process including pre- and postnegotiations and to range from conflict anticipation to conflict resolution and methods of dealing with noncompliance.[37] A spinoff from these deliberations was that Soviet scholars began to deliberate with Roger Fisher of Harvard Law School on how jointly to teach negotiating techniques and strategies. Soviet participation in these projects contributed commentaries on Western ideas and bibliographies that included a wide range of Western and Soviet writings on negotiation.[38] Soviet scholars found it more congenial to observe, learn, and comment than to venture original ideas, some Americans thought. But this process might give way, the Americans hoped, to more creative Soviet inputs. In 1988–89 Soviet participants in international conferences were volunteering papers on the most sensitive topics—from Soviet nationality policy to Moscow's foreign policy after Afghanistan (International Studies Association, London, April 1989).

Although many American research institutions (industrial as well as academic) claimed that they benefited substantially from participation in IIASA projects, the Reagan administration in 1981–82 cut off U.S. governmental funding for IIASA.[39] The National Academy of Sciences in Washington then surrendered its position as national member organization to the American Academy of Arts and Sciences in Cambridge, where private sources have sustained U.S. obligations on a tenuous basis. When the American Academy could meet only half its dues obligations in 1984, the Soviet Academy paid its 1985 dues early to cover a general shortfall.[40] Attempting to reverse course, in October 1984 former Secretary of State

[155]

George Shultz indicated that the State Department would give "sympathetic consideration" to requests by U.S. governmental agencies to fund participation in specific IIASA projects. But when the National Science Foundation, the Department of Energy, and the Environmental Protection Agency made such requests in 1985, they became stalled in the National Security Council. The result, according to an editorial in *Science* (August 15, 1986) was that "the credibility of the United States as a partner" in the IIASA consortium reached "its lowest point ever, paralleling the more general worldwide dismay at the American failure to put up funds for some of the collaborative long-term research programs interrupted by this country's walkout from UNESCO."[41]

Considering the fiscal and political obstacles to funding U.S. participation in ECOMIN and IIASA, one is struck by the contrast between U.S. rhetoric about global interdependence and U.S. action—even during the Carter years. Even when the Soviet Communist party expressed suspicion about the aims and methods of Western studies of the world problematique without a "class" perspective, elements of the Soviet bureaucracy were able actively to support such studies.

The former deputy executive director of the United Nations Environmental Program, on returning to the United States after twelve years, was struck by the "prevalence of a 'bottom line' mentality strongly resembling what used to be called 'compartmentalized thinking.' " He found this the more surprising because the United States has done much to stimulate multidisciplinary and holistic approaches and flexibility in curriculum development.[42] Apart from their sometimes Manichaean *Weltanschauung*, Americans may yearn for simple, quick answers. They may also be reluctant to invest in international inquiries that they cannot dominate. The USSR, at least in principle, looked to long-term investigations of complex phenomena.

Does Low Politics Lead or Lag High Politics?

Is arms control progress a condition for the initiation and continuation of East-West cooperation in low political activities such as IIASA? If low-level cooperation flourishes, will this promote détente? Will the domains of low and high politics converge as the globe becomes more interdependent? Answers to such questions are elusive but important. They are interesting to social scientists and vital to policy planning.

Analysis is difficult for many reasons. The dividing line between high and low politics is sometimes nebulous. Trade in computers, for example, could relate to either sphere. What seems to be a trade fair could be a front for espionage.[43]

Soviet commentators do not generally distinguish between high and low politics. Their lists of global problems include both the danger of war and such problems as environmental protection. Soviet political and philosophical analyses usually treat all global issues—even pollution—in a political-economic context. To be sure, many Soviet scholars who espouse an ecological or technocratic approach to environmental issues often attempt to minimize or set aside the political framework of their topic. In some narrow scientific settings this is feasible, but in journals such as *Voprosy filosofii* (*Problems of Philosophy*) their writings usually appear next to ideological commentaries by zealous interpreters of the Party line.

Establishing leads and lags is difficult also because scholarly and even propaganda publishing inevitably lags political events. Censors might not be able to catch up and stop publication of an article approved before a drastic change in the Party line. Further, journals such as *Priroda* (*Nature*) have operated under less political guidance than *Kommunist* or *MEMO*.

With these and other caveats, it is likely that a crude Marxist interpretation best explains the facts. Problems in the material environment motivated Brezhnev's 1971 Peace Program and its drive to expand trade with the West. Soviet attainment of strategic parity in the 1970s made it safe to downgrade the likelihood of East-West war. Meanwhile, environmental problems in the USSR were swelling to a critical mass sufficient to attract the attention of top leaders. Brezhnev needed to find an ideological rationale to justify his opening to the West. Part of it he found in the "scientific-technological revolution"; another in "global problems."

Not by accident, an enterprising Georgian, son-in-law of the Soviet premier (whose family even lived with Kosygin's for a time), led in establishing scientific links with the West. Deputy Chairman of the State Committee on Science and Technology Gvishiani carried out the logic of Kosygin's quest for trade and other tools to raise Soviet living standards. Gvishiani characterized his approach as systems analysis, a branch of science standing above ideological and political differences (but also one with some promise of salvaging the economic planning procedures of Soviet socialism).

Gvishiani's kind of low politics became more feasible when high politics embraced détente. The impetus for scientific exchanges with the West went back decades, but the Soviet stake in such exchanges grew deeper as the pace of the scientific revolution accelerated globally. The barriers to low political exchanges between East and West lowered throughout the early 1970s. As one leading Soviet scholar noted:

> The policy of détente made it possible to achieve major results in developing radically new systems of cooperation in the sphere of interstate relations in studying, protecting, and utilizing the environment. During a very brief historical period a ramified global network of cooperation systems developed at all levels—multilateral and bilateral. . . . In conditions of détente it became possible to adopt a number of measures designed to hold back the arms race, including some in the nuclear and geophysical fields that bear directly on the environment and on prospects for solving ecological problems.[44]

Soviet practitioners of low politics did not shorten their strides just because President Ford exorcised the word "détente" from his 1976 campaign. Both the Kremlin and the White House continued to give each other mixed signals for the rest of the decade. To be sure, détente was dying on the sands of the Ogaden and in the halls of Congress, but there was also movement toward curbing nuclear tests and even toward SALT II. Only when the USSR invaded Afghanistan and Washington mounted sanctions in 1980 was it clear that détente had given way to a new cold war.

Soviet supporters of East-West exchange tried to sustain the momentum generated in the previous decade. Their activities in IIASA did not slacken. Kremlin propaganda, however, now stressed that global problems could not be effectively resolved until capitalism was overthrown. This inflection—a predictable response to the cold war climate—could not contain the enthusiasm of scientists and poets who had lived too long behind an Iron Curtain and wanted to remove it.

Although Soviet-U.S. relations at the highest levels remained nearly deadlocked until Gorbachev's accession, there was movement in many arenas even in late 1984–early 1985:

—A previously scheduled bilateral consultation on nuclear proliferation was held in Moscow in November 1984, resulting in an accord to meet twice a year in alternate capitals.
—The U.S. secretary of agriculture and Soviet minister of agriculture announced in December 1984 the resumption of U.S.-Soviet scientific and technological exchanges on agriculture after a five-year lapse.
—The U.S. undersecretary of commerce led a delegation to Moscow in January 1985 to explore expanded trade in nonstrategic goods and services.

—The U.S. Coast Guard and Soviet Merchant Marine Ministry explored procedures for search and rescue missions in the North Pacific.
—Technical discussions on the Alaska boundary continued.
—Two health agreements signed in the early 1970s were continued in force through 1987.
—The 1972 U.S.-Soviet Agreement on the Prevention of Incidents at Sea was extended for another three years.
—The White House affirmed its interest in renewing the 1958 cultural agreement lapsed after the Afghan invasion; the establishment of consulates in Kiev and New York, agreed to in 1974 but moribund since the KAL incident in 1983; the 1973 oceanography agreement that expired in 1984; and plans for a space rescue mission and for top-level military exchanges.[45]

These and similar projects would gain momentum in the second half of the decade, but "life itself" had pushed for their realization even when Moscow and Washington were at loggerheads over Afghanistan and Star Wars.

The struggle of certain Soviets and Americans to keep IIASA alive through the bout of renewed East-West tensions paid off. IIASA survived, though its budget was slashed and the ratio of superpower dues to that of others was halved. When Reagan-Gorbachev summitry signaled and caused a shift back to détente, many structures of low politics were still there waiting to be reanimated. After Defense Secretary Caspar Weinberger and his arch hawk aide Richard Perle departed the Pentagon in late 1987, the Washington bureaucracy notified the American Academy of Arts and Sciences that it could count on substantial sums in 1988–89 to support specific IIASA projects (though not IIASA as an institution).[46]

Lyndon Johnson had sponsored IIASA to improve American-Soviet relations at the level of low politics; Soviet scientists and some politicians approved, probably to get access to Western science and technology more than for détentist motives. When high politics became tense, low politics helped maintain East-West working relationships. When détente returned to high politics, IIASA and the Club of Rome were among the nongovernmental bodies ready and waiting to step up the pace.

The struggle between conservative ideology and pragmatic cooperation beyond the borders represents an ancient theme in Russia's history extending back to Peter the Great and beyond. Manifestations of this contest in recent decades reflect a growing pluralism within Soviet society, triggered in part by the imperatives of modern science and the escalating interdependencies of our times. These imperatives do not support a full-

[159]

blown theory of technological determinism or convergence, but they certainly show the difficulty for any state—specially a would-be superpower—to stand aloof from the main breeding grounds of science and technology. For countries as for individual scholars and firms, breakthroughs will come more readily if they are part of the critical mass that pushes the leading edges in innovation and application. The lagging pace of Soviet economic and technological development strengthens the arguments of those who plead, in effect, "If we can't beat 'em, join 'em."

The evolution of Soviet thinking on global problems conforms to a larger pattern of secular but uneven movement in the USSR away from dogmatism, revolution, and totalitarianism toward relative pragmatism, liberalism, and cosmopolitanism. In a sense it represents a victory of Westernizers over Slavophiles. The speed and extent of this victory depends on global developments as well as those endogenous to the USSR. Soviet leaders will probably be more inclined to endorse this trend when their values are rewarded rather than frustrated or punished.

Where all life has been politicized, low politics will tend to lag high politics.[47] But low politics has its own imperatives and rewards. Absent a highly charged confrontation between the superpowers, these imperatives gain momentum and may help to shape high politics—at least at the margins. In the long run they could provide a deeper foundation for peace than tinkering with weapon counts. As the priority of world revolution was subordinated to socialism in one country in the 1920s, the late twentieth century may see Moscow reinterpret Soviet interests to accommodate the imperatives of the biosphere. This was one promise of the "new thinking" that emerged in the Kremlin in the mid-1980s.

The new thinking called for breakthroughs on all levels: East-West security and trade, cultural, and other exchanges. "Global problems" were now seen in the context of once maligned "interdependence." And the president of the Club of Rome was welcomed by Gorbachev to Moscow. Soviet ideologists no longer spoke of globalistika. Instead of claiming that Soviet science allied with Marxism had all the answers, the Kremlin now sponsored a search for answers based on the experiences of all countries. This quest is analyzed in the chapters that follow.

Notes

1. See Walter C. Clemens, Jr., "Russia's Critical Intelligentsia," *Worldview* 23, no. 8 (August 1980): 5–8; idem, "Alexander Yanov—Writing between the Lines," *Problems of Communism* 17, no. 3 (May–June 1978): 65–68. For background, see Loren R. Graham,

Science and Philosophy in the Soviet Union (New York: A. A. Knopf, 1972); Alexander Vucinich, *Empire of Knowledge* (Berkeley: University of California Press, 1984); Aleksey E. Levin, "Expedient Catastrophe: A Reconsideration of the 1929 Crisis at the Academy of Sciences," *Slavic Review* 47, no. 2 (Summer 1988): 261–79. For three letters from Petr Kapitsa to Soviet leaders protesting political repression of Soviet scientists in 1936, 1937, and again in 1980 (the cases of A. D. Sakharov and Iu. F. Orlov), see *Sovetskaia Kul'tura*, May 21, 1988, p. 6. In the late 1980s the Soviet press often cited such acts of political courage in earlier periods of Soviet history.

2. Sakharov's 1968 manifesto, however, seemed to understate the need for and feasibility of population controls in the Third World. It also proposed a rather unrealistic "fifteen-year tax equal to 20 per cent of national incomes" of developed countries to generate aid for less developed countries. See his *Progress, Peaceful Coexistence and Intellectual Freedom* (New York: W. W. Norton, 1968); for a further evaluation, see Walter C. Clemens, Jr., "Sakharov: A Man for Our Times," *Bulletin of the Atomic Scientists* 27, no. 10 (December 1971): 4–6, 51–56; idem, "Sakharov: Why He Deserves the Peace Prize," *Christian Science Monitor*, September 26, 1973.

Although Sakharov helped to instigate global thinking in the post-Stalin USSR, he told me in February 1989 (Boston) that he had never heard of globalistika and implied that he had no use for journals such as *Voprosy filosofii* and *Kommunist*. He had heard of D. Gvishiani and his systems analysis institute but expressed no enthusiasm for Gvishiani's work or that of his institute.

3. Nicholas V. Riasanovsky, *A History of Russia*, 4th ed. (New York: Oxford University Press, 1984), 296–97. On tsarist Russia's lag in organizing science, see Loren R. Graham, *The Soviet Academy of Sciences and the Communist Party, 1927–1932* (Princeton, NJ: Princeton University Press, 1967), chap. 1. Many Russian scientists of great distinction emerged in the nineteenth and early twentieth centuries, but they tended to excel in theory rather than in application. Graham evaluates the role of dialectical materialism in shaping Soviet science in *Science and Philosophy in the Soviet Union*.

4. V. F. Malinóvskii, *Rassuzhdenie o mire i voine*, 2 pts. (St. Petersburg: pri Gubernskom Pravlenii, 1803); also see his *Izbrannye obshchestvenno-politicheskie sochineniia* (Moscow: Akademiia nauk SSSR, 1958), issued in 2000 copies; on the work of Malinovskii at the lycée, see D. F. Kobeko, *Pervyi direktor Tsarskosel'skogo litseia* (Petrograd: Senatsk. tip., 1915).

5. *"No na chuzhoi maner russkii khelb ne roditsia"—Baryshnia-krest'ianka*.

6. M. Iu. Lermontov, *Geroi nashego vremeni* (Kiev: Goslitizdat Ukrainy, 1954), 23.

7. In 1880 Mendeleyev failed to gain election to the academy; he was blackballed by ten opponents, mostly Baltic Germans, who favored one of their own. See Graham, *Soviet Academy of Sciences*, pp. 16–21.

8. J. N. Westwood, *Endurance and Endeavor: Russian History, 1812–1980*, 2d ed. (Oxford: Oxford University Press, 1985), 55–56; Riasanovsky, *History of Russia*, pp. 352–53.

9. Riasanovsky uses these terms to characterize aspects of Soviet science (p. 581), but they extend back at least to Peter the Great.

10. L. N. Klingen, *Sredi patriarkhov zemledeliia narodov blizhnego i dal'nego vostoka: Egipet. Indiia. Tseilon. Kitai* (Moscow: Gosudarstvennoe izdatel'stvo sel'skokhoziiastvennoi literatury, 1960). Klingen (1851–1922) brought back over two tons of seeds and seedlings including thousands of tea plants and orange trees. Klingen's work is discussed in *Sovetskaia agronomiia*, no. 6 (1949); his monumental opus was reissued with a long introduction just after N. S. Khrushchev collected hybrid corn in Iowa.

11. Kropotkin returned to Russia after the February 1917 revolution. His name is immortalized in a Moscow metro station, if not in political practice.

12. His book *The Biosphere* was published in 1924. A Vernadskii Gold Medal and Vernadskii Prize have been established in his honor. In 1984 the Gold Medal went to Academician Aleksandr Ronov for his studies of "The Structure, Composition and Development of the Earth's Sedimentary Mantle." He is said to have initiated a new line of research—evolutionary geochemistry. The 1984 prize went to Erik Galimov for studies of

"Biological Fractionation of Isotope Methods in Oil and Gas Geochemistry." His "publications have no analogue in world literature on the subject. They validate Vladimir Vernadskii's ideas on the biological origin of the oil and gas carbon." So stated *Soviet Science and Technology 85* (Moscow: Novosti Press Agency, 1985), 172–73.

13. See, for example, Valentin Rasputin, *Povesti* (Moscow: Sovetskaia Rossiia, 1986), especially the story "Proshchanie c Materoi."

14. See also John B. Dunlop, *The Faces of Contemporary Russian Nationalism* (Princeton, NJ: Princeton University Press, 1983).

15. In 1967 Gvishiani attended a meeting in New York of the UN Committee for Science and Technology for Development. There he found a copy of a speech by Aurelio Peccei, put at the desks of all delegations by members of the U.S. delegation who found Peccei's remarks interesting. The lecture had been delivered at a military academy in Argentina, where Peccei had once been country director for Fiat. Returning to Moscow, Gvishiani read Peccei's lecture and wanted to contact him but did not know how, as his affiliations were not stated on the U.S. handout. Gvishiani then wrote to MIT Professor Carroll Wilson, a colleague at the UN Committee, asking how to find Peccei. Wilson, not knowing Peccei either, sent Gvishiani's inquiry to Dr. Alexander King, then head of the Science Department, Organization for Economic Development and Cooperation in Paris, with the terse comment: "This is what we should be thinking about."

King contacted Peccei, and the two met several times in Paris and elsewhere. The following year Peccei convened several meetings of intellectual and industrial leaders, and the Club of Rome took root. Based on an interview with Dr. Alexander King (successor to Peccei as president of the Club of Rome in 1984) in Washington, D.C., February 4, 1987, and on King, "Looking Back at the Future," *The USACoR Newsletter*, 11, no. 1 (January 1987): 23–24.

16. In the mid-1960s Jerome B. Wiesner, science adviser to former Presidents Kennedy and Johnson, flew around the USSR with Dr. and Mrs. Gvishiani. Asked whether the USSR might join the international copyright and patent systems, Gvishiani replied, "No. We just don't have the foreign currency. We wouldn't pay and then you'd be angry with us." On another occasion Wiesner sent Gvishiani a telegram asking whom he would like invited to a dinner in the United States. The modest answer: Henry Ford and Thomas Watson of IBM. At dinner Gvishiani sat between them and proposed that they build plants in the USSR. They refused. "But you could earn 200 million," Gvishiani protested. "Yes, but we'd lose our technology," one replied. Interview with J. B. Wiesner, March 25, 1987. Despite Watson's reluctance at that time, and despite some Soviet efforts in the opposite direction, Soviet computers eventually were made IBM-compatible and use MS-DOS as their program system.

17. The group included Donald Lesh, executive director of USA/COR; Gerald O. Barney, then director of the Year 2000 Project for the Council on Environmental Quality and the State Department; Thomas F. Malone, director of the Holcomb Research Institute at Butler University and foreign secretary, National Academy of Sciences; and Pierre Shostal, executive secretary for the U.S.-USSR Environmental Protection Agreement, Environmental Protection Agency. The group reported in January 1982 that the project could be best pursued under the auspices of the U.S.-USSR Agreement on Cooperation in Environmental Protection. It suggested as a candidate for analysis the impact of weather variability on world food supply and the consequences for population growth and living standards in both developed and developing countries. See "ECOMIN (ECology-Man-INteraction): A Joint USA/USSR Project to Study Trends in Human Interaction with the Global Environment." Second draft, USA/COR, January 1978. Material on ECOMIN is from USA/COR files, supplemented by interviews with Donald Lesh in 1985.

18. Letter from Gvishiani dated November 24, 1978, sent to Mesarovic and other invitees.

19. "Comments on the Tallinn Meeting," memorandum of the USA/COR, February 9, 1979, p. 1.

20. Ibid., pp. 1–3.

21. Ibid., p. 4.

22. Joint Press Release of the Commission, February 7, 1979. For a guardedly positive appraisal of Soviet-U.S. cooperation in the 1970s, see Loren R. Graham, "How Valuable Are Scientific Exchanges with the Soviet Union?" *Science* 202, no. 4366 (October 27, 1978): 383–90; also see Clemens, *The U.S.S.R. and Global Interdependence*, 86–99. All these developments are put in context in Linda L. Lubrano, "The Political Web of Scientific Cooperation," in Nish Jamgotch, Jr., ed., *Sectors of Mutual Benefit in U.S.-Soviet Relations* (Durham, NC: Duke University Press, 1985), 50–82 at 62–68.

23. Memorandum to ECOMIN Working Group from Donald R. Lesh, February 9, 1979, summarizing observations of Mesarovic and others.

24. Details of funding are summarized in a letter from Lesh to Mesarovic, September 20, 1979.

25. Letters from Donald R. Lesh to William T. Shinn, Jr., Director, Office of Soviet Union Affairs, Department of State, December 11 and December 14, 1978; Shinn to Lesh, December 27, 1978. See also Gvishiani to Mesarovic at Case Western Reserve University, January 9, 1979. Additional letter of Lesh to Shinn on February 9, 1979, and to Richard Livingston in the U.S. Environmental Protection Agency, February 15, 1979, inviting them to send observers to a meeting of an ECOMIN working group.

26. A letter from Mesarovic to USA/COR board member John A. Harris IV on January 9, 1980, speaks of the new difficulties in U.S.-Soviet relations (presumably Afghanistan) making U.S. government support "out of the question"—even from the Department of Agriculture, the best prospect until then. Mesarovic hoped still to pursue "international" avenues such as IIASA and the UN Environmental Program, but those efforts also got nowhere.

27. The Working Group wanted support for up to five person/years at the senior professional level for the first ECOMIN study, plus clerical and staff support. See Lesh memorandum, February 9, 1979.

28. Letter from William T. Shinn, Jr., December 27, 1978.

29. There was no evidence that Kirillin had ever supported Sakharov, but documentation showed that Marchuk had signed several letters protesting Sakharov's public activities. See Robert Rand, "Kirillin's Successor Said to Favor Ties with the West," *Radio Liberty Research Bulletin*, RL 47/80, January 31, 1980.

30. D. M. Gvishiani, "Nauka i global'nye problemy sovremennosti," *Voprosii filosofii*, no. 3 (1981): 97–108. His report summarized research on "Modeling of Global Development" and "Science and Social Development" led by the author at the VNIISI and GKNT. "Is Gvishiani truly a systems analyst?" some Americans were asked. "At least he is a philosopher of systems analysis," one replied. Two Soviet mathematicians who had worked at IIASA in the 1980s called Gvishiani an opportunist, not appreciating how much their own travels owed to his "opportunism." Raiffa, on the other hand, perceived him as a courageous and creative innovator.

31. Sources include Charter of the International Institute for Applied Systems Analysis (Laxenburg, Austria, 1972 and revised 1978); David Irons, "Across Political Lines," *Harvard Magazine* (May–June 1986): 32–38; Howard Raiffa, director of IIASA, 1972–75, comments at Russian Research Center symposium "Negotiating with the Soviets," Harvard University, May 5, 1986, and interview, July 28, 1986.

32. See the September 5, 1983 letter from James W. Vaupel, Duke University, to Howard Raiffa on file at the American Academy of Arts and Sciences, Cambridge, Massachusetts.

33. The number and diversity of Western organizations also increased. American institutions have included the Bureau of Industrial Economics, U.S. Department of Commerce; the Federal Reserve Board; private industrial groups such as the National Forest Products Association and the Weyerhaeuser Company; nonprofit research groups such as the Brookings Institution, the RAND Corporation, and Resources for the Future; as well as university groups such as the Institute for Demographic and Economic Studies, Yale University, and the School of Business, University of Kansas.

34. *IIASA Annual Reports* for 1979, 1981, 1983.

35. IIASA Scientific Staff List.

36. Many testimonial letters are in IIASA files at the American Academy of Arts and Sciences.

37. See *Proposal for an International Research Program on the Processes of International Negotiations* (Laxenburg, Austria, revised July 25, 1985).

38. V. A. Kremenyuk, V. B. Lukov, V. M. Sergeyev, "Toward Systemic Research of Negotiations," Background Paper for the Task Force Meeting on PIN, Laxenburg, December 9–10, 1985; "Information Document" prepared by the Institute for Scientific Information in Social Sciences (INION) of the Academy of Sciences of the USSR for the same Task Force Meeting.

39. The Reagan administration said that the $2 million annual dues could not be justified in light of budget cuts and competing requirements. Despite an incident in which a Soviet, head of the IIASA secretariat, used his appointment to pry into sensitive aspects of North Sea gas, the possibility that the West was losing technological secrets through IIASA was low. See also Chester L. Cooper, "Vienna Institute Prospers," *Bulletin of the Atomic Scientists* (December 1985): 49–51.

40. In 1984 the Soviets lowered their pledge to meet a lower U.S. target set for the United States; the Soviets paid their pledge, but the American Academy fell short. Poland, Hungary, East Germany, and Bulgaria all requested and received special treatment; and the United Kingdom withdrew from IIASA altogether. See Cooper, "Vienna Institute Prospers," p. 50.

41. William D. Carey, "The United States and the IIASA Connection," *Science* 233, no. 4765 (August 15, 1986): 701.

42. Peter S. Thacher, "Learning to Cope with Multi-Dimensional Problems," *Social Education* 49, no. 3 (March 1985): 207–10 at 209. See other articles in this issue's special section "Teaching about the Global Environment."

43. The CIA estimated in 1987 that about a third of the USSR Chamber of Commerce and Industry personnel were KGB officers. See *Intelligence Collection in the USSR Chamber of Commerce and Industry* (Washington, DC: Department of State, n.d.), iii.

44. N. N. Inozemstev, *Global Problems of Our Age* (Moscow: Progress Publishers, 1984), quoted in B. Welling Hall, "Global Problems and Nongovernmental Actors in Soviet Theory: Some Preliminary Findings" (unpublished manuscript, Ohio State University, Columbus, Ohio, July 1985), p. 10.

45. American Committee for U.S.-Soviet Relations, *East/West Outlook* 8, no. 1 (Washington, DC, January 1985), p. 5.

46. The Washington bureaucracy, including the National Science Foundation, insisted that the American Academy apply for funding for specific IIASA projects. This would help subject them to the usual NSF peer review procedure and reduce ideological criticism from the right for supporting an East-West exchange. The effect, however, was to keep IIASA insecure and minimally funded. It also created some leverage for Washington to determine the institute's agenda and modus operandi—the kind of leverage that Moscow had sought in the early years of IIASA but then surrendered under U.S. pressure.

The American Academy requested some $3 million in 1987–88 but was told that Washington might authorize about $1 million for IIASA projects in 1989; meanwhile, General Electric Company received a contract for nearly $236 million for one aspect of SDI research. See *The New York Times*, May 13, 1988, p. D1.

For background on the American Academy, the author wishes to thank Alan McDonald and Howard Raiffa.

47. On the other hand, "ping pong diplomacy" helped to usher in Sino-U.S. détente in the early 1970s, showing that low politics can sometimes be a servant of high. Athletic events can exacerbate or ameliorate political tensions. The United States led a boycott of the 1980 Olympics in Moscow because of Afghanistan; the USSR reciprocated in kind four years later at Los Angeles. The Korean Olympics had the potential to mend fences or erect barricades between Seoul and the Communist states including North Korea.

III
Gorbachev's New Thinking:
Security with Interdependence

7

A Revolution in Soviet Ideology: Speaking the Unthinkable

Multiple shock waves emanated from the Kremlin beginning in 1985 as the new general secretary launched campaigns to create a new Soviet citizen and a new orientation at home and abroad. Within the USSR the "new political thinking" was encapsulated in the slogans *glasnost'*, *perestroika*, and *demokratiia*. Deriving from the word for "voice," glasnost' sought to publicize viewpoints, grievances, and shortcomings; perestroika aimed at restructuring the economy; demokratiia sought to revitalize Soviet political life and overcome widespread apathy, stagnation, and even corruption.

A new approach gradually unfolded under Gorbachev. It built upon limited collaboration with bourgeois governments in the West and the Third World, focusing on arms control, conflict resolution, and trade; it also supported the territorial status quo. But it dropped the "kto kovo?" premise of earlier Soviet policy, urging serious efforts at mutual gain in a world of global interdependence. There was little effort at "indirect advance" of communism and none by a forward strategy.

Gorbachev wanted to integrate new political thinking into foreign as well as domestic policy. Gone was Brezhnev's complacency that strategic parity could ensure security; gone was the Brezhnev-Andropov denial of global interdependence. In place of these attitudes came a new openness and willingness to admit past mistakes including actions that made other countries apprehensive about the USSR.

Some elements of the new thinking had been virtually unthinkable before 1985—for example, letting a Polish leader hint in *Kommunist* at "blank spots" still to be addressed in the World War II history of Poland and the USSR.[1] Or if such thoughts had been thought, they would have been unspeakable except among trusted intimates.[2] Rather than ducking human rights debate, the Kremlin pressed its "Helsinki" partners to convene a human rights parley in Moscow in 1991.

But there was also much old wine in the new bottles. Many of Gorbachev's ideas—acceleration and discipline at home; interconnectedness in the world—borrowed from his predecessors. Even the term "new thinking" derived from a 1984 book coauthored by the son of the "old" foreign minister. Gorbachev's ideas were not original, nor did they come in a preset package. They grew like topsy, becoming bolder as he grew more confident and as the country's economy became more desperate.

Gorbachev came to endorse seven key propositions aimed at giving a new face and content to Soviet military and foreign policy:

(1) The needs of all humanity take priority over class, national, or other interests.

(2) All countries are now interdependent even while contradictions remain among them.

(3) Security must be mutual between the Soviet Union and the United States; among all nations it must be universal.

(4) War, in the nuclear age, cannot be an effective way to "continue" politics. Even local wars can escalate. Political dialogue and compromise are the proper way to resolve disputes.

(5) Military parity between the superpowers and the threat of nuclear retaliation do not guarantee peace; therefore arms levels must be reduced and nuclear arms gradually eliminated; the transition from the present situation to a nonnuclear world must be guided by the principle of strategic stability.

(6) Military deployments should be guided by "reasonable sufficiency"—adequate for defense but inadequate to threaten others.

(7) Comprehensive "security" must include economic as well as military-political dimensions. In short, the "all-human problems" facing the "whole of civilization" demand cooperation from and with all countries.

In these principles there was both hope and uncertainty. Although many of Gorbachev's reforms had roots in previous periods of Soviet history, they endeavored to break from the extreme alternatives of War

Communism (1917–21)—dogma, command, coercion—and the laissez-faire of the New Economic Policy (1921–27/8) with its more moderate and less overtly Communist approach to domestic and foreign policy. Could a new synthesis be reached eliciting energy without dictatorship, freedom without stagnation?[3] Another challenge for Gorbachev was to "reframe Soviet policies without jeopardizing the major strategic and political gains of the 1970s—and his own position with them." He sought to revive the instruments of Soviet diplomacy to project a more positive, dynamic, and conciliatory image of the USSR and to extricate the USSR from dead-end positions without threatening Moscow's geostrategic interests and alliances.[4]

How to implement new thinking in Soviet diplomacy was outlined in a Gorbachev speech at the Foreign Ministry on April 23, 1986, parts of which were summarized or quoted two years later in *Kommunist*. According to the paraphrase,

Gorbachev emphasized that Soviet diplomacy must be in step with the times, energetically liberating itself from the stereotypes and clichés [*shtampov*] of the past. For the transition to a qualitatively new relationship with the socialist countries, he said, it is essential to overcome the attitudes still present in some of our representatives—the preconceptions, smugness, sluggishness, and the erroneous view that we can teach them [the socialist countries]. In past Soviet policies to Europe there were many shortcomings based on an inertia of thought.

Negotiations, Gorbachev was quoted as saying, should be conducted "knowing well what we want and not creating blind alleys for ourselves or the other side. It is unforgivable to think that our partner is more stupid than we. We cannot allow persistence in upholding this or that position to grow over into a senseless stubbornness so that Soviet diplomats are called 'Mister Nyet.' "[5]

One month after summary publication of Gorbachev's talk to the Foreign Ministry veteran diplomat Viktor Israelian called on his life's experiences, readings, and recollections to issue a blistering attack on past Soviet foreign policies—Andrei Vyshinsky's propensity to use "terrible words" that would needlessly offend (what Lenin had forbidden Chicherin); Stalin's repressive policies; excessive secrecy; and—the root of many mistakes—conducting foreign policy undemocratically. Thus V. M. Molotov four times appeared at sessions of the Supreme Soviet in 1939–40 and made reports that were not debated—when the "exceptionally complex, tense situation demanded collective creativity and strengths in the making of responsible decisions." Further, Israelian wrote: "The confrontation diplomacy (if one can in general call it diplomacy) in the years of 'cold war' also did not facilitate the development of a creative, democratic approach to deciding foreign policy problems," while in the "stagnation years" the foreign apparatus was penetrated by an "infection of protectionism, nepotism and narrow-mindedness." Like the *Kommunist* review of Gorbachev's speech, Israelian praised the early years of Leninist diplomacy conducted by Chicherin, Litvinov, and others and the renewed creativity witnessed since 1985.[6]

Attempting to inject new life into Soviet foreign policy, Gorbachev drew heavily on specialists who knew the United States from lengthy firsthand experience: Aleksandr N. Yakovlev, Anatoly F. Dobrynin, and Georgii A. Arbatov. Foreign Minister Andrei Gromyko (often seen as "Mr. Nyet") was kicked upstairs to the presidency and replaced by Eduard A. Shevardnadze, inexperienced in diplomacy but flexible and outgoing.[7]

Though the senior Gromyko was seen as out of touch with the new thinking, his son, who spent part of his childhood in Washington, became one of its instigators. In the year before Gorbachev took the helm, the younger Gromyko and Vladimir B. Lomeiko, a journalist with extensive foreign experience abroad, coauthored *New Thinking in the Nuclear Age*, published with an initial printing of 103,000 copies. Their opening page quoted Einstein on the need for a new way of thinking in the nuclear age. In an era of "*overkil*" (now part of the Russian language) and growing interdependence, they wrote, "genuine security" could only be "mutual." (In line with the old but not the later thinking, they found merit in "parity" but called for arms reductions and a rejection of the Clausewitzian view that war could usefully "extend" politics.) The new thinking, they said, requires discarding "many conventional categories of thought" such as belief in the utility of "deterrence" (*ustrashenie*). Survival requires that "we live with each other—not against one another."[8]

A Holistic Paradigm? Mutual Security and Interdependence

Whereas the Gromyko-Lomeiko book dealt mainly with external policy, Gorbachev's version of new thinking embraced both domestic and external programs. It was holistic in demanding perestroika on all levels: within the individual, within society, and in the world at large. Indeed, the new thinking in foreign affairs came close to providing a new and holistic paradigm that all nations could well adopt if they wished to move toward "complex interdependence" in which military power plays an ever-diminishing role. The words of Gorbachev and his top foreign policy advisers often seemed to embody in plain language the nostrums of American academics devoted to "conflict resolution" and European defense intellectuals seeking modes of "nonprovocative defense."

Like George Bush under Reagan, Gorbachev gave little hint that his policies would differ from Andropov's and Chernenko's until he was in the saddle. Gorbachev's manner during visits to Canada and Britain struck some Westerners as promising fresh winds, but his speeches within the USSR were often simplistic and bellicose toward the West. One of his first calls for a "new political thinking" geared to an "interdependent" world took place when he visited Britain in December 1984.[9]

Gorbachev's remarks at Chernenko's funeral in March 1985, however, showed a deeper interest in energizing Soviet society than his predecessor and in removing foreign apprehensions about Soviet aggressivity. He stressed that the USSR threatened no other state and would not accept foreign dictation. "Socialism, as Lenin taught, will prove its advantages—not by force of arms, but by the force of its example in the areas of life-activity [*zhiznedeiatel'nosti*] of society—economic, political, moral-ethical."[10]

Gorbachev summed up Soviet goals in foreign policy as "peace and progress." The USSR's "first commandment" was to maintain and strengthen relations with members of the socialist commonwealth. Also, he said, "we would like a serious improvement of relations" with China on the basis of reciprocity. Implying a possible lessening of Moscow's commitment to the Third World, Gorbachev asserted that "our sympathies are on the side of the countries of Asia, Africa and Latin America," whom he called "partners in the struggle for a firm peace, for better, just relations among peoples."[11] With the capitalist world the USSR would follow the Leninist course of peaceful coexistence, he said.

Referring to the Geneva arms negotiations scheduled to resume in March 1985, Gorbachev declared that the only "rational" approach to the danger of war was to stop the arms race in outer space as well as on earth and to proceed with arms reductions, especially of nuclear arms. The USSR sought no unilateral advantage, said Gorbachev, but he warned that an attack on the USSR or its allies would be met with a "devastating return blow."[12]

Soviet foreign policy, Gorbachev explained to the editors of *Time* (September 9, 1985) was dictated by the needs of the economy. He reiterated this point to many domestic and foreign audiences.

The "evolutionary" progress of recent years in applying modern science and technology to the Soviet economy was too slow, Gorbachev declared in April 1985. "What we need are revolutionary achievements . . . a technology of the most recent generations, providing the highest efficiency." The foreign policy correlate was that Moscow wanted the "normalization of international economic relations, the securing of the economic security of states." The USSR, he said, sought improved economic collaboration with all states, beginning with its CMEA partners and extending to the developing countries and to the capitalist ones including the United States. All of Stalin's successors had agreed that war is not inevitable with capitalism, but Gorbachev went further: "There is no fatal inevitability of confrontation" between the United States and the USSR. Washington had spurned recent Soviet proposals for joint restraint in military development, said Gorbachev, but he hoped this U.S. orientation would be "corrected."[13]

In November 1985, following his Geneva summit meeting with former President Reagan, Gorbachev spoke of Soviet-American "interdependence" (*vzaimosavisimost'*). He told the Supreme Soviet that the differences between the two countries "are enormous. But in today's world the interconnection and interdependence between us are equally great." His report ended: "We propose to the entire world, including the capitalist states, a broad, long-term, all-round program of mutually advantageous collaboration. . . ."[14]

In December 1985 at the annual meeting of the American-Soviet Trade and Economic Council Gorbachev commented on the relationship between independence and interdependence. "In our century," he said, "every country, each people—the very smallest as well as the large—sees the greatest value in its independence. . . ." At the same time we confront a "growing interdependence of states. This is an objective consequence of the development of the contemporary world economy and at the same time an important factor in international stability. Such an interdependence we must welcome. It can become a mighty stimulus for the building of stable, normal and, I would not be afraid to say, friendly relations."[15]

Asked whether his policies represented a new revolution like that which took place in October 1917, however, Gorbachev replied in the negative. His policies were meant to implement, fulfill, and accelerate the revolutionary changes initiated in 1917.[16]

The Twenty-Seventh Party Congress: Contradictions

Gorbachev elaborated the new thinking in his political report to the Twenty-Seventh Party Congress in February 1986. But he began with a fulsome recital of the old thinking, laying out the major "contradictions" besetting the modern world. First of these are contradictions between the socialist and the capitalist systems. Capitalist imperialism tries to halt the course of history by force whereas "socialism has never, of its own free will, linked its future to any military solution of international problems." Today "we are firmly convinced that 'pushing' revolutions from outside, and doubly so by military means, is futile and inadmissible." Unfortunately, he went on, the USSR is dealing with a society whose ruling circles refuse to assess world realities in "sober terms." The "social senility" of this society "reduces the probability of far-reaching changes" in its policies and "augments its degree of recklessness."[17]

Second are contradictions within the capitalist world—between labor and capital, between one capitalist country and another, and between transnational monopolies and the sovereign rights of both developing and developed capitalist countries. Still, Gorbachev observed, the economic and technological superiority that the United States enjoyed over its closest competitors until the end of the 1960s "has been put to a serious test" by Western Europe and Japan.

Third, *"a new, complex, and active set of contradictions has taken shape between imperialism and the developing countries and peoples."* Imperialism has cultivated a "most refined system of neocolonialist exploitation . . . in a considerable number of newly liberated states." The consequence is that the developing countries have "become a region of wholesale poverty" coupled with illiteracy, hunger, infant mortality, and epidemics. "This is a disgrace for civilized humanity. And the guilty party is imperialism." Its techniques include "non-equivalent exchange, unequal trade, juggling and abuse of interest rates. . . ." Gorbachev contended even that there is a "causal connection between the trillion-dollar debt" of the developing countries and "the more than trillion-dollar growth of U.S. military expenditures in the past ten years." Neocolonialism provides resources that help monopoly capital to reduce tensions within bourgeois society and to bribe certain sections of the working people.

Sooner or later, Gorbachev warned, imperialism must choose between the "policy of force and plunder . . . and the opportunity for cooperation on a equitable basis." Though implying here that imperialism has a choice, Gorbachev also insisted that the "solutions must be radical—in the interests of the peoples of the developing states."

This framework provided the context for Gorbachev's analysis of a fourth set of contradictions: *"contradictions on a global scale affecting the very foundations of the existence of civilization."* Repeating the language cultivated under Brezhnev, the new leader asserted that "the global

[173]

problems affecting all humanity cannot be resolved by one state or a group of states." This argument would seem to open the door to East-West-South cooperation, but Gorbachev's next words castigated capitalism for causing an "impoverishment of culture, an erosion of the spiritual values created over the centuries." Bourgeois propaganda, corruption, and "vandaliza-tion" lead to unbridled commercialization, the cult of force, racism, propaganda of low instincts, and criminality.

A Contradictory but Integral World: Red or Green?

As if reading speeches by two different writers, Gorbachev com-pleted his dogmatic passages and then recalled that at the Geneva Summit Reagan had noted that the USSR and United States would quickly find a common language if our planet were threatened by another. Gorbachev asked whether a "nuclear disaster [is not] a more tangible danger than a landing of unknown extraterrestrials? Isn't the ecological threat big enough? Don't all countries have a common stake in finding a sensible and fair approach to the problems of the developing states and peoples?"

"The course of history," Gorbachev's political report went on, requires

> the establishment of *constructive, creative interaction [vzaimodeistviia] between states and peoples on the scale of the entire planet.* . . . The realistic dialectics of present-day development consists in a combination of competition and confrontation between the two systems and in a growing tendency toward interdependence [*vzaimozavisimosti*] among the countries of the world community. This is precisely the way, through the struggle of opposites . . . that the contradictory but *interdependent and in many ways integral [tselostnyi] world* is taking shape.

Sounding more like a Green than a Red, Gorbachev added, "the main road of march in contemporary conditions is to create worthy, truly human material and spiritual conditions of life for all nations, to see that our planet should be habitable, and to deal with its riches rationally." The chief value of all is "man himself and all his potentialities."

What policy inferences flowed from this analysis? First, said Gorbachev, "the nature of current weaponry leaves no state with any hope of defending itself using solely military-technical means. . . . Ensuring security is becoming more and more a political task. . . ." The answer, he said, is disarmament, not "terror of retribution" (*strakhe pered vozmezdiem*), not the absurdity of keeping humanity hostage to nuclear arms.

[174]

Second, security between the USSR and United States "can only be mutual, and, if we take international relations as a whole, it can only be universal" (*vseobshchei*). In a passage that could have come from a text on social psychology or the *Journal of Conflict Resolution*, Gorbachev declared:

> The highest wisdom is not to be concerned exclusively with oneself, *a fortiori* when this disadvantages the other side. It is necessary that everyone feel equally secure, since the fears and anxieties of the nuclear age give rise to unpredictability. . . . The appearance of new systems of weapons of mass destruction is steadily shortening the time and narrowing the possibilities for making political decisions on . . . war or peace in the event of a crisis.

Third, the United States and its military-industrial machine remains the "locomotive of militarism," but the goals of the military-industrial complex are not identical with those of the American people or the "true national interests of that great country."

Fourth, all states have their own "completely legitimate interests," but all must "master the science and art of behaving in the international arena in a restrained and circumspect way. . . ."

For cooperation to have real scope there must be a "comprehensive system of international economic security" that would "protect every state from discrimination, sanctions and other attributes of imperialist, neo-colonialist policy. Such a system is capable, along with disarmament, of becoming a reliable pillar of international security in general."

At present there is "equal danger" for the opposing sides. But continuing the nuclear arms race may bring the danger to a point where "even parity would cease to be a factor of military-political restraint [*sderzhivaniia*]. . . . True equal security in our age is guaranteed not by the highest possible but by the lowest possible level of strategic balance, from which it is necessary to exclude completely nuclear and other weapons of mass destruction."

Prevailing objective conditions dictate that the struggle between socialism and capitalism proceed only by way of "*peaceful competition and peaceful rivalry [mirnogo sorevnovaniia i mirnogo sopernichestva]*."

What is needed in foreign policy is "firmness in upholding principles and positions, tactical flexibility, readiness for mutually acceptable compromises [*vzaimopriemlemym kompromissam*], an orientation not toward confrontation but toward dialogue and mutual understanding."

Soviet disarmament diplomacy and military doctrine, Gorbachev asserted, harmonize with these principles. Soviet military doctrine is "unequivocally defensive." The USSR will continue to act, he promised,

[175]

so that "no one will have any reason for fear—even imaginary—for his security." Washington, London, and Paris, however, mount all manner of objections regarding Soviet peace proposals, while "counterrevolutionaries and imperialism have turned Afghanistan into a bleeding wound." This was the context for a Gorbachev pledge that Soviet forces would withdraw from Afghanistan "as soon as a political settlement is reached [ensuring] a real cessation of armed intervention from outside" in the country's internal affairs.

Declaring that peace and social progress depend on the world socialist system, Gorbachev outlined approaches to strengthen the Warsaw Treaty Organization and CMEA. But he also claimed that the best way for the USSR to promote international communism is to develop the USSR: "The CPSU sees its main internationalist duty in the successful progress of our country along the path opened and paved by October."

The report's foreign policy section ended with a listing of measures in the military, political, economic, and humanitarian fields to strengthen international cooperation. His very last recommendation was to convene a World Congress on Problems of Economic Security to discuss "everything that encumbers world economic ties." Corroborating the inference that Gorbachev was downgrading the importance of the Third World, he said nothing about it in his specific recommendations. This was in contrast to Brezhnev's reports to the Twenty-Fifth and Twenty-Sixth Party Congresses, which prominently praised Soviet allies and successes in Angola, Ethiopia, and Vietnam.

Conservative Consensus versus the Avant-Garde

Gorbachev's essay on contradictions may have been an "ideological tax" to hard-liners for advocating greater collaboration with the enemy. With all its anticapitalist hostility, however, Gorbachev's account made no claim that the correlation of forces was shifting in socialism's favor; it did not assert that the USSR would prevent the export of counterrevolution; and it did not evoke an "inexorable" advance of the world revolutionary movement. Instead the report urged more cooperation with Western European Social Democrats and with the "sober circles" of the bourgeoisie if they could overcome the militaristic "right wing" of their class.[18]

That some of Gorbachev's new thinking was unpalatable to the entire leadership was suggested by nuances in the Congress Resolution on his report and by the new Party Program adopted by the congress. The resolution reiterated Gorbachev's depiction of a dialectic between the "historical contest" of opposing systems and the "mounting tendency toward the interdependence of states in the world community"; the resolution also endorsed the report's appeal for a "comprehensive system of international security" but said nothing about "mutual" or "universal" security. The resolution struck a more revolutionary note than did Gorbachev on the "correlation of forces" question:

> The tendency toward a change in the correlation of forces in the international arena to the advantage of peace, reason and good will is steadfast [*ustoichivo*] and in principle irreversible. However this correlation is taking shape through an acute and dynamic contest between progress and reaction. Therefore the Congress reaffirms the CPSU's immutable solidarity with the forces of national and social liberation, its line on closer interaction with countries of socialist orientation, with revolutionary-democratic parties, with the Nonaligned Movement, on the development of contacts and collaboration with Social-Democracy, on the broadening of ties with all who come out against war and for international security.[19]

The newly adopted Party Program also took a less liberal line than Gorbachev's report, saying nothing about "mutual" or "universal" security. It did confirm, however, that "world war" is not fatalistically inevitable and that peaceful coexistence is desirable. It also pledged to develop the process of strengthening security, begun in Europe at Soviet initiative, so that it "embraces the whole world" with zones of peace in each region. For the first time in history a CPSU program spoke directly of "global problems" and pledged Soviet cooperation with other countries to solve them. The list of "global problems" now began with "environmental protection" and included no issues of "high politics," though the Party said that it would be easier to solve environmental problems if squandering resources in the arms race could be stopped. Other "global problems" included "energy, raw-materials, food and demographic problems, the peaceful exploration of space and of the oceans' riches, overcoming the economic lag of many newly liberated countries, eliminating dangerous diseases. . . ."[20]

Gorbachev bowed to consensus. His concluding speech to the congress reverted to the hallowed phrase of the Brezhnev era and endorsed "equal [*odinakovaia*] security" rather than "mutual security" or "interdependence."[21] The root for "equal" here is *odin* (one), connoting almost the "oneness" of each actor in a prisoner's dilemma; its connotation is sharply different from "mutual" [*vzaimo*], implying the shared destiny of a prisoners' dilemma. "Equal security" seemed also to be limited to the superpowers—much more restricted than "universal" security.

[177]

Some of Gorbachev's principles were themselves contradictory. How could one argue for "cooperation" with the "locomotive force of militarism"? How could one expect monopoly capital, making vital profits from the Third World, to acquiesce in a nonexploitative system of international economic security? How could one expect—or want—cooperation with an America denounced as the purveyor of vandalism?[22] Logical inconsistency may have been the price Gorbachev paid to elucidate his new political thinking. Perhaps he had to kowtow to old theory in order to explain the assumptions and goals he felt should underlie a new theory. If he could not persuade the Party to endorse all of his vision, he could at least lay out a good part of it for the *apparatchiki* and public to consider.

Inversion still lived. Even as Gorbachev talked of interdependence, Anatolii Aleksandrov, president of the USSR Academy of Sciences, complained to the congress that Soviet managers did not trust Soviet scientists to design what they need. Buying foreign production technology, he said, amounted to an "import plague" that often leads to "stagnation in certain branches of science and technology."[23]

And *Izvestiia* essayist Stanislav Kondrashov penned a novelette about a Soviet woman who accosts him as he returns from abroad: "Why do you keep silence? Will there be war or not? And what do they [the Americans] want? I am sure that they all have jewels and gold, and go to restaurants. What do they lack?" Kondrashov wrote that "since we are behind them in the world of shopping consumer goods, and comfort, those who hate us—the bourgeoisie—feel justified in not treating us as equal to them in the world of interstate relations."[24]

For the many Soviets who felt that their systems lag those of the West, "equal" security would be a great achievement and "mutual" security might seem an impossible dream. The defensive tendency in the Kremlin's outlook came through in the Party Program's premise that the Socialist Commonwealth should continue its "socialist integration" to "reinforce [its] technical and economic invulnerability . . . to hostile actions by imperialism and to the influence of economic crises and other negative processes inherent in capitalism."[25]

Mention in the Party Program of "global problems," V. V. Zagladin commented, was unprecedented. Previous programs had addressed global issues such as the prevention of war, but the new program documents were the first to speak of them directly. This, he said, was not accidental; it was because the problems had become so acute that they threatened many countries—indeed, all humanity. Zagladin continued to list the danger of nuclear war as the primary global problem (unlike the program itself, which omitted high political issues from its list), followed

[178]

by overpopulation and then by people's impact on nature—consuming and polluting vital resources.[26]

High priest of globalistika in the late 1970s–early 1980s, Zagladin held on to his position in the International Department of the Party Central Committee in the early years of Gorbachev's rule. In a 1986 article he softened his Manichean outlook just enough to avoid contradicting the new line on interdependence. Thus without underscoring the impossibility of resolving global problems while capitalism persists, he said that the perfecting of socialist society required the resolution of global problems in those respects that are possible within the framework of the USSR alone. The USSR's current economic plan was the fourth, he wrote, to include environmental protection measures. In the last nine years roughly 63 billion rubles had been spent on measures aimed at water purification, recycling water, removing pollutants from the atmosphere, and recultivating the land. Still, he went on, these steps did not suffice because formalism and bureaucracy in many ministries obstructed their implementation.[27]

Meanwhile, Zagladin continued, the sharpening of global problems in the capitalist world *"demonstrates that capitalism is nearing its limits, that it has become a brake on the further development of mankind. . . ."* Rising protests in the West against the global problems caused by capitalism also served to broaden the struggles against imperialism and for social progress, even when the protestors subjectively may not be against capitalism. "Scientific communism" should study the dynamics of this movement and point out the advantages of socialism in liberating humanity from today's global problems.[28]

Although dedicated to Marxism-Leninism as the source of globalistic wisdom, Zagladin also carved out a niche for philosophy, political economy, and all the natural and technical sciences to play in the analysis and alleviation of global problems. The Scientific-Technological Revolution (STR), he said, must be applied more effectively to environmental issues in the USSR, and the consciousness of Soviet citizens must be reshaped.

A skilled polemicist, Zagladin now appropriated some phrases from systems analysis, casting global problems as a subsystem of contemporary world relations—themselves part of the world historical process. But he also dismissed the efforts to date of Western and Soviet systems analysts— including D. M. Gvishiani and N. N. Moiseev (quoted later)—to model the global system. Soviet mathematics had not yet played a sufficient role in global studies, said Zagladin, and probably would some day find new methods and approaches. He managed to relegate two leading globalists to the status of amateurs and to hint that although there might be a need to resolve global problems, this could not be done effectively until socialism had triumphed.

A handbook for propagandists that Zagladin coedited and coauthored the following year asserted that "the scientific researches on global processes of world development realized from the late 1960s to the early 1970s became the theoretical foundation of the conception of new political thought" advanced at Party meetings since April 1985.[29] After 1985, however, neither Zagladin no other Soviet ideologues spoke of globalistika, the new Soviet science which, they earlier claimed, had emerged in the late 1970s–early 1980s. Perhaps the new political thinking dictated greater modesty in appraising "us and them," our achievements and theirs.[30]

While Zagladin beat a drum for the old guard, articles in the IMEMO journal sought to uphold scientifically the main thrusts of Gorbachev's congress report. The ability of Soviet writers to pound out conservative and liberal commentaries elucidating the same sacred texts demonstrated, as Gorbachev sometimes complained, that "scholasticism" still thrived in Communist Russia.

IMEMO Director Evgenii Primakov addressed the dialectical unity of the socialist and capitalist worlds and "common human problems impossible to resolve except by the efforts of all peoples and states—independent [vne zavisimosti] of their social organization." Socialism, he said, "is the model for the future of all mankind," but socialism's progress is not unilinear, for objective and subjective factors obstruct its movement. Socialism has much to learn from the ways in which capitalist countries organize science and technology, especially the manner by which individual firms support research and apply resultant discoveries.

Primakov also discussed the Party's concern for an "all-embracing system of international security," which should rest upon a base (fondament) of economic and humanitarian ties as well as political and military measures—or, one might say, of low politics underlying high. Thus Primakov laid down a somewhat idealistic rationale for learning from capitalism and cultivating trade with the West. Economic necessity, one might infer, is the mother of such learning.[31]

One of the most sophisticated expositions of the new line on interdependence was by G. Kh. Shakhnazarov also in the April 1986 issue of *MEMO*. An "entire network of interdependence," he wrote, "arises from the inclusion of an ever-broader circle of nations in economic, political, and cultural collaboration." This is related to "internationalization—the process of the drawing together [sblizheniia] of nations which is achieved by the strengthening of the interdependence of all countries,

[180]

by the gradual formation of a single economic and cultural structure of the world community." How this process and the resultant "structure" differed from "convergence" Shakhnazarov did not say. He did explain, however, that even though Marx, Engels, and Lenin perceived the trend toward "internationalization," only in recent decades has humanity become conscious that it is a world community—an awareness spurred by the threat of universal destruction and the aggravation of other global problems.

Revolutions in computers and biotechnology, said Shakhnazarov, have the power to reduce poverty and disease but also to destroy humanity. The peoples thus face a choice: "the internationalization of reason with the goal of securing a worthy future for all—or the division, the splitting of humanity no longer on the basis only of race or nationality but also by indicators of intelligence." Thus the polar choice: "internationalization or privatization." Socialism tends toward the former; capitalism, the latter. To the extent that internationalization occurs, this promotes socialism; when socialism triumphs, it will guarantee internationalization.

Because technological revolutions occur with ever-greater speed, the gap between the rich West and the poor nations is widening. Reactionary imperialists hope to dominate the STR and protect their wealth by force against the less developed countries. This view is shortsighted. The danger to the rich is not that the poor will take up arms and try to seize their wealth but that deepening inequalities and their consequences will destabilize the entire international system.

Shakhnazarov's bottom line was that the USSR should join in the global processes that bring nations closer together in networks of interdependence. No state can "successfully develop without multi-faceted connections with the world community" (*soobshchestvom*). An underdeveloped country able to feed its population can survive for a certain period, getting by without technological innovation. But sooner or later it will be compelled to take extraordinary efforts to make up for lost time.

Because of accelerating technological progress

> autarky becomes not simply disadvantageous but destructive. . . . [One] of the most important criteria of a nation's wealth becomes the degree of its participation in the international division of labor and especially its linkup to the world market of advanced scientific thought and technology. A country's development is determined not only by its own contribution to the world fund of knowledge, but in no less a way by its ability to draw from it.

Many different relationships are understood under the rubric of interdependence, but what they all have in common is "indebtedness"

[181]

(*dolzhenstvovanie*) based on formal contracts or other sources of obligation.

Independence is a prerequisite for genuine interdependence. Only a country free from external compulsion can grasp the mounting interconnections as a positive good and not view them as an extension of another's hegemony. In the colonial period interdependence meant "independence" for metropoles and "dependence" for colonies. The socialist and national liberations changed this situation, at least in the political sphere.

Today's world contains both old and forward-looking forms of interdependence: dominion of the weak by the strong as well as a collaborative relationship of equals aimed at overcoming national limitations.

In one sphere—nuclear weapons—interdependence is unambiguous: all humanity depends upon Soviet-U.S. restraint. "Genuine security in the nuclear era can only be collective." Thus whereas the Party consensus decreed that security must be "equal" and Gorbachev said it must be "mutual," Shakhnazarov put the proposition most strongly: security must be "collective."

The USSR and the United States have the means to benefit each other in the economic, scientific-technological, and cultural spheres. "They also can and must—together with the nonaligned states—begin to construct a new international order in which global problems will find a solution. . . ."[32]

Gorbachev Broadens His Horizons

Vladivostok: Power of the East

Gorbachev's July 28, 1986 speech in Vladivostok ("Power of the East") applied new thinking to the Far East.[33] In April 1986 *Izvestiia* captioned a major article: "The USSR and China—On Principles of Equality and Mutual Advantage."[34] At Vladivostok Gorbachev affirmed that the Soviet Union "is also an Asian and Pacific country." It makes no "selfish attempts to strengthen [Soviet] security at others' expense" but rather seeks to gain from cooperation with others to build "new and fair relations in Asia and the Pacific." Moscow sought to stem the militarization of Asia spearheaded by U.S. efforts to create an "iron triangle" with Japan and South Korea. Recent military activities in the Soviet Far East were strictly defensive. Still, Gorbachev allowed that the United States is "a great Pacific power"—its Little Diomede island located just seven kilometers from the Soviet Big Diomede. Gorbachev recognized that efforts to create an Asian-Pacific security system would be impossible without U.S. participation. He proposed a Helsinki-type conference with all countries having a relationship to the Pacific Ocean.

Despite his conciliatory tone, Gorbachev included many planks sure to raise American suspicions. He suggested that the Pacific security conference meet in Hiroshima. He proposed a nuclear-weapon-free zone in the southern part of the Pacific Ocean and on the Korean peninsula, two areas where Moscow has nothing nuclear to lose but the United States has a good deal. Still, he said, if the United States gave up its bases in the Philippines, "we would not leave this step unanswered." He also accused Washington of manipulating India's (not Sri Lanka's) Tamil problem and bullying New Zealand.

Gorbachev declared Moscow's readiness to deepen economic and other ties with China. Responding to Beijing's "three conditions" for improved relations, Gorbachev promised to withdraw significant Soviet forces from Afghanistan before year's end. He hoped for normalized relations between Hanoi and Beijing and between all of Indochina and ASEAN. He promised a "positive reply" regarding assistance in construction of a railroad linking [China's] Xinjiang-Uygur Autonomous Region and [Soviet] Kazakhstan. He reiterated Moscow's willingness to cooperate with China in space, including the training of Chinese cosmonauts.

He emphasized Moscow's desire for "extended cooperation" with Japan in many fields, from ocean resources to outer space.[35] On a topic of interest to Japan as well as China, Gorbachev promised that if an INF treaty were signed, missiles withdrawn from Europe would be destroyed, not transferred to Asia. In a subsequent message to the mayor of Hiroshima Gorbachev underscored the USSR's devotion to a moratorium and then a formal ban on further nuclear testing.[36]

In November 1986, as he visited India, Gorbachev and Prime Minister Rajiv Gandhi issued The Delhi Declaration calling for the creation of a "post-nuclear age": "a nuclear weapon-free world, free of violence and hatred, fear and suspicion."[37] This statement, in conjunction with others by Gorbachev, suggests that his first approximation of utopia was a nuclear-weapons-free world rather than a global classless society. Considering the murders that characterize daily life in a country founded on nonviolence—from bride-burning to regicide to regional genocide—one could easily believe that nuclear disarmament is more feasible than an end to class and ethnic conflict.

[183]

Following up on his Vladivostok themes, Gorbachev made another major speech on Far Eastern issues in September 1988 in Krasnoyarsk (*Pravda*, September 18, 1988). He pledged that the USSR would not increase the number of its nuclear weapons in the Asia-Pacific region provided the United States and other nuclear powers also refrained; invited the major naval powers to confer on limiting the size of their forces in the region; offered to withdraw Soviet forces from Cam Ranh Bay (while saying nothing about those at Danang air base in Vietnam) if the United States "dismantles" its bases in the Philippines; and called for a conference to transform the Indian Ocean into a "zone of peace" by 1990. Frustrated perhaps by the lack of positive response to his earlier overtures, at Krasnoyarsk Gorbachev courted not only Japan and China but also Australia and all ASEAN member nations.

Gorbachev's Asian strategy paid off in May 1989 when—the Kremlin having gone some distance toward meeting China's "three conditions" for normalized relations—he took part in the first Sino-Soviet summit in thirty years. The Chinese leadership welcomed Gorbachev as a reformer in foreign policy, but millions of other Chinese, led by students, greeted him as a symbol of democratic change.

Freer Thinking, Issyk-Kul, and the Club of Rome

The first constituency for new thinking is probably the intelligentsia—Soviet and foreign. *"Science is necessary for us,"* Gorbachev told an all-union meeting of social science department heads in 1986. One reason is *"to form, bring out [vospitivat'], and cultivate the capability of youth to think independently, creatively."* Citing Lenin's objections to rote learning, Gorbachev denounced tendencies in Soviet social science toward "dogmatism, scholasticism," and looking in " 'pre-scribed truths' for recipes applicable to all situations." What a paradox, he noted, that the most interesting fields of learning—people and society—have become in many lectures and textbooks something boring and formal, killing the attractions of Marxism-Leninism.[38]

"The ability to find one's way in today's complex, contradictory but interdependent world," Gorbachev went on, "is not a gift of nature" or the automatic result of "mastering special disciplines. It must be taught to future specialists. After all, a worldview [*mirovozzrenie*] is not only the totality of general information about the world. It is at once the realized [*osoznannye*] class interests and ideals, legal and moral norms, social priorities and humanistic values—all that determines the choice of a

[184]

person's line of action in life, his responsible relationship to society and to himself."

This worldview will determine, said Gorbachev, how tomorrow's engineers and scientists use their power. "This is the question of questions" —which depends on how social sciences are taught.[39] (Reading these words, I wondered whether Gorbachev knew the case of a philosopher of science at Moscow University, a man who believed that he could do nothing better for his country than to teach his subject to the intellectual elite of the USSR, but who was fired in 1983 for possessing Solzhenitsyn's writings and showing them to graduate students. Despite his numerous requests, Dr. Valeri Lebedev was not reinstated at the university as of August 1989.)

Gorbachev's message to social science departments accented freedom, whereas a report by rival E. G. Ligachev to the same audience emphasized patriotism and "constructive" truth. To be sure, Ligachev began by honoring Gorbachev's recipes about the evils of dogmatism in a contradictory but interdependent world. Ligachev then castigated political economy, philosophy, scientific communism, law, and history, all of which were failing to provide the necessary sparks for perestroika. Toward the end of his long report Ligachev went off in a different direction from the Gensec and denounced those who discuss only "negative" phenomena. "Most important," he said, "is Leninist truth—conscious and constructive truth. It calls not for conversations about shortcomings but for an active struggle against them."[40]

Gorbachev's more liberal tone waxed even stronger as he met with a group of Western and Third World intellectuals invited by Kirghiz writer Chengis Aitmatov to meet at what became known as the Issyk-Kul Forum in October 1986. The exchange was carried prominently in many Soviet publications, and Alvin Toffler wrote about it for three days on the front page of the *Christian Science Monitor*.[41] Aitmatov began by assuring Gorbachev that these were "solid, serious people" joined in a quest for "a new kind of thinking in contemporary historical circumstances." Gorbachev replied that perhaps he should become a "candidate member" of the forum, for he concurred: there is a great "deficit of new thinking."[42]

The summary of this meeting included many statements by the foreign intellectuals that seemed to confirm important elements of Gorbachev's new thinking. Thus Heidi Toffler told of her television programs in which she and her husband inserted a concluding idea: "We stand at the start of a great race into the future. Some of us have advantages; others, some kind of handicaps. But it's important that there be no victors, no defeated in these competitions for a right to the future. We must all arrive at the finish line together."

[185]

Alvin Toffler stressed that economic reform in all countries depended on "change in information policy. The necessity of free transmission of information is an immediate economic demand, because the new economics is based to a significant degree on the use of information technology."

This message may have been welcome to Gorbachev, but in reply he noted that technology can also cause great suffering. Perhaps he had Chernobyl in mind, but he spoke rather about a British automobile factory he visited in 1984. Its automation was impressive, said Gorbachev, but he worried about the displaced laborers—nearly half the factory's work force.

Toffler, who with his wife worked five years on an automotive assembly line (a fact that Gorbachev seemed to anticipate), replied that technology also promised to liberate humans from dreary, heavy work "worthy of animals—not people."

Comments by Indian cultural leader Narayan Menon helped Gorbachev get off a line that the Third World's underdevelopment is like a "long-fuse time bomb" that someday may present us with "world-scale surprises" if we defer action. Gorbachev told the assemblage that "Lenin in his time uttered a thought of colossal depth—about the priority of the interests of social development, of universal human [*obshchechelovecheskikh*] values over the interests of this or that class. Today, in the missile-nuclear age, the significance of this thought is felt especially acutely. I would like very much that in another part of the world [leaders] also understood and accepted the thesis on the priority of the universal human value of peace over all others to which one or another group of people are dedicated."[43]

Thus Gorbachev took a supraclass perspective and attributed it to Lenin, even though the Bolshevik leader had argued that the real standard of morality is what best advances the proletariat's class struggle.[44] Other Soviet commentators would later cite and expatiate on this reading of Lenin by Gorbachev, sometimes citing an 1899 draft of a Party program in which Lenin wrote that the "interests of social development are higher than the interests of the proletariat" while saying nothing about the "universal human values" priority attributed to him by Gorbachev.[45]

After the group session Gorbachev pulled Alexander King, president of the Club of Rome, aside and shattered more dogmas. As King remembers their conversation, Gorbachev said: "We esteem the work of the Club of Rome. What you could do for us is to advise how to cope with our pandemic problem of unemployment in a humane way." This one sentence, if understood and reported correctly, broke with three shibboleths: official Soviet disdain for the Club of Rome; Moscow's long-standing denial that unemployment exists in the USSR; and Soviet aversion to seeking non-Marxist advice on social problems. The first of these rules, however, had already been undermined in 1985 when Gorbachev wrote to King in reply to a Club letter on disarmament in which he expressed his wish for the Club's success in "its useful work for the advancement of the idea of peace" and halting the arms race.[46] Speaking directly to King in 1986, Gorbachev invited him to return often to the USSR.[47]

The Moscow Forum: For a Nuclear-Free World

Gorbachev made one of his most idealistic and conciliatory statements about mutual security and interdependence at the Moscow forum For a Nuclear-Free World, for the Survival of Mankind, on February 16, 1987. The Soviet leader spared the invited guests—mostly intellectuals and public leaders from many countries—the harsh class analysis of contradictions in his report to the 1986 Party Congress. Instead he warned that there "would be no second Noah's ark for a nuclear deluge" and that human survival requires profound changes in our political mentality. "A nuclear tornado," he said, would "sweep away socialists and capitalists, the just and the sinners alike. Is this situation moral?" Today's leaders must "bridge the gap between political practice and universal moral and ethical standards."

Gorbachev explained his opposition to those who see nuclear weapons as a necessary evil. First, "the bigger the nuclear arsenals, the less chance they will be kept 'obedient.' "[48] Second, the "inner logic" of deterrence increases the risk of military conflict because this threat system requires periodic military adventures to maintain its credibility. Third, deterrence theory is wrong to assume that people are inherently violent (or even, it would appear, that capitalism breeds uncontrollable violence). Fourth, it is unwise to assume that all people will respond in like fashion to certain situations because there is no common definition of "rational" and "irrational." Finally, deterrence is immoral because it posits behavior unacceptable among people as normal for relations among states.

Virtually paraphrasing John Donne, Gorbachev declared that "the Soviet Union and the Soviet people consider themselves part of an international community. The worries of all mankind are our worries, its pain is our pain and its hopes are our hopes."[49] He called for the elimination of "class narrow-mindedness, the primitive, ideological,

[187]

mechanical approach" to international affairs. Further, "we must waste no more time trying to outplay each other and to gain unilateral advantages."

This speech underscores the question of how seriously to take Gorbachev's statements—especially to foreign audiences. On one level the speech implemented Lenin's advice to play to the "pacifist wing" of the foreign bourgeoisie. Some of the arguments probably seem disingenuous or naive to "realistic" strategists—for example, the proposition that bigger arsenals are necessarily more dangerous. On the other hand, sophisticated analysts such as Donald G. Brennan and Fred Iklé have also raised major questions about the durability and morality of deterrence. Indeed, former President Reagan and Gorbachev were one in calling for nuclear disarmament, though they differed on whether disarmament can or should be supplemented with strategic defenses.

Ideological statements meant to impress foreigners cannot be made on the cheap, for they have domestic consequences. If Gorbachev is not sincere about his idealistic assertions, he risks domestic revolt merely to score debating points abroad. The February 1987 speech, as we see, formed part of a multifaceted "new thinking" advanced in many forums. On balance it should probably be taken as representing the real thrust of Gorbachev's worldview.

Kommunist *Broadens Its Horizons*

The inflections of Gorbachev's new thinking helped to trigger an upsurge of attention to environmental problems in the Party's theoretical journal. Between February 1986 and July 1987, the eighteen months following the Twenty-Seventh Party Congress and the accident at Chernobyl, the bimonthly *Kommunist* published five articles on environmental problems compared with seven in the preceding fifteen years. Three of these articles were reports on roundtable discussions involving Soviet and foreign philosophers and scientists.[50] In May 1987, for example, *Kommunist* summarized a roundtable entitled "Scientific-Technical Progress and the Role of the Human Factor" in which Soviet and Polish participants found many of Gorbachev's recent speeches worth quoting.[51] Inspired by Gorbachev's remarks to the Issyk-Kul Forum, *Kommunist* editorial board member E. A. Arab-Ogly noted that there is no contradiction between the interests of civilization on earth and those of the working class, whose historical mission is to establish a classless society. Arab-Ogly also argued that more valuable than oil or precious metals is human intellect, which will be needed to guide even supercomputers. The force of human intellect today is similar to a geological process, for it shapes not only earth but outer space.[52] Psychologists and other scientists at the roundtable concurred that "man is the genuine measure of all things." It is necessary to rethink his place in the creative process, in perestroika, and in the STR.

Carrying on the systems analysis–technocratic approach that challenged Party dogma in the early 1980s, Academician N. N. Moiseev (disparaged in Zagladin's article summarized earlier) explained to the forum how mathematical modeling permits the identification of mutually advantageous—even optimal—compromise solutions to environmental, arms race, and other problems. These solutions can be so profitable to both sides that neither will want to violate them. The only requirement for such solutions, he said, is that the parties share one overriding goal in a spectrum of otherwise conflicting aims. Modeling can proceed from the fact that at the end of the twentieth century all countries share a common goal: to preserve life on our planet. This common goal alters qualitatively the character of conflict situations, removing their antagonistic nature. Moiseev argued for the creation of "institutions for agreement [*institutov soglasiia*]" composed of competent experts able to discover variations of compromise accords and thus to eliminate confrontation and attempts to solve disputes by force.[53]

The bottom line of such presentations is to negate the "kto kovo?" outlook long cultivated in Soviet communism. Some "realists" will find Moiseev's arguments naive, but his outlook resembles in some ways the "getting to yes" and "value-creating" orientations espoused by some Western specialists on negotiation.

Strengthening the United Nations

In September 1987 Gorbachev issued a detailed call for making the United Nations an institution that could produce and maintain agreements between disputing nations.[54]

War has been avoided, Gorbachev asserted, "despite the existence of nuclear weapons," not because of nuclear deterrence. The USSR favors total nuclear disarmament, he said, and "drastically reduced levels of *nonnuclear armaments*."

The Soviet Union's "idea for the establishment of a *comprehensive system of international security"* could be worked out within the framework of the UN Charter supplemented by unilateral restraints and multilateral accords. Already the USSR and China have renounced first use of nuclear arms.

Gorbachev proposed an accord on a strategy of "military sufficiency"—restructuring armed forces so that they could repulse aggression but would be unable to conduct offensive operations. A first step in this direction could be a "controlled withdrawal of nuclear and other offensive weapons" and zones of reduced or no armaments between adversaries. He also called for accords to prevent the outbreak of nuclear war and to stop "nuclear piracy." If an "imbalance, disproportions exist" in the arms of NATO and the Warsaw Pact, said Gorbachev, "let us remove them."

He chided those who expressed satisfaction that there have been no major wars, for regional wars are quite serious. Using Litvinov's term in the 1930s, Gorbachev declared that security is "indivisible." He floated a number of tentative proposals for incorporation into an all-embracing system of peace and security: a direct communication line between UN Headquarters and "countries' permanent members of the Security Council and the location of the chairman of the Nonaligned Movement"; a UN mechanism for "extensive international verification of compliance with agreements to lessen international tension, limit armaments and monitor the military situation in conflict areas"; and wider use of UN military observers and peacekeeping forces to separate troops of warring sides and to observe cease-fire arrangements.

Gorbachev included also a number of proposals focused on economic and ecological security: reduction of interest payments under bank credits; limitation of debt payments by each developing country to the share of its annual export earnings without detriment to development; and removal of protectionist barriers by creditor-nations.

On human rights Gorbachev urged that nations bring their laws and rules into accordance with international standards; that they avoid preaching about human rights while proposing that exotic weapons hang from space as from a chandelier; that they work out a world information program to familiarize peoples with one anothers' lives, ridding the information flow of "enemy image" stereotypes, bias, and distortions of truth; and that they hold an international conference on humanitarian problems in Moscow.

Gorbachev also proposed strengthening the International Atomic Energy Agency, creating a world space organization, making more use of the International Court of Justice (ICJ)—making its jurisdiction compulsory

[190]

for all states on mutually agreed conditions, and establishing a "world consultative council under UN auspices uniting the world's intellectual elite."

The Soviet leader declared it "impermissible to use financial levers for bringing pressure" on the United Nations and pledged that the USSR would "continue to cooperate actively in overcoming budget difficulties at the United Nations."

All these ideas were integrated into Gorbachev's global vision. He pledged that the USSR would shift from confidence-building measures in individual spheres to a "large-scale policy of trust that would gradually shape a system of comprehensive security." The Soviet proposals, he said, were a first draft for "a possible new organization of life in our common planetary home."

Deputy Foreign Minister Vladimir Petrovskii termed the Gorbachev article a call for "a restructuring of international relations in all their aspects—military, political, economic, humanitarian and ecological— along the principles of democratization and law and order." The article clearly emphasizes Lenin's idea, Petrovskii declared, "that universal human values have priority over the interests of states, classes and ideologies." "Today's interrelated world," said Petrovskii, "has room neither for neoglobalism," a term often used by Soviet commentators to describe Reagan's foreign policy, "nor the policy of neo-isolationism."[55]

Gorbachev was certainly laying down a comprehensive program spanning much of the ever-widening spectrum of global security problems. But few of his ideas were original. Calls for upgrading the UN role as a mediator and peace observer had been supported for decades by the other governments. That the Kremlin now opposed financial leverage and prompt payment of UN dues was good news given that Moscow had initiated selective dues payments decades before; that Moscow now wanted compulsory jurisdiction of the ICJ was also welcome given that the USSR lagged many other nations in that regard; the Kremlin's advocacy of generosity toward Third World debtors was a cheap shot given that Western creditors—not the USSR—would be left holding the bag. The whole patchwork seemed to be meant as a speech delivered at the UN rather than as an article in *Pravda*. It was probably conceived in the spirit of the annual Foreign Ministry frenzy described by Arkady Shevchenko to produce a propaganda splash at the General Assembly. Indeed, a spokesman for the Foreign Ministry in Moscow conveyed at least one objective of Gorbachev's proposals when he said (perhaps tongue in cheek), "Not at all for polemics' sake, I would like to note that the constructive stand of the Soviet Union . . . is in obvious contrast with the mentality and methods of policy demonstrated by the U.S. leadership."[56]

[191]

Notwithstanding the possible hypocrisy and propaganda motives behind Gorbachev's article, his proposals dovetailed with and constructively enlarged his earlier statements on security and interdependence. Many of Gorbachev's proposals offered a constructive basis for making the United Nations a more dependable agency for international security. It was unfortunate that the Khrushchev or Brezhnev regime had not taken a similar line, for then Western and Soviet policies might have meshed; later they were out of phase. The Reagan administration viewed the United Nations more as a menace than as a hope for constructive cooperation. If the Soviet Union took the lead in reforming the United Nations, however, perhaps the West would come around. In fact, as we shall see in the next chapter, Soviet deeds at the United Nations and in other spheres were basically consistent with the thrust of Gorbachev's September 1987 proposals.

A plea for a more precise image of the outer world and of Soviet life appeared in *Kommunist* at the same time Gorbachev's UN proposals appeared in the central press.[57] *Izvestiia* columnist Stanislav Kondrashov argued that the USSR suffers because the ordinary citizen receives a distorted and incomplete picture of life abroad and, for that matter, at home. For example, they know that the U.S. Congress is a "millionaires' club" but do not know that its prerogatives are established in the Constitution and that its members control federal spending—that its campaigns against Watergate and Irangate help the entire society, not just a privileged few.

Soviet secrecy damages the USSR. There is a gap between what the elite and the ordinary citizens know. Soviet journalists do not even know the names, numbers, and characteristics of Soviet weapons. Uncertainty about the size of Soviet forces is manipulated by the Pentagon to demand more defense appropriations. Thus secrecy boomerangs against Soviet interests.

If Soviet citizens knew how well the federally supported Smithsonian Institution supports its museums, in shame they would do more to support Moscow's Historical Museum; if they knew more about grain purchases abroad since 1963, perhaps such imports would have ceased by now.

Soviet public opinion should help to shape the USSR's foreign policies, but this opinion must be well informed. Further, all Soviet citizens need to understand better how other people think and to know others by face, not by stereotype.

Kondrashov and other Soviet analysts in effect called for informed empathy with other peoples. "If we had thought about how our SS-20s would appear to West Europeans," researcher Yuri Davidov told me in 1987, "we could have anticipated a sharp response and might have behaved differently."

Empathy is useful for makers of foreign policy, but it is also essential for democracy. The capacity of ordinary citizens for empathy is an indicator of an ability for self-rule. It is also a prerequisite for moving out of traditional settings and developing broader horizons of all kinds, including political participation. Political subjects, of course, will then be more difficult to control because they will have opinions and greater willingness to press them.[58] When ordinary citizens cannot imagine what the government should be doing in distant places, there is no possibility of meaningful inputs to government policy.

Soviet Humanism and Russian Cosmicism

The Party's theoretical journal continued its efforts to put the new thinking in the context of a unified worldview, one that placed people squarely in the center of a humanistic synthesis of philosophy and natural and social science. As Gorbachev's UN article appeared in *Pravda*, *Kommunist* reported on the International Congress on Logic, Methodology, and the Philosophy of Science then concluded in Moscow.[59] Soviet plenary speakers P. N. Fedoseeva and I. T. Frolov told the Congress that contemporary science is characterized by a "synthesis of methodological, worldview and humanistic problematique." Moiseev argued (contrary to some Western presentations at the conference) that one cannot understand the transitions from biological to social systems merely by the thermodynamics of evolution; instead one needs a vision of the coevolution of nature and human society as laid out decades ago by the geochemist V. I. Vernadskii.

Vernadskii's importance to science in the late twentieth century is similar to that of Darwin and Newton for the previous two centuries, Moiseev argued in a follow-up article in *Kommunist*.[60] Celebrating the 125th anniversary of Vernadskii's birth, Moiseev argued that his concepts of the biosphere and noosphere help us to understand the role of man and nature in shaping our environment. Vernadskii helped to break down the traditional barriers between natural and social science. "At the basis of this revolutionary change lies Vernadskii's teaching about the noosphere, about the possibility of a gradual transition of the biosphere into a qualitatively new creation"—the noosphere. Popular misreadings of Vernadskii, according to Moiseev, expect that the biosphere will gradually

[193]

become subject to human thought and control so that the sphere of life will inexorably become the sphere of thought. Moiseev, in contrast, interpreted Vernadskii to say that human activity constitutes a great burden on the biosphere and that the human impact must be managed with great care and foresight. The biosphere can become a noonsphere, but without thought it can also degenerate.

Vernadskii's view on the coevolution of humans and the biosphere implies that society must be organized so as to thoughtfully orient the evolution of the biosphere. Attainment of the noosphere is a requirement for the flourishing of humanity.

The implications of Vernadskii's vision also confirm the inevitability—as seen over one hundred years ago by Marx and Engels—of a science that joins natural and human history. They also point to the need for a science that understands and guides people's interactions with their environment. Those implications prepare us for the necessity of studying developments without precedent and often alien to traditional science. One such event could be nuclear war—the impact of which on the biosphere has been studied at the Computer Center of the USSR Academy of Sciences. The center's studies of human interactions also showed the possibility of compromise to avert the usual explosion between antithetical social forces. In this context Moiseev repeated his proposal for "institutions for agreement" noted the previous year in *Kommunist*.

Moiseev extolled what he called Russian "cosmicism [*kosmizm*]—a unique current of thought and mental attitude, but not at all a school with its own principles and dogmas." It included a wide variety of worldviews, from Slavophile mystics to materialists such as Vernadskii. They helped to restore a view of a unified cosmos of which people are an integral part. Humans are also subject to Nature's laws and must try to ascertain them. "The development of thought, according to the world view of the cosmicists—is just as much a natural process as the movement of the heavenly bodies. Thought is the highest component of the world evolutionary process. Nature, the cosmos—they give birth to man, and he is indebted to them for his reason. Man must study nature, study himself and the place of his reason in nature. And not from the position of a disinterested observer, as a biologist researches under a microscope the movement of bacteria, but as a participant in the whole process of evolution of nature" and as one able to help shape it.

Just as the Slavophiles reacted against Western materialism, so did some Russian natural scientists insist on seeing humans as part of nature. Mystics and materialists shared the perspective of "Russian cosmicism," according to Moiseev. Slavophiles pointed out the contradiction between

[194]

confidence in "reason" and enlightened society and the irrationality of the "I." In some ways this was a return to the ancient Greek and early Christian view of a great chain of being linking the gods (or God) and man, a view that had been challenged by the Renaissance conception of objective laws that could be inferred by man standing apart from nature.

Humankind approaches a new threshold: the step toward the noosphere and directed change. Will we succeed in making this transition? We must choose from the "arsenal of possible organizational forms of [our] existence those that are most capable of ensuring this transition."

A New Paradigm? Will It Work?

The prominence given to Moiseev's views in *Kommunist* implied high-level endorsement. But his philosophy went against those who in the past hoped to reverse the directions of rivers and those who still hope for quick-fixes and nearly free lunches at the trough of Mother Russia. Even if Moiseev's reverence for life came to dominate the worldview of Soviet planners and ordinary citizens, would it suffice to pull the country from its swamp of interrelated problems? Chernobyl and a series of other environmental disasters—aggravated if not caused by people—have exposed the shortcomings of the "managed" society.[61] Can present organizational forms be trusted with powers that could destroy as well as facilitate life and thought? A special issue of *Literaturnaia gazeta* (January 25, 1989)—with reports from every corner of the USSR—found that the country's environmental problems run far deeper than the bureaucratic inertia of ministries paid to produce electricity and harness water. The Academy of Sciences has been lethargic, still lacking a special section devoted to ecology at the end of the 1980s. Indeed, even the "common man" is to blame. Drivers who bulldoze canals ruining the environment are paid 2.5 times the average wage and threaten a correspondent with death if his articles jeopardize their jobs.[62] Not only do oil wells threaten the livelihood and life style of Siberian reindeer herders, but the Russians who work the rigs at high salaries steal furs from the natives and leave them standing in the cold. As the aged father of Aleksandr Yakovlev put it, one difference between Stalin's time and Brezhnev's was that earlier a neighbor might bring wood and ask the father to make a chair, for which neither would consider payment; under Brezhnev, "it would never occur to me not to ask for payment, and it would never occur to him not to offer." The lesson that his son, a designer

[195]

of perestroika, draws for the present: "The main difficulties are not in the waves on the surface."[63]

Soviet writers complain that a nonrenewable resource—oil—has been wastefully extracted and used carelessly, its "golden rain" ($176 billion in the last decade) falling mainly in North America as payment for grain the USSR should not need to import.[64] Other analysts note that whereas Japan and the Common Market countries have lowered their energy expenditures per unit of economic output in recent decades, in the USSR the reverse trend has prevailed, worsening both environmental and economic conditions and leading the Party Central Committee to issue a decree in January 1988 entitled "On the Fundamental *Perestroika* of Environmental Protection."[65]

But even if huge sums were available, Soviet problems will not be remedied merely by spending money to clean up the environment and orders to "ecologize" production. Since the late 1960s investments in Soviet agriculture have been enormous—much higher than in the United States—with little to show for it. Work habits as well as social institutions must change, overcoming decades if not centuries of inertia.

The same cosmicism to which Moiseev looks for direction comes from roots that have also nourished Russian "titanism" and "gigantomania," tendencies that have probably done more harm than cosmicism has done good.[66] Titans see themselves not as a humble part of nature but as its masters. Nourished by Russian and Communist hubris, Soviet planners have believed "big is beautiful." For them (as for many Brazilians), "appropriate technology" has been an alien concept.

Moiseev outlined a deep foundation for new thinking, especially as it ponders the optimal relationship of humans to their environment and of social to biological science. But how to bring forth a new kind of person able to imbibe and implement the new thinking? How to inculcate altruism and deep sentiments of solidarity with and responsibility for the community? What led Martin Luther to draw a line of principle and say, "Here I stand"?

These questions brought Pavel Simonov to grapple with the ancient problem of determinism and free will in the May 1988 *Kommunist*. Simonov, a neurophysiologist, cited a wide range of viewpoints from Hegel to Stanislavskii to B. F. Skinner, but he found greatest nourishment in Ivan Pavlov's teachings on the primacy of internal need. Felt need is what shapes "will." We feel ourselves "free," as Tolstoi noted, but others see us as "determined." In fact, we are shaped by the information put to us by our upbringing. Even the freedom reflex (and its opposite, the submission reflex, both uncovered by Pavlov) is an internal "need" to overcome obstacles.

Upbringing [*vospitanie*] is the formation of internal needs for specific social and personal values in the person being educated. Educators should give primacy to the "formation of spiritual needs—the ability to live with *our* thoughts and with *other's* feelings [a phrase Simonov attributes to Lev Tolstoi], the ability to act out of respect for goodness and truth, and not from fear or from some self-seeking quest for praise or reward."

It is useless to issue appeals to be good and avoid self-seeking. "Altruism must be taught—taught like a language." All persons have altruistic drives; they must be nurtured and reinforced so that altruism becomes part of their "armor." Example plays a powerful role. "If a child from its earliest months of life lived in the company only of brave, humane and just people no special upbringing would be needed."

Though Simonov cited no Existentialist philosophers, he concluded that "personality begins with action. Attempt to fulfill your duty and you will find out what is in you. Therefore, man is an act."[67]

How shall we redirect our lives? Which roots of our civilization provide the necessary nourishment for the difficult tasks ahead? For the answers to deep problems, the authors published in *Kommunist* often survey the literature of bourgeois science and report it superficial—at best, the output of data-crunching computers. Many Soviet authors purport to find contemporary relevance in the basic insights of Marx, Engels, Lenin, and, as of 1987–89, Nikolai Bukharin.[68] But for real sustenance they return to native roots—from Slavophiles to Tolstoi to the great men of Russian science before and shortly after the October Revolution. The apostles of the new thinking promote a worldview unashamedly idealistic. In print if not in person, they tend to be quite hopeful. Is this optimism justified?

One problem is that their idealistic generalizations are difficult to operationalize. How does one put human survival over more limited but still burning national interests? How does one entrust one's own interests—not someone else's—to an international tribunal? How will a construction engineer tailor his project so that it helps the biosphere become a noosphere, especially when the immediate economic incentives run the other way? How can we infuse others (or even ourselves) with a "spiritual need for altruism"? How can we proceed with perestroika of ourselves and those around us—much less with the nation or the globe? Will Gorbachev's new thinking succeed where Socrates, Christ, Woodrow Wilson, and the United World Federalists have made such limited progress?[69]

Were Gorbachev's utterances about mutual security credible? To foreign audiences they were often mixed with jokers placing unequal burdens on the United States (as in specifics of the Vladivostok speech).

[197]

At times the Gensec seemed to practice an approach-avoidance syndrome, inviting but also sabotaging prospects of U.S. cooperation with Soviet initiatives. Some of his ideological boilerplate on contradictions could have been meant to assuage conservatives at home, but its venom was easily the match of Reagan's "evil empire" language that Moscow found so distasteful.

Despite Gorbachev's attempt to promote new thinking, the general secretary maintained two dogmas that produced blindspots in the emerging Kremlin worldview. One was Gorbachev's insistence on retaining Communist party leadership in the USSR. To be sure, he wanted the Party to retire from active management of government and the economy, but he wanted it to remain the ultimate authority and source of government policy. In 1988 he tolerated "Popular Fronts" and demands for greater autonomy in the Baltic and Caucasian republics, but in early 1989 he spoke against a multiparty system or republic veto of central legislation.

Gorbachev's dilemma was that he encouraged freedom but wanted to set limits to its evolution. Having permitted the genie of freedom to come halfway out of its bottle, how could he stuff it back? And if he could do so, would this not throttle the very energies and innovations he had wanted to unleash?

Another blindspot was Gorbachev's rather self-righteous critique of capitalism as the main source of militarism and uneven development. This lopsided appraisal lifted too much responsibility from the Communist and Third Worlds for problems of their own making. And it could only interfere with attempts at deeper mutual understanding among peoples.

Challenges to Gorbachev's new thinking about mutual security and interdependence came from both outside and within the USSR. If Gorbachev's overtures to the Kremlin's principal adversaries failed, his paradigm would be discredited. As Charles Osgood has warned, a strategy of conflict reduction must be sustained over a rather long period to persuade skeptical adversaries of its merit. By the time the adversaries begin to reciprocate, the initiator of tension-reducing moves may become disenchanted and shift back to traditional power politics. To cope with this problem the initiator must clearly announce his strategy—to potential domestic critics as well as to the foreign adversary—and then stick with his plan despite initial rebuffs.[70]

Osgood's cautions were well placed. The United States and its allies did little initially to reciprocate Gorbachev's overtures, probably making his position more tenuous. Over time, however, Reagan and other Western leaders agreed with Margaret Thatcher that Gorbachev was a man with whom they could conduct useful business. Even then, however, none of the Western countries went very far toward matching the unilateral force reductions and other concessions made by Gorbachev. Still, at the end of the 1980s there was nothing in the global arena that showed his new paradigm to be fundamentally unworkable.

Gorbachev's foreign policy initiatives could also be torpedoed at home. Conservative opponents could accuse him of naiveté or treason—that he placed trust in the good intentions of class enemies and persisted in unilateral restraint even when rebuffed by the foe. Despite the rather radical changes in the ideology and practice of Soviet *foreign* policy championed by Gorbachev, they evoked little overt domestic opposition. When questions were raised in the Supreme Soviet and elsewhere about asymmetrical force cuts in the INF Treaty, Soviet military and diplomatic representatives silenced doubters with powerful rejoiners. Some military writers, however, sniped at the new thinking on reasonable sufficiency and deterrence as well as the "vegetarian pacifism" sprouting under the auspices of glasnost'. Indeed, the last article by Marshal S. L. Sokolov (in *Pravda*, May 9, 1987) shortly before his dismissal as defense minister asserted that *world* war in the cosmic-nuclear era has outlived its usefulness, implying that other wars had not. His successor, Dmitrii Yazov, explicitly supported the notion of military sufficiency (*Pravda*, July 27, 1987), but he has also expressed concern about the impact of glasnost' on morale.[71] There were indications in 1988–89 that many military professionals were unhappy with asymmetrical cuts in Soviet forces. Whether their doubts and disillusion would find serious political expression was uncertain. Soviet Russia had no Bonaparte tradition, but a general had recently restored some law and order to Poland.

The largest threat to the new thinking in foreign affairs came from conservative opponents of Gorbachev's domestic programs. If efforts to restructure the country's internal life collapsed, the general secretary and his mutual security line would likely crash as well—probably to be replaced by more conventional ways of thinking and acting at home and abroad.

Gorbachev's style marked him as a potentially successful entrepreneur of ideas and action. He despised the low-risk, no-breakthrough posture of the last decade's stagnation, but he also avoided the extremely high-risk adventures of the Khrushchev era. He sized up problems and embarked on policies that were risky but had a good prospect of breaking from the deadends facing Soviet communism inside and outside the USSR. He endeavored to build up support for his ideas and policies in many quarters and sometimes retreated or tacked when faced with serious opposition. Thus his November 2, 1987 speech on the seventieth anniversary of the Bolshevik Revolution managed to mention Bukharin, but mainly in a negative way; it said the Party had gotten off the track here and there but that the October Revolution opened a "new dawn" for mankind. Gorbachev even had good things to say about collectivization, the Molotov-Ribbentrop pact, and Stalin's wartime leadership.

Still, Gorbachev's domestic program faced serious dangers in many arenas. Economic reform, even if promising in the long run, initially yielded chaos, unemployment, lowered living standards and challenge to privilege. All this stimulated unrest among laborers and unhappy bureaucrats. Glasnost', in turn, opened the floodgates to a torrent of denunciations of the Soviet past harmful to the Party's legitimacy. Glasnost' plus demokratiia aggravated ethnic unrest, leading minority nationalities to denounce Great Russians and one another. Kremlin tolerance of such unrest encouraged anti-Soviet activism in Eastern Europe as well.

Gorbachev ran some risk that he would be believed neither abroad nor at home. Foreigners might not believe he was really a supporter of mutual security and total disarmament. Hard-liners in the Communist world might doubt his dedication to Communist ideals and institutions. Intellectual dissidents would doubt that glasnost' and demokratiia would go very far or that they would endure. Ordinary Soviet citizens might doubt his assurances that their lives would improve when, at least in its first few years of perestroika, the Soviet economy yielded less rather than more for the average worker earning only 220 rubles per month.

A kind of conservative manifesto appeared in the newspaper *Sovetskaia Rossiia* in mid-March 1988. Ostensibly written by a Leningrad teacher, it breathed the spirit of neo-Stalinism, questioning whether the new policies were not recklessly and sacrilegiously overthrowing the sound policies and institutions of the past. Nearly three weeks passed before an authoritative rebuttal appeared in Moscow *Pravda* (April 5, 1988) and was then reprinted in many papers including *Sovetskaia Rossiia*. The *Pravda* article charged that certain people are striving "to turn democratization and *glasnost'* against the very same democratization and *glasnost'*, against *perestroika*." And one Soviet citizen snarled that the conservatives should not be given a microphone to broadcast their views, for they will use it as a stick.[72]

When the Party prepared to hold its June 1988 Conference—the first since 1941—many local party groups conspired to exclude candidates who might support the new thinking and nominated only one candidate, a solid supporter of the old thinking. When the conference convened, it heard

Gorbachev turn Marx upside down again. The Soviet economy, he said, could not be restructured unless the political mechanism was changed. Transforming the base would depend on a new superstructure.[73] The delegates approved Gorbachev's plan to create a more powerful Supreme Soviet headed by a president—a post that he snatched from Gromyko in October 1988.

Reforms were still proceeding from the top down rather than from grass-roots initiatives. Still, Gorbachev worked harder at building a consensus before announcing some initiative than that other reformer, Nikita Khrushchev.[74]

When Gorbachev called repeatedly for placing human above class interests, however, this opened him to conservative charges that he had renounced communism for humanism. In July 1988 a major statement by his close aide Shevardnadze refused to identify peaceful coexistence with class struggle. "The struggle between two opposing systems is no longer a determining tendency of the present-day era." Instead, "joint efforts to restore and protect the resources necessary for mankind's survival acquires decisive importance."[75]

A few days later Ligachev rebuffed this line. He told Party workers in a speech later carried on national television:

> We proceed from the class nature of international relations. Any other formulation of the issue only introduces confusion into the thinking of Soviet people and our friends abroad [a sentence omitted in a version printed in *Sovetskaia Rossiia*]. Active involvement in the solution of general human problems by no means signifies any artificial 'breaking' of the social and national liberation struggle.[76]

By the end of September Ligachev seemed no longer to be number two Party secretary and had been given the daunting task of supervising Soviet agriculture. Human interests rather than class struggle remained the official criterion of Soviet policy. Moscow's new chief ideologist, Vadim A. Medvedev, asserted that "universal values" such as avoiding war and ecological catastrophe must outweigh the idea of the class struggle (*Pravda*, October 5, 1988). Still, if Gorbachev stumbled, this revision of Party doctrine would probably be held against him.

Gorbachev faced an uphill struggle in which he had to win battle after battle. If he lost any major encounter, his momentum could be stalled and perestroika might slip back toward the old ways. Gorbachev had to move uphill on many fronts—economic reform, political participation, nationality policy. If he made headway in each domain, synergy might make his overall advance easier. He could afford some slippage in one domain—at least for a time—but not in all simultaneously. If he lost across the board, his job and the fate of his policies would be in grave jeopardy.

Gorbachev's ability to carry out the new thinking abroad depended on his success with political and economic perestroika at home.

Notes

1. Polish leader W. Jaruzelski was allowed to make this argument in an article, "K novym gorizontam," *Kommunist*, no. 11 (July 1987): 59–73 at 63–64.

2. Gorbachev encouraged discussion of blank spots in Polish-Soviet relations. In February 1989 the Polish weekly *Odrodzenie* published details of the 1940 Soviet massacre of more than four thousand Polish officers while a Polish-Soviet study of this event was still under way.

3. This "bi-model pendulum" is described by Moshe Lewin, *The Gorbachev Phenomenon* (Berkeley: University of California Press, 1987); Fyodor Burlatsky also notes a vacillation between militant and NEP-style communism, which he associates with Bukharin, schematically suggesting that Gorbachev embodies the latter tendency.

4. See Gail W. Lapidus, "Gorbachev's Agenda: Reforms and Foreign Policy Assessments," in Peter Juviler and Hiroshi Kimura, eds., *Gorbachev's Reforms* (New York: Aldine de Gruyter, 1988), 1–20 at 14.

5. G. Seleznev, "V interesakh mira i progressa" [A review of a new three-volume history of Soviet foreign policy], *Kommunist*, no. 7 (May 1988): 124–26. This Gorbachev speech does not appear with his collected speeches cited in note 9. One irony: Seleznev attacks the three-volume history for "being without people"—omitting the names of Lenin's "coworkers" in foreign policy, Soviet diplomats responsible for various achievements; but Seleznev does not tell us the names of the authors of the work being reviewed.

6. V. Israelian, "Mir ne mozhet byt' zakliuchen tol'ko sverku" [Peace cannot be concluded only from above], *Literaturnaia gazeta*, June 15, 1988, p. 14.

7. Dobrynin, long-time ambassador to the United States, became director, International Department, CPSU Central Committee. Yakovlev, exchange student at Columbia in 1958–59 and former ambassador to Canada, became a Politburo member responsible for propaganda and, in 1988, for foreign affairs. Yuli Vorontsov, Dobrynin's chargé in Washington for a time and then ambassador to Paris, became deputy foreign minister and roving ambassador to arms control and Afghanistan negotiations. Arbatov, head of the Institute for USA and Canadian Studies, also became a Gorbachev adviser. Andrei Gromyko had long experience in American affairs but was probably seen as too rigid for the new diplomacy. I. T. Frolov, globalistics expert with close ties with Boston University and MIT philosophy of science programs, became chief editor of *Kommunist* for a time. The other globalistics high priest, V. V. Zagladin, remained in the International Department under Dobrynin. Gvishiani was promoted to deputy director of Gosplan but shortly lost that position and, in 1987, his position as chairman of IIASA; the staff at his systems analysis institute was also cut back.

There were also personnel and institutional changes at the Soviet Foreign Ministry and IMEMO intended to strengthen the role of civilian specialists in security policy, a point made to me when I visited IMEMO in March 1989. For background, see Jeffrey Checkel, "Gorbachev's 'New Political Thinking' and the Formation of Soviet Foreign Policy," *Radio Liberty Research Bulletin*, RL 429/88, September 23, 1988, pp. 4–5; also see F. Stephen Larrabee, "Gorbachev and the Soviet Military," *Foreign Affairs*, 66, no. 5 (Summer 1988): 1002–26 at 1012; and Vernon Aspaturian, "The Soviet Foreign Policy Apparatus," *Meeting Report*, Kennan Institute for Advanced Russian Studies (Washington, D.C.), summary of talk on November 16, 1987. Dobrynin retired in 1988; Gromyko died, 1989.

8. *Novoe myshlenie v iadernyi vek* (Moscow: Mezhdunarodnye otnosheniia, 1984), 4, 232–33, 268. Signed to press in June 1984.

9. "The nuclear age inevitably dictates new political thinking." See M. S. Gorbachev, *Izbrannye rechi i stat'i*, 3 vols. (Moscow: Izadatel'stvo politicheskoi literatury, 1987), II: 112–4. This collection of Gorbachev's "Selected Speeches and Articles" presents one article from 1967, twenty-two items from the 1970s, and then moves on to the 1980s. The first speeches included in an American collection are from 1983. See M. S. Gorbachev, *A Time for Peace* (New York: Richardson & Steirman, 1985), where each item before 1985 "is included in the book because of its significance." One such item is Gorbachev's speech to the British Parliament on December 18, 1984, at pp. 39–46.

10. "Rech' M. S. Gorbacheva na traurnom mitinge 13 marta 1985 goda," *Kommunist*, no. 5 (March 1985): 16–17.

11. Andropov had also spoken of Soviet "sympathies" for Third World struggles—a far cry from the "international duty" to aid such efforts in the Brezhnev years.

12. Speech at Central Committee plenum, March 11, 1985, in ibid., pp. 8–11.

13. "O sozyve ocherednogo XXVII s"ezda KPSS i zadachakh, sviazannykh s ego podgotovkoi i provedeniem," Doklad na Plenume TsK KPSS, 23 aprelia 1985 goda, *Izbrannye rechi*, II: 152–73 at 156–57, 168–72.

14. Ibid., III: 88–110 at 98, 109.

15. December 10, 1985 in ibid., III: 111–17 at 112.

16. Answers to questions posed by the French Communist newspaper *L'Humanité* in Gorbachev, *Izbrannye rechi i stat'i*, III: 154–70 at 154.

17. Gorbachev's "Political Report of the CPSU Central Committee to the 27th CPSU Congress," on February 25, 1986, in *Pravda* the next day and in *Kommunist*, no. 4 (March 1986): 5–80; "contradictions" are discussed in part 1, "The Contemporary World"; policy inferences are in part 4, "Basic Goals and Directions of the Party's Foreign Policy Strategy." All emphases in the excerpts quoted here are in the original.

18. See Abraham Becker et al., *The 27th Congress of the Communist Party of the Soviet Union: A Report from the Airlie House Conference* (New York and Santa Monica: Columbia University and RAND Corporation, December 1986), 57–58.

19. *Kommunist*, no. 4 (March 1986): 81–98 at 83, 93.

20. Ibid., pp. 99–152 at 112, 145.

21. Speech of March 6, 1986 in ibid., pp. 172–76 at 175.

22. See also Becker et al., *27th Congress Report*, p. 74.

23. See Vladimir Shlapentokh, "Goodbye to an Old Soviet Dream: Catching up with the West," *Christian Science Monitor*, April 8, 1986, p. 21.

24. Ibid.

25. See the Program's Part 3, I. "Cooperation with the Socialist Countries," *Kommunist*, no. 4 (March 1986): 139–42.

26. V. V. Zagladin, "Programmnye tseli KPSS i global'nye problemy," *Voprosy filosofii*, no. 2 (1986): 3–15. Written on the eve of the Party Congress, the article addresses the "draft new edition" (*Proekt novoi redaktsii*) of the Party Program circulated in late 1985.

27. See ibid., pp. 8–9, 12.

28. Ibid., pp. 10–12.

29. V. V. Zagladin and N. V. Shishlin, eds., *Spravochnik propagandista-mezhdunarodnika* (Moscow: Politizdat, 1987), p. 80. Zagladin could claim some paternity of the researches referred to in this quotation.

30. See, for example, I. T. Frolov, ed., *Sotsializm i progress chelovechestva: global'nye problemy tsivilizatsii* (Moscow: Politizdat, 1987); V. S. Buianov, *Nauchnoe mirovozzrenie* (Moscow: Politizdat, 1987). The latter book gives a more temperate review of bourgeois works on global issues—Theilhard de Chardin, the Club of Rome, others—than Khozin's book and others cited in chapter 5. For a pre-Gorbachev book stressing "we and they," see Stanislav Kondrashov, *My i oni v tesnom mire* (Moscow: Politizdat, 1984)—the same author who became an exponent of "getting a more precise image of the world" after 1985.

31. E. Primakov, "XXVII s"ezd KPSS i issledovanie problem mirovoi ekonomiki i mezhdunarodnykh otnoshenii," *MEMO,* no. 5 (April 1986): 3–14, esp. 4–7, 12–13.

32. G. Kh. Shakhnazarov, "Internatsionalizatsiia—istoki, soderzhanie, stupeni razvitiia," *MEMO,* no. 5 (April 1986): 21–33. Compare also his 1981 and 1985 books: *Griadushchii miroporiadok* (Moscow: Politizdat) and *Kuda idet chelovechestvo* (Moscow: Mysl) set in type in February 1984 but not approved for printing until July 1985.

33. *Pravda,* July 29, 1986, pp. 1–3.

34. The article reported on the first meeting of the Soviet-Chinese Commission on Economic, Trade, Scientific, and Technical Cooperation. It dated the all-around improvement in Sino-Soviet relations to 1983–84 (i.e., the Andropov-Chernenko years). *Izvestiia,* April 19, 1986, p. 5.

35. A visit by Foreign Minister Shevardnadze to Japan in January 1986 seemed to offer some hope for improvement in Japanese-Soviet relations. Moscow agreed to consider Japanese requests to visit relatives' burial places, but both sides remained deadlocked over Japanese claims to the southern Kuriles. See Yu. Vdovin, "Crucial Choice," *Pravda,* January 8, 1986, p. 4 and a Soviet-Japanese communiqué in *Pravda,* January 20, 1986, p. 5.

36. Foreign Broadcast Information Service (FBIS), *Daily Report: Soviet Union,* January 16, 1987.

37. "The Delhi Declaration," November 27, 1986 as printed in FBIS-SOV- December 3, 1986, p. D14.

38. Judging from my experiences in the History and Law Faculties of Moscow University in 1958–59, shortly after Gorbachev studied there, the emphasis on rote learning was probably much stronger when he studied than when he spoke in 1986. Still, readers of *Kommunist* are expected to know the meaning of "scholastic." Do they? In 1986 I asked a former KGB border guard what this term means. He gave an accurate, precise answer—one few American college students could match.

39. *Kommunist,* no. 15 (October 1986): 3–7. All emphases in the original.

40. Ibid., pp. 8–23 at 19.

41. Besides the Tofflers, attendees included Alexander King, president of the Club of Rome; a member of the UNESCO Secretariat; actors, artists, and writers from England (Peter Ustinov), Cuba, Ethiopia, France, India, Spain, Turkey (two), India, and the United States (Arthur and Inga Miller; actor David Baldwin; writer James Baldwin). The listing showed six Americans, two Englishmen, two Turks, two from Soviet client states, one each from several other countries, and no participants from the Warsaw Pact countries except Aitmatov. For the most authoritative Soviet account, see "Vremia trebuet novogo myshleniia," *Kommunist,* no. 16 (November 1986): 3–14.

42. Gorbachev has said that he has read and appreciated Aitmatov's work. Aitmatov's short stories condemned collectivization and Communist fanaticism in Kirghizia long before Gorbachev took power—not in polemics but in highly textured depictions of a region whose peoples are quite different from urban or rural Russians and where CPSU directives were often strikingly inappropriate. See his *Tales of the Mountains and Steppes* (Moscow: Progress Publishers, 1973); also *Sobranie sochinenii v trekh tomakh* (Moscow: Molodaia gvardiia, 1982).

43. *Kommunist,* no. 16 (November 1986): 12.

44. See, for example, Lenin's speech to the Young Communist League, October 2, 1920, in V. I. Lenin, *Polnoe Sobranie Sochinenii,* 5th ed., 55 vols. (Moscow: Gospolizdat, 1958–65), 41: 298–318.

45. Lenin argued the importance of pointing out the "class character of contemporary Russian absolutism and the necessity of overthrowing it—not only in the interests of the working class but in the interests of all [*vsego*] social development." See ibid., 1959, IV: 211–39 at 220. Because the class interests of the proletariat depended on social development, a skeptic might argue, Lenin was ultimately arguing the importance of class interests. In any case, this page of Leniniana says nothing about "common human values." Perhaps Soviet commentators believe that the end of humanism justifies the means of lying. Anatoly Dobrynin wrote in *Kommunist* immediately following the Issyk-Kul discussion about "the

humanistic essence of the proposition *on the universal historical mission of the working class.* . . ." See his "Glavnaia sotsial'naia sila sovremennosti," *Kommunist*, no. 16 (November 1986): 15–25 at 24. Emphasis in the original.

46. The letter appeared in *Pravda* on October 27, 1985. The editor's note in Gorbachev's *Izbrannye rechi*, III: 40–42 at 40 calls the club "one of the most influential international organizations" working to halt the arms race. The Soviet statements cited were silent on the Club's efforts to promote discussion of environmental stress in the world problematique, but Gorbachev's request for advice on unemployment showed his awareness of the club's broad agenda. (Replying to questions posed by *L'Humanité* on February 4, 1986, however, Gorbachev denied that unemployment existed in the USSR and indicated that with proper planning, it would never be a problem. Ibid., III: 158.)

47. The Club of Rome invited several Soviet citizens to become members: E. Primakov, Ch. Aitmatov, and Rektor Lagunov of Moscow State University. D. Gvishiani invited the executive board of the club to meet in the USSR. A Polish chapter was founded in 1987.

48. *Pravda*, February 17, 1987. Partly in response to Reagan's confidence in SDI, Soviet commentators in 1985–87 spoke more and more frequently against misplaced confidence in computer-operated defenses and warned about machines out of control.

49. This slogan, according to the staff of the American Committee on U.S.-Soviet Relations in Washington, was first proposed by Anatoly Gromyko and Vladimir Lomeiko in "Son razuma rozhdaet chudovishch," *Novyi mir*, no. 10 (1984): 181. The title of their article——"Reason's Sleep Gives Birth to Monsters"—appears on the frontpiece of their 1984 book cited earlier where it is attributed to Goya.

50. B. Welling Hall, "The Influence of Soviet Security Ideas and Assumptions" (unpublished manuscript, Earlham College, Richmond, Indiana, 1987), 11.

51. "Chelovek—Tekhnika—Priroda," *Kommunist*, no. 7 (May 1987): 81–89. The same issue carries Gorbachev's preface to a book of his speeches for American readers; an essay by Gyorgy Lukacs on the interconnection of Lenin's ideas; and an article on genetics, society, and the individual. To see which party is more interested in theory, one could compare *Kommunist* with the monthly reviews published by the Republican and Democratic think tanks in Washington—the American Enterprise Institute and the Brookings Institution. Despite their Marxism, many Soviet writers seem to believe that "in the beginning was the Word," whereas their American peers tend to consider interests and actions as more important than words.

52. Ibid., pp. 81–82.

53. Ibid., p. 83.

54. "The Reality and Guarantees of a Secure World," *Pravda*, September 17, 1987, pp. 1–2 and FBIS-SOV, September 17, 1987, pp. 23–28. Emphases in the following quotations appear in the original.

55. Moscow TASS in English, September 18, 1987 in FBIS-SOV, September 18, 1987, pp. 5–6; see also Petrovskii's remarks to Flora Lewis in *The New York Times*, July 6, 1988, p. A23.

56. Boris Pyadyshev on Moscow TASS in English, September 17, 1987 in FBIS-SOV, September 18, p. 6.

57. S. Kondrashov, "Tochnyi obraz mira," *Kommunist*, no. 14 (September 1987): 51–59.

58. See Daniel Lerner, *The Passing of Traditional Society* (New York: Free Press, 1958), 50–51.

59. "Gumanisticheskii vektor nauki," *Kommunist*, no. 14 (September 1987): 74–83. The first such congress, *Kommunist* reported, took place at Stanford in 1960. Soviet scholars first took an active part in the 1967 (Amsterdam) Congress. Some 100 Chinese scholars were among the over 1,200 participants in the Moscow Congress.

60. "V. I. Vernadskii i estestvennonauchnaia traditsiia," *Kommunist*, no. 2 (January 1988): 72–81.

61. See the cutting remarks of economist Gavril Popov about his Belorussian relatives ill from radiation sickness brought on by poisoned food sold in local markets. Their illness,

he said, may be ultimately traced to "bureaucratic socialism." Popov and other critical minds contributed to a symposium, "What If Even This Perestroika Fails?" *Moscow News*, no. 23 (1988): 8–9.

62. Sergei Zalygin, "Professionaly ot gigantomanii," *Literaturnaia gazeta*, February 8, 1989, p. 11.

63. Bill Keller, "Moscow's Other Mastermind," *The New York Times Magazine*, February 19, 1989, pp. 30 ff. at 40.

64. Iurii Chernichenko, "Zemlia, ekologiia, perestroika," *Literaturnaia gazeta*, January 25, 1989, pp. 3–4 at 3.

65. See V. Koptiug, "Ekologiia: ot obespokoennosti—k deistvennoi politike," *Kommunist*, no. 7 (May 1988): 24–33 at 24–26.

66. On gigantomania, see Zalygin, "Professionaly ot gigantomanii."

67. P. Simonov, "Priroda postupka," *Kommunist*, no. 8 (May 1988): 87–94.

68. A survey of 939 Muscovites with telephones showed that 42 percent gave Bukharin a positive evaluation; Khrushchev, 23 percent; Brezhnev and Stalin, 12 percent each; and Trotsky, 11 percent. See *The New York Times*, May 27, 1988, p. 1.

69. These questions occurred to me when, after reading Simonov, I went out to Walden Pond for a dip. Seeing that a log had floated away from the support structure holding up the fragile banks, I asked two healthy specimens to help me move it back into place. One was turning lobster red while lying on a cot in the shallow water and could not be disturbed; his partner, sitting in the shade, also refused to help, even after he roused himself for a vigorous swim.

70. See his *An Alternative to War or Surrender* (Urbana: University of Illinois Press, 1962).

71. See Tsuyoshi Hasegawa, "Gorbachev, the New Thinking of Soviet Foreign-Security Policy and the Military: Recent Trends and Implications," in Juviler and Kimura, *Gorbachev's Reforms*, pp. 115–47 at 134–42; also Alexander Dallin, "Gorbachev's Foreign Policy and the 'New Political Thinking' in the Soviet Union," ibid. pp. 97–113 at 112–113.

72. Vladimir Reznichenko in *Moscow News*, 25 (June 25–July 3, 1988): 2.

73. Coverage of the conference was extensive in most Soviet papers—for example, *Literaturnaia gazeta*, June 22, 1988. For analysis, see Seweryn Bialer, "The Changing Soviet Political System: The Nineteenth Party Conference and After," in Bialer, ed., *Politics, Society, and Nationality Inside Gorbachev's Russia* (Boulder, CO: Westview, 1989), 193–241.

74. See Checkel, "Gorbachev's 'New Political Thinking,' " pp. 7–9.

75. Shevardnadze addressed a conference at the Ministry of Foreign Affairs on the recent Party conference. Text in *Vestnik ministerstva inostrannykh del SSSR*, no. 15 (August 15, 1988): 27–46. See especially pp. 35–36.

76. "Vremia" newscast, Moscow Television Service, August 5, 1988, in FBIS-SOV, August 8, 1988, p. 41. The passage quoted here was truncated in *Sovetskaia Rossiia* (August 6, 1988) and *Pravda* (August 6, 1988), which rendered Ligachev's comments only on domestic affairs.

8

Actions Louder than Words?
Doing the Unthinkable

The words of Russia's new leaders were revolutionary, but what of their deeds? Did Gorbachev say one thing and do another? Were there spheres in which it proved easier to convert rhetoric to action and others in which old ways tended to hold on? In foreign affairs would change come more readily in high or in low politics?

Gorbachev began radical change in two areas that might be judged most sensitive: freedom of expression and international security policy. More slowly than in high politics, the Kremlin also moved toward greater cooperation with the non-Communist world in economics and other domains with low political saliency. Perestroika moved most slowly in remolding Soviet economic practices. Sixty years earlier Stalin had stood Marx on his head using political power to transform the economic base. Now Gorbachev found that it was easier to change the superstructure than the production and social relations created by Stalin.

The optimum strategy for coping with a distrustful rival, one Western study concluded, is to match his every move tit for tat. If he cooperates, match his cooperation; if he breaks faith, repay him in kind. Such behavior, however, could put rivals on an endless spiral of conflict damaging to both sides. To escape such dead-ends, one party must initiate cooperative moves that persuade the other to reciprocate. The initiator will probably have to make several such moves before his message is clear. The first initiatives must be sufficiently significant to impress the antagonist that they are not empty propaganda; yet these steps must open the initiator to coercion by the other side. If both parties begin to reciprocate each other's moves, each can afford larger steps toward accommodation.[1]

Gorbachev broke from tit for tat with a series of initiatives or concessions to Western demands which included the following:

—Maintaining an eighteen-month moratorium on nuclear testing and permitting U.S. scientists and seismic equipment near Soviet test sites

—Agreeing to a treaty requiring the USSR to remove more warheads and destroy more intermediate- and shorter-range missiles than the United States

—Opening to Western scrutiny a Soviet radar station with possible ABM significance as well as other military installations and activities

—Unilaterally cutting Soviet military forces by one-tenth and pledging to restructure remaining units in a strictly defensive configuration

—Withdrawing Soviet forces from Afghanistan by February 15, 1989

—Supporting arrangements to end regional conflict in Kampuchea, southern Africa, the Persian Gulf, and the Middle East

—Easing emigration barriers for Soviet citizens and repression of political dissidents

—Tolerating organized calls for greater autonomy and even for "sovereignty" in the Baltic and other border republics

—Putting the USSR's record on the line by summoning a human rights conference in Moscow in 1991

—Inviting joint ventures and sponsoring other moves to make the USSR a partner in world commerce and science

These and other Gorbachev actions will be examined in this chapter. Although each move departed radically from Soviet precedent, none ensured that other nations had nothing to fear from the Russian Bear. Each action could be read as trivial—even a trick to heighten ultimate Soviet advantage. Still, their cumulative impact persuaded many in the West that a historic opportunity had arisen in which to supplant the cold war with mutually advantageous cooperation.

Abolishing All Nuclear Arms by A.D. 2000

In line with Western theories of conflict reduction, Gorbachev laid out his broad strategy in advance, affirming his priority for domestic perestroika and his rejection of nuclear deterrence as a basis for security.

[208]

He emphasized dialogue and compromise as the ways to resolve disputes—not force of arms. On January 16, 1986, he issued a "declaration" (*zaiavlenie*) outlining a plan to eliminate all nuclear arms by the year 2000 and sharply limit other weapons as well.[2]

Was the plan feasible? Was it even desirable from the standpoint of Soviet security? American interests? those of other countries?

Stage 1 of the January 1986 proposal could benefit all parties: Soviet and U.S. strategic arsenals would shrink by 50 percent over the next five to eight years to a total of no more than 6,000 warheads each. A reduction of this magnitude (suggested by George F. Kennan five years before) would leave each superpower with more than enough arms to deter attack from any quarter. The USSR and United States would also eliminate all their ballistic and cruise medium-range missiles in Europe—a step that would leave them with many other nuclear and nonnuclear arms in that theater. France and Britain could keep their present arsenals but not enlarge them. The key component of NATO's "trip wire"—forward-based U.S. troops with nuclear weapons—could remain.

Stage 1 included two features that Washington rejected: a moratorium on U.S. and Soviet nuclear tests and a ban on the testing or deployment of space strike weapons, thus confining Star Wars to laboratory research. The White House replied that strategic defense provided a kind of "insurance" policy supplementing—not contradicting—nuclear disarmament. But arms control specialists asked how either power could cut its missiles if meaningful defenses curtailed their deterrent threat.[3]

The Gorbachev plan was also explicit that whereas Britain and France would not immediately be required to reduce their missile forces, Washington could not transfer medium-range missiles to its allies—a point that, Soviet commentators argued, distinguished Moscow's position from Reagan's "zero option" offer, which did not close U.S. options for missile proliferation.

Stage 2 (1990 to 1995 or 1997) required Moscow and Washington to cut further their medium-range and strategic nuclear forces and the other nuclear powers to begin reducing their nuclear arms, though Gorbachev did not specify the permitted levels. All nuclear states in Stage 2 would have to halt nuclear testing, join the ban on deployment of cosmic strike weapons, and eliminate all tactical nuclear arms (range up to 1,000 kilometers).[4]

Some NATO strategists worried that dispensing with tactical nuclears would remove the firebreak between conventional and all-out nuclear war. Other Western analysts called the firebreak theory a dangerous illusion and said that there are better ways to stop a Soviet offensive if Moscow should ever contemplate one.

[209]

Gorbachev's Stage 2 also called for a ban on development of nonnuclear arms based on new physical principles giving them a capacity for mass destruction. This proposal—reminiscent of tsarist proposals in 1899 and 1907—could inhibit NATO's quest for a nonnuclear defense. Holding back the momentum of military R&D might be feasible only if political relations between East and West were transformed.

Stage 3 raised the deepest questions. Between 1995 and the end of 1999 all nuclear weapons would disappear. There would be a universal accord "that such weapons will never again come into being." Elaborate measures would be undertaken to verify the accords.

Gorbachev also proposed immediate steps to ban the use of chemical weapons and then to destroy chemical weapons stockpiles. Their industrial base would be eliminated under international inspection. He urged reductions of conventional forces in Europe and adoption of confidence-building measures including advance notification of large-scale troop maneuvers ("putting off the question of naval activity until the next stage of the conference").

Gorbachev flouted the conventional wisdom that the quest for perfection is the enemy of the good: that piecemeal arms limitation is more feasible than comprehensive disarmament. He finessed whether it is wiser to concentrate on the Big Two or factor in all nuclear powers. Ultimately the Kremlin could hardly accept far-reaching arms limits unless all its potential foes were constrained.[5]

Received wisdom asks: Can we hold back the clock? Gorbachev would ban all nuclear tests, prohibit all testing of space strike weapons, limit the power of new nonnuclear weapons, and destroy the industrial base for chemical weapons. Utopian? Perhaps, but why curb today's weapons if tomorrow's will be more threatening?

A grave theoretical problem was Moscow's refusal to recognize that nations arm because they distrust one another. Gorbachev said that the "Soviet Union is opposed to making the implementation of disarmament measures dependent on so-called regional conflicts." Moscow, he averred, wanted a speedy, just, collective resolution of such conflicts, but the Kremlin resisted efforts to "impose on sovereign peoples an alien will." As in the 1920s, the USSR rebuffed the notion that "moral" disarmament must precede "material" disarmament. In short, the Kremlin opposed "linking" arms limitation with extraneous matters. In practice, however, Gorbachev's diplomats worked to moderate "regional conflicts" *in tandem* with Soviet-U.S. arms limitations.

A provisional reading of Gorbachev's plan indicated that all sides could gain from implementing Stages 1 and 2. But the total elimination of nuclear arms envisioned in Stage 3 appeared potentially destabilizing as well as politically remote. So long as nations compete for dominion, most governments will resist closing military workshops or dismantling the forces on which they stake their security.

Nuclear weapons have probably helped to prevent major wars since 1945. Might we not face a heightened danger of war if all nuclear arms disappeared? And what if one nation cheated and cached, say, a hundred nuclear weapons? Could it not blackmail and command others? It would therefore be more realistic to permit each power to retain a nuclear umbrella—its size carefully calculated—until all parties feel deterrence is unnecessary.

Most Soviet commentaries on the January 1986 proposal amounted to knee-jerk praise, but veteran diplomat Viktor Israelian thoughtfully compared it with Soviet proposals for comprehensive disarmament in 1927–32 and 1959–62. The earlier plans, he wrote (*Literaturnaia gazeta*, June 15, 1988), were unrealistic in proposing total disarmament in one to four years; the late 1950s–early 1960s proposals were out of tune with that era's cold war spirit. Gorbachev's proposals, by contrast, were realistic and did not play into the hands of the foes of disarmament.

Asymmetrical Moves

Although Gorbachev kept his nuclear-free utopia in view, he moved on many fronts to accomplish limited measures of arms control. Soviet commentators affirmed that the USSR possessed military assets so large that some could be sacrificed to improve East-West relations. Gorbachev's Kremlin often did the unthinkable: curtailing its forces unilaterally or to a greater extent than the other side.

Halting Nuclear Tests: From Unilateral Moratorium to Joint Verification Experiments

Gorbachev argued that halting nuclear tests is a promising way to constrain new engines of destruction. The Reagan administration, on the other hand, opposed halting nuclear tests because it wanted to test new weapons for SDI and other programs.[6] It asserted that Soviet underground tests had often exceeded the limits of the Threshold Test Ban Treaty (TTBT) signed in 1974 but still unratified.[7]

Taking a cue from Khrushchev's 1958 test moratorium initiative,[8]

[211]

Gorbachev announced in July 1985 that the USSR would observe a unilateral testing moratorium beginning August 6 (the anniversary of the bombing of Hiroshima) and continuing until January 1, 1986. It would "remain in effect, however, so long as the United States, for its part, refrains from conducting nuclear explosions." In January Gorbachev extended the moratorium for another three months. Responding to an appeal from six world leaders, the Kremlin announced its willingness to refrain from nuclear explosions even after March 31, 1986—until the first nuclear explosion in the United States. Following another U.S. test in April 1986, the Soviet government announced its intention to resume testing but reiterated its willingness to take part in a bilateral moratorium. In the wake of the Chernobyl accident, however, Gorbachev stated on May 14 that the USSR would extend its moratorium once again, to August 6; on August 18 he announced a further extension to January 1, 1987.[9]

Considering that Gorbachev was new to the job and that he must have wanted the military's loyalty, it was remarkable that he persisted in this unilateral restraint for eighteen months—a fortiori given that the United States was actively testing components of a new high-tech arsenal.[10] As Gorbachev put it in his January 1986 declaration, "it was far from easy for us to adopt the decision to continue the moratorium for another three months. The Soviet Union cannot go on displaying unilateral restraint . . . ad infinitum." Indeed, insiders reported the Soviet Defense Council voted 3–2 to initiate the moratorium; 3–2 to continue it in January 1986; and 3–2 (contra Gorbachev) to resume testing. Soviet underground testing recommenced in February 1987.

The Soviet government, ever concerned to demonstrate the feasibility of monitoring a test ban, opened its territory to a team from the Natural Resources Defense Council (a private agency) that placed seismic monitoring equipment in three locations some two hundred miles from the Semipalatinsk testing site in July 1986 and sent Soviet scientists to Nevada to test equipment that November. Also in July 1986 the USSR proposed developing a second-level system as a foundation for international seismic monitoring of a test ban.[11] Neither government allowed the scientists direct access to the test sites but did enable them to place monitors nearby.[12] The experiments, conducted in 1987–88, showed that in comparison with the Soviet test area in Kazakhstan, seismic signals travel poorly through the porous and fractured geology of southern Nevada.

What considerations drove Gorbachev's efforts to halt nuclear testing? "It is not a propaganda war that we seek to win," he declared (TASS, September 8, 1986). A test ban "is organically linked with nuclear arms reductions"; it would help to overcome distrust and would stop the squandering of "forces and funds for an evil cause. . . ."

Are Soviet weapons so much simpler than U.S. that they need no reliability tests? Did modernization of Soviet forces overtake the United States before the moratorium? Gorbachev denied both charges on September 8, 1986. He argued that experience shows that one can be sure of nuclear munitions by checking their nonnuclear components. "Since 1974 the USA and the USSR do not conduct tests with a yield of over 150 kilotons in compliance with the existing [threshold] treaty. Meanwhile, munitions with yields over that 'threshold' make up 70 per cent of the nuclear arsenal. . . ."

Gorbachev attacked the U.S. position that both sides should agree to "regulate" rather than end nuclear testing, saying there could be no halfway solution to the problem of nuclear tests. All the evidence, he said, indicated that a complete ban could be monitored with assurance.

Despite such categorical statements, Moscow agreed in 1986 that Soviet and U.S. experts could meet to discuss methods for verifying the TTBT and Peaceful Nuclear Explosions Treaty (PNET) signed in 1976. And the next years found the two countries cooperating to improve verification procedures. Whereas the NRDC experiments aimed at demonstrating the feasibility of a comprehensive test ban or a ban on explosions larger than one kiloton, the intergovernmental study sought only to test methods to verify a ban on tests over 150 kt.

In 1987–88 the U.S. government engaged Moscow with a variety of plans to improve the reliability of nuclear test monitoring.[13] Critics called such moves transparent gestures to appease the naive. This interpretation dovetailed with secret testimony to Congress of Deputy Assistant Secretary of Energy James W. Culpepper who asserted that research on nuclear-powered beam weapons promised the United States an edge over the USSR because of America's superiority in high technology.[14]

Test ban or no, the United States went to great lengths to improve monitoring of the USSR, utilizing Chinese-manned seismic stations in Xinjiang (some six hundred miles from Semipalatinsk) and in Manchuria to measure Soviet blast yields. The Pentagon also used the *Glomar Challenger* drilling ship to test the ocean floor six hundred miles from Kampchatka to see if such a site were sufficiently free of background noise to monitor shock waves from Central Asia.[15]

Although the Kremlin remained dubious about U.S. motives, in spring 1987 Moscow agreed to permit use of a Corrtex cable at Soviet test sites as a way of checking and improving America's capability to monitor Soviet tests with seismic instruments based around the world.[16] In

September Moscow even reversed gears and accepted the sequence demanded by Washington: first, explorations of "effective verification measures"; then, assuming their success, talks on "intermediate limitations" such as the number and size of permitted tests. Ultimately "complete cessation of nuclear testing" was the goal adopted in a communiqué issued by Secretary of State George Shultz and Soviet Foreign Minister Eduard Shevardnadze.[17] Both sides then carried out a Joint Verification Experiment in 1988 using two different monitoring systems—teleseismic and hydrodynamic—at the Nevada and Semipalatinsk sites to study explosions in the range of 100 to 150 kt.[18]

Both sides made concessions. Soviet behavior implied that the U.S. demand for better test monitoring methods might have legitimacy; joint experiments might show that existing technologies were weak. Reagan now treated a test ban as a worthy goal to be implemented if proper verification procedures became available. He no longer made U.S. acceptance of a comprehensive test ban hinge on nuclear arms cuts.

Global "Double Zero"

Soviet concessions and American steadfastness produced a December 1987 accord to eliminate within three years two classes of missiles: longer-range intermediates (LRINF, 1,000–5,500 kilometers) and shorter-range intermediates (SRINF, 500–1,000 km). Because most of the deployed Soviet IRMs carried three warheads and all the U.S. missiles carried only one, the USSR was obliged to retire several times more warheads than the United States. The warheads and missile guidance systems had to be removed but could be recycled.[19]

The origins of the INF problem could be traced back to the 1950s when NATO deployed "battlefield" nuclears and the Kremlin held Europe hostage with hundreds of medium-range missiles. Both sides talked of "disengaging" and "thinning" European forces, but German rearmament and recurrent Berlin crises reinforced the lines of confrontation.

In the 1970s the USSR acquired rough intercontinental parity with the United States and began in 1977 to modernize its Euromissiles, supplementing or supplanting older weapons with the RSD-10—what the West called the SS-20—a solid-fueled, mobile missile able to fire its three nuclear warheads with great accuracy some 5,000 kilometers and then reload. From deployments in Soviet Central Asia it could hit targets in all of Western Europe and China; from the Urals, Iceland and Greenland; from the Western USSR, half of Africa; from eastern Siberia, Alaska, Japan,

[214]

Okinawa, Guam, the Philippines, and Indochina—falling just short of Wake Island and Midway.[20]

The SS-20 was a much more formidable weapon than its predecessors. Further, like the new Soviet Backfire bomber, the range of the SS-20 fell just short of the 5,500 kilometers necessary to be defined as a "strategic" weapon to be limited under SALT II. As Strobe Talbott notes,

> The SS-20 was a classic example of the Soviet penchant for playing as close as possible to the edge of what is permissible under existing or prospective arms-control agreements, stopping just short of violating the letter of these agreements but nonetheless upsetting the stability and predictability that arms control is meant to help achieve.[21]

The SS-20 deployment deepened NATO worries about parity, coupling and deterrence. The United States had no comparable missiles, therefore the SS-20 created a significant asymmetry in theater weapons. Formalization of strategic parity would tend to decouple U.S. security interests from Europe, especially when Soviet strike forces against Europe were becoming more formidable.

German Chancellor Helmut Schmidt in 1977 had called for moves to recouple U.S.-European security and to make extended deterrence more credible. One avenue could be through deployment of U.S. intermediate-range missiles then being developed. French President Valéry Giscard d'Estaing suggested that NATO join its own INF deployment with an arms control initiative. Following on the SALT II Treaty signed in June 1979, NATO adopted a "dual-track" approach in November: negotiate to reduce the SS-20 threat while proceeding to deploy 572 American IRMs (464 Tomahawk cruise missiles and 108 ballistic Pershing 2s)—a number that would not match Soviet warheads but would suffice for NATO's objectives. NATO also agreed to withdraw 1,000 of its approximately 7,400 nuclear warheads then in Europe—a step that, however rational, added to worries about decoupling.

Ignoring this background, the newly elected Reagan administration picked up an idea from the German left and proposed in fall 1981 a "zero option"—no NATO INF deployment in exchange for SS-20 disarmament. Moscow's response under Brezhnev and then Andropov was to propose a freeze on *new* INF deployments. Soviet diplomats contended that Soviet forces were already matched by British and French forces and U.S. forward-based systems. Brezhnev rejected as "absurd" the idea of unilateral Soviet disarmament to reach zero-zero; other Soviets called the U.S. proposal an "insult." To break the impasse top U.S. and Soviet negotiators in Geneva in 1982 sketched a tentative "walk down the

[215]

mountain" agreement to restrict NATO's IRM deployment to GLCMs in exchange for substantial reductions in SS-20s, but this deal was not attractive to the Kremlin or White House.[22]

In 1983 the West began its INF deployment and the Soviet diplomats walked out of strategic as well as INF negotiations. Having threatened compensatory moves, the USSR deployed more submarines close to U.S. shores. It also began to deploy "shorter-range" SS-12 (OTR-22 in Soviet terminology) missiles in East Germany and Czechoslovakia and SS-23 (OTR-23) missiles in East Germany, supplementing deployments of both weapons in the USSR. NATO ministers at Montebello in 1983 voted to modernize NATO's theater nuclears but also to withdraw another 1,400 atomic warheads from the present deployment.

Soviet and U.S. diplomats returned to negotiations in March 1985 when new "umbrella" talks linking strategic, space, and theater arms got under way. Negotiators at one table focused on strategic arms (what Washington called START—Strategic Arms Reductions Talks); another on space weapons and the ABM treaty; the third table concentrated on INF issues.

Only limited progress was registered at the first two tables, but the INF negotiations yielded a treaty signed in December 1987 and ratified May 1988. After much zigging and zagging, the Kremlin had made ten basic concessions.

(1) Moscow agreed to proceed on the INF even though no accord had been reached reaffirming the traditional interpretation of the ABM Treaty and limiting the scope of Reagan's SDI. The Kremlin had insisted on linking INF and ABM at Reykjavik in 1986 and in the aftermath of the 1987 "Yeltsin affair," only to discard this condition shortly before the December 1987 Washington summit.

(2) The Kremlin agreed to omit U.S. forward-based systems (FBS) from the INF equation, perhaps judging that U.S. aircraft in Europe and at sea represented a secondary threat compared with Euromissiles.

(3) Moscow agreed in February 1987 to ignore the expanding intermediate-range arsenals of France, Britain, and China even though Gorbachev's January 1986 proposal said that these forces should be frozen in Stage 1 of a progressive disarmament package and reduced in Stage 2. Now Moscow said only that the other nuclear powers must be brought into the next disarmament accords.

(4) The USSR agreed in April 1987 to make the treaty a "double zero." When Shultz proposed a freeze on Soviet SRINFs deployed with a right for the West to build up to parity, Gorbachev replied by proposing a second zero —SRINFs. NATO at first hesitated, but this was a deal too sweet to pass up.[23]

(5) Moscow also agreed to ignore West Germany's force of seventy-two aging shorter-range missiles (Pershing 1A), even though they carried nuclear warheads owned by the United States. Because France and Britain were not limited by this treaty, the Federal Republic resented any hint that its forces would be constrained in what was basically a bilateral treaty. Bonn agreed, however, to eliminate its SRINFs "with the final elimination" of Soviet and U.S. INF missiles.

(6) The Kremlin agreed in July 1987 to global limits: eliminating its LR/SRINFs in Asia as well as in Europe even though its adversaries could offer no quid pro quo. Initially Moscow wanted to retain all or at least one hundred of its missiles deployed in the Far East. But the United States claimed the right to deploy a comparable force. Any residual forces permitted in Soviet Asia would also raise objections from Tokyo and Beijing. Moscow finally agreed that it would be easier to ban the production, stockpiling, and deployment of all INF missiles rather than permit a selected few to remain. Officials later explained to the Supreme Soviet that Moscow's relations with Asian countries (presumably China) had improved in recent years and that the United States had not increased its nuclear forces near the Soviet Far East.

(7) Soviet negotiators worked to incorporate in the treaty a pledge not to circumvent the treaty by sharing INF technology. They settled for a promise not to "assume any international obligations or undertakings which would conflict with its provisions."

(8) The Kremlin agreed essentially to whatever kinds of verification procedures the United States proposed, whether intense or confined. When the Americans wanted extremely intrusive on-site inspection, Moscow agreed, leading the Pentagon and certain military manufacturers to object, fearful that Soviet inspectors would ferret out high-tech secrets. Washington then proposed a "portal and perimeter" watch around one Soviet and one American factory to check what came out rather than to examine what was done inside. That the Soviet factory (the Votkinsk Machine Building Plant some six hundred miles northeast of Moscow) was still producing missiles (the SS-25), whereas the American (Hercules Plant in Magna, Utah) had ceased producing missiles made the inspection procedures more intrusive for the USSR than for the United States. So long as SS-25 production continues at Votkinsk, both parties are entitled to keep their inspectors on watch for thirteen years.

U.S. negotiator Paul Nitze acknowledged that "only 'anytime, anywhere' inspection without a possibility of refusal" would provide high-certainty verification. But ceding "the same right in the INF treaty to Soviet inspectors on our territory is not in our interest." Inspectors are permitted

[217]

to observe only those sites where each country reported it had once produced, deployed, or tested its LR/SRINFs. All but a tiny fraction of Soviet and U.S. territory is off-limits to inspectors. On national technical means of inspection will fall the task of monitoring the rest of each country—supplemented perhaps by spies or vigilant citizens. Nitze said that the verification procedures aimed to make militarily significant violations impossible.[24]

At Washington's behest the treaty did not require INF warheads and missile guidance systems to be destroyed. The United States wanted to recover the nuclear material and safeguard secret information about the warhead designs.[25]

In early 1988 Soviet negotiators seemed to renege on several inspection commitments. When the Senate threatened to delay ratification, the Soviets signed a memorandum on May 12, 1988 explicitly supporting the broader and more intensive procedures the United States maintained were in the December 8, 1987 accords. The Kremlin also agreed to an exchange of notes specifying that deployment and testing of IRMs carrying weapons based on future technologies were also banned by the treaty. The American note stated the principle, and the Soviet note (both dated May 12, 1988, Geneva) declared that the USSR fully shared the U.S. view on this matter.[26]

(9) The Kremlin did not insist on a "third zero": eliminating all nuclear arms with ranges less than 500 kilometers. West Germans found it unpleasant to think that the only territory on which nuclear exchanges might occur would be their own. Even though Moscow could easily have manipulated German sentiments, it did not. To do so would have agitated still further the NATO strategists already complaining about the dangers of weakening U.S. ties with Europe.

(10) The bottom line was that the USSR agreed to destroy missiles carrying many more warheads than the missiles eliminated by the United States (a discrepancy arising because the SS-20 carried three warheads whereas all the U.S. missiles carried only one; because the USSR had a monopoly on SRINFs; and because some Soviet missiles were equipped with refire warheads). The Pentagon talked of recycling the warheads on SLCMs or ALCMs; the Kremlin decried Western talk of "compensation."

Why did the Soviet Union agree to these apparently asymmetrical obligations? Kremlin spokesmen warned Soviet doubters against taking a simplistic, arithmetical approach to analysis. Many of the Soviet missiles were old, and none could reach the United States except for Alaska. The American missiles were new and could strike Soviet territory.

[218]

The Pershing 2 missile sounded special alarms, leading Moscow's "walk down the mountain" negotiator to offer a high price to ban the P2 but to let many Tomahawks be deployed. Fired from southern Germany, the P2 could hit the Kremlin in six or seven minutes—too quickly for Kremlin occupants to reach deep shelters. Deep-penetrating warheads would add to the dangers. Carrying a 150-kt warhead, the P2 could fly only 1,850 kilometers, falling just short of Moscow; if loaded with a lighter warhead (40 to 50 kt) its range could reach 2,100 km, sufficient to hit Red Square. In addition to worries about their personal safety, the Politburo may have worried about the undefined chain of command inside the Kremlin. If the top man were eliminated, who could push the "fire" button? Unless this question were resolved, the Soviet deterrent might not function, thus increasing Western incentives to strike first. The P2's short flight time added to Moscow's reasons to adopt a "launch on warning" posture that could be triggered by a false signal.

The GLCMs had a somewhat longer range than the P2s and were more accurate; their low flight might evade Soviet radars, but their longer flight time made them somewhat less threatening than the U.S. ballistic missiles.

The American threat to convert P2s to Pershing 1-Bs or to deploy some other form of shorter-range missile doubtless helped to stimulate Gorbachev's offer to establish a "double-zero." The U.S. demand for parity in residual IRMs—a threat to add one hundred American missiles to balance those in the Soviet Far East—probably helped to induce the Kremlin to accept global limits.

The USSR had responded to NATO INF by moving submarines closer to U.S. coasts. These weapons too may have presented some danger of an unauthorized Soviet launch or tempting Washington to launch on warning. In early 1988 they were redeployed closer to the United Kingdom, perhaps to compensate for withdrawal of the SS-20s.

Both sides retained an abundant and redundant supply of planes and long-range missiles by which to attack each other's targets in or near Eurasia; they could also keep or increase their supply of short-range missiles (up to 500 km range), in which the USSR had a decisive lead. They could also deploy more missiles at sea or in the air, even using warheads and guidance systems salvaged from the scrapped INF missiles. But if NATO now diverted some of its dual-capable aircraft to nuclear missions, this would weaken the West's conventional capabilities. In addition, the F-111 bombers based in England probably had insufficient range to fly to the USSR and return, though they could conceivably land in West Germany.

The Kremlin may have guessed that the INF Treaty would stir up a hornet's nest within NATO as each country asked, "What's in it for me?" and "What do we do next?" While some NATO governments worried how to compensate for the removed missiles, the Kremlin's Eastern European allies expressed relief that all IRMs would be destroyed.[27]

Soviet leaders seem to have concluded that limited nuclear exchanges are uncontrollable and should be avoided. Soviet military planning appeared "increasingly focused on prosecuting a conventional-only war instead of initiating hostilities with a nuclear strike as appeared to be their approach in the early 1970s"[28]—before Brezhnev's 1977 speech at Tula questioning the value of nuclear superiority. From this standpoint any steps toward denuclearization of Europe are desirable for Moscow.

To eliminate forces that had no practical use—and persuade the other side to do the same—meant little sacrifice, especially given that Warsaw Pact forces outnumbered Western in most conventional arms. The USSR could then concentrate on modernizing its conventional forces even if it pared the East's quantitative advantages.

Eliminating all IRMs would also impede NATO's plans to deploy smart conventional warheads on missiles that could strike deep into Warsaw Pact territory. Given that NATO's smart weapon technology led Soviet, this would stall another round of arms competition disadvantageous to the USSR. It could make it more difficult for the West to maintain "escalation dominance" at every rung of the ladder. Also barring all IRMs with futuristic technology weapons could constrain America more than the USSR, even though this ban was demanded by the U.S. Senate.

Beyond such military gains, the INF accord could provide what Soviet commentators portrayed as one of the first tangible results of the "new thinking." Probably the treaty enhanced the Gensec's status and support.[29] It opened the way to détente, trade, and other arms control measures. Had Gorbachev had nothing substantial to show for his summit meetings with Reagan and Soviet unilateral restraints, his authority would have slipped at home and the East-West atmosphere could easily have become more tense. Instead the INF provided the justification for two summits—a signing ceremony in Washington and ratification in Moscow—accompanied by a small explosion of joint venture and other exchange deals.

Although the INF Treaty netted few economic gains and entailed some costs, it could permit future savings if it tempers future arms competition. The treaty strengthened Moscow's new image of peace and conciliation not only in the West and in Eastern Europe but in more suspicious Beijing and Tokyo.

[220]

To make these gains, the USSR eliminated some of the newest and most formidable weapons in its arsenal; withdrew many more nuclear warheads than its rival; opened military facilities to on-site inspection; failed to curtain French, British, and Chinese forces; and did not stop America's expanding SLCM and ALCM deployment. While winning applause for "reasonableness," Soviet behavior also vindicated the hang-tough, negotiate-from-strength school of Western diplomacy. Gorbachev even risked domestic opposition to his asymmetrical concessions.

Conventional Force Imbalances

Most NATO planners choked at the notion of removing all nuclear arms from Europe—the West's ace against Russian mass and proximity. The major NATO governments except Bonn balked at a "third zero." Instead they wanted to proceed with nuclear force modernization.[30] The rationale for modernization became stronger after the INF Treaty accentuated Soviet conventional strengths.

Instead of upgrading nuclear or other arms, the USSR proposed shifting Warsaw Pact and NATO forces toward a posture of "reasonable sufficiency"—adequate for defense but insufficient to threaten attack. Gorbachev's Kremlin declared itself willing to make conventional reductions as well as nuclear. If there were asymmetries in the assets of both sides, Soviet spokesmen stressed Moscow's willingness to remove them, even if this meant reducing more Eastern than Western forces. Gorbachev proposed at the Moscow Nuclear Forum in February 1987 steps to maintain a balance at ever lower levels.

Gorbachev's inflection conflicted with NATO's modernization plans and its recently adopted concept of Follow-On Forces Attack (FOFO) strategy—deep air strikes against second-echelon Warsaw Pact forces far behind the lines. Some U.S. strategists were also urging an "offensive defense" posture that could send Western ground as well as air forces against Dresden or Smolensk while Soviet forces approached Hamburg. Thus NATO hoped to counter Pact numerical superiority not only by exploiting Western advantages in high tech but by transforming a passively waiting victim into an active threat against Pact residual forces and core values.[31]

Many Western critics (for example, Senator Carl Levin and Ret. Rear Admiral Gene R. La Rocque) denied the premise that Pact forces possessed significant advantages over NATO. They argued that Pact forces were unreliable, inefficient, undertrained, and not in possession of the ratios of

[221]

advantage needed for attackers to overwhelm a stout defense. Not only quality but terrain and other factors favor Western defense. Soviet planners would never attack westward because China might then open a second front.

Most NATO governments, however, backed State Secretary Shultz when he stated that the West could not renounce its battlefield nuclear weapons unless the Kremlin made large cuts in conventional forces. Some Western analysts feared that small conventional reductions, though tilted in NATO's favor, could worsen imbalances.[32] Even if Pact forces were cut to equal Western, residual forces in the USSR would remain closer to Central Europe than forces based in North America. Further, Soviet reserves could be kept at higher readiness than Western. The Pact would retain the advantages of the attacker, perhaps aided by deception and surprise. One study concluded that "the Soviets can unilaterally reduce their forces, cut defense spending and still retain a range of warfighting options against NATO. . . . [Probably the] Soviets, for the foreseeable future, will merely seek to 'repackage' their military superiority in Europe."[33]

Confirming Pentagon fears, on December 7, 1988, Gorbachev announced that in 1989–90 the USSR would unilaterally reduce its armed forces by 500,000 men, 10,000 tanks, 8,500 artillery pieces, and 800 aircraft. Some 50,000 Soviet troops and 5,000 tanks (including six tank divisions) would be withdrawn from East Germany, Czechoslovakia, and Hungary. These reductions would come from 380,000 serving in East Germany, 80,000 in Czechoslovakia, and 65,000 in Hungary, leaving the 40,000 Soviet troops in Poland (many of them engaged in maintaining electronic and other logistic links between the USSR and the GDR) largely unaffected. Airborne assault and river-crossing units as well as six tank divisions would be withdrawn from Eastern Europe and disbanded.

Soviet analysts endeavored to explain why the USSR could disarm unilaterally. In *Red Star* (December 22, 1988) military observer M. Ponomarev said that Soviet forces were switching from "overarmament" to "reasonable sufficiency." S. A. Karagonov from the Western European Institute told Soviet television audiences on December 14, 1988 that the USSR was decreasing not its defensive but its offensive capabilities, which had been built up earlier to counter NATO's nuclear superiority. Because Western advantages had been "liquidated" in the 1970s, the need to compensate against them had fallen away. Karagonov added that "a smaller but more efficient and more professional Armed Forces" would help to counter the "decline in prestige" suffered by the Soviet military. Karagonov and two colleagues had already argued in *Kommunist* (No. 1,

1988) that another invasion from the West as occurred in 1941 was most unlikely. Instead, they said, the main threat to the USSR is "economic exhaustion" from attempting to match the West's arms buildup.

On January 18, 1989, Gorbachev spelled out that the half-million-troop reduction would include 240,000 from the west of the Soviet Union, 200,000 from the east, and 60,000 from the south (*Pravda*, January 19, 1989). The cut would include three-fourths of the 55,000 Soviet troops in Mongolia. The president declared that Soviet spending for "armaments and military hardware" would decline by 19.5 percent and the "military budget" by 14.2 percent (from unspecified totals). Meanwhile, Shevard-nadze made clear that troops pulled from Eastern Europe would take their "organic" nuclear arms—missiles and artillery—with them; he also announced that the USSR would begin destroying its chemical weapons.

The military significance of the proposed reductions was unclear. A half-million men amounted to 10 percent of total Soviet forces as calculated in the West at just over 5.0 million. Gorbachev, however, said they represented 12 percent of Soviet forces, implying a total of 4.2 million troops (a plausible number if railroad and construction forces are excluded). U.S. forces, by comparison, totaled just over 2.0 million backed by 1.0 million civilians in 1988. Half a million is significant compared with total Red Army cadres in the late 1920s–early 1930s (just under 600,000) and current West German forces (under 500,000). But the 1989–90 cut would be much smaller than unilateral reductions in Soviet forces in 1922, 1946–48, 1955, and 1960, as shown in Table 3.1. In 1960, for example, Khrushchev initiated a cut of 1.2 million from a baseline of only 3.6 million, a lower starting point than in 1989. After demobilizing about 600,000 in 1960–61, however, the Kremlin stopped and then reversed the reduction during the 1961 Berlin crisis.

Gorbachev's Russia, like most of Europe, faced a demographic squeeze and wanted to engage more of its young men in constructive work. Without the force reduction, some analysts said, the Kremlin might be compelled to extend compulsory military service from two to three years. (Chancellor Helmut Kohl's cabinet in early 1989 voted to stretch Bundes-wehr service from fifteen to eighteen months but then decided to stay with a fifteen-month tour.) Half a million men would represent some .04 percent of the 118 million Soviet work force—about equal to the present yearly increment in the labor force. Given that 40 percent of Soviet troops are from Central Asian and Caucasian republics, their demobilization could *add* to local unemployment and underemployment.

In January 1989 the defense ministers' Committee of the Warsaw Treaty Organization (WTO) at last published its version of the relative levels of armed forces and armaments of both alliances in Europe—from the Atlantic to the Urals—and Europe's off-shore waters. As an exercise in glasnost' it was unprecedented. By this reckoning the Warsaw Pact led the West in many departments. Some were "defensive"—civil defense forces and air defense interceptors "that cannot be employed against ground targets"—but other weapons of Pact superiority could be used for offensive purposes, such as tanks and infantry fighting vehicles. WTO logistical units were also much more numerous than NATO's.

Both the WTO and various Western estimates (presented in Table 8.1) gave the Pact a large superiority in tanks and infantry-fighting vehicles and armored personnel carriers. Indeed, the WTO estimates showed a higher number of tanks for both alliances than did Western calculations. These discrepancies probably derived from many unresolved issues, including whether to count tanks in storage and whether to include older as well as newer tanks and light as well as heavy tanks.

But the WTO statement gave much lower total numbers for Pact manpower than did Western estimates. If the WTO count were correct, the unilateral troop reductions announced by Moscow and other Pact members altered the balance more than if the starting levels were higher, as Western observers believed.

Judging by the discord among the various estimates—even between the Pentagon and NATO—the parties were far from possessing a common conceptual framework or empirical data foundation. The WTO estimates included naval forces in Europe's off-shore waters in the balance, whereas NATO omitted them, allegedly because they are mobile and could be dispatched elsewhere. So long as Western navies cruise Europe's waterways, however, they add substantially to NATO's tactical and strategic assets, leading the East to compare the asymmetries at sea with those on the ground and in the air.

No mere "bean count" could answer *qualitative* questions such as the value of NATO's antitank forces against Pact tanks, the utility of NATO's jet bombers against Soviet defenses, or the impact of differential rates in mobilization capability. These and sundry related questions have been studied, but the answers to them are even more subjective than the relatively hard data cited in Table 8.1—by themselves a vortex of contention. Figure 8.1 underscores the range of estimates on the crucial dimensions of manpower, combat aircraft, and tanks.

None of the estimates dealt realistically with the perennial wild card: whether in a crunch to count the various WTO armies with or against the USSR. The Kremlin might hope that its officers were still in charge and that former satellites would be thankful for Moscow's less bellicose posture,

TABLE 8.1

European Balance of Power, "Atlantic to the Urals (ATTU)" (1988)

	WTO			NATO			PENTAGON			IISS		
	WTO	Ratio	NATO	WTO	Ratio	NATO	WTO	Ratio	NATO	WTO	Ratio	NATO
PERSONNEL (in thousands)												
Command and control personnel: general staffs (main headquarters), directorates, departments of ministries of defense	30.2	1:1.6	49.47									
Ground forces, airborne troops, army aviation personnel	1,823.5	1:1.2	2,115.36									
Air defense personnel	550.5	4.0:1	137.7									
Air force personnel	425.1	1:1.1	482.3									
Naval personnel	338.0	1:2.0	685.0									
Personnel in units subordinated to the central command and control agencies (intelligence, communications, radio-electronic warfare, higher educational establishments, others)	225.4	2.3:1	96.9									
Logistic units and establishments of the armed forces	146.3	1.7:1	87.5									
Civil (territorial) defense personnel	34.1	5.7:1	6.0									
TOTAL strength of the armed forces in Europe and adjacent water areas	3,573.1	1:1	3,660.2									
[minus air defense, air force, and naval personnel]	−1,313.6		−1,305.0									
[Total ground forces in Europe]	2,259.5		2,355.2	3,009	1.4:1	2,213.6				2,143	1:1.1	2,340
[Reserve personnel]										4,239	1:1.1	4,543

Table 8.1 contd.

WEAPONS	WTO			NATO			PENTAGON			IISS		
	WTO	Ratio	NATO	WTO	Ratio	NATO	WTO	Ratio	NATO	WTO	Ratio	NATO
Tactical combat aircraft of the air forces, air defense, and navies including	7,876	1.1:1	7,130	8,250	2.1:1 (includes land-based naval)	3,997	7,120	1.3:1 (excludes naval)	5,360	8,535	1.5:1	5,588
Tactical combat aircraft of the air forces and air defense forces	5,355	1:1	5,450				3,100	2.7:1	1,140	4,432	3.8:1	1,178 [air defense/fighters]
Air defense interceptors that cannot be employed against ground targets	1,829	36:1	50									
Naval combat aircraft	692	1:2.4	1,630							885	1:1.3	1,175
Total number of attack aircraft (bombers, fighter-bombers, ground attack aircraft) in the air force and naval tactical aviation	2,783	1:1.5	4,075				3,450	1:1.1	3,850	3,598	1:1	3,648
[Total combat aircraft]	10,659	1:1.1	11,205	8,250	2.1:1	3,997	10,570	1.2:1	9,210	12,133	1.3:1	9,236
Combat helicopters (including naval in WTO count but not in Western)	2,785	1:1.9	5,270	3,700	1.5:1	2,419	1,250	1:1	1,300	1,220	1.4:1	864
Tactical missile launch systems (IISS figures omit Soviet SRINF to be destroyed under INF)	1,608	11.8:1	136				1,400	16:1	88	1,420 (Frog, Scarab, Scud)	22:1	65 (Lance)
Tanks	59,470	1.9:1	30,690	51,500	3.1:1	16,424	53,100	2.1:1	25,900	53,000	2.4:1	22,200
Anti-tank missile launchers	11,465	1:1.6	18,070	44,200	2.4:1	18,240						
Infantry fighting vehicles and armored personnel carriers of which	70,330	1.5:1	46,900	93,400	2.4:1	39,494	60,000	1.7:1	34,400	23,600	3.8:1	6,200
Armored Infantry Fighting Vehicles				22,400	5.4:1	4,143						
Light Armored Vehicles				71,000	2.1	35,351						

Table 8.1 contd.

	WTO			NATO			PENTAGON			IISS		
	WTO	Ratio	NATO	WTO	Ratio	NATO	WTO	Ratio	NATO	WTO	Ratio	NATO
Multiple launch rocket systems, artillery pieces (75-mm calibre and larger) and mortars (50-mm calibre and larger—NATO estimate is for 100-mm and larger)	71,560	1.3:1	57,060	43,400	3.1:1	13,857	44,000	2.4:1	18,500	44,300	3.3:1	13,500
Anti-aircraft artillery and surface-to-air missiles				24,400	2.4:1	10.109				23,400	2.1:1	11,400
Submarines (except strategic ballistic missile submarines)	228	1.1:1	200				258	1.3:1	206	190	1:1.1	206
including nuclear-powered subs	80	1:1	76				130	1.3:1	103			
Large surface ships (aircraft carriers, battleships, cruisers, destroyers, frigates, amphibious ships with 1,200-ton displacement and over)	102	1:5	499							303	1:1.4	434
including												
Ships capable of carrying aircraft, aircraft carriers	2	1:7.5	15				2	1:5.5	11	2	1:7.5	15
[Helicopter carriers]							2	1:3	6			
Cruise missile ships	23	1:11.9	274									
Amphibious ships (1,200-ton displacement and over)	24	1:3.5	84				25	1:2.3	57	84	1.2:1	69

SOURCES: For WTO, Novoe Vremia, no. 6 (February 6–13, 1989), 5–6; for NATO, "Conventional Forces in Europe: The Facts" (Brussels: NATO, November 25, 1988), 6–28; for Pentagon, Soviet Military Power: An Assessment of the Threat 1988 (Washington, DC: U.S. Department of Defense, 1988), 106–15; for IISS, The Military Balance, 1988–1989 (London: International Institute for Strategic Studies, 1988), 20, 35, 233–37.

NOTES:
1. All estimates purport to cover all WTO (Warsaw Treaty Organization) and NATO forces in Europe from the Atlantic to the Urals (ATTU). They exclude U.S. and Canadian forces stationed outside Europe. All estimates except the Pentagon's include French and Spanish forces in NATO totals.
2. Categories in the first column are given by WTO sources except for those in brackets. Some Western estimates do not fit WTO categories precisely. In some cases Western estimates reported here sum distinct categories.
3. NATO estimate for anti-tank weapons includes not only guided missiles but recoilless rifles and anti-tank weapons on armored fighting vehicles and helicopters.
4. The International Institute for Strategic Studies (IISS) is a nongovernmental organization.

Personnel (ground forces)

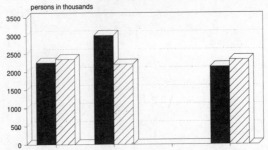

Combat Aircraft (excluding helicopters)

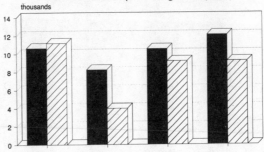

Battle Tanks

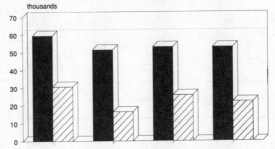

Large Surface Ships

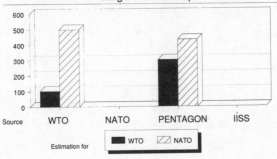

but the "freedom complex" of Polish, Hungarian, and other Eastern European nationalists would probably lead them to intensify efforts to throw off all alien restraints. Whether they succeeded or failed, the result would be to undermine the Pact cohesion needed for a *Drang nach Westen*. If so, conventional arms reductions that weakened Russia's control of Eastern Europe would neutralize Moscow's proximity advantages.

Indeed, as demands for more autonomy arise in the Baltic and other border republics, similar questions must be posed about the minority nationalities of the USSR: would they fight with or against Russia if push came to shove? Baltic popular fronts demand that their youth serve only in the home republic. They protest not only futile sacrifices in Afghanistan and dangerous duty at Chernobyl but "non-regulation relations"—brutal hazing of minority troops, a practice acknowledged by officials such as Major Yu. Rutsov (in *Red Star*, December 21, 1988). Indeed, many Soviet military as well as political leaders in 1988–89 commented on the shortcoming of "internationalist education" and the deleterious consequences for USSR military and other operations. They note the open hostility of Balts, Caucasians, and other minorities toward nonindigenous Soviet servicemen and their families.

In 1989, as in 1960, some Soviet military writers suggested placing demobilized soldiers in a territorial militia to supplement the regular army. In 1988–89 even more than in 1960, Soviet officers and their families expressed strong anxieties about losing their jobs in the wake of INF and other force reductions. Yazov and other spokesmen said that employment needs would be looked after and that only those officers would be laid off who had completed their terms of duty.

Many reports from inside and outside the USSR indicated considerable reluctance among Soviet officers to accept military perestroika and force reductions even if these moves aimed at producing a more efficient force armed with modern communications and weaponry. Yazov warned also that impending force reductions could increase "pacifist sentiments and lack of perspectives," especially among officers (*Red Star*, December 23, 1988). He and other military leaders lamented that drunkenness, poor discipline, and poor training stymied efforts to reform the army.

Still, Pentagon and RAND analysts found little comfort in morale problems within the Pact or in Soviet pledges to move toward "defensive defense." They noted the continued modernization of Soviet forces under Gorbachev. They observed too that geographic proximity and the capacity to plan a surprise attack would favor the USSR regardless of troop cuts.[34]

Western skeptics calculated that the six divisions to be withdrawn from Eastern Europe would possess only 24 Scud and other short-range missiles, leaving Soviet forces there with another 1,376 such weapons against a mere 65 to 88 Lance missile launchers deployed by NATO armies. NATO had successfully excluded nuclear arms from the "stability" talks commenced in March 1989, and Western officials complained that announced Soviet missile withdrawls reintroduced the issue through the back door.

The Kremlin underscored the dimensions of the unilateral cuts in Pact forces. Replying to Western charges that the Kremlin intended to get rid of obsolete tanks, Gorbachev asserted on January 18, 1989 that "we are withdrawing 5,300 of the most advanced tanks from our troop groups." Half of the 10,000 tanks withdrawn would be destroyed and half converted to tractors.

Most Eastern European countries also announced unilateral cuts in 1989: East Germany, 10,000 men (some 6 to 10 percent of its total), 600 tanks, and 50 combat aircraft; Czechoslovakia, 12,000 troops (8 percent of its total) and 850 tanks (25 percent of its total); Hungary, 9,300 men and 251 tanks; Bulgaria, 10,000 men and 200 tanks; and Poland, reductions to the level of "indispensable defense." The allies also promised defense spending cuts, ranging from 10 percent (East Germany) to 17 percent (Hungary). Soviet and East European tank cuts were to total 12,000.

More important than quantitative changes, Soviet leaders (for example, Major General V. Kuklev of the General Staff in a *Red Star* interview, December 28, 1988) pledged that Soviet forces remaining in Eastern Europe would be reorganized into strictly defensive postures with fewer tanks and airborne units.

Because the USSR had not divulged its entire arsenal (a point lamented by Stanislav Kondrashov in *Izvestiia*, January 3, 1989), the impact of the announced withdrawls could be assessed only by reference to Western estimates. A withdrawal of 10,000 tanks would affect nearly one-fifth of the total Soviet holdings of battle tanks (estimated at 53,000 by the IISS). A reduction of 5,000 from Eastern Europe would cut Soviet tanks there by one-half. Some Westerners opined that the tank divisions removed from East Germany and Czechoslovakia were "Operational Maneuver Groups" specially trained as a possible spearhead against the West. Their withdrawal, together with that of specialized air assault groups and river-crossing brigades, would reduce the WTO capacity for a surprise attack.

In 1988 NATO had called for WTO cuts in front line offensive forces; in 1989 the Pact purported to do just that.

Even though the two alliances differed on present numbers, there was hope for accord in Soviet acceptance of the notion of parity in conventional forces. Thus, WTO negotiators at Conventional Armed Forces in Europe (CFE) held in Vienna in spring 1989 endorsed Western proposals that both alliances cut tanks to the same level—20,000. For artillery, the Pact proposed a ceiling of 24,000 for each side, while NATO called for one of 16,500. They seemed also to be calling for parity in armored vehicles, although NATO's definition stressed troop carriers. No matter what base line one used, parity at these levels would require highly asymmetric WTO reductions.

The huge Soviet arsenal and Gorbachev's spirit of innovation permitted him to wave one carrot on a stick after another, adding to NATO's disarray. Thus, in May 1989 he pledged to cut 500 tactical nuclear weapons from the Kremlin's European forces. Western skeptics replied that this would trim the Pact's estimated 10,000 tactical nuclear warheads by only 5 percent, while NATO in the past decade had trimmed its tactical nuclears from more than 7,000 to less than 4,000 warheads. Still, Gorbachev's announcement strengthened Germans and other Europeans anxious to negotiate the reduction or elimination of nuclear arms not covered by the INF Treaty.

Moscow's carrot in this case came with a stick: Shevardnadze departing Bonn in May 1989 threatened that the USSR would stop eliminating its 239 SS-23 missiles as required by the INF Treaty if the West developed and deployed comparable missiles. The SS-23, Soviets said, had a range less than 500 km. and thus fell outside the scope of the INF Treaty. If NATO modernized and stretched its Lance missiles to a comparable range, there was no reason why the Kremlin should eliminate the SS-23s. Here was an issue where both sides could charge bad faith.

The real meaning of "new thinking" in Soviet military affairs would lie not in quantitative reductions but in whether, as Moscow pledged, the residual forces were configured in purely defensive ways. This configuration would eventually need to be translated into doctrine, training, deployment, and exercises. Doubts were raised in 1988 when NATO observers were shown one Soviet exercise that was strictly defensive, only to learn through "national means" that offensive maneuvers were conducted after the Westerners had gone home. Questions arose from the vagueness with which Soviet doctrine began to be formulated in 1987–89: USSR forces should suffice only for "defense," some commentators said, leaving unspecified whether this required a capability to preempt a Western attack or recover lost territory. Still, as Gorbachev persuaded Westerners that Soviet priorities were domestic, talk of an active Soviet menace to the West became less credible.[35]

Moscow has long been of two minds whether American forces in

[231]

Europe are a boon or a bane. As of 1988 some 320,000 U.S. soldiers were still stationed in Europe along with equipment for two or three army divisions. The perennial pressures on Washington to withdraw some or all U.S. troops from Europe could be assuaged or stimulated by progress toward conventional disarmament. Analysts at IMEMO in March 1989 averred that the presence of U.S. and Soviet troops in Europe was desirable for stability under present circumstances but that future conditions might permit them to withdraw.

Détente and arms control gained from greater Soviet flexibility on human rights. The Conference on Security and Cooperation in Europe meeting in Vienna from November 1986 through January 1989 recorded many Soviet concessions on emigration, travel, and religious freedom. In late 1988 Moscow stopped jamming all Western radio broadcasts. The final Vienna accord committed signatory governments to deal with urgent family reunification cases in three days. Moscow even agreed to a new CSEC mechanism allowing individuals to monitor their governments' adherence to the Vienna document. The January 1989 agreement opened the way to new conventional arms talks, negotiations on confidence- and security-building measures, and the scheduling of a human rights meeting in Moscow in 1991.

Military Glasnost'

"Spy-mania," as Sergei Khrushchev and Sergo Mikoyan put it in February 1989, went back to Lenin and perhaps to Ivan the Terrible, making it unlikely that the Kremlin would accept serious on-site inspection for arms control. Foreign ambassadors to ancient Muscovy described this obsession in terms similar to those posted to Stalin's Kremlin. Not only did the tsars hide military and economic data from public view, they also tried to prevent unmonitored meetings between their subjects and outsiders. Sometimes tsar or commisar tried to keep some asset from foreign view; often they wanted to conceal real or imagined weaknesses. Even when the Soviet regime gained more confidence, the old patterns—some would say inferiority complexes or paranoia—persisted.

The Kremlin rejected most Western arms control schemes from the late 1940s through the 1950s as positing "inspection first, disarmament later." The Kremlin's tendency to downplay the importance of "compulsory international inspection," Israelian wrote, hurt the cause of disarmament. The Soviet penchant for depending on unilateral verification measures (*samokontrol'*) "did not win wide support." To think that Moscow's many proposals without compulsory international inspection would be adopted was to "trust in miracles."

Still, the Kremlin's growing interest in achieving significant arms controls gradually softened its resistance to foreign inspection. From the mid-1950s through the early 1960s Moscow expressed a willingness to consider inspection by "mixed commissions" of Central European disengagement, seismic stations to monitor a test ban, measures to lessen fear of surprise attack, Antarctic station visits, and limited numbers of on-site inspections to police a nuclear test ban. Despite such movement, the USSR accepted outside inspection with extreme reluctance. Only when Washington confirmed that it would not need to inspect Soviet space launchers close up did Moscow agree to enter the gentlemans' agreement of 1963 not to deploy mass destruction weapons in outer space.[36]

Satellite observation changed all previous rules. In 1960 the Kremlin vigorously protested U-2 overflights, but when the USSR acquired its own spy satellites in the early 1960s (roughly two years after the United States), Moscow acquiesced in an understanding that satellite reconnaissance from outer space did not violate international law. In SALT I and II the superpowers enshrined a new rule: verification by national technical means was not only permitted, but each side was obligated not to "impede" this process by camouflage or, the U.S. argued, by excessive encryption.

The burden of the past could be seen in the fact that the USSR did not at first publish the complete text of SALT I with its enumeration of present and permitted missile forces. Looking back, Israelian in 1988 lambasted Moscow's refusal to publish key SALT I and II documents for the Soviet people and reporters.

Israelian also complained that as Soviet ambassador to the chemical weapons talks in Geneva, for years he could not even give a straight answer to the question, "Does the USSR possess chemical weapons?" Soviet diplomats, he said, were often poorly informed on the arms they were negotiating. All these problems were being rectified, he said, since 1985.

In the 1970s few Soviet civilian researchers had access to data about Soviet or Western forces except through Western publications. Responding to the slick Pentagon annual *Soviet Military Power* (first edition, September 1981), the Soviet Defense Ministry—even before the Gorbachev era—issued booklets under such titles as *Whence the Threat?* Despite several years of glasnost', however, awkward questions were posed at the Supreme Soviet's INF hearings in 1988: When will the USSR publish its version of the military balance comparable to data published in the West? Marshal Akhromeev was evasive and belittled the accuracy of data published by the International Institute for Strategic Studies in London and the Stockholm International Peace Research Institute (SIPRI). At year's end, however, Major General Kuklev (*Red Star*, December 28, 1988) commended reports published by both institutes and studies of the East-West balance by the U.S. Office of Technology Assessment and Congressional Research Service. The January 1989 WTO presentation of the East-West balance marked a major step toward "parity" of public information.

The Gorbachev leadership agreed to or produced a number of proposals for verification departing from past Soviet practice:[37]

(1) Responding to U.S. complaints about encryption of Soviet missile test data, Soviet representatives at the Standing Consultative Commission asked their American counterparts to specify the parameters for which the United States needed to receive unencrypted data to verify SALT II. (The United States refused to provide those parameters, saying that this would reveal too much about data collection sources.)

(2) Accused of noncompliance with the Biological Weapons Convention, Soviet representatives in 1986 provided more (but still quite limited) information concerning the 1979 anthrax outbreak near Sverdlovsk.

(3) In 1986 the USSR permitted private U.S. scientists to install and observe seismic stations about two hundred miles from Semipalatinsk and in 1988 permitted U.S. government scientists to install and test seismic and hydrodynamic equipment at a Soviet nuclear test site.

(4) In August 1987 the USSR complied with a snap U.S. request under a 1986 Stockholm agreement for American observers to observe announced Soviet maneuvers and verify that they were not larger than forecast. American and other Western officials had previously observed other Soviet exercises at the invitation of Soviet officials. This inspection was the first on Soviet territory in accordance with an agreement specifying that U.S. observers could not be refused entry. The Soviets announced the exercises, responded within twenty-four hours to the U.S. request to inspect them, and received the Americans within thirty-six hours of the request and provided them with two helicopters, vehicles, and drivers as requested. The Americans were allowed to use maps, cameras, binoculars, and tape recorders. They walked tank lines, visited units, and photographed equipment and personnel without interference.[38] Doubts remained, however, as to whether they had seen the entire picture.

(5) In October 1987 the USSR opened its chemical warfare center in Shikhany to experts from forty-five countries including the United States to observe what Soviet officers said was the USSR's entire range of chemical weapon delivery systems and a process for destroying toxic agents in the

field. Why? "To help create the right atmosphere at the Geneva disarmament talks for a convention banning chemical weaponry," said General Vladimir Pikalov, commander of Soviet Chemical Forces. U.S. delegate to the forty-nation Geneva Disarmament Conference Max L. Friedersdorf said he believed the display had been complete but that "we still don't know what the Soviet stockpiles are."[39] The USSR announced in December 1987 that its chemical weapons stocks contained no more than 50,000 tons of toxic agents; Lt. General Anatoly Kuntsevich estimated that the United States possessed twice that amount (TASS, January 6, 1989). Only NATO has deployed toxic weapons in advance positions, he said, which would poison the West if detonated. Soviet negotiator Viktor Karpov claimed that the USSR had successfully tested a way to verify a weapons production ban in the chemical industry (TASS, December 29, 1988). But reports in the Soviet media that Interior Ministry troops had used poison gas against Georgian demonstrators on April 9, 1989, did not inspire confidence in Kremlin commitments to chemical weapons disarmament.

(6) In September 1987 the USSR permitted a congressional delegation and expert staffers to look at, walk through, and photograph the Abalakovo radar near Krasnoyarsk—the very installation that Washington regarded as the clearest Soviet violation of the ABM Treaty. "If we were building the Krasnoyarsk radar in violation of the ABM Treaty," Shevardnadze said later that month in Washington, "we would not have invited U.S. congressmen, U.S. experts, to see that radar. . . . I really hope now that the U.S. will reciprocate, and that our people will be able to see the controversial radar in Greenland." Although opening Abalakovo to U.S. visitors proved nothing about the intentions behind the installation a decade or more earlier, this unprecedented glasnost' certainly implied a willingness to reach some compromise about contentious radars on both sides.[40] The next month Moscow officials told Shultz they were suspending work on Abalakovo for one year and offered to allow U.S. officials to inspect two other radars at Gomel, Belorussia, which Washington suspected of being mobile radars in violation of the ABM Treaty (but which some private analysts thought were being used for spare parts or experiments).[41]

(7) Also in September 1987 the USSR invited the International Atomic Energy Agency (IAEA) to carry out a thorough review of operating and safety procedures at Soviet atomic power reactors.[42] Military glasnost' escalated in May 1989 as Gorbachev announced the "real figure" for USSR defense outlays—77.3 billion rubles—four times higher than previously stated, but far below CIA estimates; as ten Americans in July tested radiations tests on a Soviet cruiser, visited the Kyshtym plutonium complex, and walked through the Sary-Shagan laser proving grounds; and

as Soviet and U.S. negotiators in July agreed on procedures for chemical weapons disarmament.

What lay behind military glasnost'? Such openness would help to build confidence in Soviet intentions and was probably a prerequisite for far-reaching arms control. Further, mutual on-site inspection would give Soviet observers better access to American industrial know-how. Finally, as the world becomes more transparent, secrets are in any case harder to maintain. Soviet citizens are more likely to talk to foreigners about subjects previously off-limits. In a world of expanding technology, reconnaissance gains against the art of *maskirovka*—camouflage and other deceptions. Satellites are becoming more maneuverable and less visible, making it harder to anticipate their orbits or to hide from or disinform their cameras. Their sensors are becoming more powerful, able to penetrate through clouds and shrouds to the physical composition of hidden objects.[43] If maskirovka is impossible, why not be more open?

Strategic Arms Reductions

Before 1985 Soviet diplomats negotiated seriously only to place ceilings on expansion of strategic forces. Both Reagan and Gorbachev seemed uncomfortable depending on MAD ("mutual and assured destruction"), and each wanted to curtail the other's nuclear war-fighting capabilities. As Table 8.2 shows, negotiators had to cope with great asymmetries. Glib assertions of superpower "parity" masked the fact that U.S. warheads, concentrated on submarines and bombers, outnumbered Soviet; and that the USSR deployed over half its warheads on ICBMs—vulnerable to a U.S. first strike but also menacing to America's land-based forces.

Despite many asymmetries in both capabilities and requirements, Soviet-U.S. negotiations in 1986–88 produced understandings on the framework of an agreement for a strategic arms reduction treaty (START) including these points:[44]

—a limit of 1,600 on launchers (ICBMSs, SLBMs, bombers);
—a limit of 6,000 on certain classes of warheads;
—a sublimit of 4,900 on ballistic missile warheads;
—a sublimit of 1,540 warheads on 154 "heavy" missiles such as the Soviet SS-18 ICBM; and
—a reduction of about 50 percent in the Soviet aggregate ballistic missile throw-weight, to a level not to be exceeded by the United States.

[236]

TABLE 8.2
Soviet and U.S. Strategic Forces, 1987–88, and under START

	UNION OF SOVIET SOCIALIST REPUBLICS				UNITED STATES OF AMERICA			
	1987 (SALT II Counting Rules)	1988 (SALT II Counting Rules)	1988 (START Count)	START Limits	1987 (SALT II Counting Rules)	1988 (SALT II Counting Rules)	1988 (START Count)	START Limits
Launchers								
ICBMs	1,418	1,386	1,386		1,000	1,000	1,000	
SLBMs	928	942	942		640	640	640	
Bombers	165	175	175		317	362	362	
Total	2,511	2,503	2,503	→ 1,600	1,957	2,002	2,002	→ 1,600
SLCMs	?	?	?	?	?	?		
Warheads								
On ICBMs	6,440	6,412	6,412		2,261	2,373	2,373	
On SLBMs	3,344	3,662	3,378		6,656	6,656	5,632	
Subtotal								
ICBM + SLBM	9,784	10,074	9,790	→ 4,900*	8,917	9,029	8,005	→ 4,900*
On bombers	1,260	1,620	805 (665)**	→ 1,100	4,956	5,608	1,784 (2,580)**	→ 1,100
Total	11,044	11,694	10,595	6,000	13,873	14,637	9,789	6,000
On SLCMs	?	?	?	?	?	?	?	?

SOURCES: *The Military Balance, 1987–1988* (London: International Institute for Strategic Studies, 1987), 224–25; *The Military Balance, 1988–1989* (London: IISS, 1988), 230–32; Walter B. Slocombe, "Force Posture Consequences of the START Treaty," *Survival* 30, no. 5 (September/October 1988): 402–8; Union of Concerned Scientists, *Nucleus* (Cambridge, MA) (Winter 1988): 4.

* Sublimit of 1,540 warheads on 154 "heavy missiles." Total throw-weight not more than half present Soviet throw-weight.

** IISS estimate of maximum bomber loading.

Both sides sacrificed some advantages to arrive at this framework, but the Kremlin's concessions were larger. As Table 8.2 shows, the "counting rules" adopted by both sides in 1986–88 understated the actual number of SLBM- and bomber-carried weapons by a large fraction. Given that American forces were more numerous in these domains, U.S. weapons would be "undercounted" more than Soviet, pressuring the USSR to alter its force structure more radically than the United States in order to deploy the largest permissible arsenal.

At Reykjavik in 1986 the USSR accepted a rule counting the entire load of gravity bombs and short-range attack missiles (SRAM) carried on a bomber as a single weapon in the 6,000-weapon limit. (In 1988 it was agreed that bombers equipped to carry air-launched cruise missiles [ALCMs] would be counted differently, but the sides failed to resolve just how to count ACLMs. Washington wanted to limit only ACLMs with a range greater than 1,500 kilometers whereas Moscow wanted to ban those with a range over 600 km. Washington wanted to count each bomber with ACLMs as having only ten—even if more were on board—because ACLMs are less threatening than fast-flying ballistic missiles, whereas Soviet diplomats wanted each ACLM counted with a sublimit of 1,100 ACLMs per country. The American approach—attributing 10 ACLMs to each ACLM carrier—is used in Table 8.2.)

Rules for counting warheads were altered in 1987 away from the premise that each missile carries the maximum number of warheads with which it has been flight-tested. The previous rule was dropped because it did not necessarily conform to actual deployment and because it created incentives to deploy the largest number of warheads possible. The new approach specified numbers of warheads for each missile type contingent on implementation of strict verification procedures. This approach did not alter the number of warheads posited for ICBMs, but it significantly reduced the numbers attributed to SLBMs. America's Poseidon C-3 missile warhead count dropped from 14 to 10 whereas the figure for the Trident II/D-5, when deployed, will be set at 8. The Soviet SS-N-20 was changed from 9 to 10; the SS-N-23 was reduced from 10 to 4.

A Soviet critic might complain that this is a numbers or shell game in which what you see is not what you get: the parties promise to cut their weapons to an aggregate of 6,000. Because the Americans have more weapons than the USSR—nearly 15,000 to nearly 12,000—the appearance is that Washington makes the greater concession and both arrive at "coequal security." In reality, airborne and submarine-launched weapons are undercounted, permitting both sides to have far more than 6,000 strategic warheads. Given that the United States leads in these domains, Washington gains—at least so long as Soviet lags persist. To make matters worse, no limits have yet been set on SLCMs, another area of American advantage. Further, the USSR must halve its unique ace: heavy missiles, cutting them to 158 with 10 warheads on each. Meanwhile, American forward-based aircraft on aircraft carriers and in Europe are not counted at all, nor are French and U.K. weapons even though all can hit Soviet territory.

The Soviet analyst might note also that the 1987 rules on counting warheads gave both sides great leeway to break out from a START accord because the front-end "bus" of their missiles could be rapidly filled with additional warheads; the bus space on existing U.S. SLBMs, however, could hold another 1,024 warheads whereas Soviet subs were already close to full and could house only another 384. The new D-5 missile might

[238]

expand this disparity still further, given that it had been tested with 12 warheads but was counted as having only 8.

A Western strategist, in turn, could complain that a START accord along these lines would increase the Soviet capacity to wipe out U.S. land-based ICBMs. The ratio of highly accurate SS-18 warheads to U.S. silos would increase from 3:1 to over 4.4:1. If the treaty permitted mobile ICBMs and if Washington deployed some ICBMs in a mobile mode, however, this ratio could be reduced or nullified. Even without a shift toward mobile ICBMs, more than 80 percent of U.S. warheads would remain at sea or on bombers. Although submarines and bombers might be less vulnerable to a surprise attack that would silo-based ICBMs, however, far fewer can be kept on alert. One estimate assumes alert rates to be 90 percent for America's ICBMs, 70 percent for strategic submarines, and 20 percent for aircraft. Rates for Soviet forces might be much lower, especially for submarines. From this perspective the concentration of Soviet forces in ICBMs remains a plus for Moscow. Washington has sought a sublimit of 3,300 warheads on ICBMs but has rejected the Soviet counterproposal of a maximum of 3,300 warheads on SLBMs as well as ICBMs.

A critic suspicious of both superpowers might object that they had not in fact reduced their arsenals by one-half. A supporter of arms control could reply that the START cuts amount to substantial reductions—one-third if not one-half of both sides' strategic warheads—and that under-counting bomber and submarine weapons is good for strategic stability because it encourages movement away from the weapons most conducive to first-strike thinking: ICBMs. Absolute ceilings on launchers and warheads would militate against profligate targeting to barrage deployment areas for mobile ICBMs or strategic submarines.

Broader-based arguments for START are that it would permit strategists in both countries to plan their forces on the basis of finite rather than virtually limitless parameters. The result would be a far cry from "minimum deterrence" measured in hundreds of weapons, but it would shift sharply away from the endless spiral that could otherwise suck the two countries' forces toward infinity. If Moscow and Washington embarked on START, the directions and distances they would cover in arms control could not be predicted. The likely requirements for on-site verification procedures could be expected to enhance mutual confidence.

Despite intense efforts to bridge differences before Reagan left office, however, negotiators failed to remove obstacles to a treaty. One was Reagan's insistence on keeping the door open for a strategic defense system. Indeed, on the eve of the 1988 Moscow summit the United States advanced as an avenue to compromise a proposal to designate certain earth orbits as test ranges, thereby creating what one critic called "legal shooting galleries in space."[45] Another U.S. proposal authorized unlimited testing and even deployment of space-based sensor systems, which, if capable of substituting for radars, would probably be banned under any treaty interpretation. The Kremlin agreed to some forms of research and testing of potential SDI weapons, but basically Moscow insisted on adherence to a narrow interpretation of the ABM Treaty as a precondition for strategic offensive weapon reductions.

SLCMs presented an even less tractable problem because of sharp asymmetries in the technologies, forces, and objectives of each side. The United States (as of 1987) planned to deploy 3,994 SLCMs; of those 758 would be nuclear-armed, with 270 on submarines and 488 on surface ships. The USSR, though trailing American technology, was developing a Tomahawk-like cruise missile and a larger one for submarine deployment. CIA estimates held that by the mid-1990s the USSR could have as many as 1,500 nuclear-tipped SLCMs.

At Reykjavik the two sides agreed to exclude SLCMs from the 6,000 limit on warheads and to negotiate a separate SLCM provision. In July 1987 Moscow put forward a draft treaty with a sublimit of 400 nuclear SLCMs deployed only on specified classes of submarines. American officials spurned the Soviet proposals as unverifiable because (1) it is impossible to distinguish conventional- and nuclear-armed SLCMs and (2) SLCMs could easily be hidden and evade detection. The USSR maintained that means exist to distinguish warheads, such as electronic tagging of nuclear variants of missiles at the production stage with follow-on checks during transportation to ships and finally on the vessels. But if these or other means were not acceptable, Soviet diplomats called for a ceiling of 1,000 to be placed on all SLCMs—about one-quarter of the American deployment plan.

The United States stood pat and offered no compromise plan on SLCMs during the 1988 Moscow summit. Washington, critics said, was repeating its MIRV mistake from 1969–70. Claiming a free hand for itself, not only did the United States deploy a weapon that made arms verification much more difficult, but it opened the way for the USSR to catch up with and soon outnumber American forces.

American diplomats in 1988 wanted a ban on flight testing of the Soviet Union's SS-18 heavy missile to prevent Moscow from developing new versions of the weapon and to undermine reliability of existing versions. Some U.S. officials in early 1989 wanted to ban the SS-18 altogether. But this was the USSR's most accurate strategic missile, and few U.S. specialists expected Moscow to accept such a ban. Still other Bush administration officials favored a ban on mobile missiles with multiple warheads, a move that would outlaw Moscow's deployment of its ten-warhead SS-24 missiles on rail cars. Both sides disagreed also on what limits should be set on land-based mobile missiles, whether there should be a separate ceiling on the number of warheads on land-based ballistic missiles, and on what verification procedures were needed. In early 1989 the Bush administration made no hard decision on what kinds of ICBMs to deploy or curb, preferring to keep its options open with multiple warhead MX missiles—mobile as well as in silos—and with continued development on a single-warhead Midgetman missile.

The United States was trying to push the Soviet triad away from its emphasis on heavy land-based missiles and toward greater dependence on submarine and bomber forces. Moscow rejected U.S. proposals not in principle but rather for their specific content, which may have stressed near-term Soviet capacities for change. Conversely, Washington's reluctance to contain significantly its ACLM and SLCM deployments introduced wild cards into negotiations that ostensibly aimed at reducing strategic arsenals.

Other Arms Controls

Soviet naval activity rose steadily from 1965 until 1984 when deployment of submarines averaged 46 per day and other warships 31; these averages fell in 1987 to 25 submarines and 24 other warships. Marshal Akhromeev said the USSR had cut back on distant naval maneuvers in line with its defensive doctrine; American skeptics thought the motive was to cut costs. They also saw no decrease in Soviet shipbuilding patterns.[46]

In February 1988 the USSR became the first nuclear power to ratify the South Pacific Nuclear Free Zone (SPNFZ) Treaty. China had signed but not yet ratified, and the Western Big Three had refused to sign. Moscow, in signing the protocols in December 1986, interpreted the treaty as prohibiting visits to treaty states of foreign ships that might be nuclear-armed. When Australia disputed this interpretation, the USSR replied that if other signatories violated their treaty obligation, the USSR would "retain the right to review its commitments" not to use or threaten nuclear weapons against treaty parties. Canberra again urged the Kremlin to change its position. In ratifying the treaty Moscow indicated that it was taking into account the wishes of the South Pacific signatories—an ambiguous hint that it might accede to Australia's interpretation.[47]

Moscow's broad agenda was set out by Shevardnadze in a June 8, 1988 speech to the UN General Assembly's Third Special Session on Disarmament. Because the nuclear stalemate catalyzes conventional arms competition, he said, nuclear arms must be scrapped. *"Ensuring security by non-nuclear means is possible. It is possible on the basis of sufficiency"* (emphasis in the original). Suffiency, he said, is "a political disposition toward ever smaller arsenals—sufficient for defense but not for attack." It is "a concept of security as driving from collective actions of states." Therefore the United Nations and its institutions must be strengthened.

Shevardnadze said conventional arms reductions should "start with eliminating imbalances . . . on the basis of a reciprocal exchange of data"— *official* data from governments. Once negotiations began, on-site inspections would be conducted to check the baseline data and to remove differences in assessments. At that stage ways of eliminating imbalances could be identified and methods of carrying out reductions devised. In a second stage negotiations would "deal with cutbacks in the armed forces of both sides by approximately 500,000 men each." In a third "forces on both sides would be given a defensive character and their offensive nucleus . . . dismantled."

The Shevardnadze cafeteria included "reciprocal reductions" in tactical nuclears, attack aircraft, and tanks. He endorsed Eastern European suggestions for "disengagement" and for zones free from nuclear and chemical weapons. He approved a proposal of Nonaligned states for "the cessation and prohibition of the use of scientific and technological achievements for developing" new kinds of conventional and mass destruction arms such as laser, genetic, and electromagnetic systems. He also noted Sweden's call to ban the use of battlefield lasers for blinding personnel. He wanted restrictions on sales and supplies of conventional arms.

Putting Washington on the defensive, Shevardnadze called for naval disarmament, asking: "What is the number of, say, tanks, that would be equal to the fire-power of this floating armada" of aircraft carriers? He called for limits on naval activities in the Pacific and Indian oceans, the northern seas, and the Mediterranean; for advance notifications of maneuvers; for lowering the density of arms in major ocean lanes; for precluding any surprise attack from sea; for a policy of announcing the presence or absence of nuclear weapons on ships calling at foreign ports; and for the elimination of all overseas military bases by the year 2000. He proposed creation of a UN naval force.

Along with this pack of jokers Shevardnadze offered other, perhaps more promising ideas for multilateral action:

[242]

—Establishment of a UN International Monitoring and Verification Agency to monitor arms controls and verify compliance with agreements on lessening tension
—Establishment of a World Space Organization (as proposed by the USSR in 1985) and of an International Space Monitoring Agency (as suggested by France), an accord preventing the introduction of weapons into outer space, cooperation to prevent pollution of outer space, and a joint Soviet-U.S. mission to Mars
—Establishment of a Disarmament for Development Fund

Many of Shevardnadze's ideas seemed, if not "loaded," at least visionary. But a follow-on speech on June 13, 1988 by Soviet Ambassador A. S. Piradov to the UN Committee on Peaceful Uses of Outer Space outlined many actions or agreements already undertaken by the USSR showing what can be done to internationalize space research:

—The Soviet *Mir* space station, in orbit since February 1986, carried an X-ray observatory built by Soviet and Western European specialists and a telescope built with Swiss participation.
—A Syrian cosmonaut visiting *Mir* helped to conduct a space survey of natural resources in Syria.
—Projects with Bulgarian, French, Afghan, and Austrian cosmonauts had already been conducted or were planned.
—The *Phobus* project launched in July 1988 entailed Soviet cooperation with eleven Eastern and Western European countries and the European Space Agency.[48]
—The USSR, France, and Poland cooperated in developing a large Gamma-l telescope.
—The 1988 Moscow Summit produced agreement to expand Soviet and U.S. cooperation by placing instruments on one another's spacecraft and by exchanging national studies of future unmanned solar system exploration missions.

Russian cosmicism, discussed in the preceding chapter, seemed to have penetrated the new thinking on international relations. How it would blend with American pragmatism remained to be seen.

[243]

Afghanistan and Other "Regional Conflicts"

In the late 1980s the USSR cut back Soviet involvements in costly Third World ventures—from Nicaragua to Africa—under whatever face-saving arrangements could be created.

Stymied by Afghan tribesmen armed with Stinger missiles, Soviet forces initiated an orderly withdrawal from Afghanistan in early 1988 and completed it on February 15, 1989, under a deadline set by Gorbachev. Washington committed itself to "positive symmetry" in April 1988: U.S. aid to the rebels would decrease and halt only as Soviet aid to the Kabul regime halted. Like Americans in Vietnam a generation before, Soviets asked: "Why are we here?" Perhaps they had been invited by some leaders in Kabul, but it was clear most Afghans wanted them out. The glasnost' of *Ogonek* and *Literaturnaia gazeta* brought the bitter realities to Soviet readers in 1986–88. Well before the "new thinking," however, many young Soviet men went to extreme lengths to avoid "internationalist" military duty.

Soviet forces performed worse in Afghanistan than those of the United States in Vietnam. The USSR had the advantage of short supply lines, better knowledge of the country and its language, a mountainous terrain rather than jungle, a fractious and disunited foe without heavy weapons or equipment, and little organized resistance or stomach-wrenching television coverage at home. When shoulder-fired missiles began blasting Soviet helicopters and airplanes from the skies, the Kremlin recognized the realities and did its best to retreat in dignity.

Fyodor Burlatsky argued that the Afghan expedition, like the massive SS-20 deployment, testified to an excessive dependence on force in Soviet foreign policy under Brezhnev.

The old-style thinkers could be blamed for bad judgment; the new thinkers claimed good sense. The "Theses of the CPSU Central Committee for the 19th All-Union Party Conference" conceded that

> our foreign policy, too, did not escape dogmatic and subjective attitudes. It trailed behind fundamental changes in the world and missed chances to reduce tensions and enhance understanding among nations. In our bid for military-strategic parity we occasionally failed to use opportunities available to attain security for our nation by political means, and, as a result, allowed ourselves to be lured into an arms race, which could not but affect this country's social and economic progress and its standing on the international scene.[49]

Removing Soviet forces from Afghanistan and thinning Soviet forces on the Chinese border would address two of Beijing's "three conditions" for improved Sino-Soviet relations. The Kremlin seemed to be working on the third condition as well—urging Vietnam to withdraw from Kampuchea.[50] The Kremlin was also removing the SS-20s once targeted on China, Japan, and Korea; it was opening the border with China and encouraging trade and other exchanges. With China, as in other spheres, Soviet concessions promised large dividends.

Deputy Foreign Minister Vladimir Petrovskii asserted that the USSR now sought a "constructive role" in solutions for conflicts in Angola, Cambodia, the Middle East, and elsewhere. Moscow's approach, he said, is "to create external conditions for people to settle the issues themselves, to remove foreign interference. We want to take the superpowers out of crisis situations." Asked if this meant the USSR was becoming a status quo power, he only replied, "Good question."[51]

The new thinking, Petrovskii added, called for democratizing foreign policy, involving more people than the tight little groups that prepared decisions in the past. "The pluses of democratizing the foreign policy process are greater than the minuses,"[52] a view supported also by the balance sheet drawn in chapter 1.

In line with these views in December 1988 Moscow endorsed a U.S.-brokered accord to end Angolan-South African fighting and create an independent Namibia, accompanied by withdrawal from Angola of Cuban forces.

In early 1989 the Kremlin indicated to Norway its willingness to "alter moderately" proposals for a boundary in a strategically vital zone of the Barents Sea.[53] The 1989 move deviated from general Soviet refusal to negotiate any of its borders. An inch to Norway could become a mile to China.

Transforming the Struggle for Power?

The cumulative effect of these initiatives was to persuade even former President Reagan of Gorbachev's devotion to perestroika within the USSR. The Soviet leader seemed ready to sacrifice face as well as tangible assets to disentangle the great Bear from the thickets and swamps of overseas adventure.

Gorbachev wanted progress in low as well as high politics, but the pace of change in that domain was slower. The USSR wanted to join GATT and take up observer status at the International Monetary Fund; the Kremlin declared that it welcomed joint business and space ventures with the West. As the Central Committee's May 1988 theses put it: "The radical economic reform and our new approach to foreign economic contacts have produced the first shoots needed for more efficient involvement of our country in the world economy." Still, there was no economics or low politics equivalent of the INF Treaty or the Afghan pullout. Perhaps economic relationships were more complex than INF trade-offs. Perhaps the top Kremlin leadership invested less attention in such matters or knew less about them. Washington did not rush to welcome the USSR into the community of world commerce until the drift of high politics was clearer.

Unless the Kremlin went much further toward reducing its military arms and spending, the USSR's neighbors would still have cause for worry—even if Moscow's intentions were currently benign. Gorbachev's policies, moreover, aimed at making Russia stronger. His successors might then have more expansionist ideas. Westerners pondered whether "best safety lies in fear"—treating the Bear as a potential killer even if it now appeared docile—or whether the moment was ripe to bring Russia into a relationship in which the law of the tooth, fang, and claw gave way to transnational cooperation.

Notes

1. On the success of tit for tat in prisoner's dilemma computer tournaments, see Robert Axelrod, *The Evolution of Cooperation* (New York: Basic Books, 1984); on graduated initiatives and tension reduction, see Charles E. Osgood, *An Alternative to War or Surrender* (Urbana: University of Illinois Press, 1962).

2. Gorbachev implied that the declaration derived from decisions by the Party Politburo and the Soviet government. Text in *Pravda* and *Izvestiia*, January 16, 1986, pp. 1–2. But the general secretary's leading role in arms control contradicted his thesis that the Party should withdraw from day-to-day affairs more properly conducted by the government. The unity of Party and state was implied by the composition of a January 18 press conference conducted by G. M. Korniyenko, first deputy minister of Foreign Affairs; General Staff chief S. F. Akhromeev; and L. M. Zamiatin, head of the Central Committee's Department of International Information. For V. Israelian's commentary see "Mir ne mozhet byt' zakliuchen tol'ko sverkhu," *Literaturnaia gazeta*, June 15, 1988, p. 14.

3. On the inherent linkage between defense and offense, see Walter C. Clemens, Jr., "Good Offense Beats a Good (Star Wars) Defense," *Wall Street Journal*, April 24, 1985, op-ed.

4. For several years China had offered to take part in arms control talks only if the superpowers first cut their nuclear arsenals by half. Gorbachev previewed his plan for French parliamentarians and stressed Moscow's readiness for "direct conversations with France" on arms limitations. See *Pravda*, October 4, 1985, pp. 1–2.

5. A multilateral accord could benefit the smaller nuclear powers as well. France, Britain, and China would all gain from curbs permitting them to retain a relatively small deterrent, as in Gorbachev's Stages 1 and 2. So long as U.S. forces match Soviet, any

additional French and British forces tilt the balance westward. As nuclear arms go down, the leverage of China's mass, reinforced by a small nuclear arsenal, rises. See also Walter C. Clemens, Jr., *National Security and U.S.-Soviet Relations*, 2d ed. (Muscatine, IA: Stanley Foundation, 1982), 31–32.

6. See letter of Frank Gaffney, deputh assistant secretary of Defense, Nuclear Forces and Arms Control Policy, in Center for Defense Information, *The Defense Monitor* 14, no. 8 (1985): 6. The Reagan administration also refused to continue talks on a Comprehensive Test Ban Treaty (CTBT) drafted by Britain, the Soviet Union, and United States in 1977–80.

7. By the mid-1980s the CIA and nongovernmental analysts concluded that the size of Soviet underground tests had been exaggerated by U.S. seismic identification procedures and that probably the USSR had complied with the TTBT. See *F.A.S. Public Interest Report* (Washington, DC: Federation of American Scientists), 38, no. 7 (September 1985), special issue on Test Ban.

8. The Kremlin initiated a moratorium on Soviet nuclear testing on March 31, 1958, and called on the United States to reciprocate. Eventually a de facto moratorium took shape that lasted until September 1, 1961, when the USSR launched a massive test series. For opposing interpretations, see Jerome B. Wiesner, "Setting the Moratorium Record Straight," *The New York Times*, January 3, 1986 op-ed; Robert K. Squire, "The Russians Broke 1958–61 Test Moratorium," in ibid., January 19, 1986, letter to editor; and Wiesner rejoinder, in ibid., March 30, 1986, p. E18.

9. For relevant documents on each Soviet move, see *Current Digest of the Soviet Press (CDSP)* 38, no. 3: 7, no. 11: 9, no. 13: 5, 16, no. 15: 6, no. 20: 20; *The New York Times*, August 19, 1986, pp. 1, 12, 13.

10. U.S. government sources acknowledged fifteen underground tests in the first year of the Soviet moratorium; Gorbachev claimed there were eighteen. See *The New York Times*, August 19, 1986, p. 12; Chief of Staff Akhromeev said the absence of Soviet testing caused some "damage to us, although for the time being we consider the damage acceptable." Ibid., August 26, 1986, p. A4.

11. Press briefing by Col. Vitalii Kotuzhanskii, August 27, 1986, USSR Mission to the United Nations, no. 118; see also Conference on Disarmament, Geneva, Document CD/778, August 10, 1987.

12. The NRDC worked with scientists from three U.S. universities; their Soviet counterparts were with the USSR Academy of Sciences.

13. The U.S. intelligence community was deeply divided, however, on the technological requirements for a test ban and the utility of the Corrtex system based on a cable inserted into the ground close to the blast.

14. For the views of many critics and supporters of nuclear testing, see *The New York Times*, October 18, 1987.

15. See Michael R. Gordon, "U.S. Uses Seismic Devices in China to Estimate Size of Soviet A-Tests," *The New York Times*, April 4, 1987, pp. 1, 4, citing documentation obtained under the Freedom of Information Act by William M. Arkin.

16. Michael R. Gordon, "Soviet Offers to Allow Some On-Site Test Monitoring," *The New York Times*, June 4, 1987, p. A3. Moscow later agreed to permit Corrtex cables to be placed at such sites "if there will be negotiations about complete prohibition of nuclear tests." Col. Gen. Nikolai F. Chervov, head of the Arms Control Directorate of the Soviet General Staff, on August 31, 1987, quoted in *The New York Times*, September 1, 1987.

17. See Peter Grier in the *Christian Science Monitor*, September 25, 1987, pp. 1, 32.

18. The Soviet hydrodynamic method was similar in some ways to Corrtex. See "Testing the Waves for a New Agreement," interview with Troy Wade, in *Arms Control Today* 18, no. 5 (June 1988): 21–24.

19. The USSR had to destroy some 826 IRMs (470 of them deployed) and 926 SRINFs (387 deployed); the United States, 689 IRMs (429 deployed) and 170 SRINFs stored in Colorado. By a collateral understanding West Germany would destroy 72 SRINFs "with the final elimination" of Soviet and U.S. INF missiles. The treaty also stipulated elimination of missile support facilities and banned INF production and flight testing.

These numbers derive from data provided in the documents signed on December 8, 1987, but both sides entered minor changes in their self-inventories in 1988. The U.S. intelligence community was itself divided over the probable number of Soviet reserve missiles. The Treaty on the Elimination of Intermediate-Range and Shorter-Range Missiles was accompanied by three other documents: Protocol on Procedures Governing the Elimination of the Missiles Systems Subject to the Treaty; Protocol Regarding Inspections; and Memorandum of Understanding Regarding the Establishment of a Data Base. The treaty text was carried in *Pravda*, December 9, 1988, p. 2; the other documents were only summarized. Soviet papers gave much space, however, to Gorbachev's and Reagan's speeches during the Washington summit.

20. *IISS Map of Intermediate-Range Ballistic Missile Coverage* (London: International Institute for Strategic Studies, 1986).

21. Strobe Talbott, *Deadly Gambits: The Reagan Administration and the Stalemate in Nuclear Arms Control* (New York: A. A. Knopf, 1984), 30.

22. The USSR could have deployed 225 intermediate-range warheads against Europe; the United States, 300 in Europe; Moscow would have to trim its existing SS-20 deployment by two-thirds; the Americans would be banned from deploying the Pershing 2; there would be a freeze on SS-20s in Soviet Asia. Ibid., pp. 126–28; idem, *The Master of the Game: Paul Nitze and the Nuclear Peace* (New York: A. A. Knopf, 1988), 174–81.

23. There were hundreds of Soviet SRINFS deployed in East Germany, Czechoslovakia, and the USSR able to hit most Western European targets (but not southern Italy, where some U.S. GLCMs were deployed) and much of Turkey. The West had no comparable force, though the United States could produce SRINFs within a year or two. Indeed, in March 1987 the Pentagon talked of converting the P2s covered by the INF Treaty into shorter-range Pershing 1-Bs—identical to the P2 but without the second rocket stage. This led Moscow to worry that the P1-B could be stretched to reach Soviet territory.

24. Quoted in Lynn E. Davis, "Lessons of the INF Treaty," *Foreign Affairs* 56, no. 4 (Spring 1988): 720–34 at 728–29.

25. Ibid., p. 729. Shevardnadze told the United Nations on June 8, 1988, that his government would respond positively if the General Assembly asked both Moscow and Washington "*not to use for military purposes the materials released as a result of nuclear disarmament agreements*" (emphasis in original).

26. See *Vestnik Ministerstva Inostrannykh del SSSR*, no. 10 (July 1988): 6–7.

27. See Lewis A. Dunn, "NATO after Global 'Double Zero,'" *Survival* 30, no. 3 (May–June 1988): 195–209; and Robert E. Hunter, "Will the United States Remain a European Power?" ibid., pp. 210–31; on the present strengths of NATO vis-à-vis the Pact, see *The Defense Monitor* 17, no. 3 (1988).

28. See *Soviet Military Power: An Assessment of the Threat, 1988* (Washington, DC: Department of Defense, 1988), 113.

29. Feodor Burlatsky wrote that the INF and Moscow summit proved that Soviet skeptics were wrong and promoters of new thinking were right in their assessment of potential accords with the hitherto obdurate Reagan White House. See his "Kto okazalsia prav," *Literaturnaia gazeta*, June 8, 1988, pp. 1, 9.

30. Bonn feared that modernization could spark a replay of antinuclear demonstrations. It preferred that NATO and WTO tactical nuclears be reduced to equal levels and eventually eliminated.

31. Asked in March 1989 whether they saw FOFO as an "offensive" posture quite out of step with Gorbachev's troop reductions, civilian strategists at IMEMO replied "not necessarily." The nature of FOFO would depend on how it evolved and what kinds of technologies emerged.

32. See also James A. Thomson and Nanette C. Gantz, *Conventional Arms Control Revisited: Objectives in a New Phase*, Report No. N2697-AF (Santa Monica, CA: RAND Corporation, December 1987), cited in Davis, "Lessons of the INF Treaty," p. 754.

33. Davis, "Lessons of the INF Treaty," p. 753.

34. See Edward L. Warner III, "New Thinking and Old Realities in Soviet Defence Policy," *Survival* 31, no. 1 (January/February 1989): 13–33 and essays in *Adelphi Papers*, no.

236 (London: IISS, 1989), especially James A. Thomson, "An Unfavourable Situation: NATO and the Conventional Balance" at pp. 49–71. On the sources of conflicting appraisals of the East-West balance, see forthcoming reports by Randall Forsberg, Steven M. Lilly-Weber, and others at the Institute for Defense and Disarmanent in Boston.

35. Even the Reagan-appointed Commission on Integrated Long-Term Strategy concluded that the possibility of a large-scale Soviet attack in Central Europe was becoming remote. It therefore called for greater attention to regional instabilities outside Europe. See the commission's report, *Discriminate Deterrence* (Washington, DC: U.S. Government Printing Office, 1988).

36. In August 1963 a Soviet official asked U.S. diplomats if Washington still stood by its 1962 position that on-site launcher inspection would not be needed for a ban on bombs in orbit. See Walter C. Clemens, Jr., *Outer Space and Arms Control* (Cambridge: MIT Center for Space Research, 1966), 54.

37. See also Gloria Duffy et al., *Compliance and the Future of Arms Control* (Cambridge, MA: Ballinger, 1988), 159–61.

38. See Michael R. Gordon, "U.S. Praises Soviet for War Games' Role," *The New York Times*, September 22, 1987, p. A3.

39. Gorbachev had announced in April 1987 that the USSR was halting production of chemical weapons including toxic gases and other agents of the type used in World War I. But Western experts estimated the Soviet stock of chemical arms from the 1970s and early 1980s at between 200,000 and 500,000 tons. The United States claimed to have stopped producing chemical weapons in 1969 but planned to begin producing binary weapons. See *The New York Times*, October 5, 1987.

40. See Walter C. Clemens, Jr., "*Glasnost* on the Arms Front," *Christian Science Monitor*, September 24, 1987, p. 13.

41. See Michael R. Gordon, "Soviet Offers U.S. Inspections of Additional Radar," *The New York Times*, October 28, 1987, p. A6.

42. Czechoslovakia and Hungary issued similar invitations. See Paul Lewis, "Soviet Invites Inspection of Atom Power Plant," *The New York Times*, October 18, 1987:

43. See William J. Broad, "U.S. Designs Spy Satellites To Be More Secret Than Ever," *The New York Times*, November 3, 1987, pp. Cl ff. On Soviet *maskirovka* in many domains, see Brian D. Dailey and Patrick J. Parker, eds., *Soviet Strategic Deception* (Lexington, MA: Lexington Books and Hoover Institution Press, 1987).

44. On START, see Robert Einhorn, "The Emerging START Agreement"; Walter B. Slocombe, "Force Posture Consequences of the START Treaty"; and Jeremy K. Leggett and Patricia M. Lewis, "Verifying a START Agreement"—all in *Survival* 30, no. 5 (September/October 1988): 387–401, 402–8, 409–28, respectively.

45. Spurgeon M. Keeny, Jr., "Moscow Opportunity: Lost in Space" and "News and Negotiations," *Arms Control Today* (May 1988): 2, 19–21. For background, see Michele A. Fournoy, "A Rocky START: Optimism and Obstacles on the Road to Reductions," *Arms Control Today* (October 1987): 7 ff.; Michael R. Gordon, "Outlook for the Summit," *The New York Times*, May 26, 1988; *Peace Research Centre Newsletter* (Canberra: Australian National University) 3, no. 1 (May 1988): 1–2.

46. *The New York Times*, July 17, 1988, p. 13.

47. *Peace Research Centre Newsletter*, p. 7.

48. The laser aboard the *Phobus* was too small to have military value but raised the question of how to decide when a laser is worrisome militarily and violates the ABM treaty. Ashton Carter quoted in *The New York Times*, July 17, 1988, p. E6.

49. *Pravda*, May 27, 1988.

50. On May 29, 1988, TASS announced with some fanfare that "recently the Socialist Republic of Vietnam and the People's Republic of Kampuchea announced a decision to withdraw 50,000 Vietnamese volunteers from Kampuchea this year, that is, half of the personnel of the SRV's military contingent stationed in that country"—as part of Hanoi's plan to withdraw all its troops from Kampuchea.

51. Interview with Flora Lewis in *The New York Times*, July 6, 1988, p. A23.

52. Had there been democratic participation in decision making, would the USSR have invaded Afghanistan? Petrovskii replied, "I don't know. We had no idea of our public opinion. We've only begun polls." Ibid. Western analysts found considerable support in the Soviet public— at least among Russians— for the "internationalist" action for several years, followed by a disillusionment by 1987 and then a broadening opposition. See Radio Free Europe/Radio Liberty, "The Soviet Public and the War in Afghanistan: Discontent Reaches Critical Levels," *Soviet Area Audience and Opinion Research* AR 4-88 (Paris, May 1988).

53. For eighteen years the USSR had insisted that the line follow the meridian due north from the western edge of the Soviet coast, whereas Oslo wanted a line equidistant from each country. Unwilling to compromise, the USSR had complained that Oslo's formula gave Norway a disporportionately large share of the Barents Sea. For a Soviet perspective, see Alexander Kan, "Naboskap under Kald Krig og Perestroika," *Forvarsstudier* (Norwegian Institute for Defence Studies) 6 (1988).

9

What Makes Arms Accords Possible?
Necessary and Helpful Conditions

What are the underlying conditions that make arms control agreements feasible and useful for East and West? What are the necessary and sufficient conditions needed to bring each side to an accord? The experiences of the mid-1980s suggest that some lessons based on case studies from earlier periods need to be revised. Human imagination and political will, it turns out, can outstrip the limits of economic, technological, or strategic-military determinism. But material incentives and negotiating from "positions of strength" have also played important roles—more weighty than some idealistic precepts predicted.

Putative Principles

The following principles—a sometimes self-contradictory array gathered from hawks, doves, and owls, East and West—are all now in doubt:

(1) Radical measures of *negotiated* disarmament are impossible, though governments may be willing to engage in token reductions or to place ceilings on existing forces.[1] Western "realists" point to the "Cain" in human nature: relations among nations being nasty and brutish, weapons are useful to intimidate or coerce and prevent others from doing the same—the powerful will never surrender their assets voluntarily.[2]

[251]

Dogmatic Communists reach a similar conclusion: *Capitalist* regimes will never voluntarily enter into arms reduction agreements; their class interests lead to war and, in the interim, depend on the maintenance of a substantial arms industry.[3]

(2) Step-by-step arms reduction measures can never get very far; comprehensive packages are necessary to overcome asymmetrical advantages.[4]

(3) Even when governments make ostensibly generous disarmament offers they usually include a joker in the pack that is unacceptable to the other side.[5]

(4) "Arms control agreements of an unambiguously substantial character tend to be negotiable only between states whose mutual relations are sufficiently good that arms control is irrelevant." This is the "arms control paradox."[6] It follows from the realpolitik paradigm of politics among nations as a zero-sum struggle for power.[7]

(5) Arms control is a poor way to break the ice of cold war competition. Consistent with the arms control paradox, arms control agreements become feasible only when rivals are both wary and weary—still afraid of each other but weary of competition. Thus arms control will be the consequence rather than the source of any overall improvement in a hostile relationship.[8]

(6) Arms limitations or reductions are impossible unless there is parity or near-parity in the weapons to be regulated. Progress in arms control generally takes place only when neither side has an advantage.[9]

(7) "Weapons systems are more amenable to limitation before they become operational or as their operational utility begins to decline"—the "abortion or euthanasia" principle."[10] A related problem is that the Soviets are usually unwilling to dismantle operational systems.[11]

(8) Soviet leaders and defense planners, "much like defense planners and conservative analysts in the United States, tend to prefer a free hand for themselves, even if this means giving a free hand to the other side, rather than to constrain themselves in constraining the other side. Thus, they have never been much taken with the strategy of attempting to forestall the development of new or substantially enhanced American capabilities by mortgaging the future of their programs."[12]

(9) Arms control negotiations are more likely to be undertaken—and more likely to succeed—in a period of stable military technology than in a time of great technological ferment.[13]

In a different vein from these skeptical analyses, some idealists hold the following:

[252]

(10) Unilateral restraint is useful to stimulate "disarmament by mutual example" or movement toward agreement in arms negotiations.[14]

(11) Accumulating bargaining chips intensifies arms racing, not movement toward arms control.[15]

(12) Backing the Bear or the Eagle into a corner leads to confrontation, not accommodation.[16]

Neither skeptical not idealistic, some analysts dwell on the sheer technical and political complexity of arms control:

(13) Economic considerations are virtually irrelevant to arms control motivations and outcomes.[17]

(14) Arms control is usually possible only when there is substantial intramilitary discord or when military opposition is mollified by an appropriate quid pro quo.[18]

(15) The complexity of modern arsenals makes both the political and the technical requirements for arms control verification more difficult. Because the USSR will never permit on-site inspection, only those arms controls are feasible that can be monitored by national means of verification. Alternatively, whatever verification procedures are instituted, human ingenuity will outwit them. Arms control will then self-destruct as it leads military planners to produce weapons whose control would be impossible to verify.[19]

(16) Alleged Soviet noncompliance with past accords has taken on major political implications. Compliance issues, "if not resolved, will prove to be a major (perhaps insurmountable) barrier to significant progress in arms control."[20]

(17) Superpower arms accords are unlikely if they are opposed by allies of either country.[21]

(18) The Soviets are unlikely to negotiate seriously unless they perceive "sober" forces as well as hard-liners in Washington and believe that they can exploit differences between them.[22]

(19) The top leader must throw his or her weight behind any agreement for it to be signed and ratified.[23]

(20) U.S. arms control policy has generally focused on narrow military objectives; Moscow has proved more adept than Washington at integrating its arms control stance with military programs, general foreign policy objectives, and domestic political imperatives.[24]

(21) Neither side is likely to achieve a security benefit through arms control that it is unable or unwilling to create by its own unilateral actions.[25]

Lessons Questioned

Let us review the implications of the INF accord and other arms control developments in the 1980s for each of the foregoing "lessons." Most of these propositions are too cynical to account for the movement toward arms control in this period, but some are too idealistic to explain what has happened.[26]

(1) The fundamental reason lessons derived from previous experience have proved faulty is that the 1987 INF agreement represents the first case in which major, rival powers have agreed voluntarily to disarm, in this case eliminating two classes of weapons under foreign inspection. The Versailles Treaty and other peace treaties *imposed* disarmament on defeated countries, but these measures were by no means voluntary and were repudiated when circumstances changed. The 1922 Washington Naval Treaty required the great naval powers to scrap many ships already built or under construction to comply with their alloted quotas; similarly, the 1972 and 1979 SALT treaties compelled the superpowers to retire some delivery systems if they chose to build and deploy new ones beyond permitted ceilings. A whole series of treaties have precluded weapons testing or deployment in certain domains (e.g., Antarctica) or have limited the quantity or characteristics of agreed-on weapons (such as ABM systems). But the closest move toward negotiated disarmament before the INF agreement came in 1972 when the Biological and Toxin Weapons Convention was signed. Unlike the INF accord, however, the BWC was spurred by unilateral—not negotiated—disarmament. President Nixon announced in 1969–70 that the United States would destroy its existing stocks of biological and toxic weapons. Unlike INF, the BWC contained no provisions for international inspection.

Still, analysts debate whether the INF cuts were significant disarmament or trivial steps intended to deceive the gullible. Whereas earlier arms treaties reduced or limited weapons thought to be obsolete, redundant, or unusable, the INF eliminated nuclear-tipped missiles among the newest and most formidable in the two countries' arsenals. Its on-site inspection features were unprecedented.[27] The USSR had to remove from its LRINF arsenal 3.6 times as many warheads, eliminate three times as many launchers, and twice as many missiles as NATO, while also eliminating three times as many SRINF. Still, the treaty removed only a small portion of the superpowers' arsenals; it did not prevent "compensating" measures nor did it require destruction of INF warheads and guidance systems. The Pentagon debated recycling removed warheads onto air-launched cruise missiles (ACLMs) and even issued two contracts to convert ground-

[254]

launched to sea-launched missiles—implying that 145 GLCMs had not been properly reported and destroyed. Even if the conversion used unassembled components rather than completed missiles, compliance issues needed resolution. The USSR also investigated ways to modernize its intermediate-range weaponry.

Transferring warheads to other kinds of missiles might result in a more crisis-stable environment, but this would be "redeployment" rather than "disarmament." Perhaps only time will tell whether the INF pact was a major step toward a demilitarized world. For all its limitations, however, its scope and depth were unparalleled in Soviet-U.S. relations. It was at least a potentially if not assuredly significant breakthrough in arms reduction.

The INF Treaty—along with Reagan's support at Reykjavik for complete nuclear disarmament—suggested that capitalists were not inherently against arms reductions.[28] To be sure, the Reagan administration backed away from the most intense on-site verification measures, apparently in deference to industrial sensitivities, but it accepted external observation of some key defense installations. The American stock markets, already buffeted by serious blows, did not decline further when the INF agreement and the 1987 summit meeting were announced; rather, stock market averages bounced up and then down, responding to production and trade figures rather than to changes in Soviet-U.S. relations.[29]

(2) All or nothing? The importance of creating a "package" trading off assets of both sides was underscored by Paul Nitze and Yuli Kvitsinsky as they drafted a deal to limit Euromissiles in July 1982.[30] Gorbachev's January 1986 call for complete nuclear disarmament put forward a much more complex package with many trade-offs for all nuclear powers.[31] But the complexity as well as the radical goals of this scheme aroused skepticism in the West.

Soviet diplomats also tried to condition an INF agreement on a variety of other arms curbs.[32] The December 1987 treaty, however, was not conditioned on limitation of SDI or other superpower weapons programs. It did not hinge on reciprocal or parallel moves by any other countries except West Germany, which pledged eventually to eliminate its Pershing 1-A missiles. Probably the Kremlin hoped that the INF Treaty would lead to other, farther-reaching accords, but it adopted a "peace in parts" approach.

The INF Treaty demonstrated that disarmament measures are possible even though they entail asymmetrical burdens and do not require across-the-board superpower reductions or even reciprocity by other nuclear powers. Disarmament need not be a matter of all or nothing.

(3) Each side's INF negotiating pack contained "jokers," but they were gradually discarded. Reagan's zero option may have aimed primarily at impressing the Western European peace movement.[33] No realistic analyst, critics averred, could expect the USSR to give up something for nothing. The Kremlin countered in 1982–83 with an offer to halt its SS-20 deployment if the West deployed no Pershing 2s or Tomahawks, but his deal contained a joker: the West could not accept a Soviet monopoly on Euromissiles.[34] Even after negotiations resumed in earnest in 1985, many moves by each side were quite one-sided—for example, Moscow's demand to keep its Asian missiles where America had none; the Western demand for limits on "shorter-range" as well as "longer-range" intermediate missiles (given that the West had only 72 "shorter-range" missiles deployed).

The joker concept has always been ambiguous. Are unacceptable jokers inserted into disarmament proposals to kill any prospect of an accord or only to safeguard one's own interests?[35] An apparently one-sided proposal could imply that its advocate wants no agreement—or only that he or she is starting with stiff terms in a negotiation process that might evolve toward an agreement. The Reagan White House may well have put forward its zero option thinking the Kremlin would not accept it but believing that, were it accepted, Western interests would gain. The Reagan administration also rejected the 1982 Nitze-Kvitsinsky formula on the ground that it was stacked against American interests.[36] Because the Kremlin eventually agreed to a zero option (indeed, a double zero option) in 1987, it can be argued that Washington's earlier position was not merely a propaganda gesture but the *only* ground on which it was willing to come to terms with Moscow. The Kremlin did not hold out on its own conditions (such as SDI and limits on other nuclear powers); therefore the Kremlin's potential jokers turned out only to have been opening gambits. Thus possibly "unacceptable" positions on both sides proved to be only bargaining ploys or perhaps the only grounds on which West could meet East. In time the stipulations that could have prevented an agreement were either withdrawn or accepted. Because we cannot know when a proposal is meant to frustrate agreement or even when it will necessarily prevent agreement, the term "joker" loses most of its analytical value. In the INF what seemed impossible turned out to be necessary.

(4) Must good relations already exist between nations for them to agree to limit their arms? The "arms control paradox" derives from the abstract logic of Realpolitik more than from historical fact. It flows from the simplistic dogma that arms races spring from distrust and not the other way around. But relations among nations are not so clear cut. Often distrust is exacerbated—even generated—by arms competition.

[256]

History provides many cases in which arms accords have helped to diminish tensions between rivals. Thus the 1817 Rush-Bagot agreement to limit military vessels on the Great Lakes did not arise simply because British-U.S. relations were euphoric. It came on the heels of a war, the passions and memories of which were still fresh. Indeed, there was even a possibility of another war arising out of confrontation on the Great Lakes. The Rush-Bagot agreement helped to quiet those anxieties and, over many decades, contributed to the general pacification of British and Canadian relations with the United States. Similarly the 1922 Washington Naval Treaty eased tensions between and among Britain, Japan, and the United States. It helped to curtain navalism and the militarization of the Pacific until a more militaristic orientation came to power in Japan.

There is no assurance that arms limitations will ensure détente forever. Thus Japanese hawks resented the "middle" ratio assigned to Japan at Washington and at the 1930 London Conference extending the Washington formula to cruisers. They assassinated the prime minister after the 1930 accord, abrogated arms control obligations, and instituted policies that led to Pearl Harbor. Thus the longer-term impact of the Washington limitations on U.S.-Japanese relations was anything but beneficent.

Many Soviet-U.S. arms accords have been signed during or immediately after times of strong East-West tensions, as detailed in analysis of the next proposition. But the INF agreement puts the nail in the thesis of an arms control paradox. It was negotiated when the United States was supporting anti-Soviet guerrillas in more than half a dozen countries in an effort to collapse what Reagan termed the "evil empire."

(5) Is arms control a poor way to break from cold war competition? What is the nexus, if any, between arms control and détente?

If arms diplomacy is only gamesmanship, it will probably deepen mutual hostilities, as happened in the late 1940s. But if East-West exchanges demonstrate a shared desire to reduce the risks and costs of arms racing, this can diminish East-West tensions. One outcome of the 1955 Geneva summit, French participant Jules Moch told me, was that each side came to believe that the other deeply feared a nuclear exchange and wanted steps to prevent one.

Arms negotiations became a way to sustain dialogue between Moscow and Washington when communications in other realms withered. Thus serious negotiations on a nuclear test ban and on preventing surprise attack took place in the late 1950s despite confrontations in the Middle East, divided Germany, and the Taiwan Straits. Kennedy and Khrushchev used the hot-line agreement and nuclear test ban to demonstrate, after the Cuban

[257]

crisis, the will to improve relations. Negotiations on outer space, the NPT, and SALT helped to sustain American-Soviet dialogue despite conflicts in Indochina and the Middle East. To be sure, a drastic downturn in East-West relations, as occurred in 1956 and 1968, can disrupt détente. But arms control has also proved to be a powerful way to resurrect East-West dialogue and to take the edge off mutual tensions. Gorbachev's words and deeds on arms control broke the tension spiral between the superpowers in the 1980s.

The record of Soviet-U.S. relations since the mid-1950s shows that arms control can brake competition and put both sides on the road to détente. Progress toward arms control has sometimes occurred when superpower relations were generally tense, but there has never been a broad trend toward improved Soviet-U.S. relations not trigered in part by movement toward arms control. Arms control has been a virtual sine qua non for détente.

Arms control can generate détente, but it cannot ensure that it lasts—witness the decline of détente after SALT I and II. Moreover, if a Soviet or American administration were effectively tarred with "selling out" through arms control—as Japanese moderates were accused after the naval limits of 1922—the backlash could easily intensify tensions and arms competition between the superpowers.

(6) Can progress in arms control occur only when neither side has an advantage? This view is supported by much but not all history before the INF. Thus America's initial nuclear monopoly meant that either Washington or Moscow would have to take an enormous leap of faith to ban the bomb. Even after the USSR broke the U.S. monopoly the Kremlin refused to consider freezing strategic arsenals until it achieved rough parity. And only after Washington announced plans to end Russia's ABM monopoly did Moscow agree to negotiate defensive as well as offensive systems.

The failure of efforts to ban antisatellite weapons (ASAT) weapons also implies that arms accords are unlikely if either side has the upper hand. Washington opposed a ban on ASAT that would leave the USSR with a demonstrated capacity to intercept and destroy some low-orbit U.S. satellites while prohibiting the United States from obtaining a comparable capability. The Kremlin refused to dismantle its ASAT capability as the price for precluding an American ASAT. As happened in the ABM case, Moscow showed more interest in mutual restraint only when the Pentagon moved closer to testing an ASAT better than the Soviet.[37]

But even the ASAT case is oversimplified. Thoughtful members of Congress argue that an ASAT test ban would benefit U.S. interests even though American technology may be superior to Soviet. The existing

Soviet capacity, they contend, poses little threat to most U.S. satellites; but an unfettered competition in antisatellite warfare could jeopardize reconnaissance and communications systems based in outer space. Thus asymmetries in ASAT weapons need not prevent an accord if top leaders saw things differently. What would be needed is a change of perspective similar to that underlying the ABM agreement—a recognition that even if technology improved, the resulting competition could make security even more fragile.[38]

The "no advantage" thesis oversimplifies other realities even before the mid-1980s. The 1963 limited test ban was concluded despite two American advantages: many more tests already conducted and better capabilities for the underground testing now permitted. Washington welcomed the 1972 ABM Treaty even though only the USSR had a deployed ABM force. SALT I permitted the Kremlin numerical advantages that, Henry Kissinger argued, were compensated by American qualitative strengths. Besides, as he asked after the 1974 Moscow summit, "What in the name of God is strategic superiority?"

The evidence suggests that *arms controls are negotiable when each side is willing—given the overall situation—to surrender or trade off some military or other assets.* Specialists at IMEMO argued in March 1989 that the INF Treaty made possible Moscow's decision to go beyond a purely "mathematical" or "mechanical" approach to arms control; to consider the limited role that military force can play in a world where power comes first of all from mastery of science and technology; to understand the tremendous destruction that would result from use even of a handful of nuclear arms—or even a conventional strike against a nuclear reactor; and to take account of the prestige factor behind British and French insistence on upgrading their nuclear arsenals. They also allowed that the threat posed by the P2 was unique but argued that this was only one of many considerations leading the Kremlin to the various concessions embodied in the INF accord.

No matter how formally symmetrical the treaty, asymmetries usually persist. For example, if each side were left with 100 weapons, the accuracy and throwweight of those weapons may differ; America's may be closer to Moscow than Russia's to Washington. Many Soviet-U.S. accords have been reached when there was no clear way to measure the utility of the forces limited and those not curbed. Throughout the 1970s, for example, the USSR worried about America's forward-based systems in Europe and at sea but agreed to omit them from strategic arms accords.

The INF agreement was concluded despite enormous asymmetries in the forces eliminated and those that remained. To be sure, the "no advantage" school can contend that despite asymmetries, there was "rough equivalence" between the Soviet and U.S. forces destroyed and those that would remain.[39] But analyzing INF trade-offs is like comparing apples and oranges. The no advantage argument can be made only by blurring the quite different assets each side surrendered and retained. The argument could become tautological: "Because an arms accord has been concluded, it must be that there existed no advantage for either side."

The INF and other arms controls might be better compared with negotiations for a used car. Both the seller and the buyer must see advantages for the transaction to take place. The fact that each side has different values facilitates the deal. Some Soviet and U.S. values ran parallel in the INF accord: improving crisis stability; getting an accord that appeals to domestic constituencies. But the Kremlin was more interested in first derivatives, whereas Washington focused on present values, especially its 1:4 warhead gain.[40]

The no advantage school implies a strategic determinism that need not hold if statesmen exercise vision and free will. To demand precisely equal sacrifices and outcomes could preclude accords to mutual but unequal gain. No matter what arms accords are reached, each side will retain certain geopolitical economic advantages and liabilities.[41] Because the negotiating process has involved trade-offs in multiple currencies (military, alliance cohesion, domestic politics, and so on), "it is unlikely that the preferred outcome in any currency will be achieved in an agreement acceptable to both sides."[42] *Arms accords and other agreements may be in the national interest even though one side must give up more than the other.*

(7) Are the only weapons that can be controlled those that are unborn or about to pass into obsolescence? Battleships, the argument runs, were virtually obsolete when they were limited in 1922, whereas the Washington Treaty did little to curb development of more promising weapons—aircraft carriers and submarines. The 1967 outer space treaty worked because it prevented deployment of a new type of weapon rather than attempting to eliminate it after deployment; the ABM treaty was another example of successful abortion—at least so long as technology promised high costs and little gain from ABM deployment.

The "abortion-euthanasia" principle was already challenged by certain limitations set down in SALT I and II because these treaties placed ceilings on some weapons already developed but far from obsolescence. But these were both interim agreements. Indeed, SALT II contained an ALCM ban set to last only two years.

The INF accord demonstrates that political actors can, if they so will, limit—even destroy—weapons in their prime. The weapons eliminated under INF may be undesirable for other reasons (conducive to preemptive moves or launch-on-warning responses), but they are hardly obsolete. The Pershing 2s and GLCMs were by no means antiquated; they were among the most accurate, difficult-to-intercept weapons in the U.S. arsenal, even offering some promise of waging a controlled nuclear war. Some of the Kremlin's intermediate-range arsenal is quite old, but its main component—the SS-20s—is a mobile, solid-fuel, multiple warhead weapon impossible to treat as "over the hill." Though deployed long before America's Euromissiles, the SS-20 was incrementally improved over the years.

(8) Do Soviet planners prefer a free hand to forestalling foreign technological dynamism? The answer seems to be "yes" if we consider the lack of serious interest under Stalin to the Baruch Plan or under Brezhnev to throttling the U.S. lead in MIRV. But Kremlin attitudes changed in the 1980s as Soviet planners worried that the USSR was falling further and further behind Western and Japanese technology. The Pentagon in 1986 rated the United States as superior to the USSR in fourteen of twenty fields of basic technology, with a widening lead in computers and software; the two countries as equal in six domains (including lasers and electro-optical sensors); the USSR ahead in none. If Soviets share such perceptions, this would help to explain why the Kremlin has sought to ban all testing of ASAT systems and to halt development of the hydra-headed SDI. This interpretation—contrary to the original proposition—is supported by Matthew Evangelista's research showing that U.S. weapons innovations have usually come "from the bottom" spurred by corporate or government researchers and military officials, whereas the centralized Soviet system has produced innovations "from the top" in response to foreign developments.[43] In short, the Soviets have been far more reactive than the Americans, often lagging for years.

(9) "Arms control negotiations are more likely to be undertaken and are more likely to succeed in times when military technology shows little dynamism." This principle seems almost self-evident, but when did it hold? Looking back we find that ferment in military technology has often *sparked* arms control efforts—to limit the crossbow, to prohibit larger cannon and more powerful explosives (1899), to constrain projectiles from dirigibles (1907), and so on. Generally it was the less advanced party that sued for restraint, such as tsarist Russia in 1899/1907. But the United States has also led in initiating arms control moves, as it did after each world war, even though it was the technological leader.

[261]

Soviet anxiety about the "ferment" in American R&D stimulated Moscow to limit ABM defenses, seek ASAT constraints and opposed SDI. The other side of this coin is that in the early 1970s Washington had little faith in the ability of U.S. technology to produce an effective ABM and, with Reagan gone, to create some other form of antimissile shield. When Moscow fears that the United States may succeed and the Americans fear they may fail, the chances for an accord improve. Thus technological ferment may generate arms control negotiations, but accords are most likely when no technological breakthrough is in sight.

There is also a prescriptive lesson: it is unwise to test and deploy weapons that are redundant or destabilizing. Both sides should have banned MIRV and cruise missiles even though one party had a temporary "lead" because their proliferation aggravates many other security problems.

(10) What has been the role of unilateral restraint in generating superpower arms controls? There are grounds to argue that it has had no effect, or even that it has been counterproductive. But there are also reasons to believe that, combined with the threat of playing other cards, unilateral restraint has been conducive to joint accords. Evaluation is difficult because there are few instances "of one side's abstaining from an activity of significant military utility over a period of time sufficiently long to induce an observable and unambiguous response by the other side."[44]

Psychologist Charles Osgood called in the early 1960s for a strategy of GRIT ("graduated and reciprocal initiatives in tension reduction"), suggesting that the stronger side should take the first steps in a long-range plan to reverse the spiral of hostility. Similarly, Khrushchev at the end of 1963 spoke of "disarmament by mutual example," and in 1985 Gorbachev proposed "an eye for an eye" in arms restraints.[45]

American hard-liners contend that U.S. restraint on ABM development in the 1960s induced no Soviet reciprocity and that a whole series of U.S. policies in the 1970s—reduced defense spending, leveling off in numbers of strategic delivery vehicles deployed, cancellation of the B-1 bomber and neutron weapons—had no impact on Soviet military spending and deployment. An opposing view holds that cuts in U.S. military outlays came primarily from ending the Vietnam engagement and secondarily from winding down cycles of ICBM and SSBN deployments. The most important index of power—the number of strategic warheads—increased sharply throughout the decade without ballooning the U.S. defense budget. Carter's decisions on the B-1 and neutron bomb were made on grounds of cost-effectiveness and not as inducements to the USSR to negotiate.[46]

[262]

Nor is it clear that Soviet restraint has made a dent in American planning. The Kremlin after 1976 seems to have suppressed the growth in its military spending to no more than the sluggish expansion of the Soviet economy.[47] Soviet moratoria on SS-20 deployment in 1982–83, on nuclear testing in 1985–86, and in other domains were ignored or written off as meaningless gestures by top Washington officials. Indeed, if the Kremlin demonstrated some restraint and sued for American reciprocity, some Pentagon officials argued that this implied a weakness that America should exploit by stepping up arms development. Gorbachev's policies thus risked that they would generate not American restraint but heightened competition. He complained in September 1985 that instead of reciprocating Soviet restraint, Washington was "defiantly" conducting more nuclear tests, carrying out the "first operational test" of an ASAT weapon, and launching another hate campaign against the USSR.[48]

Still, the accumulating evidence of Gorbachev's interest in restraining the arms race probably induced Reagan to think more favorably about a deal with Moscow. The general secretary spoke and acted in conformity with Osgood's injunctions to (a) announce a long-term strategy of initiatives in tension reduction; (b) start with small steps, promising that they will be amplified if the other side reciprocates; and (c) be persistent and patient, giving the other side sufficient time to see that you are serious and to plan his response. Perceptions of Soviet restraint helped to eliminate dissonance between earlier images of Soviet evil and Reagan's wish that he be remembered as a man of peace. Indeed, in 1987 Reagan declared that Gorbachev was the first Soviet leader who said nothing about expanding communism worldwide.[49]

Unilateral initiatives, pursued in conjunction with other carrots and sticks, can help to open the way to joint arms control. But history shows that the superpower juggernauts tend to run on their own momentum, impelled more by technological feasibility and domestic pressures than in response to pacific gestures or deeds by the adversary. Still, if neither side makes the first move, both sides will be condemned in perpetuity to the mounting risks and dangers of a tit-for-tat competition.

(11) Are bargaining chips counterproductive to arms control? Only when the United States threatened to deploy ABM did the Kremlin (in the late 1960s) agree to negotiate on defensive as well as strategic nuclear arms. Only when NATO decided to deploy Euromissiles did Moscow initiate a moratorium on its SS-20 deployments. Only after the Pershing 2 and GLCM deployments were under way did the Kremlin accept Washington's zero option proposal. It is surprising that the Gorbachev regime agreed to remove 2,210 LRINF warheads in exchange for only 676 American, but

[263]

it would have been still more surprising had Moscow agreed to remove its SS-20 force without a substantial quid pro quo.

Without bargaining chips on both sides, Moscow and Washington would have less incentive to negotiate seriously. Why should either give up some asset without getting something in return? A skillful security policy, however, must be wary of developing bargaining chips but then refusing to put them on the table. It should avoid transforming chips into "solid assets not to be traded at any price."[50] Thus MIRVed-missiles and cruise missiles, conceived in part as bargaining chips, became so "sweet" technologically that they quickly became integral to the American arsenal without any serious attempt to limit them on an East-West basis.

Without chips one cannot bargain; but in arms control one must remember the goal of the game: enhanced security.

(12) To what extent can either superpower be pressured into a positive negotiating posture? A kind of folk wisdom says not to push the Bear into a corner. But analogies of this kind oversimplify. To be sure, the most dangerous moments in East-West relations came in 1961–62 as the strategic balance of power tilted away from Moscow. Similarly, the perceived power shift to Russia's advantage in the late 1970s coupled with more aggressive Soviet behavior elicited a new American determination to stand up to the Bear. The Eagle retreated for five years after Vietnam and then came out "defiant" and sometimes fighting.[51] The Reagan administration then pushed the Bear against the wall and talked derisively of the Soviet system as an experiment destined for the garbage heap of history. When the USSR halted nuclear tests for eighteen months, Washington did not reciprocate. When Moscow began to budge on INF, Washington asked for more, repeatedly upping the ante until the Kremlin gave in on most Western demands.

Our image of the cornered Bear needs to be refined. How the Kremlin responds to pressure depends on the nature and intensity of the threat; the other domestic and foreign problems and opportunities it perceives; the way in which particular leaders think, feel, and act under pressure. Probably there are multiple and interacting thresholds that outsiders can barely guess at. Below a certain level of economic duress, for example, Moscow may feel little reason to curtail arms spending; given the transformation that Gorbachev envisions, however, the Kremlin has been willing to follow the Brest-Litovsk model, surrendering a great deal in order to win a substantial *peredyshka* (breathing space) for perestroika. (The play *Brestkii mir*, or *Brest Peace* became popular in Moscow in the late 1980s, showing how Lenin traded territory and revolutionary dreams for peace.)

The fact that Reagan's pressure tactics "worked" does not mean that they were or will be optimal for U.S. interests. A combination of positive as well as negative inducements would probably have more success over time in bringing the USSR out of a zero-sum and into a positive-sum orientation in foreign affairs. Still, the Reagan-Gorbachev interactions showed that sustained pressures on the USSR, at a time when the Kremlin is becoming acutely aware of mounting problems at home and abroad, can elicit a conciliatory inflection in Soviet policy.

It is probably impossible to prescribe the optimum blend of conciliation and firmness in adversary relations. But it seems clear that until humans become far-sighted angels, some combination of both elements should be applied in each negotiating situation. Gorbachev's conciliation was probably necessary to evoke a positive response from Reagan, but American steadfastness increased Moscow's willingness to make the necessary concessions. But this particular intersection of individuals and forces will never recur.

(13) Is economics irrelevant? So far there has been little "peace dividend" from arms control. The decline in U.S. defense outlays for most of the 1970s was caused by withdrawal from Vietnam, not by SALT I. The tapering off of Soviet defense outlays after 1976 was probably dictated by the decline in growth of the overall economy rather than by arms control.

Fears about the burden of defense spending on general economic performance seem to have played little or no role in the Oval Office as Reagan continued to request substantial increases in defense spending through 1987 while cutting taxes. There is no evidence that the rising U.S. budget deficit and America's new role as global debtor made the president more responsive to Soviet arms initiatives. Many Democrats and some Republicans in Congress, however, worried about military outlays and did what they could to curb them. Congressional authorizations for defense declined after 1985, even though military spending continued to climb. The October 1987 global stock market crash suggested that many investors also worried about the American imbalances, a worry little assuaged by the prospect of an imminent Soviet-U.S. summit accord on INF.

Economic concerns pinched more perceptibly in Moscow. The Soviet growth rate had crawled for a decade; export earnings were down principally because oil and gas prices had retrenched; Kremlin planners were awed by the emerging gap between CMEA and OECD technological capabilities. Gorbachev believed that the ills of the Soviet economy and society demanded revolutionary restructuring. He told the editors of *Time* (September 9, 1985) simply to look at his plans for the Soviet economy;

[265]

from these plans they should be able to deduce the peaceful thrust of Soviet foreign policy. The Party leadership, he said, does not seek "new records in producing metals, oil, cement, machine tools or other products. The main thing is to make life better for the people." The key change in the world that would benefit the Soviet economy would be "an end to the arms race," which he described as wasteful as well as immoral. Gorbachev denied that the USSR is dependent for modernization on import of U.S. technology, but he expressed a wish to return to the mutual advantages provided by "reciprocal scientific and technological cooperation" that existed in the 1970s. If foreign policy is the continuation of domestic policy, he asked, and if the USSR has "truly grandiose plans in the domestic sphere, then what are the external conditions that we need to be able to fulfill those domestic plans?"

It was probably not clear even to Gorbachev's top planners just how savings in military outlays would translate into general economic improvements. High Soviet officials have quipped that even their staffs do not know how to calculate the total value of USSR military outlays. But given that the Soviet defense burden is over twice the American, any steps to ease its weight must be welcome to Soviet policymakers. Fewer soldiers could mean more workers. Fewer scientists devoted to military R&D could mean more research in basic science and technology—essential for civilian or military applications. The INF agreement and even a cut in strategic weapons would provide only marginal savings because such weapons have already been paid or planned for. Nor does the INF accord diminish the threat to Soviet interests from Western military technology. But heading off new rounds of competition in exotic weapons—those developed under SDI and explorations into new conventional arms—could permit more Soviet scientists to attend to basics instead of pursuing crash programs to keep up with the West. Withdrawing from Afghanistan should also permit various economies.

In early 1987 Gorbachev termed defense a "great burden" for the Soviet economy and indicated that in the future military requirements would have to be based on the principle of "reasonable sufficiency." But the early years of his regime saw little change either in military procurement or in overall economic growth from the decade 1975–85. Military spending continued to increase at about 2.0–3.0 percent above inflation, estimated to run 2.0–4.0 percent annually. The situation resembled "stagflation," with overall economic growth at between 0.5 and 2.3 percent annually. Consumers suffered more than generals as living standards went down in the chaos that accompanied perestroika. Defense plants, however, had the advantage that much of their modernization and retooling had already been accomplished.[52]

Feeling a need to provide ordinary Soviet citizens with some boon, the Kremlin established an emergency fund in December 1988 and used it to import Western goods ranging from razor blades to soap powder. Economist Leonid I. Abalkin averred that the USSR's most pressing economic problem was the deficit, which he put at 100 billion rubles—a sum three times higher than earlier acknowledged and equivalent to 11 percent of Soviet GNP (compared with a U.S. deficit equal to about 4 percent of GNP). Abalkin, a close adviser to Gorbachev, also pledged steep slashes in Soviet outlays for troops, arms, and military hardware. Meanwhile, cuts in the USSR space budget were also demanded from various quarters—including Gorbachev ally Roald Z. Sagdeev and Gorbachev critic Boris N. Yeltsin, who called for "stretching out" space research.[53]

As military power appears redundant or unusable, economic incentives have become more powerful to Gorbachev's Kremlin than to previous Soviet regimes. In Moscow (and to a lesser degree in Washington) economic considerations have reinforced the movement toward arms control in the mid-1980s. They have been neither a necessary nor a sufficient cause for agreements, but—especially for the Kremlin—they have been mighty inducements toward arms limitation. Western economic strength thus created both sticks and carrots by which to move Moscow toward serious arms negotiations. Looking beyond immediate savings from détente and arms control, the Gorbachev regime looks forward to enhanced East-West trade and broader Soviet participation in the global economy.

(14) The argument that arms control is usually possible only when there is intramilitary discord or when military opposition is mollified by an appropriate quid pro quo comes mainly from the American experience, not the Soviet. Many in Congress as well as the military are dubious about arms control as a way to improve security. Therefore the administration that negotiates an arms treaty must "deliver" the blessing of the uniformed military to secure the approval and consent of the Senate for arms control. Approval of the Washington Naval Treaty was facilitated by an alliance between civilian and pro-naval arms control segments in the military over the opposition of other military leaders. The Joint Chiefs of Staff extracted four safeguards for supporting the 1963 test ban and three for endorsing SALT I.

Outgoing NATO commander Bernard Rogers joined a Cassandra chorus with Al Haig, Henry Kissinger, and others who warned that INF could lead to a denuclearized Europe. When Frank C. Carlucci became defense secretary, however, carping about INF from the Pentagon ceased and the uniformed military offered no deep objections to the treaty. Threatened by radical cutbacks in defense spending, the military were in no position to demand compensation for signing off on INF.

The military can obstruct but not stop arms control in Washington provided the president and Congress want an agreement. Congressional criticisms of SALT II, for example, were more influential than any comments from the Joint Chiefs, which saw value in limiting Soviet missiles.

As noted in chapter 3, the military-industrial complex as an interest group is much weaker in the USSR than in the United States. The Communist party chief heads the Supreme Defense Council and is joined there by other top Politburo members whose vision and responsibilities are for the entire country, not just the military. If a Marshal Zhukov shows signs of becoming a political rival, he is dismissed. A civilian, Dmitrii Ustinov, was responsible for the military industry from before World War II until he became defense minister in Brezhnev's last years. Uniformed officers have often served as Soviet defense minister, but they have often lacked a seat on the Politburo, even as candidate members. Ustinov, a full member of the Politburo, was succeeded as defense minister by two uniformed officers who were made candidate (notvoting) Politburo members.[54]

It is said that the military complained about Khrushchev's 1960 proposal to cut the armed forces by one-third, but the plan went ahead—until East-West tensions rose over Berlin the following year. It is said that Soviet marshals opposed omitting America's forward-based systems from SALT I and II, but they were omitted. Brezhnev seems to have favored all military branches (unlike Khrushchev, who backed the Strategic Rocket Forces and denigrated other branches). Regardless of grumbling from some elements of the military, Gorbachev extended the U.S.-Soviet moratorium over eighteen months in the face of continued U.S. testing. Until 1987, of course, no branch of the Soviet military suffered from arms control except the PVO (Anti-Air Defense) limited by the ABM accords. But the military has not been in a strong position to do more than snipe at Gorbachev's 1987–89 moves to cut INF forces, trim conventional forces, and reduce defense spending. Unless the military finds strong backers in the Politburo opposition, Gorbachev will be under little pressure to "compensate" the military to gain its approval. He stands at the pinnacle of the military-industrial complex as well as the Party; with continued centralization and without free enterprise, arms controls approved at the top are unlikely to meet much resistance from the ranks.

Thus the argument of proposition 14 undervalues the tradition of civilian dominance in both countries, particularly the USSR. If domestic resistance to Gorbachev's reforms mounted, of course, some military leaders would be tempted to side with conservatives. A possible straw in the wind: in January 1988 Defense Minister Yazov spoke out against excesses of glasnost' in a way that seemed to align him with then KGB chief Chebrikov and other advocates of caution.[55]

Indeed, some Soviet civilian analysts complain that the Moscow "Pentagon" still plays a disproportionate role in shaping Soviet arms control policy—exploiting its near monopoly of classified military information—and that the upper ranks are still dominated by tank officers reliving 1943. IMEMO gets requests for studies from the Defense Ministry but little feedback, the officers questioning the competence of civilians to do serious research. Not intimidated, IMEMO sector chief Aleksandr Saveleev attacks the competence of the Soviet military even in the realm of doctrine (for example, the objectives of war). He would have U.S. experts such as Edward Luttwak lecture the Soviet officers on strategy.

Although Soviet civilian analysts do not think a military coup likely, this possibility is not excluded if crises mount within the USSR.

(15) Must arms controls go no further than measures that can be verified by "national means" such as satellites? This argument has long been exaggerated. As early as 1955–56 the USSR advocated "mixed commissions" to police arms controls in Central Europe.[56] On-site inspections are authorized to verify the demilitarization (since 1959) of Antarctica. The Kremlin agreed in 1958 to a system of seismic stations on Soviet and U.S. territory to police a comprehensive test ban; Khrushchev later offered to allow several intrusive inspections a year to verify a test ban.[57] Western negotiating behavior, however, deepened Moscow's suspicion that the West was more interested in inspection than in arms reductions—that its goal was to undermine a valuable Soviet asset: secrecy. Kremlin spokesmen often voiced this charge, helping thereby to "confirm" Western suspicions that the Kremlin would never permit intrusive inspections.

Moscow probably proposed a limited test ban in 1963 more to wrap up a treaty quickly than to avoid intrusive inspection. The ABM Treaty and both SALT accords dealt with weapons whose numbers and characteristics could be reasonably well monitored by "national means"—again eliminating any requirement to spell out verification procedures in the treaties. The USSR balked until 1987 at permitting intrusive inspection of chemical weapons disarmament, perhaps because it would have to be extremely extensive to be credible. (In August 1987 Foreign Minister Shevardnadze stated that the USSR accepted in principle the U.S. proposal for short-notice inspections, but many verification and other problems remained before a chemical weapons treaty could be signed.) Even before Gorbachev, however, the Kremlin permitted IAEA inspection of some Soviet nonmilitary nuclear reactors.

Is it possible that military refinements will produce weapons incapable of verification and thus give arms control its coup de grace? This argument is plausible in the abstract and gains some support from the manifest difficulties in regulating multiple warheads and cruise missiles. But the question cannot be definitively resolved by deductive logic. Verification technology has been inventive; where there is a will for arms control, modes of verification may be discovered; the prospect of detection will also inhibit cheating. As glasnost' expands, public-spirited Soviets as well as Americans would be tempted to report any arms violations by their government.

Under Gorbachev glasnost' has been extended to the arms front. The Kremlin has welcomed and called for more intrusive inspection than the United States: it has permitted a private group to set up seismic stations on Soviet territory to monitor Soviet nuclear tests, helped NATO observers to watch Soviet maneuvers, guided American congressmen and their staff experts through the notorious Krasnoyarsk radar, offered to permit American inspection of other radars suspected of violating the ABM Treaty, and agreed to whatever on-site measures that Washington wanted to police the INF agreement.[58]

Soviet interests in becoming part of the world economy call for joint ventures and, generally, more penetration by outsiders of Soviet society. Television and radio also help to make the USSR part of a global village.[59] All these forces help to render anachronistic the security concerns and xenophobia that once resisted international inspections. If the price is right— if Moscow gets arms controls it wants—Moscow seems willing to permit many kinds of on-site inspection. Part of the deal, of course, will be that Soviet representatives can look closely at Western installations of some interest. Western concern to protect industrial secrets may become as formidable an obstacle to on-site verification as traditional Soviet secrecy.

Future arms controls may require more on-site verification than did those of the 1970s. Limits on cruise missiles, mobile missiles, multiple warheads, and so on will be more difficult to monitor by satellite than the requirements set by SALT I and II. Conventional ideas about military and industrial security may need to be sacrificed in both societies. Analysts at IMEMO assert that the USSR wants chemical and biological disarmament and is ready for extremely intrusive inspection—provided it can retain a nuclear umbrella.

(16) Would an American administration that has repeatedly accused the USSR of cheating on arms control sign a new arms accord with Moscow while previous charges remain unresolved? Recent history, contrary to logic, says "yes." Less than a week before Gorbachev landed in Washington to sign the INF Treaty, Reagan sent another of his reports on "Soviet Noncompliance with Arms Control Agreements" to Congress. His cover letter asserted that "the Soviet Union to date has not corrected its noncompliance activities. Indeed, since the last report, there has been an additional case of Soviet violation of the ABM Treaty in the deployment of an ABM radar at Gomel, and other violations are continuing." But the report also noted progress in monitoring Soviet military activities under the Helsinki Final Act, in plans for joint verification experiments at nuclear test sites, and in a more forthcoming Soviet attitude toward providing information on bacteriological warfare programs. Still, the White House emphasized the "discrepancy between Soviet public and private arms control diplomacy" and charged that the "Soviets have maintained a prohibited offensive biological warfare capability" and were conducting ambiguous behavior in other domains.[60]

Despite the administration's continued charges of Soviet noncompliance, it found a simple answer to the apparent inconsistency in pursuing further arms controls with Moscow. The INF had a more detailed data base and much more stringent provisions than had previous agreements; because it entirely eliminated two classes of weapons, there would be less room for deception than in less sweeping agreements. The Reagan administration promised that any additional accords (for example, on strategic arms) would also be accompanied by vigilant verification procedures.

(17) What is the role of allies? For the United States it is secondary; for the USSR, tertiary or lower. Washington has often attempted to anticipate and to meet most security concerns of its European partners. Partly because it trusts its partners more than it does Moscow, Washington has long shared part of its nuclear arsenal under two-key arrangements. Thus Washington sponsored the idea of a multilateral force in the mid-1960s to give Germany a greater role in nuclear operations. The inspiration for NATO's Euromissiles was a complaint by German Chancellor Helmut Schmidt that SALT II failed to address the SS-20 threat to Europe. Some U.S. initiatives such as the proposed zero option sought to win propaganda points that would makes its Euromissile deployment more palatable. Indeed, the difference between the two alliance systems is underscored by the fact that parliamentary approval was needed in each NATO country before U.S. theater weapons could be deployed there, a situation completely absent in Eastern Europe.[61]

But the Reagan administration, like its predecessors, sometimes acted first and consulted second. Reagan struck out in uncharted waters, ready to jettison deterrence—announcing the SDI and endorsing (at Reykjavik) complete nuclear disarmament—without vetting these iseas through the American bureaucracy, much less that of NATO. The reservations of Europe and Japan about SDI were muffled by offering contracts and subcontracts to their industries. Reservations of Chancellor Helmut Kohl and other Europeans about INF—including the de facto inclusion of German missiles in INF—were overwhelmed by Prime Minister Margaret Thatcher and Reagan emissaries. Kohl found a graceful way to go along, and Moscow accepted. Still, it was not clear that he who pays the piper (Americans spend more than twice as much per capita on defense as their NATO partners) would always call the tune.[62]

The Soviet Union gives even less heed to its allies in formulating its policies on arms and arms control. Khrushchev made some effort in the mid-1950s to defer to Mao Zedong's view that the East Wind should be prevailing over the West. But Moscow's concerns for Chinese sensitivities dropped away in 1960 and Khrushchev denounced Beijing for "dogmatism."

Despite periodic joint maneuvers of most Warsaw Pact forces and meetings of WTO political and military leaders, most Eastern European spokesmen (except for Romania's) acted as sounding boards for Soviet views. Does Moscow want an all-European security conference? "Fine." Does the Kremlin want Helsinki and Helsinki review conferences? "Good." Does Moscow want to deploy nuclear-capable launchers in Eastern Europe? "Well, all right." Does it want to stockpile nuclear warheads as well, at least in some countries? "*Ja, wenn es sein muess*—if it can't be helped."

If other Pact members had reservations about the wide-scale deployment of SS-20s in the USSR or Moscow's subsequent walkout from arms negotiations, these views were ignored. To be sure, some Warsaw Pact communiqués lacked the threatening language sometimes found in Soviet statements about Euromissiles. And some Soviet carrots—promises to curtail SS-20 deployments—were probably intended for Eastern as well as Western European audiences. But the naked fact of a massive SS-20 deployment remained, one likely to trigger Western countermeasures. When those steps came, Moscow proceeded to deploy new shorter-range missiles in some Eastern European countries even though their governments showed some reluctance to accept (and pay) for them. Adding insult to injury, Soviet pressures led to cancellation of Erich Honecker's planned trip to Bonn in 1984. Earlier that year at the Stockholm Conference on

Confidence- and Security-Building Measures and Disarmament in Europe, some Eastern European diplomats told Western officials that they had been instructed to do no more than reinforce the themes of Soviet diplomacy, though this did not keep Romania from introducing a plan with measures different from Moscow's standard package.[63]

Gorbachev's January 1986 declaration presumed to speak for all Warsaw Pact members in affirming their readiness to reach accords in the Vienna and Stockholm negotiations on arms control and security. He posited that all parties in the MBFR negotiations would freeze their conventional forces after U.S. and Soviet forces in Europe were reduced, and that all countries would permit international inspection posts to monitor military contingents in the zone of arms limitation. Outside Europe, China was cited approvingly for having pledged, like the USSR, never to be the first to use nuclear arms. India, party to Friendship Treaty with Moscow, was not mentioned in the declaration, but Gorbachev posited that all nations would eventually join in a nuclear test ban and other universal measures of arms control.

NATO as well as the Warsaw Pact approved the INF accord within days of its signing, the Eastern Europeans immediately signing a pledge presented by Gorbachev to permit the necessary on-site inspections on their territories.

In the 1980s both superpowers lost power relative to the rest of the world, but both remained hegemons within their alliances. How long the old patterns would continue was unclear. Researchers at IMEMO said that Moscow could tolerate a neutral Hungary and Poland—even a reunited Germany—if overall conditions were right.

(18) Divisions in the capitalist ranks: From the time of the 1922 Genoa Conference the Soviets have sought to manipulate differences within and among capitalist countries using the issues of peace and disarmament. Even under Stalin the Kremlin and its front organizations mounted peace offensives aimed primarily at Western audiences. As the Soviet regime has become more serious about wanting arms accords, however, it has sometimes portrayed ruling circles in the West as split between sober, realistic forces and madmen bent on aggression. With the former group, Soviet media suggested, it was possible to deal. The Kremlin then acted in accordance with Lenin's 1922 recommendation to do everything possible to strengthen pacifist tendencies among the bourgeoisie. Soviet media portrayed such cleavages in the West at the time of the 1963 "Spirit of Moscow" and again in 1972, before and after the Moscow summit.[64] An essay entitled "The Genoa Formula" in *Pravda* (September 2, 1988) again recalled the relevance of Lenin's 1920–22 thinking to contemporary times.

Reagan presented a problem for Soviet analysts: his fundamentalist attitude toward Soviet communism placed him among the hard-liners. For most of his two terms he dominated Congress so that liberals there had little clout. Despite this situation, Gorbachev chose to meet and negotiate with Reagan and his deputies. In short, the Gorbachev regime struck a major deal—not with moderate liberals but with the American far right. Gorbachev's efforts to negotiate with Reagan one on one also deviated from the premises of Marxism. If Reagan were only an instrument of a class, what value were personal relations with him? Gorbachev ignored these niceties and, with persistence and skill, sought to push on to the INF and behond.[65] Printing an essay by Adam Ulam ("Remember Past Mistakes to Avoid Them in the Future"), *Izvestiia* (March 10, 1989) explained that even a critic could produce books and articles from which Soviet readers could learn. Other Soviet publications printed statements by hard-liner analysts Richard Pipes and Zbigniew Brzezinski and by moderates likes Raymond Garthoff and Alexander Yanov.

(19) A review of successful and unsuccessful negotiations over the last three decades finds that the active involvement of the U.S. president is required to overcome the obstacles to signing an arms control accord. Where an American president demonstrated his interest in getting an agreement, obstacles were overcome to conclude the 1963 test ban and the various accords of 1972 and 1979; where the president held back—as on a comprehensive test ban or ASAT—no accord was reached.

If this proposition were true, it could help to explain why Gorbachev ignored Marxist logic and courted Reagan the man. But the argument seems somewhat overstated both historically and in the mid-1980s. There was not heavy White House support for the Antarctica accord in 1959, for the outer space treaty in 1967, or for the NPT in 1968. In the mid-1980s Mr. Reagan did not put his weight firmly behind the negotiations. For six years he emphasized an arms buildup and sponsored arms control jokers. A vehement critic of arms control well before he became president, Reagan treated the ABM Treaty with disdain and authorized SDI tests that may well have violated it; meanwhile he charged in the most cavalier manner that the Kremlin was breaking many if not most of its previous arms control commitments; he declared SALT II a dead letter in 1986. Reagan's hands-off style of "management," as the Tower Commission so euphemistically termed it, could hardly be expected to provide strong support for any complex enterprise; at most he could tell subordinates, "This is the direction I want to move; take the ball and run there."

Torn between the opposition to arms control and an impulse to "rid the world of nuclear weapons" and secure a place in history as peacemaker, in 1986–88 Reagan tilted in the second direction. This gave Shultz and the U.S. negotiators in Geneva the leeway to push toward accords with Moscow. To compare this situation with the leadership provided by Kennedy, Nixon, and Carter in previous administrations, however, would be quite misleading. Still, the former president's blessing and support for the INF were critical to securing its approval by Congress.

Whereas Reagan's attitude toward arms control was mixed, Gorbachev's has been enthusiastic and determined. Without the full weight of the general secretary behind each move of recent years, it would have been nearly impossible to adopt a long, unilateral moratorium on nuclear testing, invite Americans to Krasnoyarsk, or sign a treaty so asymmetrical as the INF. In these respects Gorbachev follows on the heels of Khrushchev and Brezhnev, who staked their reputations on their ability to reach far-reaching accords with the West.

Although Washington's leadership vacuum in the mid-1980s did not give active support to the U.S. arms negotiators, it permitted them to proceed. Reagan's well-known skepticism about any agreements with Moscow may have induced greater Soviet concessions than would have been offered, say, to Jimmy Carter. Soviet fear of a crazy streak in Reagan may have made his Euromissiles look more menacing to Moscow. Reagan's anti-Communist record then ensured congressional approval for INF. The ironies of history again performed an end-run around logic and social science.

(20) Have Soviet leaders better integrated arms control into their broad foreign, defense, and domestic policies than American? Has U.S. arms control policy been primarily an exercise in shaping the military force architecture—its force levels and characteristics—to strengthen stability and promote U.S. security interests? One U.S. negotiator maintains that Soviets, unlike Americans, have viewed arms control not as a narrow technical device to achieve isolated military goals but as "an integral part of a broad foreign and defense policy in which all the elements are intended to be mutually reinforcing and in which the nonmilitary objectives of arms control can be just as important as the strictly military ones." Moscow's interest in the broad correlation of forces—not merely in the military balance of power—alerts it to the impact that arms control may have on the USSR's international standing, the coherence of NATO, the great power triangle, and domestic political alignments in the West.[66]

This argument is surely overdrawn. Both in 1963 and 1972, for example, the Kennedy and Nixon administrations intended that arms controls signed with Moscow contribute to a larger strategy of tension reduction and low-politics cooperation. They hoped arms control would

[275]

influence Soviet behavior in the Third World. Presidents Nixon, Ford, Carter, and Reagan hoped that arms controls would strengthen them domestically. And although Western Europe has not been Washington's prime consideration when negotiating arms control, it has not been forgotten. Thus Kennedy asserted *"Ich bin ein Berliner"* on the eve of the 1963 nuclear test ban.

The Carter and Reagan administrations coordinated America's Euromissile policies through NATO's dual-track strategy. The United States readied its Pershing 2s and GLCMs for deployment, helped European governments deal with their publics, and took a firm stance in negotiating with Moscow. The INF was negotiated and signed in the context of a strategy of maximum pressure against the USSR on its domestic and external fronts. Surely this represented a successful case of integrating arms control with other foreign and domestic political goals. The Reagan team's failure to appreciate the deleterious impact its combined policies would have on the American economy amounted to hubris rather than a refusal to assess the interaction of defense programs with other goals.

The Kremlin, to be sure, has generally tried to integrate arms control with other policy goals at home and abroad. But Soviet arms policies have often operated in ways that did not optimize broad Kremlin objectives. Unilateral force cuts from 1955 to 1960, for example, could have been better integrated with arms control negotiations, as in 1922. Arms shipments and other Soviet activities in the Third World have taken place—from 1955 through the early 1980s—with little consideration of their likely impact on East-West tensions. Soviet bluster and smiles toward Western Europe have rarely worked in harmony.

Moscow has also been interested in negotiating to achieve improvements in "force architecture." For decades Soviet negotiators have labored diligently to preserve Soviet assets and reduce those of the West. Even the asymmetrical cuts in Soviet missiles required by the INF can be rationalized on military as well as foreign policy grounds.

In short, both sides have often used arms control negotiations and outcomes to influence domestic and foreign policy goals as well as military force structures. Often, of course, various government policies, both U.S. and Soviet, have pulled in different directions. Neither side has had a monopoly on wise or counterproductive behavior.

(21) Is it true that neither side is likely to achieve a security benefit through arms control that it is unwilling or unable to achieve by its unilateral actions? The argument holds that neither superpower is likely to give something to the other unless compelled to do so by the other's

leverage. Leverage comes from the ability and willingness to implement military programs costly to the adversary's security. Only when the Americans threatened to overwhelm the Soviet ABM did Moscow negotiate strict limits of ABM; only when the West threatened to deploy Euromissiles did the Kremlin show a willingness to curb its SS-20s.

This argument is too simplistic. If both sides have weapons peculiarly suited for a preemptive first strike, such as P2 or MX missiles, and if an effective defense screen against such an attack is not available, only by joint force reductions can such a threat be diminished. The Pershings were tempting targets for Soviet preemption and were themselves weapons that would be useful in wiping out Soviet command and control centers. Both sides are better off without them.

Howard Raiffa effectively argues the opposite of this proposition. A third party can often suggest a negotiated settlement more advantageous for both sides than they could achieve through bilateral bargaining. Given that neither superpower is likely to call in a mediator, the best alternative is to conduct long negotiations aimed at finding negotiated settlements that improve on the status quo.[67] This is the approach of value-creating rather than value-claiming.

Evaluation: From Duress, Enlightenment?

The movement toward arms control and improved Soviet-U.S. relations in the 1980s defied any simple analysis.[68] The INF Treaty represented enlightened self-interest, but its evolution could not be readily explained by any rational theory of behavior. Many independent variables contributed to the treaty—many of them functioning quite differently from the way they were intended. Pentagon planner Richard Perle, for example, may well have endorsed the Social Democrats' *Null-Loesung* ("zero solution") in the early 1980s as a joker that the Kremlin would surely reject, one that would help to justify deployment of Euromissiles. If so, Perle's game plan worked smoothly for a few years—until Gorbachev came to power and accepted not only the zero option but most other associated demands that Western negotiators threw his way. Reagan, who may have initially viewed the game as Perle did, would later claim authorship of the zero option and proudly sign the INF Treaty. Not only had Soviet views changed, but so had the former president's. When Soviet concessions left him with a deal difficult to refuse, he found himself castigating fellow Republicans opposed to the treaty as believers in the inevitability of war—

[277]

taking a line from Khrushchev's rebuffs to Communist dogmatists a generation before.[69]

The Joint Chiefs of Staff were also confounded by Soviet flexibility. Reluctant to open the Lockheed "skunk works" and other U.S. defense plants for visits by Soviet inspectors,[70] the JCS signed off on a proposal for intensive on-site inspection only on the assurance that the Kremlin would never accept such measures. When Moscow said "*da*" rather than "*nyet*," Washington had to backtrack and find a reason to propose a less free-wheeling system of inspection than it originally demanded. If the Americans wanted less, that was also OK by Moscow. But when the Pentagon in December 1987 voted against publishing an INF memorandum listing America's Euromissile sites (lest the list facilitate terrorist attacks), Soviet negotiators said they would publish the lists of both countries' installations.[71] Who would have predicted that the USSR and the United States would switch sides on verification and openness? Back in 1972 the USSR withheld publication even of the SALT I Protocol enumerating the weapons on each side to be constrained.

Personality variables leave us with enormous imponderables. What if Gorbachev had been general secretary in the 1970s? Might he have accepted Jimmy Carter's "deep cuts" disarmament proposal in 1977? restrained SS-20 deployment and accepted a zero option before both sides spent billions on missiles later destroyed? Many of the problems facing Gorbachev in the mid-1980s were already acute in the previous decade. Did their severity have to pierce some threshold to jolt the Kremlin into "new thinking"? Might not an enlightened leader have perceived and acted on them much earlier?

Alternatively, what if Leonid Brezhnev or Yuri Andropov had still held power and been fully alert in the mid-1980s? Might they have responded to the same basket of mounting domestic and foreign challenges similar to Gorbachev? Brezhnev had backed the CPSU Peace Program and approved some defense and foreign policy innovations throughout the 1970s. Andropov, for his part, wanted to innovate but suffered debilitating illness from the onset of his brief reign. It was Andropov who moved up Gorbachev and poised him at the brink of power, perhaps sensing the need for innovation.

Determinism or voluntarism? No doubt a combination of each, but it is difficult to weigh the impact of each. Still, it seems evident that the problems of the USSR became cumulatively more serious in the 1980s *and* that Gorbachev and his immediate advisers were more likely to respond to these challenges creatively than the leaders whom they displaced. In part this was because they belonged to a generation too young to have worked for Stalin and been threatened by him. Instead, most of Gorbachev's team had just reached formative years when Khrushchev announced and denounced the excesses of the personality cult.

What about brain power? Gorbachev and many of his advisers have received better educations than earlier top leaders and their cronies. Many of his foreign policy advisers had extensive experience in the United States. Conversely, Andropov is widely regarded as having been more intelligent than Gorbachev. And some exponents of new thinking had also been exponents of old thinking.[72] Chameleon Vadim V. Zagladin, for example, as secretary of the Supreme Soviet's Foreign Affairs Commission appeared to discuss with foreign parliamentarians environmental problems of the polar North.[73]

Considering everything, Lenin's maxim, "The worse, the better," applied to the Socialist Fatherland: crises had to mount before new personalities emerged to change the system.

Did Gorbachev conciliate Washington because the balance of power by the mid-1980s was tilting against the USSR?[74] It is difficult to disentangle fact from perception, propaganda from operational code. The USSR steadily gained on the United States in several measures of power throughout the 1970s. But perceptions of this trend were amplified by Kissinger's Spenglerian warnings about the decline of the West and Republican charges that Carter had neglected defense. Soviet spokesmen asserted that the correlation of forces had shifted and that the West should accept the consequences. After the Pentagon budget went up in the early 1980s, however, Reagan claimed that American was standing tall and could negotiate from strength. After 1985 Gorbachev told audiences at home and abroad that the Soviet economy was in trouble. He conceded that the USSR needed to take radical measures to overcome its technological backwardness. For several years Moscow worried that Star Wars might radically alter the rules of the game. Just as public perceptions in the 1970s exaggerated America's military weaknesses, so the *Zeitgeist* amplified U.S. gains under Reagan, even though the USSR had drawn close to the United States in strategic warheads and accuracy. The difficulties experienced by U.S. forces in Lebanon, Grenada, and the Persian Gulf showed that increased military spending did not automatically convert into effectiveness or wise strategy.[75] Still, the *direction* of change in the military balance and the broad correlation of forces probably shifted in America's favor in the mid-1980s. Thus the Kremlin possessed 10,716 strategic warheads to 12,846 American in 1986; but the United States expanded its lead in 1987 to 13,873 versus 11,044; and in 1988 to 14,637 against 11,694.[76]

A majority of the foregoing propositions are rooted in Realpolitik or

Communist suspicion and "kto kovo?": because governments are engaged in a struggle for power, they will negotiate or curb their arms only for tactical reasons, hoping for one-sided advantage. They will put on a show of limiting capital ships or bacteriological weapons while devoting more resources to weapons judged more useful in the future. They will be little concerned about the opportunity and other costs of military competition, for these are a necessary input to the business of power politics and trivial on the scale of superpower activity.

This viewpoint has underestimated the ways in which some Soviet and American leaders have perceived the dangers and costs of the military confrontation. Seeing them not as trivial but as life-threatening, these leaders have gone beyond business as usual to pursue not merely arms control but substantial arms reductions, accepting the sacrifices and risks entailed.

Idealistic propositions on the utility of unilateral restraint and the dysfunctions of bargining from strength, however, also need qualification. The Kremlin often gave way to American pressure. The pressures generated by Reagan's arms buildup, the Euromissile deployment, and various programs to destabilize Communist regimes worldwide helped to trigger Moscow's "new thinking." From duress, enlightenment. The seeds of Gorbachev's new thinking germinated in Soviet soil for nearly thirty years, but they sprouted and received official sanction only when the domestic and external problems facing the Kremlin crossed new thresholds of discomfort.

Beyond these contextual variables there has been the contribution of hard work, patience, and growing experience on the part of Soviet and U.S. officials concerned with arms and arms control. Both sides have learned a great deal in recent decades.[77] Knowing how to proceed, they proceeded surely and quickly when given the green light.

East-West relations have also been graced with luck—luck that the hostile exchanges of the early 1980s did not spill over into some uncontrolled confrontation; luck that NATO did not collapse but grew stronger as it implemented its two-track decision; luck that the P2 did not trigger some launch-on-warning accident in the USSR; luck that Gorbachev with his risks for peace was not quickly replaced by a more hard-line regime; luck that Eastern Europe bubbled but did not boil over; luck that Gorbachev persisted in dealing with the Reagan administration despite its penchant for anti-Soviet jokes and speeches, its embarrassment with the Iran scam, and its growing senility and lame-duck status; luck that Mr. and Mrs. Reagan could recognize a gift horse when they saw one and distinguish it from a Trojan horse. A purist may say all this was not luck but skill. If so, we were lucky to have such skill on both sides.

Notes

1. This assumption underlay much if not most of the American arms control literature of the 1960s and 1970s. It posited that "arms control offers an approach to peace that is at once less hopeful but more attainable than disarmament." See "The Arms Control Road to Peace: Pros and Cons," chapter 4 in Walter C. Clemens, Jr., *The Superpowers and Arms Control* (Lexington, MA: Lexington Books, 1973), 89–104 at 89. Like most of the propositions cited here, this one was often accompanied by various caveats and qualifications, many of which are omitted in order to emphasize the thrust of their logic.

Whereas many Western analysts have doubted whether disarmament is possible or even desirable, many Soviet writers have argued that it is desirable but not attainable because of the class interests of capitalism. They condemned proposals for "mere" arms limitation as symptoms of capitalism's inability and unwillingness to take part in comprehensive measures of disarmament. See, for example, E. A. Korovin and V. V. Egor'ev, *Razoruzhenie* (Moscow: Gosizdat, 1930), 151–54. Non-Marxists have expressed skepticism about disarmament on other grounds; for example, see Merze Tate, *The Disarmament Illusion* (New York: Macmillan, 1942) and Inis Claude, *Power and International Relations* (New York: Random House, 1962).

2. Claude recalls that "man cannot unlearn what he knows about the means of creating power." Therefore the capacity to devise instruments of destruction would remain even if all weapons were destroyed. See Claude, *Power and International Relations*, pp. 7–8. Some Western liberals concur with Communist doctrine, however, that human nature is not inherently aggressive. See Walter Hollitscher, ed., *Aggressionstrieb und Krieg* (Stuttgart: Deutsche Verlags-Anhalt, 1973).

3. This view derives from Lenin. See Walter C. Clemens, Jr., "Lenin on Disarmament," *Slavic Review* 23, no. 3 (September 1964): 504–25. Soviet views on the role of the military-industrial complex and the impact of arms spending on Western economies have zigzagged. In 1959 Khrushchev reversed the thrust of most previous Soviet commentary, arguing that arms spending was detrimental to *all* economies. This view was elaborated in I. S. Glagolev, ed., *Ekonomicheskie voprosy razoruzheniia* (Moscow: Akademiia Nauk SSSR, 1961). M. S. Gorbachev has cited Wassily Leontief to make the same point.

4. See Philip Noel-Baker, *The Arms Race* (New York: Oceana, 1958), 557–59, where he also quotes Thomas K. Finletter and Leo Szilard to the same effect. Noel-Baker won the Nobel Peace Prize one year after this book's publication.

5. John W. Spanier and Joseph L. Nogee, *The Politics of Disarmament: A Study in Soviet-American Gamesmanship* (New York: Praeger, 1962), 53–54.

6. Colin S. Gray, "The Purpose and Value of Arms Control Negotiations," in U.S. Senate Committee on Foreign Relations, *Perceptions: Relations between the United States and the Soviet Union* (Washington, DC: U.S. Government Printing Office, 1978), 365.

7. See, for example, Hans J. Morgenthau revised by Kenneth W. Thompson, *Politics among Nations*, 6th ed. (New York(A. A. Knopf, 1985), esp. 439–50.

8. Joseph J. Kruzel, "The Preconditions and Consequences of Arms Control Agreements" (Ph.D. thesis, Harvard University, 1975), 364–65, 389. The thesis is updated in Kruzel, "From Rush-Bagot to START: The Lessons of Arms Control," *Orbis* 30, no. 1 (Spring 1986): 193–216.

9. Albert Carnesale and Richard N. Haass, "Conclusions," in their edited work, *Superpower Arms Control: Setting the Record Straight* (Cambridge, MA: Ballinger, 1987), 330–33. The authors caution, however, that "this does not mean that success [in arms control] comes only when the forces subject to negotiation are identical. Overall parity does not require precise equality in every measure of military strength."

10. Kruzel, "Preconditions and Consequences," pp. 352–56.

11. Robert J. Einhorn, *Negotiating from Strength* (New York: Praeger, 1985), 54.

12. Robert Legvold, "Strategic 'Doctrine' and SALT: Soviet and American Views," *Survival* 21, no. 1 (January/February 1979): 11.

[281]

13. Kruzel, "Preconditions and Consequences," pp. 349–51. "The introduction into the structure of the strategic forces of one or both sides of still one more, qualitatively new component greatly complicates the entire system of the strategic balance, and creates additional complications in calculating the correlation of forces." E. Velikhov and A. Kokoshin, "Iadernoe oruzhie i dilemma mezhdunarodnoi bezopasnosti," *Mirovaia ekonomika i mezhdunarodnye otnosheniia*, no. 4 (1985): 33–43 at 40.

14. Successful negotiations leading to agreements have "tended to be characterized by instances of restraint or initiative to encourage progress and by mutual willingness to reciprocate concessions made by the opponent, including the search for packages that exchanged diverse compromises," according to William B. Vogele, "Strategy and Policymaking in Arms Control Negotiations," presented at the Annual Meeting of the Northeast Political Science Association, Boston, November 1986, p. 13. See also his "Negotiating Arms Control Agreements: The Conditions for Success in US-Soviet Arms Control Negotiations, 1954–1980," presented at the Annual Meeting of the American Political Science Association, Washington, D.C., August 1986. For the classic statement on the need for a strategy of graduated reciprocity in initiatives for tension reduction, see Charles E. Osgood, *An Alternative to War or Surrender* (Urbana: University of Illinois Press, 1962).

15. Even if a weapon is developed to be a bargaining chip, it may gain too much momentum to be bargained away. See, for example, Robert J. Bresler and Robert C. Gray, "The Bargaining Chip and SALT," *Political Science Quarterly* 92, no. 1 (Spring 1977): 65–88. While stressing the utility of bargaining chips, Einhorn warns that sometimes they have not been cashed in—to the detriment of arms control. See his *Negotiating from Strength*, chap. 6.

16. This is one of the maxims many analysts have derived from study of the 1962 Cuban missile crisis. It has been applied in other contexts—for instance, that of the 1980s when the Reagan administration pressured the USSR on many fronts at home and abroad.

17. Kruzel, "Preconditions and Consequences," pp. 368–69, 395–97; for evidence that past arms controls have often led to intensified defense efforts rather than "lulling," see Sean M. Lynn-Jones, "Lulling and Stimulating Effects of Arms Control" in Carnesale and Haass, *Superpower Arms Control*, pp. 223–73.

18. Kruzel, "Preconditions and Consequences," pp. 369–72, 397–99.

19. Spanier and Nogee, *Politics of Disarmament*, p. 54, held that "the Soviet Union considers all controls as espionage." For an argument that an essential condition for agreement is the existence of arms control measures that can be verified without "intensive physical intrusion by foreign inspectors," see Clemens, *The Superpowers and Arms Control*, p. 63. Kruzel puts the argument in a more generalized form, without emphasizing the security consciousness of the USSR: "The less a proposed limitation is dependent upon high-confidence verification procedures, the more likely it is to be negotiated," Kruzel, "Preconditions and Consequences," pp. 356–61. For Luttwak's paradox, see his *Strategy: The Logic of War and Peace* (Cambridge, MA: Harvard University Press, 1987), p. 187.

20. Carnesale and Haass, *Superpower Arms Control*, p. 348.

21. For the United States to reach an arms control agreement *"requires our success in at least three negotiations*: . . . within the U.S. government . . . among the NATO allies, and between the United States and the Soviet Union—though not necessarily in that order." Graham Allison and Albert Carnesale, "Can the West Accept *Da* for an Answer?" *Daedalus* 116, no. 3 (Summer 1987): 69–93 at 79. In a similar vein Kruzel argues that "the smaller the number of nations involved in an arms control negotiation, the more likely it is that an agreement will be concluded." "Preconditions and Consequences," p. 361. Few analysts would contend that a middle power such as West Germany or China could veto an action that Washington or Moscow wished to undertake; it is more plausible that the opposition of an influential ally could lead either superpower to actions that would make an arms accord unlikely. Thus Konrad Adeneauer worked with John Foster Dulles to make arms control less likely in the mid-1950s; and Mao's China kept up a drumbeat of opposition to East-West accords that influenced (but did not determine) Khrushchev's arms control policies. For an investigation of this point, see Helmut Sonnenfeldt, "The Chinese Factor in Soviet

Disarmament Policy," in Morton H. Halperin, ed., *Sino-Soviet Relations and Arms Control* (Cambridge: MIT Press, 1967), 106–8.

22. The importance of Soviet perceptions of Western elites has been stressed in many works by Franklyn Griffiths: e.g., "Genoa Plus 51: Changing Soviet Objectives in Europe," *Wellesley Paper* 4 (Toronto: Canadian Institute of International Affairs, June 1973); also his "The Sources of American Conduct: Soviet Perspectives and Their Policy Implications," *International Security* 9, no. 2 (Fall 1984): 3–50. Despite the importance that Griffiths and the present author attribute to Genoa as a symbol for a certain orientation in Soviet policy, the term means almost nothing to several Soviet specialists at IMEMO and the USA-Canadian Institute interviewed in March 1989. Still, the intermittent use of the term in the Soviet press implies that the top authorities wish it to signal a special message—even if not many Soviet citizens absorb it!

23. "High priority and presidential sponsorship was important for willingness of the US to reciprocate Soviet concessions" in a series of successful arms control negotiations, according to Vogele, "Strategy and Policymaking," p. 13.

24. Einhorn, *Negotiating from Strength*, pp. 57–58.

25. Ibid., pp. 105–12.

26. This analysis is based on the text, "Treaty between the United States of America and the Union of Soviet Socialist Republics on the Elimination of Their Intermediate-Range and Shorter-Range Missiles" (Washington, D.C., December 1987), and the accompanying "Memorandum of Understanding Regarding the Establishment of the Data Base" for the treaty.

27. For agreements before 1987, see Coit D. Blacker and Gloria Duffy, eds., *International Arms Control: Issues and Agreements*, 2d ed. (Stanford: Stanford University Press, 1984).

28. By 1921–22 Lenin came to support disarmament negotiations, albeit with little hope that they would produce agreements. See Clemens, "Lenin on Disarmament."

29. The New York Stock Exchange responded more directly to the Indochina War, averages declining in response to escalation and recovering losses only with deescalation. See Walter S. Jones, *The Logic of International Relations*, 5th ed. (Boston: Little, Brown, 1985), 429.

30. Strobe Talbott, *Deadly Gambits* (New York: A. A. Knopf, 1984), 128.

31. "Zaiavlenie General'nogo Sekretaria TsK KPSS M. S. Gorbachev," *Pravda*, January 16, 1986, pp. 1, 2.

32. For a summary of this history, see Elizabeth Pond, "Summit Scorecard," *The Christian Science Monitor*, December 7, 1987, pp. 18–19.

33. Richard Perle endorsed the *Null-Loesung* idea conceived by German Social Democrats as a way to "put the Soviets on the defensive" and keep them there. See Talbott, *Deadly Gambits*, p. 60.

34. Contrary to some accounts, the Soviets observed a long moratorium on the deployment of SS-20s until NATO's Euromissile deployment began. See Raymond L. Garthoff, *Détente or Confrontation* (Washington, DC: Brookings Institution, 1985), 884–85.

35. These distinctions are recognized by Spanier and Nogee, *Politics of Disarmament*, p. 4; because they then perceived the superpower confrontation as virtually zero-sum, however, the distinction had little practical meaning for them.

36. See Talbott, *Deadly Gambits*, chap. 6.

37. Carnesale and Haass, *Superpower Arms Control*, p. 332.

38. For a balanced treatment, see Joseph S. Nye, Jr. and James A. Schear, eds., *Seeking Stability in Space* (Lanham, MD: Aspen Institute for Humanistic Studies and University Press of America, 1987); for a Soviet acknowledgment of profound asymmetries in the Soviet and U.S. force structures, see Velikhov and Kokoshin, "Iadernoe oruzhie," p. 41; see also Richard Halloran, "Air Force Proposes Abandoning Anti-Satellite Weapon to Reduce Budget," *The New York Times*, December 18, 1987, p. A35.

39. Although Moscow had to destroy more warheads, its missiles were older and less accurate than America's; the U.S. missiles could hit the USSR whereas the SS-20 could reach

only Europe or Alaska; the Pershing 2 could strike the USSR in 6–7 minutes, giving Soviet leaders even less time to scurry to shelter than it might take an SLBM to land (eight minutes). (Such distinctions, Arkady Shevchenko told his debriefers, were important to top Soviet leaders.) The Kremlin also stood to gain because Soviet ICBMs, airplanes, and subs could still hold Europe "hostage," because the INF Treaty would partially "decouple" Western European and U.S. security stakes and enhance the role of Soviet conventional force advantages, and because it would prevent NATO's using the banned missiles with conventional warheads.

The U.S. alliance system also gained in many ways. NATO's Euromissiles were basically unusable unless Washington surrendered decision responsibility to field commanders. Eliminating Pershing 2s and GLCMs removed weapons that militated for dangerous launch-on-warning procedures in the East and invited preemptive attack. Not only did the Kremlin eliminate more warheads than the West, but the treaty removed more Soviet targets (the SS-20 and other missiles destroyed) than NATO missiles; removing SS-20s from Asia, it gave a free ride to Japan and other U.S. friends; it slightly loosened military integration within the Warsaw Pact by removing shorter-range weapons from East Germany and Czechoslovakia; its inspection procedures might disrupt the relatively closed societies of the East more than those of the West; NATO's dual-track orientation was vindicated; Britain and France were free to continue present plans to expand their arsenals from present numbers of roughly 200 to about 1,200 strategic warheads by 1995; other U.S. forces able to strike Soviet targets from submarines, surface ships, and ground-based aircraft were unfettered; and dual-purpose Soviet rockets in Eastern Europe were also removed.

40. This distinction was suggested by George Rathjens at a faculty seminar of the "Avoiding Nuclear War Project," Harvard University, December 9, 1987.

41. See Clemens, *Superpowers and Arms Control*, pp. 60–61; also see Richard N. Haass, "The Bottom Line on the INF Accord," *Chrisian Science Monitor*, December 7, 1987, p. 16.

42. See this and other propositions advanced in Allison and Carnesale, "Can the West Accept *Da?*" pp. 77–78.

43. See Matthew Evangelista, *Innovation and the Arms Race: How the United States and the Soviet Union Develop New Military Technologies* (Ithaca, NY: Cornell University Press, 1988). This situation has prevailed despite the fact that according to the Pentagon, Soviet military R&D outlays over the past decade exceeded American by two to one. See Casper W. Weinberger, *Annual Report to the Congress Fiscal Year 1987* (Washington, DC: U.S. Government Printing Office, 1986), pp. 255–56. Another report found that the United States held strong leads in most critical technologies in 1980–85 but that Soviet R&D competence was superior in many fields including vacuum tube electronics, ceramics, and innovative ABM interceptors. See John M. Collins, *U.S.-Soviet Military Balance 1980–1985* (Washington, DC: Pergamon-Brassey's, 1985), 37–42.

44. Carnesale and Haass, *Superpower Arms Control*, p. 336.

45. "If all that we are doing is indeed viewed as mere propaganda," Gorbachev asked, "why not respond to it according to the principle of 'an eye for an eye and a tooth for a tooth'? We have stopped nuclear explosions. Then you Americans could take revenge by doing likewise. You could deal us yet another propaganda blow, say, by suspending the development of one of your new strategic missiles. And we would respond with the same kind of 'propaganda.' " *Time*, September 9, 1985.

46. See, for example, Lynn-Jones, "Lulling and Stimulating Effects of Arms Control," pp. 223–73, esp. 235; also pp. 255–56. For an explanation why states respond with diffidence to an adversary's moves toward cooperation, see George W. Downs and David M. Rocke, "Tacit Bargaining and Arms Control," *World Politics* 39, no. 3 (April 1987): 297–325 at 322–24.

47. See, for example, Richard F. Kaufman, "Causes of the Slowdown in Soviet Defense," *Soviet Economy* 1, no. 1 (January-March 1985): 9–41.

48. *Time*, September 9, 1985.

49. For an evaluation, see William Safire, "The Fawning After," *The New York Times*, December 13, 1987, p. E25.

50. See William G. Hyland, "Foreword," in Einhorn, *Negotiating from Strength*, p. viii.

51. See Kenneth A. Oye, Robert J. Lieber, and Donald Rothchild, eds., *Eagle Defiant* (Boston: Little, Brown, 1983).

52. The more optimistic estimates derive from Soviet sources and the more pessimistic from American. CIA and the Defense Intelligence Agency believed that Kremlin outlays increased in 1987 for sophisticated submarines, ships, the I1-76 aircraft, and the strategic SA-10 missile system. See presentations and answers in *Allocation of Resources in the Soviet Union and China—1987*, Hearings before the Subcommittee on National Security Economics of the Joint Economic Committee, U.S. Congress, pt. 13 (Washington, DC: U.S. Government Printing Office, 1988), 23, 34, 73, 80, 102, 104.

53. See Bill Keller, "Adviser's Soviet-Deficit Figure Is Triple Kremlin's," *The New York Times*, January 26, 1989, p. A4. Abalkin and other economists argue how to proceed with perestroika in *Kommunist*, no. 6 (April 1989): 10–23. On Soviet inflation, see V. Bogachev, "Eshcho ne pozno: *Denezhno-finansovoe ozdorovlenie v sisteme antikrizisnykh mer*," *Kommunist*, no. 3 (February 1989): 31–41. On the emergency fund, see Bill Keller, "Moscow Importing Consumer Goods to Appease Public," *The New York Times*, April 17, 1989, pp. 1, 8. Eastern Europeans in 1989 also stepped up import of Western consumer goods. See *Financial Times*, March 1, 1989, p. 8. For "Space Rockets vs. Butter Is Talk of the Soviet," see John Noble Wilford in *The New York Times*, April 17, 1989, p. A13.

54. For background, see Jiri Valenta and William Potter, eds., *Soviet Decisionmaking for National Security* (Boston: Unwin Hyman, 1984); also Condoleezza Rice, "The Party, the Military, and Decision Authority in the Soviet Union," *World Politics* 40, no. 1 (October 1987): 55–81.

55. For a report on Yazov's comments about the ways that glasnost' harms martial spirit, see Bill Keller in *The New York Times*, January 21, 1988, p. A3.

56. A letter from John Foster Dulles to the Kremlin "inadvertently" omitted Eisenhower's wish to accept the Soviet proposal for ground teams if Moscow would accept his plan for aerial inspection. See Dwight D. Eisenhower, *Mandate for Change* (Garden City, NY: Doubleday, 1963), 527.

57. See Glenn Seaborg, *Kennedy, Khrushchev, and the Test Ban* (Berkeley: University of California Press, 1981).

58. See, for example, Walter C. Clemens, Jr., "*Glasnost* on the Arms Front," *Christian Science Monitor*, September 24, 1987, p. 13; also David Aaron, "Verification: Will It Work?" *The New York Times Magazine*, October 11, 1987, pp. 37 ff.; and Michael R. Gordon with Paul Lewis in *The New York Times*, November 16, 1987, p. A6.

59. See Don Carlson and Craig Comstock, eds., *Citizen Summitry* (Los Angeles: Jeremy P. Tarcher, 1986).

60. "The President's Unclassified Report on Soviet Noncompliance with Arms Control Agreements" (Washington, DC: U.S. Government Printing Office, December 2, 1987).

61. For background, see F. Stephen Larrabee, "Westeuropaeische Interessen im amerikanish-sowjetischen Dialog ueber Kernwaffen und Waffen zur strategischen Verteidigung," *Europa-Archiv*, Folge 6 (1985): 165–74.

62. For a series of arguments why the INF benefits the Atlantic Alliance, see Allison and Carnesale, "Can the West Accept *Da?*" esp. pp. 86–87. In early 1988, however, NATO found itself in some disarray as Kohl resisted U.S., British, and French pressures to modernize short-range Lance missiles in Germany. NATO leaders signed bland communiqués promising to upgrade the alliance's nuclear and conventional forces when necessary.

63. See Kenneth Hunt et al., "New Soviet Missiles for Eastern Europe," in Vojtech Mastny, ed., *Soviet/East European Survey, 1983–1984: Selected Research and Analysis from Radio Free Europe/Radio Liberty* (Durham, NC: Duke University Press, 1985), 93–97; also Ronald Eggleston et al., "The Stockholm Conference," in ibid., pp. 97–109 at 100.

64. See Clemens, *Superpowers*, pp. 85–86.

65. The complexities of the American scene were suggested in a front-page story in

Literaturnaia gazeta on the eve of the 1987 summit. American peace marchers, it said, presented roses to the Soviet embassy, where they were gratefully accepted; roses presented at the White House, however, were thrown in the trash by guards—an act for which a White House spokesman later apologized. Zionists, conservatives, and other intriguers were trying to organize opposition to improved Soviet-U.S. relations, but public opinion polls showed that Americans thought quite favorably of Secretary Gorbachev as well as Mr. Reagan and trusted their determination and ability to progress on arms control and other matters. The former president himself lashed out at conservative critics as believers in the inevitability of war, while one of them called the president an "idiot" agent of Soviet propaganda. Meanwhile, in a Washington cathedral, bells rang incessantly and many clergymen from both countries prayed for peace and to appeal to Gorbachev and Reagan to end the arms race. Front-page photos showed a rather thin line of Americans forming a human chain from the White House to the Soviet embassy and a joyous, more robust line of Muscovites from the Supreme Soviet to the USA embassy. See Iona Andronov, "Istoricheskaia vstrecha," *Literaturnaia gazeta*, December 9, 1987, p. 1. Elsewhere in this issue (p. 9), *LG* reported that NBC had run Gorbachev's hour-long interview without its usual commercial interruptions to avoid distracting the viewers' attention, that *Perestroika* is a best seller in Paris, and that the Soviet Writers' Union sent consolations to the brother of James Baldwin on the writer's death. On pp. 12–13 there were discussions of violations of socialist justice by responsible Soviet organs and the preface to a new and quite critical book on Stalin.

66. Einhorn, *Negotiating from Strength*, p. 57.

67. See Howard Raiffa, "Post-Settlement Settlements," *Negotiation Journal* 1, no. 1 (January 1985): 9–17.

68. The following discussion owes much to a faculty seminar, "Avoiding Nuclear War Project," Harvard Center for Science and International Affairs, December 9, 1987—especially comments by Avner Cohen, Graham Allison, Albert Carnesale, Joseph S. Nye, Jr., George Rathjens, and Richard Garwin.

69. For divergent evaluations, see Andronov in *Literaturnaia gazeta*, and Safire, "The Fawning After," note 49.

70. See William Safire, "Horror at the Skunk Works," *The New York Times*, September 2, 1987.

71. The United States decided to publish the memorandum immediately after the Washington summit. See "Memorandum of Understanding," data base for the INF Treaty, cited in note 26.

72. Burlatskii was a speech writer for Khrushchev but claims to have been out of favor during 1964–85. Father and son Georgii and Aleksei Arbatov, however, were not nearly so prominent under Brezhnev as under Gorbachev. Virtuoso diplomats such as Vorontsov carried out their missions no matter the regime. Some of Gorbachev's brain trust, however, had been exiled under Brezhnev—Aleksander Iakovlev to Canada, some liberal economists to Novosibirsk.

73. See interview with Zagladin: "Nel'zia razrivat' ekonomiku v ushcherb' ekologii," *Izvestiia*, March 10, 1989, p. 5.

74. The view from the International Institute for Strategic Studies, however, was not so euphoric. *Strategic Survey 1986–1987* (London: IISS, 1987) emphasized the disarray in American leadership and the retrenchment in U.S. defense spending (pp. 5–24); budgetary limitations on U.S. power were also underscored in *Military Balance 1987–1988* (London: IISS, 1988), 12–14.

75. See Walter C. Clemens, Jr., "Goliath and the Exocet: Have Americans Gone Soft?" *Christian Science Monitor*, August 18, 1987, p. 11.

76. Totals given in *Military Balance, 1986–1987* (London: IISS, 1986), 222; ibid. for 1987–88, p. 225 and for 1988–89, p. 230.

77. See Joseph S. Nye, Jr., "Nuclear Learning and U.S.-Soviet Security Regimes," *International Organization* 41, no. 3 (Summer 1987): 371–402; also George W. Breslauer, "Ideology and Learning in Soviet Third World Policy," *World Politics* 39, no. 3 (April 1987): 429–48.

10

Can the Kremlin be Trusted?
Can Washington?

Doveryai no proveryai—"Trust but verify." The Russian proverb became one of former President Reagan's favorite sayings as he signed the INF Treaty. This folk wisdom sums up a central dilemma of all efforts at arms control. Trust alone can be abused; verification cannot be foolproof. Both are needed if adversaries are to mute their conflict to mutual advantage.

The USSR, like the United States, has shown that it can be trusted to seek and enter arms controls that would enhance its strategic and other interests. Can Moscow also be trusted to *comply* with agreements it has entered? To what extent has the USSR violated either the spirit or the letter of its commitments? And what of America's record? Is either side in a position to throw the first stone? Apart from lapses by either side, what has been the positive side of their compliance? And what problems may cloud the future? These are the concerns of this chapter.

Arms accords can be thought of as a point on a spectrum between unilateralism and cooperation—a point where adversaries perceive their interests to intersect or overlap at that time. But perceptions and interests may shift, leading one or both sides to place more value on self-help and less on coordination.[1]

The Nixon and Carter administrations seemed to value the arms control accords reached between Washington and Moscow; when questions arose about Kremlin compliance with these accords, U.S. and Soviet negotiators were able to resolve most of them. The Reagan White House,

[287]

however, until 1986 seemed more interested in denouncing Soviet noncompliance than in reaffirming, upholding, or creating arms controls.

The main charges against Moscow were summarized in Reagan's "Report on Soviet Noncompliance with Arms Control Agreements" sent to Congress on January 23, 1984. It asserted that "the Soviet Union is violating the Geneva Protocol on Chemical Weapons, the Biological Weapons Convention, the Helsinki Final Act, and two provisions of SALT II: telemetry encryption and a rule concerning ICBM modernization." In addition, "the Soviet Union has almost certainly violated the ABM Treaty, probably violated the SALT II limit on new types, probably violated the SS-16 deployment prohibition of SALT II, and is likely to have violated the nuclear testing yield limit of the Threshold Test Ban Treaty."

These and other charges of noncompliance with arms control commitments are reviewed here. The record, we find, is mixed. Soviet behavior has repeatedly pressed against the permissive limits of many arms accords and has probably exceeded them in several cases. But on balance Moscow's compliance with arms control obligations—especially the arms cuts carried out to stay within the limits of SALT I and II—has been more significant, both militarily and politically, than Soviet evasions.

Most U.S. charges of Soviet noncompliance have not been substantiated. Some derived from ambiguities in the treaty language or difficulties in verification procedures. Many charges seemed inspired by a determination to justify U.S. military programs confined or prohibited by arms accords of the 1970s.

Compliance or Evasion? The Spirit and Letter of Arms Control Commitments

Propaganda versus practice. Our survey begins with cases in which Moscow has preached one thing and done another. At the 1922 Genoa Economic Conference, for example, Foreign Commissar G. V. Chicherin called for a "general limitation of armaments" and "the absolute prohibition of [the] most barbarous forms" of warfare "such as poison gas, aerial warfare, etc., and in particular the use of means of destruction against peaceful populations." Chicherin's appeal came at the very time the Soviet republic was opening its territory to Germany so that it could evade the arms limitations of the Versailles Treaty. Germany developed and tested not only planes and tanks but also chemical weapons on Soviet territory all through the 1920s and into the early 1930s. The Soviet republic, of course, had been excluded from the Versailles deliberations, and Chicherin's proposals were turned down as irrelevant at Genoa, but there was a sharp contrast between Chicherin's castigation of the "most barbarous forms" of warfare and Soviet clandestine practices with Germany.[2]

In the late 1940s there was another break between word and deed as Stalin spurred development of an atomic bomb even as his diplomats and World Council of Peace called for banning the bomb. Moscow's disarmament campaign served as a political tool rather than a medium to reach East-West agreements.

In 1961 the USSR broke the moratorium on nuclear testing by unleashing a series of tests that included the largest thermonuclear explosion of all time. The Soviet government had complained about the initiation in 1960 of French nuclear tests; Moscow also took note when former President Eisenhower twice warned that the United States did not consider itself obliged to continue the moratorium. The deepest motive to resume testing, however, was probably to display Soviet power in the face of Kennedy's missile buildup and the acute Berlin confrontation. Moscow's ICBM force was still minuscule and primitive, but at least the USSR could explode the largest bombs ever tested.

Neither in 1961 nor in 1948 or 1922 did Moscow's actions violate a Soviet treaty commitment. The Kremlin simply preached one thing and did another. Other governments, of course, have also had such lapses—as when the Reagan administration quietly sold arms to Iran in 1985–86 while enjoining others to boycott Teheran and not to bargain with kidnappers. Or, more to the point here, it seemed incongruous to many Soviets that Washington would dispatch a U-2 spy plane over their territory on the eve of the 1960 Paris summit.

The broad reality is that East, West, and South have been known to practice gamesmanship, injecting "jokers" into their proposals known to be anathema to their negotiating partners.[3] Both Moscow and Washington have helped to make public diplomacy an art form. The Kremlin has had its "ban the bomb" signature campaigns; the United States has had its appeals for "open skies" (to legitimate U-2 flights) and "zero options" (a public relations gambit that turned out to be a powerful negotiating ploy). Gamesmanship has also been practiced by China and various Third World governments, many of which call for superpower arms control even as they accelerate their own arms buildups.

The Turkish Straits. There is one case in which the USSR has already broken a treaty obligation from the interwar years or plans to do so—with the acquiescence of Western governments. The 1936 Montreux Convention prohibits aircraft carriers from transiting the Turkish Straits.[4] But Soviet helicopter carriers have been passing through the Dardanelles since 1968 and V/STOL carriers since 1976 without protest by Ankara or other NATO signatories of the convention. Even Kiev-class vessels that carry thirty Yak-36 jet aircraft, Turkish officials say, may be regarded as "antisubmarine cruisers"—not as true aircraft carriers. To support this claim they sometimes refer to classifications in *Jane's Fighting Ships*. Turkey and its Western allies seem reluctant to rock the boat by raising questions that could undermine the stability of a 1936 regime that suits the evolving interests of many parties.[5] The West may fear a showdown with the USSR in a region where the Soviet shadow looms large. Ankara also winks at other Soviet violations of Montreux—misrepresentations of what kinds of Soviet ships are passing, passage of submarines in darkness, inaccurate advance notice of intentions to transit—perhaps in return for Soviet favors or perhaps to avoid unpleasant confrontations. The accumulated record of this permissiveness will make it difficult to close the Straits when the USSR completes trials of the large aircraft carrier being tested in the Black Sea in recent years. Indeed, a Soviet naval officer wrote in 1976 about the "bankruptcy of the claims that certain new Soviet ships do not fall into the category of ships that . . . have the right to transit through the Straits." He asserted that "transit through the Straits of *any* ships of states on the Black Sea does not contradict the letter and spirit of the Convention."[6]

Nuclear Cuba. The Kremlin's mendacity and evasiveness entrapped it in one problem after another. Before the October 1962 crisis, Soviet representatives denied that the USSR was placing "offensive" weapons in Cuba—a denial that later fanned American anger when spy planes discovered the reality. Even after Moscow decided to withdraw its weapons, Soviet diplomats refused to accept the U.S. terminology and referred instead to the weapons "you say are offensive." Taking advantage of this lapse, the Americans then included not only missiles and bombers but torpedo boats. Because the boats had already been transferred to Cuban control, Anastas Mikoyan had great difficulty persuading Castro to release them. Infuriated by the whole affair, Castro refused international inspection on Cuban territory and forced the Americans and Soviets to find another way to verify removal of the offending weapons—displaying them on the deck of Soviet ships.

The Kremlin later tested how far it could stretch the vague 1962 understanding before meeting a stiff response. In July 1969 and May 1970 the USSR upgraded its naval presence in Cuban waters with flotillas that included two old diesel torpedo attack submarines and then a nuclear-powered cruise missile-launching submarine. In August 1970 the Soviet charge d'affaires, Yuli Vorontsov, raised with Henry Kissinger the question of reaffirming the 1962 Kennedy-Khrushchev understanding on Cuba, which former President Nixon and his national security adviser were glad to do, but secretly, without informing even the U.S. secretary of state. This occurred at the very time that the USSR was building a naval base and a facility for tending submarines at Cienfuegos. When the construction was discovered by a U-2 plane in September, the United States protested in strong terms. Moscow obliquely replied in October, proclaiming that it was not doing and would not do anything to "contradict" the 1962 understanding. "The outcome of the various statements was that the United States got a greater degree of Soviet commitment against permanent basing of missile submarines in Cuba, while the Soviet Union finally got American commitment to the 1962 understanding and pledge not to invade Cuba"—on which Washington had hedged because there had never been any international inspection to verify the absence of offensive arms in Cuba.[7]

Nixon specified in a television address on January 4, 1971, that if "nuclear submarines were serviced either in Cuba or from Cuba, that would be a violation of the understanding." This interpretation broadened the 1962 understanding to include "nuclear submarines" (which might be nuclear powered without carrying nuclear arms) and their tenders.[8] Washington, of course, insisted that its interpretation be accepted by the other side. The Kremlin, however, probed again in February 1971, sending another tender and a nuclear-powered but not missile-launching submarine to Cuba, soon withdrawing them after further U.S. protests. Occasional visits were made in subsequent years, but never by a nuclear-powered ballistic missile-launching submarine, and a Soviet submarine base was not established.

An Egyptian-Israeli standstill. Another "understanding"—this one made in 1979—fell apart almost immediately. An American initiative led to a standstill/ceasefire agreement among Egypt, Jordan, and Israel that officially began on August 7. The outline of the accord had been communicated by Washington to those countries plus Britain, France, and the USSR on June 19. After initially rejecting the proposal, Egypt accepted the plan in July, followed by Jordan and Israel, during a time when Soviet-built SAM-2 and SAM-3 defenses continued to shoot down Israeli planes over Egypt. When the United States then sent Cairo a demand that the ceasefire begin within twenty-four hours, the Egyptian Foreign Ministry indicated that Washington could *state* that the accord would enter into effect at the deadline proposed but that in fact several days would be needed for Egypt to complete its hardware operations in the ceasefire/standstill zone. When Ambassador Jacob Beam presented details of the plan to Soviet Deputy Foreign Minister Vasily V. Kuznetsov only a short time before the ceasefire/standstill was to begin, Kuznetsov asked, "Are you asking for our concurrence?" Beam replied in the negative, saying that he was merely informing Kuznetsov of the plan.[9]

When the USSR did not prevent Egypt from erecting new SAMs in the standstill zone and Soviet personnel helped in the operation, U.S. Ambassador Charles Yost told the UN General Assembly on October 30 that the "country from which these highly advanced missiles came, as well as the government on whose territory they were placed, is responsible for these developments." Professor Hans J. Morgenthau charged the Kremlin with "agreeing to a ceasefire for the Middle East and violating the agreement from the very moment of its coming into operation."[10] The reality was that the USSR had never stated that it would adhere to the ceasefire and that Israel as well as Egypt violated the agreement from the outset. Despite the fact that there were many sides to this story, Americans tended to stick to their self-righteous version of the events.

FOBS. Another instance in which Moscow pushed the limits of an arms accord occurred when the USSR paraded and flight-tested a fractional-orbital bombardment system (FOBS) despite a 1963 "gentleman's agreement" and a 1967 treaty prohibiting the deployment in outer space of mass destruction weapons.[11] The USSR proceeded with at least eighteen tests of FOBSs between 1966 and 1971, fifteen of which were successful.[12] The United States accepted the argument that a "partial orbit" did not amount to an orbit and that therefore the Soviet tests did not break the understanding or the treaty. FOBS was explicitly banned in SALT II, in which the Second Common Understanding to Article 7.2 required dismantling twelve Soviet FOBS launchers and conversion of the remaining six for testing missiles undergoing modernization. These obligations were to be carried out on entry into force of the treaty. Although Washington never ratified this pact, no more FOBS tests have been noted.

"Venting." Both superpowers have violated arms accords without intending or wanting to do so. Underground nuclear tests by the United States as well as the USSR have occasionally vented, releasing radioactive substances beyond the national borders—thereby violating the strictures of the 1963 Limited Nuclear Test Ban Treaty. The first time this happened seems to have been in 1965, when a Soviet test vented, probably carrying radioactive material beyond the borders of the USSR. Moscow's initial response to U.S. inquiries was to deny that such an event had occurred. Because the venting was probably not deliberate, the State Department

decided not to carry its protests further. Since that time, however, U.S. as well as Soviet tests have occasionally vented, each side acquiescing in the other's explanations that it had no intention to violate the 1963 treaty. When the USSR reproached the United States in January 1984 for a vented test, the State Department replied that "both the United States and the USSR have encountered some difficulty in containing all their underground nuclear tests. The United States, however, has had only a few problems in the past with . . . venting. . . . As more experience was gained with the containment of underground tests, venting from U.S. tests became even more rare. Over the past decade there has been only one incident of local and minor venting. The Soviets had not raised their concerns about U.S. venting with us" from 1976 until the January 1984 complaint.[13] In 1986, however, in yet another case of Energy Department malfeasance, a U.S. test had to be vented when it proved more powerful than expected.[14]

Fissionable materials production. In at least one case both sides have permitted joint pledges of restraint to lapse without protest. Thus American officials doubted in the mid-1960s that the USSR had in fact substantially reduced the production of uranium-235 for nuclear weapons, as Khrushchev had promised to do in a statement issued simultaneously with similar declarations by the United States and the United Kingdom in April 1964.[15] This informal understanding was much more vague and difficult to monitor than other parallel commitments by the Soviet Union and Western governments in the 1960s and later. This vagueness plus a desire in Washington, as well as Moscow to produce weapons-grade material for expanding arsenals, turned the 1964 statements into a dead letter.

SALT I. The 1972 ABM and SALT I accords were much more comprehensive and complex than any previous arms limitations. Both accords provided that "assurance of compliance" would be achieved through "national technical means of verification" and that neither party would "interfere" with the other's national technical means of verification or use "deliberate concealment measures which impede verification." Questions of SALT I compliance were to be considered by a Soviet-U.S. Standing Consultative Commission. Through the 1970s the SCC heard questions about the behavior of each side. Both the USSR and the United States, for example, sometimes delayed retiring older weapons to compensate for introduction of new ones to stay within SALT limits. Both governments put up structures that in effect camouflaged ICBMs, making it impossible to verify their characteristics by "national technical means." When these issues were raised in the SCC, the offending party took

[293]

measures to remove the grievance.[16] As former CIA Director William Colby summarized the record: "There were a few ambiguous situations that arose under SALT I which we took up with the Soviets, and we have been satisfied that the activity was explainable and not in violation of the treaty, or we saw a modification of Soviet behavior to comply with the treaty. The record is that the Soviets essentially complied with the treaty."[17] Experience with the 1972 verification procedures was so satisfactory that they were incorporated into the 1979 SALT II Treaty, which also pledged noninterference with national technical means and referral of compliance questions to the SCC.

The Conservative Critique: Public Accusation

Contrary to Colby and others who expressed satisfaction with Moscow's compliance record, the 1980 Republican party platform charged the Carter administration with covering up "Soviet noncompliance with arms control agreements." And the newly elected Reagan administration dropped the quiet diplomacy approach of its predecessors and proceeded to make public accusations of Soviet violations or "near violations" of many arms agreements. Ranking administration officials began making such charges in 1981 and 1982. In January 1984 the White House sent to Congress the report cited at the outset of this chapter charging Soviet violations or probable violations of many commitments.

One of the broadest-ranging assaults on Soviet behavior was the report, *A Quarter Century of Soviet Compliance Practices under Arms Control Commitments: 1958–1983*, by the General Advisory Committee on Arms Control and Disarmament, a panel of private citizens appointed by the president with the advice and consent of the Senate. The White House sent this scathing document to Congress on October 10, 1984, with the strange caveat that neither the report's methodology nor its conclusions had been "formally reviewed or approved by any agencies of the U.S. Government." Still, the White House cover letter indicated that the committee's "full report" contained extensive classified intelligence and that the classified version was being transmitted to the two Select Committees of the Congress on Intelligence.[18] This approach permitted the White House to imply that "you can't trust the Russians" while disavowing any responsibility for some of the more extreme judgments in the report.

Assistant Secretary of Defense Richard N. Perle often made

[294]

statements to the press, attributed and otherwise, alleging Soviet violations of arms obligations. Many of his charges were included in a twenty-seven page pamphlet issued in 1985 over the signatures of Caspar W. Weinberger and George P. Shultz: *Soviet Defense Programs*. With no publisher and no date listed, the pamphlet seemed to have less than official standing, thereby permitting its authors to denounce the USSR without fully committing the U.S. government.

The Reagan White House sent other reports to Congress somewhat less extreme in their charges than the General Advisory Committee report but putting the president's full authority behind them. These included the January 1984 report cited earlier, an update of that report in February 1985, and another on December 23, 1985, which, Mr. Reagan wrote, should "significantly increase understanding of Soviet violations and probable violations."[19] In November 1985 Secretary Weinberger sent a memorandum to the president, *Responding to Soviet Violations Policy (RSVP) Study*. In February 1986 the Arms Control and Disarmament Agency issued a report entitled *Soviet Noncompliance*. All this helped to set the stage for the president's announcement in May 1986 that he was abandoning the restraints of the SALT II treaty, citing Soviet violations as a primary justification. He issued another noncompliance report in March 1987 reiterating previous charges but offering no new evidence or analysis. Meanwhile the Reagan administration prevented the U.S. delegation to the Standing Consultative Commission from adopting a problem-solving approach and blocked efforts to make the SCC more effective. The result was to "make it far more difficult to resolve the very compliance problems the administration claims it desires to resolve."[20]

"Yellow rain" and anthrax. One of the first Reagan administration attacks on Soviet treaty observance came in September 1981 when Secretary of State Alexander Haig accused the USSR of using chemical weapons in Afghanistan and of supplying toxins to its Vietnamese ally for use in Southeast Asia in violation of the 1925 Geneva Protocol (a ban initiated with U.S. backing in the early 1920s but not approved by the U.S. Senate until 1974).[21] This charge was repeated by the White House on many occasions. Independent researchers, however, have been unable to document these accusations and point to other, more likely explanations of the "yellow rain" phenomenon.[22] Still, even when the U.S. Army's chemical laboratory and those of Canada and Britain were unable to confirm the presence of toxin in yellow rain samples, the United States continued to press its charges at a 1986 Geneva conference.[23]

The U.S. government stood on firmer ground in raising questions about Soviet compliance with the 1972 Biological and Toxin Weapons

[295]

Convention. The Reagan administration charged that the USSR retained production facilities and continued biological weapon production, storage, and use in violation of the 1972 BWC. This accusation was also made by Arkady Shevchenko in 1985; he reported that the Soviet military in the early 1970s opposed any agreement limiting chemical or biological weapons. Shevchenko maintained that the Kremlin leadership—Gromyko in particular—felt it necessary for propaganda purposes to respond to the West's proposal and sign the convention. The Soviet military then agreed that Moscow should sign, but it refused to consider eliminating stockpiles or halting production. "The Politburo approved this approach. The toothless convention" established "no international controls over the Soviet program, which continues apace."[24]

Contra Shevchenko, it is unlikely that the Politburo would hold back from signing or implementing an arms accord because of pressures from the Soviet military establishment. But the charge that Moscow has maintained biological weapons production facilities and weapons stockpiles gains credence from the unusually large outbreak of anthrax that occurred at Sverdlovsk in 1979. A biological warfare facility is long thought to have existed at Sverdlovsk and would be permitted under the 1972 convention if confined to research. Some evidence suggests that the anthrax was contracted by breathing in the spores—proof of a warfare agent. But the prolonged time course of the epidemic points to a gastric anthrax acquired by eating the bacteria. Soviet spokesmen, in fact, have attributed the epidemic to tainted meat. Still, the suspicion remains that the USSR may have illegally stockpiled anthrax spores, and the borderline between a "research" and a "production" facility is not sharply defined.[25]

The lack of an institutionalized structure for resolving concerns about compliance with the 1972 convention (such as the Standing Consultative Commission or some form of on-site inspection) "make it exceedingly difficult . . . to resolve compliance questions satisfactorily. Likewise, the absence of clear guidelines as to the types or quantities of agent that may be retained for 'peaceful' purposes makes it nearly impossible to determine whether a country is engaged in activities that violate the convention." The convention was signed at a time when the West did not regard biological weapons as militarily useful and when détente lessened incentives to establish high standards for verification.[26]

Maneuvers. The Reagan administration also faulted the USSR for violating not only the human rights but also some arms control provisions of the 1975 Helsinki Final Act. Moscow, said Washington, violated the commitment to notify Final Act Parties and provide specified data twenty-one days before conducting exercises of more than 25,000 troops when it conducted major military maneuvers in March and September 1981 and in June 1983. The act, however, is not a legally binding treaty but only a statement of intent. The Soviets, for their part, claimed that the United States has acted contrary to Helsinki commitments to promote East-West trade.

An SS-20 moratorium? Defense Secretary Weinberger and SACEUR General Bernard D. Rogers in autumn 1982 charged the Soviets not only with violating treaties but with failing to observe a self-imposed moratorium on additional deployment of SS-20 missiles targeted on Europe so long as the United States did not begin deployment of intermediate-range missiles in Europe. A close study by Raymond L. Garthoff, however, indicates that following the counting rules evolved in SALT I, the Brezhnev and Andropov regimes observed this restraint and began no *new* deployment sites within range of central Western Europe after the moratorium was announced in March 1982 until after it was revoked in December 1983, following the first U.S. INF deployments.[27]

Unilateral declarations. The General Advisory Committee in 1984 and other U.S. government statements complained that the USSR has "disregarded all six unilateral declarations made by the U.S. in SALT I to clarify constraints upon Soviet forces under this agreement." As the chief U.S. SALT I negotiator has written, however, Soviet representatives made clear *during* the SALT I negotiations their rejection of the U.S. interpretations.[28] Washington should have insisted on *joint* understandings or refused to sign rather than crying "thief!" after leaving the barn door open for the mare to depart.

Encryption. Another U.S. complaint has been that Moscow has encoded the results of missile tests, violating its SALT obligation not to impede U.S. verification programs. There is no agreement, however, even within the Washington bureaucracy as to what level of encryption would be permitted under SALT. Some Western observers see Soviet encryption in the 1980s as an act of defiance: "Since the United States feels free not to ratify SALT II, we Soviets feel free to encrypt when we want to." Were the USSR encrypting telemetry on MIRV bus maneuvers and hiding a potential to multiply warheads, this would have serious military significance. But there seems to be no evidence in the public domain that this has occurred. Soviet encryption practices have had "virtually no military impact."[29] When asked by Soviets if the level of encryption would be acceptable, U.S. representatives have refused to say because this would reveal too much about U.S. "national means"!

ABM radars, new and modernized. Probably the clearest Soviet challenge to an arms treaty has been the construction of a large, phased array radar (LPAR) in the interior of the USSR near Krasnoyarsk. If completed and switched on this installation would almost certainly violate the ABM Treaty's stricture against deployment of "radars for early warning of strategic ballistic missile attack except at locations along the periphery of [the] national territory and oriented outward." The Krasnoyarsk site is far inland; the closest border is with Mongolia more than five hundred miles distant. The 1972 treaty also permits radars for "purposes of tracking objects in outer space or for use as national means of verification," but it contains no criteria to distinguish prohibited LPARs from those permitted for space tracking or verification. Still, Soviet spokesmen conceded in 1987 that Krasnoyarsk is poorly oriented for tracking satellites.

The characteristics of the Krasnoyarsk radar had been under scrutiny by U.S. satellites for some years and the target of U.S. noncompliance charges since 1983. In 1987 a delegation of U.S. congressmen with expert staff members was allowed to visit the installation and photograph its interior as well as exterior. From their on-site observations and from other information it appears that Krasnoyarsk has not been built as a battle-management radar.[30] More likely its function is to fill an important lacuna in the USSR's early warning system, giving notice of missiles fired by U.S. submarines in the northern Pacific. The Kremlin may have hoped to plug this gap by erecting two radars close to its Far Eastern borders, as permitted by the ABM Treaty, only to give up the idea because construction on Siberian permafrost would be too difficult. Krasnoyarsk, far inland—on firm soil and close to a railroad—would fill the breach.[31]

If Washington charged that the Krasnoyarsk installation violated the ABM Treaty, Moscow may have hoped to finesse this problem in the Standing Consultative Commission. The Kremlin, for its part, has voiced many complaints about American radar construction, which could be put on the table in any discussion of a resolution acceptable to both sides. In 1975 the USSR charged that the Cobra Dane radar the United States was building in the Aleutians had been tested as part of an ABM system. Washington countered that the radar's function was to monitor Soviet missile tests—a purpose permitted by the ABM Treaty. The Kremlin also charged that the "PAVE PAWS" radars erected in many locations around the United States "can serve as the basis for providing radar backing for the ABM defense" of the entire U.S. territory. But Washington has replied that these radars are oriented outward and are close to the U.S. periphery as required by the treaty.

Moscow's most serious charge has been that the United States has also been upgrading radars in Greenland and England so that they can fulfill ABM roles well beyond their capacity when the 1972 treaty was signed. Since October 1985 the USSR has offered to stop work at Krasnoyarsk if the United States halts what Washington calls "modernization" of its two overseas radars. "If we were building the Krasnoyarsk radar in violation of the ABM Treaty," Soviet Foreign Minister Eduard Shevardnadze said in Washington in September 1987, "we would not have invited U.S. congressmen, U S. experts, to see that radar. . . . I really hope that now the U.S. will reciprocate, and that our people will be able to see the controversial radar in Greenland."

The ABM Treaty does not prohibit modernization of existing radars, but upgrading of the U.S. radars at Thule, Greenland, and Fylingdales Moor in the United Kingdom employs electronic scanning much more powerful than the mechanical steered devices they replaced. This technology, that of a LPAR, was restricted by the ABM Treaty to the territory of each signatory. The U.K. radar is being built several miles from the original site.

The Greenland facility became operational in 1987, but the Krasnoyarsk radar appeared then to be at least two years from an operational capacity. Some in the U.S. congressional delegation argued that the Soviet radar would not violate the ABM Treaty until it was switched on.

The Krasnoyarsk and other Soviet radars could help the USSR to rapidly break out of the ABM Treaty regime. In practice, however, they were not linked to launchers or other components needed to create a wide-scale defense. The technology for an "Astrodome" shield was not in sight in the United States; it was even more remote in the USSR.[32]

If the main function of the disputed radars is early warning, they should present no major problem if both sides wish to maintain the ABM Treaty. One approach would be to permit both sides to perfect their early-warning systems making allowances for geographical peculiarities such as Siberian permafrost. Perhaps some form of on-site inspection could be introduced to ensure that neither side converted its early-warning radars into more threatening battle management systems. Alternatively, construction could be halted at both the Krasnoyarsk and U.K. radars, permitting both sides to reaffirm the 1972 treaty and clarify distinctions between early-warning and other radars. Halting work would leave both sides with gaps in their early-warning systems, especially the Soviet Union. But Moscow may be willing to live with such a gap: in October 1987 Soviet officials informed George Shultz that the USSR was stopping construction at Krasnoyarsk for a year without demanding any quid pro quo.[33]

"Light" ICBMs. Another serious U.S. charge was that the USSR

[299]

broke the SALT II limitation that "each party may flight-test and deploy only one new type of light ICBM." In 1982 the USSR began testing the SS-24 (U.S. designation) and subsequently informed the United States that this missile would be the new light ICBM permitted under the treaty. In February 1983, however, the Soviets began testing a smaller, single-warhead ICBM, the SS-25. Washington claimed that development of the SS-25 violated SALT II. Moscow replied that the SS-25 was merely a permitted modification of an existing weapon, the SS-13, over ten years old at the time of the SALT negotiations.[34]

Such wrangling is inherent in negotiations to constrain weapons development. Virtually all the issues in the SS-25 dispute were prefigured in 1899 when Russia proposed to ban the use of any new kinds of firearms, new explosives, or powders more powerful than in current use. The Russian representative said that "new kinds of firearms" meant "an entirely new type, and should not include transformations and improvements."[35] His reasoning, if applied today, would permit the SS-25. Given that Soviet practice tends toward incrementally improving weapons rather than embarking on drastically new approaches—often the American style— a "new form" of Soviet weapon is more likely to build on an older model than is the case in the United States.

The Pentagon reported in 1988 that the USSR was deploying both road-mobile SS-25 ICBMs and rail-based SS-24 ICBMs ("which apparently will also be silo-based").[36] Like the projected U.S. Midgetman missile, the SS-25 is comparatively "crisis stable." Mobile, it could not be eliminated readily by a first strike; with only one warhead, it would not be so useful for preemption as the SS-24 or American MX Peacemaker missiles, each of which can carry ten warheads. Mobile missiles, of course, are harder to track than those kept in silos; as of 1988, however, U.S. planners believed they could count the total number of Soviet land-based missiles on wheels or rails. But Washington also worried that the USSR was flight-testing a follow-on to its giant SS-18 ICBM, a weapon well suited to a preemptive, counterforce mission. Two new classes of submarine—the Typhoon and Delta IV—when deployed, would further add to Moscow's first-strike capacity.

Lulled by "Peaceful Coexistence"?

None of the Soviet actions alleged to violate arms accords in the 1970s–80s seriously affected the balance of power. But has the Kremlin exploited arms treaties and détente to overtake the United States militarily and to intensify a forward strategy in the Third World? There is no clear evidence that arms treaties and negotiations have produced either a "lulling" or a stimulative effect on U.S. military spending and procurement. "Levels of [U.S.] military spending do seem to rise and fall in tandem with public support for the defense budget, but these fluctuations do not seem to be influenced by arms control agreements."[37] To be sure, R&D for missile defense plummeted after the ABM Treaty, but the Pentagon has often intensified aspects of its buildup to compensate for agreed limitations. After SALT I the Soviets vastly increased their launchers but the Americans multiplied their warheads. The Americans lost their will to intervene in the Third World, but that was more a result of a Vietnam hangover than of détente.

The main thrusts of the Soviet buildup have not been constrained by treaty. Both sides have been free to deploy multiple warheads because neither worked hard to prohibit them in SALT I. The Soviets were permitted to build more nuclear-missile submarines than America because Dr. Kissinger in 1972 granted them higher ceilings—to the chagrin of the "front-channel" U.S. negotiators—as part of an overall package.[38]

Granted that the USSR has endeavored to improve its strategic-military posture through negotiation and arms accords, *there is no evidence that Moscow also welcomed arms control because it intended to exploit certain agreements by cheating*. What rather seems to happen is that Soviet leaders, marshals, and technocrats ask, "What can we do within the limits of this treaty?" As in foreign trade, Soviet arms negotiators may even have taken a certain pleasure in outwitting "bourgeois" specialists at their own game. The Kremlin has brazenly affronted the spirit of some accords by pushing the letter to its far limits— for example, testing fractional-orbital bombardment systems. The Krasnoyarsk installation seems to violate even the letter of the ABM Treaty and is regarded by some Soviet officials as a "stupid mistake."

Another Side: Mutual Compliance

More significant than the shortcomings of treaty language and observance has been the positive record of Soviet and U.S. compliance with arms control commitments—a record without parallel in world history. (Despite complaints from Sparta, the Athenians insisted on building long walls to their port even though this defensive system, combined with the Athenian navy, threatened to nullify Sparta's land power—a condition that helped to spark the Peloponnesian wars.) From Antarctica through the INF Treaty, the world's two major antagonists have, since 1959, curbed their arms in accordance with many treaties, including two that have now expired (SALT I and II), the second of which was never even ratified! When the United States chose not to ratify SALT II, Carter in March 1980 and Reagan in March 1981 pledged that they would take no actions to undercut existing agreements so long as the USSR exercised the same restraint (a position that accorded with the 1969 Vienna Convention on the Law of Treaties). Washington reiterated this position in 1985 but kept open its option to exceed treaty limits in the future as part of a "proportionate response" to alleged Soviet violations. Working under the no-undercut policy the United States deactivated 320 ICBMs, 544 SLBMs, and 10 Polaris submarines; in 1985 it dismantled a Poseidon submarine as a new Trident submarine began sea trials. Although some of these weapons were dated and some may have been redundant, most were still quite formidable.[39]

In signing SALT II in 1979 the Kremlin undertook an obligation to reduce its aggregate force of ICBMs, SLBMs, and heavy bombers from 2,505 to 2,250 by late 1981. Because the treaty did not go into effect, this requirement has not been operative. Like the United States, however, the USSR pledged not to undercut the treaty. Though the White House charged in December 1985 that the total of Soviet strategic systems exceeded the "2,504 cap in violation of its political commitment," the order of battle given in the Joint Chiefs of Staff report, *United States Military Posture* (January 1986), showed the total of such weapons at 2,477—well below the permitted ceiling. Analysis by the Arms Control Association found in 1985 that the USSR had deactivated even more weapons than had the United States to comply with SALT I and II: 1,007 ICBMs, 233 SLBMs, and 13 Yankee-class nuclear-missile submarines. It found that since 1979 the USSR had not constructed a single new fixed ICBM silo, not increased the number of reentry vehicles on existing ICBMs, not exceeded fractionalization restrictions on tests of multiple warheads, kept the production rate of the Backfire bomber at 30 per year or less; and removed refueling probes from this aircraft so as to limit its ability as an intercontinental weapon.[40]

The Present Danger—as Seen from Moscow

The rules of the game—what is acceptable behavior in arms control—have been formed by the words and deeds of both sides. Many Soviet specialists regard the United States as highly fickle and self-serving in arms control matters. When in May 1955 Moscow accepted in principle many Western arms proposals, Washington shifted and pushed for "open skies"—hardly an attractive prospect for the USSR at that time. After the 1955 Geneva summit the State Department even placed a "reservation" on Washington's pre-Geneva positions.[41] After East and West agreed in 1958 on the technical requirements for a nuclear test ban, in 1959 Washington decided that this machinery would be inadequate. Eisenhower twice announced that the United States no longer felt obliged to observe the nuclear test moratorium initiated by Khrushchev in 1958; Kennedy later railed at Moscow for breaking it. U.S. negotiators in SALT I often changed and even retracted their positions on the number and location of permitted ABM sites.[42]

A U.S. signature on an arms treaty by no means implies it will be ratified. Washington has signed but not ratified the 1974 threshold nuclear test ban, the 1976 peaceful explosions ban, and SALT II. Washington took a leading role in the 1970s in drafting a comprehensive Law of the Sea, which the Reagan administration refused to sign. Reagan's diplomats walked away from lengthy but promising negotiations for a comprehensive nuclear test ban and from important talks to limit antisatellite weapons. A Soviet analyst asked rhetorically: "How can one reach agreements with a country the President of which cannot reach agreement with the Congress, and when even the Congress in an officially adopted resolution says one thing and then demands something quite different?"[43]

The Reagan administration became judge and executioner of previous arms accords. It treated unilateral U.S. interpretations of SALT as though they bound both sides. It shunned serious explorations of compliance issues in the Standing Consultative Commission and instead "went public," often shooting from the hip, often confusing possible with certain violations. Sometimes it had to eat crow, as when the CIA announced that improved Western seismic detection methods demonstrated that the USSR probably had not violated the threshold nuclear test ban, as previously charged.[44] When independent researchers and even U.S. government labs could not confirm reports of Soviet and Vietnamese use of chemical weapons and pointed to better explanations of yellow rain, Washington explained that its publicity had led Moscow to desist.

Having condemned SALT II even before he became president, for five years Reagan continued the no-undercut policy established in 1980. In 1985, however, as U.S. deployments pushed at SALT II limits, Reagan waited until the last minute to indicate whether the United States would continue to dismantle older weapons to stay within authorized ceilings. He made clear that he was not obliged to adhere to the SALT limits indefinitely because the treaty, even if ratified, would expire in 1985 and because Soviet violations justified a "proportionate response." In May 1986 Reagan declared SALT II a dead letter. In November the United States exceeded the treaty's limits on strategic delivery vehicles with multiple warheads. SALT II no longer existed as a legal obligation or political commitment, so Washington refused to discuss SALT II compliance in the SCC. [45]

In its first term the Reagan White House seemed not to believe in the long-term benefits of collaboration between adversaries; hence it did not mind undermining whatever arms control arrangements had been worked out under previous administrations. A profound change overtook the president in 1985–86, one that led him even to endorse radical disarmament at Reykjavik and later. But he demonstrated in his first four or five years in office that the United States is quite capable of backing away from its arms control commitments.

Soviet observance of arms control accords also left much to be desired. Pushing at the limits of each treaty, seeing how far it could be stretched before Washington complained, the Soviet Union stirred American suspicions.

The most blatant American challenge to arms control was Reagan's Strategic Defense Initiative, which, if implemented, would render the ABM Treaty another dead letter. Even "development and testing of ABM systems or their components which are sea-based, air-based, space-based, or mobile land-based" would violate the treaty. Nonetheless in the mid-1980s the United States conducted tests of lasers and antisatellite weapons. [46] When Moscow protested the research and testing conducted or planned under SDI, [47] the State Department's chief lawyer defended a "broad interpretation" of the ABM Treaty—an interpretation not supported by the negotiating record or Senate hearings on the treaty. [48] The White House showed disdain for the ABM Treaty and proceeded with steps that could lead to much more significant changes in the balance of power than Soviet development of two light ICBMs.

If technology progressed so as to make feasible a highly effective defense of the entire country, a prudent leader would probably prefer that approach over the Damocles' sword of deterrence, but few scientists believed this possible for decades, if ever. Despite this the Reagan administration put in jeopardy the main safeguard of stabilized deterrence: mutual restraint in ABM systems. It did so without serious discussions with its treaty partner, with the Western allies, or even within the concerned branches of the U.S. government.

The administration's decision to deploy the MX Peacemaker missile in old, relatively vulnerable silos was another destabilizing move. It placed a weapon exquisitely suited for a first strike in a mode ill-suited to ride out a Soviet first strike. From Moscow's perspective, the combination of the MX plus an improved but not leakproof ABM could be quite threatening. America could strike first and then hope that even an imperfect SDI might thwart a ragged Soviet reply.

Perhaps all these contingencies are as fanciful as the angels dancing on the pinheads of medieval scholastics. But Russia has been hit twice in this century by massive surprise attacks; the United States only once, and with less lethal consequences. U.S. arms policies in the 1980s looked at least so ominous to the Kremlin as Soviet policies did to Washington.

Can Military R&D Be Constrained?

Despite an unprecedented variety of arms limitations negotiated and implemented, arms racing outpaces arms control. The problems inherent in limiting each side to one "light" ICBM raise a fundamental question: *How can arms negotiators ban what they cannot entirely foresee?*[49] As Captain Alfred Mahan noted in 1899, it is possible that some technological invention has diminished "the frequency and indeed the exhausting character of war."[50] If not the general good, innovation may benefit one side. Even if negotiators seek to forestall development in a certain domain, their net may prove too fine or too open. Whether the obstacles erected to new weapons are broad or narrow, technology and technocrats may punch through or run an end sweep; alternatively, if the obstacles work, military R&D may shift its energies to another domain.

The difficulties of eliminating present weapons and banning future ones are illustrated in the 1987 INF Treaty. Under Articles 2 and 7 only new missile types that are unarmed or dedicated to air defense are allowed. Yet as then Senator Dan Quayle pointed out, there is no definition of what a new "type" is. Could either side paint an existing missile a different color, claim it is unarmed, and deploy it?[51]

Critics also complained that the INF ban on GLCMs prevents the United States from deploying conventional as well as nuclear warheads

[305]

on such missiles, depriving the West of a promising way to improve the conventional balance. U.S. officials replied that a broad ban is needed because it is virtually impossible to distinguish GLCMs with conventional warheads from those with nuclear. Their critics persisted: "Why do you then permit ground-launched reconnaissance drones?" U.S. negotiators responded that drones can be identified by a flight pattern quite different from that of a true GLCM.[52] Other analysts held, however, that even drones are outlawed under the treaty unless their external characteristics distinguish them from weapon-carrying missiles. The Senate Armed Forces and Foreign Relations committees also asked if the treaty limited exotic weapons such as lasers and particle beams; the administration replied that the subject was not discussed in the INF negotiations but that the "commonly understood" reading of the treaty banned them, with which Soviet spokesmen concurred in April 1988. Former Pentagon Secretary Weinberger demurred, saying that such a ban was not implicit or even desirable. The Armed Forces Committee failed to get a clear answer to another question: Does the treaty ban a possible new type of missile known as a hypersonic boost glide vehicle, which, if developed, would take off like a ballistic missile and then glide toward its target?[53] As the treaty is implemented, even more questions will surely arise from Pandora's box; even the numbers of systems to be eliminated aroused dispute—the Defense Intelligence Agency accused Moscow of understanding the number of missiles at stake.

The Soviet government has its own concerns about the viability of the INF. The chief Soviet negotiator, Yuli Vorontsov, told the Foreign Affairs Commission of the Supreme Soviet:

> Our experience in conducting negotiations with the United States on disarmament, extending over decades, confirms that it is necessary to trust but verify—a proverb that President Reagan also likes to repeat . . . . It is essential to verify whether the USA will not attempt in some way to circumvent the [INF] treaty and thus destroy the obligations taken on itself by some kind of acts outside the treaty framework.[54]

To constrain the United States, Vorontsov explained, Moscow proposed in April 1987 that the treaty stipulate the following: "With the aim of securing [its] viability and effectiveness . . . each of the Parties commits itself not to circumvent the provisions of the present Treaty in any way including by means of transferring to any other party missiles or components of such missiles, launchers of such missiles, or technical documentation relating to such missiles and launchers. Each of the Parties commits itself not to take on any international obligations that contradict the present Treaty." When the Americans "decisively opposed" such a clarification, this strengthened the Soviets' determination to include one. The Americans, according to Vorontsov, fought any provision that might keep them from rendering the treaty meaningless. The Soviet delegation remained firm and finally settled for what became Article 14: "The Parties shall comply with this Treaty and shall not assume any international obligations or undertakings which would conflict with its provisions." This sentence, Vorontsov declared, contains Moscow's initial demands but in highly general phrasing.

For his part, Senator Quayle complained that there is no explanation in the text to clarify what "obligations" would conflict with the treaty. If Britain or France developed weapons using guidance systems similar to those in the banned INF missiles, would this be a U.S. "undertaking" that "conflicts" with the treaty?[55] Adding to the complications, "undertakings" is rendered in the Russian version of the text as "actions" (*aktsii*, which could also mean "shares"). The last part of Article 14 in the Russian text reads "and will not undertake any kind of international actions"—thus using the adjective "international" twice, whereas it is specified only once in English.

Moscow objected to NATO efforts to "compensate" for the weapons eliminated. Such plans were resented the more because the INF Treaty imposed asymmetrical obligations on the USSR. "Compensation," said Vorontsov, is "blasphemy." The idea of compensation derives from the "old military-political thinking and directly contradicts the new thinking to which we summon the USA and other countries." Compensation would be like a surgeon who cuts out an ulcer and implants cancer cells in its place. Article 14 has practical—even philosophical—meaning, Vorontsov claimed, because it prevents anyone from thinking that it is possible to evade—at first in part and then entirely—the disarmament obligations of this treaty.

Marshal S. F. Akhromeev, also testifying before the Supreme Soviet, noted the military's concern at Western plans to modernize and expand NATO's short-range nuclear and dual-capable (nuclear and conventional) arsenals. Formally speaking, Akhromeev granted, nothing in the treaty prohibits such "compensation," but the Americans never talked about it during seven years of negotiations.

There are no loopholes, weaknesses, or ambiguities in the INF Treaty, Vorontsov maintained, for it was carefully drafted. Especially there are no provisions that could be used against Soviet interests. Still, questions could arise as the treaty is implemented. They are to be referred to the Soviet-U.S. Special Verification Commission. Some U.S. senators

[307]

have said that they want to exclude missiles with conventional warheads, but this would undermine the treaty and change its character. Some want to inspect SS-4 and SS-5 missile sites in Cuba, but that issue was resolved in 1962, and the INF concerns only existing missiles. Americans forget, said the chairman of the Supreme Soviet's Foreign Affairs Commission, G. M. Kornienko, that Moscow could demand to check former U.S. missile sites in Turkey and Italy.

Defense Ministry representative V. I. Medvedev noted that as of February 1988, the Reagan administration had not itself looked for loopholes in Senate hearings but that many Senate witnesses had done so. *Amerikanist* G. A. Trofimenko added that "realistic thinkers" in the Senate sought a definitive and binding interpretation of the treaty from the administration so as to avoid a replay of the ABM "broad interpretation."

One questioner asked when Soviet military authorities would publish their version of the military data now issued by the International Institute for Strategic Studies (London) and the Stockholm International Peace Research Institute on the military balance in Europe. To this challenge Akhromeev replied old style: "Data on the composition of armed forces in Europe is not just data; it is also a weapon in the hands of those with whom we afterwards must conduct negotiations. The West only asserts that it publishes such information. The IISS is not an official organ. We are ready to publish the data if the NATO bloc, in its turn, publishes its own—a pledge Moscow fulfilled in early 1989."

Responding to another question, Medvedev exaggerated the scope of the INF verification provisions. He claimed that the INF inspection system "comprehends all objects where intermediate- and shorter-range missiles could be deployed" and that the on-site inspections permitted under yearly quotas may check out "any object [*liuboi obekt*] of the other side." In reality, the INF Treaty limits on-site inspection to specified sites, thus leaving most of each country inaccessible except to "national technical means" of verification.

Both Vorontsov and Akhromeev boasted that the "offensive, active position" of Soviet delegations to the INF and subsequent strategic arms talks put the Americans on the "defensive." This was done, said Vorontsov, in accord with our long-standing principle: If disarmament is at issue, we are interested in effective controls no less and perhaps more than the United States. Many inspection provisions of the INF Treaty were initiated by the Soviet side, but some Soviet proposals were turned down by the United States. For example, the Americans rejected inspection of enterprises that produce missiles and countered with their plan to monitor only the portals and periphery of such plants. "To some extent this approach is sufficient, though we believe that if you are going to control—then control completely." The Americans also refused Moscow's proposal to inspect a whole list of specified enterprises and agreed to just one. But Vorontsov was sure INF verification procedures would work and—supplemented by national means—would be sufficient.

A similar conclusion was reached by the U.S. Senate Select Committee on Intelligence. The committee's March 21, 1988, report stressed that on-site inspections under the treaty are applicable only to declared facilities; hence the burden of detecting banned activities at undeclared sites would fall on national technical means. The treaty's bans on production, flight testing, and storage would inhibit Soviet (and presumably U.S.) ability to maintain nondeployed missiles in a high state of readiness. If the USSR covertly maintained some SS-20s, their military utility would be eroded over time by the ban on flight testing.

GLCMs, however, pose a difficult monitoring problem because they are interchangeable with SLCMs. Testing an SLCM would permit a Soviet planner to fulfill the technical requirements for testing a covert GLCM. Lack of ground forces infrastructure for such weapons, however, would lessen the value and probability of cheating. There is also the possibility that the Soviets could develop a GLCM with a prohibited range (500 to 5,500 km) but test it only at shorter ranges. But reliability questions would be significant if the missile were untested at its intended range. Unless the USSR's present 10,000 strategic warheads were substantially reduced, however, the Soviets "have little or no incentive to cheat" on the INF.[56]

Can the Kremlin Be Trusted? Can Washington?

Unambiguous language is helpful but not sufficient to ensure compliance; it may not even be necessary. If either party believes a treaty no longer serves its interests, tight legal language will not prevent circumvention. If either side wishes to evade restraints, it can probably find a way to do so—backed by legalistic (perhaps sophistic or demagogic) justifications for this course. Similarly, if either party seeks to denounce the other for noncompliance, the multifaceted research and development programs carried out by each superpower will create convenient targets for criticism. As in a marriage that is falling apart, actions by each side can be treated as grounds for divorce.

Trouble arose in May 1989 as Shevardnadze threatened that Moscow would halt dismantling of its SS-23 missiles as required by the INF Treaty

[309]

if the West modernized and stretched its Lance missile. Both sides accused each other of duplicity. The Kremlin had agreed to remove the SS-23s even though, it said, their range fell just short of the 500 km scope of the INF accord. But why should it disarm if NATO were going to produce a comparable missile with a range just below 500 km? Western spokesmen replied that NATO's determination to modernize its missiles was well known during the INF negotiations and that now Moscow should stick to its word and avoid blackmail. Western optimists said Shevardnadze was only bluffing and had committed a tactical blunder; pessimists said his threat revealed that Gorbachev's regime, like its predecessors, viewed arms control pacts as mere scraps of paper.

The basic question is whether the superpowers can manage their adversarial relationship so that they gain more from coordination than from unrestrained competition.[57] The bottom line is that governments adhere to commitments so long as they believe it is in their interest to do so.

Perceived self-interest may be different from enlightened self-interest. What governments believe to be to their advantage may be short-sighted or based on incomplete information.[58] Still, perceived self-interest is the most dependable predictor of Soviet and U.S. adherence to international agreements. In short, Moscow and Washington will do what each thinks will be good for it.

National egotism helps to explain an apparent paradox: each superpower has behaved more willfully in its traditional sphere of interest than with its major adversary.[59] As noted in chapter 4, the USSR has been more concerned with Western opinion than with commitments toward its neighbors, friends, and allies. The Bolsheviks preached national self-determination but used force to bring all non-Russian republics into the USSR and keep them there. The Kremlin breached its 1920 "peaceful coexistence" treaties and later mutual aid pacts with the Baltic republics when it invaded and annexed them in 1940; it mocked Yalta commitments to broaden the Polish government and hold free elections in liberated Eastern Europe; it built a powerful "People's Police" in East Germany despite promises to keep Germany disarmed. The USSR interpreted the 1955 Warsaw Treaty to mean that Moscow had the right and duty to intervene militarily in its allies' internal affairs. From Beijing's perspective, Moscow violated its 1950 mutual assistance treaty with China and the 1957 new defense technology pact. More recently, the Kremlin used the pretext of a 1921 treaty and alleged requests for aid from Kabul to terminate the Amin regime and attempt implanting others, not hesitating at genocide.

[310]

The United States has also stretched or ignored its treaty obligations in seeking to maintain friendly regimes south of the border. Washington has created "doctrines" with "corollaries," interpreted and implemented them, and sometimes ignored or ended them. It has sought to keep out nonhemispheric powers and to maximize hemispheric integration orchestrated by the United States. This tendency commenced under Thomas Jefferson and persisted under liberal presidents Wilson, Kennedy, and Johnson; it emerged strongly also under conservatives Theodore Roosevelt, Taft, and Reagan. To promote its aims in Nicaragua the Reagan administration abused not only international law but domestic; it retracted America's acceptance of the ICJ's compulsory jurisdiction as regards Central America and yawned as members of the National Security Council and CIA schemed to circumvent restrictions on Contra aid imposed by Congress.

If the superpowers act willfully in their own backyards, does this mean they will be perfidious toward each other? Security treaties and nonaggression pacts, like arms control, bear on life-and-death issues—even the survival of a political system and its people. When adherence to a treaty seems to jeopardize vital interests, governments usually disregard its obligations, sometimes adding a legalistic defense of their actions. When vital interests are at stake, governments sometimes justify self-aggrandizement by twisting or expanding the terms of an existing treaty. When a treaty is ambiguous, governments often interpret vague clauses to suit their expedient interests. One or all of these conditions has usually been present when Moscow or Washington flouted the law seeking to get its way in Eastern Europe or south of the border.

The USSR has entered arms control accords with the United States because Moscow hoped that they would enhance Soviet security and other interests. This calculation usually looked toward long-term goals that would be undermined by any effort to squeeze immediate gain from cheating on arms obligations. Given the modest scope of all arms controls to date, cheating could create little useful gain. The ultimate sanction is not a slap by "world opinion" or the ICJ; nor is it a threat from some UN Police Force. Rather, it is the likelihood that the other superpower will respond with countermoves that undo the very ends for which arms controls were established. Whereas neither superpower is inclined to intervene to uphold justice in the other's sphere, both Moscow and Washington stand ready to act if the other violates an arms accord.

Although not much could be gained by violating SALT I or II, the Soviet Union's interests were strongly enhanced by its actions to dominate its neighbors. In many cases Moscow's hegemonic moves came in

[311]

response to *crisis* situations—the threat of a German attack, the collapse of Communist regimes, the possibility of a catalytic war brought on by China. No such crises have existed in the realm of Soviet-U.S. arms control: even Pershing 2s and SDI presented no immediate threat similar to Hungary in 1956.

Whereas Russia's neighbors could be abused at low risk because they were weak, the United States is powerful and dangerous. The neighbors are close at hand; America, remote.

Arms control agreements, finally, usually allow less scope for free interpretation than do friendship treaties or promises of free elections or free movement.

If Moscow thought that serious security gains could be achieved by violating an arms control obligation, the Kremlin might be tempted. Because deterrence systems are redundant, however, neither side is likely to achieve a "usable superiority" whether by stepping up the arms race or by cheating. In short, neither Moscow nor Washington has had a pressing incentive to evade its arms control obligations. If either side cheats on any of the accords of recent decades, it is unlikely to achieve an advantage that the other could not nullify before being pressed to its knees. Even the 50 percent cuts considered in recent years (assuming their stipulations gave neither side an edge in hard-target kill capability) would probably leave little incentive to cheat because no decisive advantage could be achieved.

The utility of "defecting" could increase dramatically if the superpowers reduced their arsenals by a large factor—say, another 50 to 100 percent. If each side were entitled to only 1,000 or 2,000 weapons, hiding an extra 500 or 1,000 might yield great bargaining power. If Moscow and Washington agreed to eliminate two legs of their triads and depend only on submarines, the side that cached 100 ICBMs might have a substantial advantage. If they agreed to depend only on submarines but to ban antisubmarine warfare, the side that kept up and improved its ASW might destabilize deterrence. Such dangers—the "clandestine weapon problem"—could emerge in the world of total nuclear disarmament proposed by Gorbachev in January 1986.

Some leading Soviet scholars (discussions at IMEMO, March 1989), however, dismissed such worries. So long as any power possesses even a small umbrella of *invulnerable* nuclear weapons, they said, it need not fear *diktat* by another or even by an array of others. Hence the USSR can readily contemplate reducing its strategic arsenal to a low level, at parity with the United States, even though Washington's partners have minimal nuclear forces of their own.

[312]

This kind of thinking becomes more powerful if we accept that military power—especially nuclear weapons—is losing its relevance in a world dominated by information technology and characterized by greater transparency, mutual understanding, and ever-broadening interdependence. Conversely, it seems unhistorical if not naive to assume that aggression and the feelings that weapons induce—fascination as well as fear—will disappear because of changes in our material-spiritual environment. Even if most Americans and Russians become enlightened, may not some rogues appear who try to play by the old game? If one side suddenly produces an extra 100 or 1,000 atomic bombs, may this not engender some special bargaining power even though rationally it remains vulnerable to a counterblow?

Leaving such questions for the future, the record indicates that the Kremlin and the White House can probably be trusted to abide by their arms control and other obligations so long as each believes its interests will best be served thereby. Arms controls that are militarily asymmetrical will probably be spurned unless they include offsetting trade-offs in other domains.

If each thinks that a particular arms control arrangement serves as a tool to enhance its survival and prosperity, enlightened self-interest dictates faithful adherence to this accord unless underlying conditions change a great deal. If the Soviet or U.S. government succumbs to myopia and wishful thinking, the prospect of immediate gains may blind it to long-term enhancement of intrinsic interests. Each side may try to go it alone, trusting in its superior power unfettered by negotiated constraints. As the decision tree in Appendix I shows, however, each superpower might be better advised to maintain a cooperative approach than attempt to overwhelm the other, only to find that this approach backfires.

Even if both sides want coordinated solutions, they face deep problems: How does one contain military technology when experts disagree how it may evolve? For example, how does one evaluate the utility of lasers and stealth aircraft in an age when nuclear exchanges would be suicidal? How to constrain dual-use technologies with legal constructs? How to bind two powers in a world where other countries, large and small, are acquiring mass destruction weapons? What is the trade-off between secrets lost through on-site inspection and security gained?

Today's nuclear armed rivals have reason to manage their engagement so as to avoid self-destructive actions. If either side could gain a decisive technological breakthrough or alliance reversal, we would have to expect a short life span for many arms accords. But in today's superpower competition—for better or worse—a meaningful "upper hand" is probably not attainable.

[313]

Preventive arms control measures, history and common sense suggest, are more feasible than corrective therapy. East and West have agreed—probably to mutual advantage—to limit arms in Antarctica, outer space, and the seabeds; they have agreed to severe restraints on ABM and certain other weapons; they have attempted to halt nuclear proliferation. Facing at least some of the broader challenges of modern technology, they have also agreed to limit further depletion of the ozone layer. Granted that such measures are extremely difficult to negotiate and implement, they may enhance the self-interest of East, West, and South more than unfettered competition.

Notes

1. Gloria Duffy, "Conditions That Affect Arms Control Compliance," in Alexander George, Philip J. Farley, and Alexander Dallin, eds., *U.S.-Soviet Security Cooperation: Achievements, Failures, Lessons* (New York: Oxford University Press, 1988), 270–92 at 270.

2. On German-Soviet military cooperation, see sources cited in Robert M. Slusser and Jan F. Triska, comps., *A Calendar of Soviet Treaties, 1917–1957* (Stanford, CA: Stanford University Press, 1959), 403–12.

3. John W. Spanier and Joseph L. Nogee, *The Politics of Disarmament: A Study in Soviet-American Gamesmanship* (New York: Praeger, 1962).

4. Annex II of the 1936 Montreux Convention excludes aircraft carriers from the categories of capital ships permitted to transit the Straits under specified conditions. The reason aircraft carriers are not allowed to transit has nothing to do with their tonnage or whether they make use of their aircraft while in transit, as suggested in Christos L. Rozakis and Petros N. Stagos, *The Turkish Straits*, IX. *International Straits of the World*, ed. Gerard J. Mangone (Dordrecht: Martinus Nijhoff, 1987), 54–55, 108–10. The authors do, however, argue persuasively the political backdrop to Turkey's permissiveness.

Soviet practice has probably violated Article 12 of the convention as well, for it limits submarine egress from the Black Sea to cases in which the vessels are to be repaired in dockyards outside the Black Sea.

For a detailed analysis of the burdens placed on Soviet naval movements by the Montreux Convention, see Gordon McCormick, "Soviet Strategic Aims and Capabilities in the Mediterranean," *Adelphi Papers*, no. 229 (Spring 1988), 32–48, notes 4–7.

5. Author's interviews with responsible officials in the Turkish Ministry of Foreign Affairs, Ankara, in 1971. British and U.S. officials interviewed in Ankara in 1971 and in Washington in later years also showed no disposition to rock the boat of the Montreux Convention.

6. V. Serkov, "Pravovoi rezhim chernomorskikh prolivov," *Morskoi sbornik* (Summer 1975): 86, quoted in Alvin Z. Rubinstein, *Soviet Policy toward Turkey, Iran, and Afghanistan* (New York: Praeger, 1982), 45, emphasis added.

7. Raymond L. Garthoff, *Détente and Confrontation* (Washington, DC: Brookings Institution, 1985), 76–83 at 81.

8. See George H. Quester, "Missiles in Cuba, 1970," *Foreign Affairs* 49, no. 3 (April 1971): 493–506; also Walter C. Clemens, Jr., *The Superpowers and Arms Control* (Lexington, MA: Lexington Books, 1973), 152, notes 38 and 39.

9. See also the more detailed account and notes in Clemens, *The Superpowers and Arms Control*, pp. 18–21.

10. Hans J. Morgenthau charged that "it is peculiar to the Soviet approach to negotiated settlements to enter sometimes into such settlements with the intention not to honor them." See his article, "Changes and Chances in American-Soviet Relations," *Foreign Affairs* 49, no. 3 (April 1971): 429–41 at 440–41.

11. The October 1963 understanding affirmed the intentions of the United States and USSR "not to station in outer space any objects carrying nuclear weapons or other kinds of weapons of mass destruction." Two forms of "stationing" were mentioned: placing weapons in orbit around the earth and installing them on celestial bodies. See Walter C. Clemens, Jr., *Outer Space and Arms Control* (Cambridge: MIT Center for Space Research, 1966), 60–61. The 1967 outer space treaty also banned placing "in orbit around the earth any objects carrying" mass destruction weapons.

12. See Stephen M. Meyer, "Space and Military Planning," in William J. Durch, ed., *National Interests and the Military Uses of Space* (Cambridge, MA: Ballinger, 1984), 61–88 at 78.

13. Soviet aide-mémoire dated January 29, 1984, and State Department reply dated January 31, 1984, in *Survival* 26, no. 3 (May/June 1984), which also excerpts a State Department fact sheet summarizing Reagan's classified "Report on Soviet Noncompliance with Arms Control Agreements," sent to Congress on January 23, 1984.

14. Matthew L. Wald, "Errors Cut Safety Margin in Bomb Tests," *The New York Times*, February 17, 1989.

15. Texts of the U.S., Soviet, and U.K. declarations are in *Documents on Disarmament 1964* (Washington, DC: U.S. Arms Control and Disarmament Agency, 1965), 165–71. The U.S. commitment was for four years; the Soviet, for "the next few years."

16. See Sidney N. Graybeal and Michael Krepon, "Making Better Use of the Standing Consultative Commission," *International Security* 10, no. 2 (Fall 1985): 183–99.

17. *Military Implications of the Treaty on the Limitation of Strategic Offensive Arms and Protocol Thereto (SALT II Treaty)*, Hearings before the Committee on Armed Services, U.S. Senate, July-October 1979 (Washington, DC: U.S. Government Printing Office, 1979), pt. 3, p. 1018.

18. White House letter to the Honorable Thomas P. O'Neill, Jr., Speaker of the House of Representatives, dated October 10, 1984. The unclassified version of the report runs fifteen single-spaced pages.

19. Letter to Speaker of the House dated December 23, 1985.

20. See Allan Krass and Catherine Girrier, *Disproportionate Response: American Policy and Alleged Soviet Treaty Violations* (Cambridge, MA: Union of Concerned Scientists, 1987), 24–26; see also Stuart D. Goldman, *Verification: Soviet Compliance with Arms Control Agreements* (Washington, DC: Congressional Research Service, August 1, 1986).

21. See *The New York Times*, September 14, 1981, p. A1, and the more formal *Special Report to Congress No. 98*, Alexander M. Haig (Washington, DC: U.S. Department of State, March 22, 1982); also U.S. Department of Defense, Defense Intelligence Agency, *Soviet Biological Warfare Threat* (Washington, DC: U.S. Government Printing Office, 1986).

22. Joan W. Nowicke and Matthew Messelson, "Yellow Rain: A Palynological Analysis," *Nature* 209, no. 5965 (May 17, 1984): 205–6; letters by Peter S. Ashton and others in *Science* 222 (October 28, 1983): 366, 368. For a broader picture, see Philip M. Boffey, "Evidence Is Fading as U.S. Investigates Use of 'Yellow Rain,' " *The New York Times*, May 15, 1984, pp. A1, B6. Counterevidence is summarized in Thomas D. Seelye et al., "Yellow Rain," *Scientific American* 253, no. 3 (September 1983): 128 ff. For a review of pros and cons, see letters to *The Atlantic* (January 1986): 12 ff., replying to Peter Pringle, "Political Science," in ibid. (October 1985).

A U.S. government team scouring Southeast Asia from late 1983 to late 1985 was unable to find evidence supporting charges of Soviet and Vietnamese chemical warfare. On the team's hitherto classified reports, see *Washington Post*, August 30, 1987, and *The New York Times*, August 31, 1987.

23. *The New York Times*, July 15, 1986, p. C8; and editorial, in ibid., September 20, 1986.

24. Arkady N. Shevchenko, *Breaking with Moscow* (New York: A. A. Knopf, 1985), 174.

25. *The New York Times*, September 20, 1986, editorial.

26. Elisa D. Harris, "The Biological and Toxin Weapons Convention," in Albert Carnesale and Richard N. Haass, eds., *Superpower Arms Control* (Cambridge, MA: Ballinger, 1987), 191–219 at 208.

27. Brezhnev offered in March 1982 and again in May 1982 not to deploy additional SS-20s against Europe so long as the United States did not deploy intermediate-range missiles in Europe. Several months after he spoke the USSR activated a few SS-20 groups within range of Europe, but their construction was already under way when the moratorium was offered. This practice was permitted under the counting rules that evolved during SALT I. The moratorium was reaffirmed by Andropov in December 1982 and again in 1983; it was revoked in December 1983 after U.S. INF deployment began. See Garthoff, *Détente and Confrontation*, pp. 884–85.

28. Gerard Smith, *Doubletalk: The Story of SALT I* (Garden City, NY: Doubleday, 1980), 468–69.

29. Krass and Girrier, *Disproportionate Response*, p. 65.

30. It appeared that the Krasnoyarsk installation was not hardened, would not be able to operate at the correct frequency for battle management, and had no independent power-generating capacity. See *The New York Times*, September 9, 1987, pp. A1, 6; September 20, 1987, p. E3; and Jim Moody, congressman from Wisconsin, "A Visit to Krasnoyarsk," *Christian Science Monitor*, October 5, 1987, p. 14. For historical background, see Sayre Stevens, "Ballistic Missile Defense in the Soviet Union," *Current History* 84, no. 504 (October 1985): 313–16, 344–47.

31. Much of the following analysis is based on Krass and Girrier, *Disproportionate Response*, pp. 33–46; see also Walter C. Clemens, Jr., "*Glasnost* on the Arms Front," *Christian Science Monitor*, September 24, 1987, p. 13. On Krasnoyarsk and related problems, see James A. Schear, "Arms Control Treaty Compliance: Buildup to a Breakdown?" *International Security* 10, no. 2 (Fall 1985): 141–82 at 154–59.

32. Other analysts, however, continued to see Krasnoyarsk and other Soviet radar developments as threatening and as significant violations of the ABM Treaty. See "ABM Antics," *Wall Street Journal* editorial, September 9, 1987, p. 32; and William V. Kennedy, "Radar Enigma," *Christian Science Monitor*, September 24, 1987, p. 13. The "President's Unclassified Report on Soviet Noncompliance with Arms Control Agreements," December 2, 1987, expressed concern over Soviet testing and development of ABM components that could be deployed in months rather than years, the concurrent operation of air defense and ABM components, the development of modern air defense systems with possible ABM capabilities, and the demonstration of a rapid reload capability for ABM launchers. It also noted the construction of three new LPARs on the USSR's western periphery. The report inferred that "the USSR may be preparing an ABM defense of its national territory."

33. Soviet officials also offered to allow the United States to inspect two radars that some conservative senators argued violated the ABM Treaty, though the radars were situated next to an electronic installation and, some Western experts thought, were being cannibalized or used for experimental work. See Michael R. Gordon, "Soviet Offers U.S. Inspections of Additional Radar," *The New York Times*, October 28, 1987, p. A6.

34. The SS-25 may be permitted under the letter of SALT II. The targeting device of the SS-13 remains attached to the third-stage booster, whereas that of the SS-25 is mounted on a post-boost vehicle that detaches from the booster before sending the warhead on its desired trajectory. SALT II defines the targeting device as part of a missile's throw-weight. This definition permits Moscow to argue that the SS-25's *throw-weight* differs from that of the SS-13 by less than 5 percent, in compliance with the treaty, even though the *weight thrown* by the SS-25 is much greater. See Krass and Girrier, *Disproportionate Response*, pp. 52 ff.

35. See William I. Hull, *The Two Hague Conferences and Their Contributions to International Law* (Boston: For the International School of Peace, Ginn & Co., 1908), 83–85.

36. *Report of the Secretary of Defense Frank C. Carlucci to the Congress on the Amended FY1988/FY1989 Biennial Budget*, February 18, 1988 (Washington, DC: U.S. Government Printing Office, 1988), 26.

37. Sean M. Lynn-Jones, "Lulling and Stimulating Effects of Arms Control," in Albert Carnesale and Richard N. Haass, eds., *Superpower Arms Control: Setting the Record Straight* (Cambridge, MA: Ballinger, 1987), 223–73 at 238.

38. Smith, *Doubletalk*, chap. 13; Garthoff, *Détente and Confrontation*, pp. 158–68.

39. *Countdown on SALT II: The Case for Preserving SALT II Limits on U.S. and Soviet Strategic Forces* (Washington, DC: Arms Control Association, 1985), 14.

40. *The New York Times*, February 8, 1986; *Countdown on SALT II*, p. 14.

41. Statement by Deputy U.S. Representative Harold E. Stassen to the UN Disarmament Subcommittee, September 6, 1955. *Documents on Disarmament, 1945–1959*, 2 vols. (Washington, DC: U.S. Department of State, 1960), I: 510–14 at 513.

42. Smith, *Doubletalk*, p. 465; Garthoff, *Détente and Confrontation*, pp. 151–55.

43. G. Trofimenko in *Voprosy istorii*, no. 11 (1983), cited in Garthoff, *Détente and Confrontation*, p. 826.

44. Michael R. Gordon, "New Measure Seen for Soviet A-test," *The New York Times*, November 4, 1985, p. A13; idem, "CIA Changes Way That It Measures Soviet Atom Tests," *The New York Times*, April 2, 1986, p. A1; Len Ackland, "Testing—Who Is Cheating Whom?" *Bulletin of the Atomic Scientists* (October 1986): 9–11.

45. Krass and Girrier, *Disproportionate Response*, pp. 23–24.

46. For observations by members of the Arms Control Association, see Charles Mohr in *The New York Times*, February 9, 1985.

47. Akhromeev called the Reagan administration interpretations of the ABM treaty a "deliberate deceit." TASS, October 18, 1985.

48. For the heavily documented analysis by Senator Sam Nunn, see *Congressional Record* 133, no. 38 (March 11, 1987): 1–15; Abraham D. Sofaer, legal adviser to the State Department, comments at pp. 14–15. Mr. Nunn's analysis continues in ibid., nos. 39 and 40 (March 12 and 13, 1987). A principal author of the ABM Treaty maintains that the treaty was intended to restrict systems based on new technologies such as those being cultivated in the SDI. See Raymond L. Garthoff, *Policy versus the Law: The Reinterpretation of the ABM Treaty* (Washington, DC: Brookings Institution, 1987).

49. Agreed Statement D of the ABM Treaty attempted to set out guidelines for future systems based on "other physical principles" not known at the time the treaty was drafted.

50. See Hull, *Two Hague Conferences*, pp. 84–85.

51. Dan Quayle, "INF Treaty's Dangerous Vagueness," *The Wall Street Journal*, February 8, 1988 (op-ed). For a more detailed statement of Quayle's reservations and the views of other senators and senate witnesses, see Committee on Armed Services, U.S. Senate, *NATO Defense and the INF Treaty* (Washington, DC: U.S. Government Printing Office, April 1, 1988), esp. 45–54.

52. Michael R. Gordon, "Former Officials Propose Changes in Missile Pact," *The New York Times*, February 4, 1988, p. A3.

53. Michael R. Gordon, "Missile Pact's Application to Exotic Arms Debated," *The New York Times*, April 14, 1988, p. A20.

54. The following references to statements by Vorontsov and other Soviet commentators on the INF Treaty are to ratification hearings by the Preparatory Commission, Foreign Affairs Commission, Supreme Soviet, February 19, 1988 and published in *Vestnik Ministerstva Inostrannykh del SSSR*, no. 5 (March 15, 1988): 16–25.

55. Quayle in *Wall Street Journal*.

56. "The INF Treaty: Monitoring and Verification Capabilities," U.S. Senate Select Committee on Intelligence (Washington, DC: U.S. Government Printing Office, March 21, 1988), 8, 12, 13. The most serious question arising from the INF was that there were contracts awarded by the U.S. Navy to convert GLCMs to SLCMs, implying that 145 GLCMs had not been properly reported and destroyed.

57. For the theory, see David A. Lax and James K. Sebenius, *The Manager as*

[317]

Negotiator: Bargaining for Cooperation and Competitive Gain (New York: Free Press, 1986), chap. 5.

58. See also Steven J. Brams, *Superpower Games* (New Haven, CT: Yale University Press, 1985), 112–15.

59. For background, see Jan F. Triska, ed., *Dominant Powers and Subordinate States* (Durham, NC: Duke University Press, 1986).

Appendix I: A Nonmyopic Rationale for Arms Control Compliance

At first glance game theory suggests that two rivals would be well advised to evade arms control restrictions so as to minimize damage and maximize possible gain. Whether the problem is seen as "prisoner's dilemma" or, more realistically, as "negotiator's dilemma" (in which communications between players are possible), the rational strategy for each rival is to "defect" and not "cooperate." If one cooperates and the other defects, the cooperator will suffer terrible consequences and his cynical opponent will score a big gain. Therefore it is wiser for each to defect, even though that course brings on losses for both sides and prevents them from achieving mutual gains.

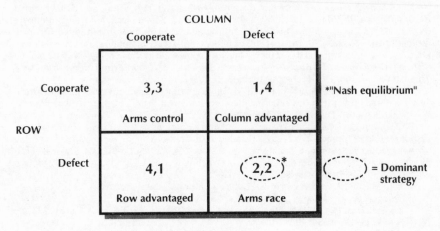

Figure 10.1 Compliance as Prisoner's Dilemma ·

The structure of this game is shown in Figure 10.1. This approach, however, is short-sighted. Defection is motivated by myopia—the prospect of immediate gain—and by fear that the rival may defect. Defection is myopic because in today's superpower arms competition a meaningful "upper hand" is probably not attainable by intensified arms

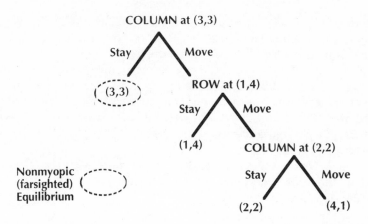

Figure 10.2   A Compliance Decision Tree

development or by cheating on arms control agreements. A game tree analysis of the decision-making process shows a paradoxical outcome.

Starting from a mutually advantageous arms accord, one super-power actor—"Column"—chooses to move from (3,3) to (1,4) hoping to gain an advantage over its rival "Row." But Row will not choose to remain at (1,4) because this is its worst outcome; Row moves instead to (2,2), its second worst outcome. Both players have now landed at (2,2)—a "Nash equilibrium" in which neither side has an incentive to depart unilaterally because it would immediately do worse or at least not better if it moved. Column remains at its second worst outcome rather than moving to its very worst (4,1). The treaty now collapses and gives way to an intensified arms race.

If Column uses the "Backward Induction" mode of analysis, however, it will look ahead and discover that the mutually cooperative outcome (3,3) is a Nonmyopic equilibrium. Working backward, we see that Column, given the choice between its worst outcome (4,1) and its second worst, should choose (2,2). This effectively cuts the bottom branch to (4,1). Row, given the choice between (2,2) and its worst outcome (1,4), will also pick (2,2). This effectively cuts the (1,4) branch. As a result the game comes down to a choice for Column between its second worst outcome (2,2) and its second best (3,3). Logically, Column chooses (3,3), thus cutting the top "move" branch.

In sum, if one superpower uses foresight to trace the ramifications of its actions, it will not defect but continue to cooperate in adhering to the arms limitation accord (perhaps pushing its interpretation to the limits

[319]

acceptable to its rival). The other superpower, if it looks ahead, will reach the same conclusion. Thus in far-sightedness there is a remedy to the instability in arms control regimes from the myopic tendency to defect.

This decision tree analysis seems to harmonize with the realities—probable payoffs and values—of the late twentieth century. But if some mode of cheating could be discovered having a truly decisive effect on the immediate ability of one side to dictate to or wipe out the other, myopia could become far-sightedness and the logic of the decision tree would be cut short.

This appendix owes a great deal to the more complex arguments found in Brams, *Superpower Games*, and to research by Michael D. Libenson of Boston University.

IV.
Creating the Future

11
Alternative Futures:
Détente, Confrontation,
Transformation?

Can we control our own destinies? Tolstoi noted the paradox: Individuals feel free—that they have options and can choose among them. But others see these persons as limited, their possibilities determined by genetics, nurture, and environment.[1] Americans and Russians as peoples even in recent decades have seen their horizons as unlimited: each believed that if it only wished, it could move in any direction over its vast continent; expand abroad; even fly to Mars. In the 1980s, however, many Americans and Russians (like individuals in middle age) doubted their country's prowess and became deeply aware of its limitations. Some outsiders saw the "superpowers" as blind giants—perhaps as crippled giants. Marshall Shulman has compared them with dinosaurs and asked whether they could adapt to changing conditions.[2]

Looking at the rhythms of Soviet-U.S. relations since 1945—long periods of confrontations interrupted by hopeful but brief moments of détente—Tolstoi (joined by a Greek chorus) might argue that the superpowers are predestined to tragedy. The general secretary and American president may think they are free, but forces larger than they cast whole nations on the waves of Fate.

Can the dinosaurs learn to adapt to the challenges facing their societies and the world? Both societies have gone far toward aborting their ideals and squandering their assets, both moral and physical.[3] Their global influence is declining and their own environments despoiled. To some extent this was because of their competition with one another, for this rivalry distracted them from attending to other needs. Some of their failures derived from the same sources that made for achievement—in the Soviet case, a centralized capacity to command. Both societies suffered from hubris and overreaching; the United States had become "soft" and complacent; the USSR was exhausted. Both suffered from the same intangibles ascribed by Gorbachev in 1986 to many Soviet diplomats: preconceptions, smugness, narrow-mindedness, arrogance.[4]

The obstacles to recovery and successful adaptation are enormous, but some conditions are favorable. Both societies still possess enormous material assets—more than any other countries in the world—and deep intellectual and spiritual resources on which to draw. Regardless of what Tolstoi said about determinism, individuals ultimately make history. Individuals and groups in the United States and USSR might still develop and carry out action plans that would help their societies (and perhaps others) to cope with domestic problems and global challenges that no society can resolve alone.

Renewed Détente

Before surveying alternative futures, let us first review the tremendous changes that transformed Soviet policies in the 1980s, for they illustrate how individuals can shape events. Gorbachev's multiple revolutions profoundly altered the thrust of Soviet policies at home and abroad. The "tendencies most useful to global problems" (as set out in chapter 2) came to the fore after 1985, reversing the policy trends of the previous five and more years. The new regime worked out a new approach to foreign policy premised on interdependence and mutual security. Support for this concept—in word but also in deed—climbed to the top of the ladder while "inversion" and "forward strategy" moved to the bottom. Limited collaboration with the West, more aspiration than reality in the early 1980s, became a fact of life, one that steadily increased both within the USSR and in international affairs. The new leadership portrayed its first steps toward arms control and trade as part of a strategy that would adapt to and profit from the realities of an integral but still contradictory world. These departures in foreign policy derived from and were consistent with Gorbachev's domestic reforms.

Autarky, the new thinking asserted, is possible only for agrarian countries that do not mind falling behind; the USSR should try to raise its technology to world standards, depending both on self-reliance and interaction with the outside world. Forward strategy seemed to play almost no role in Gorbachev's policies; he seemed intent on eliminating asymmetrical advantages that either the Warsaw Pact or NATO might possess for bullying each other. He slowly reduced Soviet commitments to leftist regimes in the Third World.

What forces brought on the détente of the late 1980s?

Domestic Politics and Economics

Domestic factors within the USSR and the United States encouraged the détente of the late 1980s. Severe economic problems in both countries— but especially the USSR—pressed for curtailing defense expenditures.[5] Soviet economic growth and per capita consumption figures showed a steady decline from 1966 to 1985 and beyond.[6] The Gorbachev regime concluded that the entire Soviet way of life needed to be restructured. It needed no "foreign bogey," as Stalin did, to justify sacrifice; instead the new leadership wanted a relaxed international atmosphere in which to carry out domestic reform and move toward closer engagement with multinational business.

Ideology was reshaped to downplay class struggle and to emphasize global problems needing global solutions. Instead of pretentious claims to having created a science of globalistika, the Kremlin took sober note of its environmental as well as economic difficulties and the painful connections between them. "Kto kovo?" apparently ceased to be a fundamental guide to foreign policy.

Détente gained from glasnost'. Greater openness at home makes it easier to pursue greater openness abroad. Freer dialogue at home fits well with more dialogue abroad; less coercion and secrecy at home with less coercion and secrecy abroad.

The new foreign policy drew little serious criticism, even from ideological puritans and vigilant members of the military-industrial complex. The new thinking about the world, however, was dependent on the fate of domestic perestroika—resisted actively or passively by thousands of Party, industrial, and government bureaucrats whose privileges it threatened and by the amorphous masses accustomed to low but secure pay for little work. The main supporters of the new thinking were intellectuals—a necessary bulwark for modernization but hardly a decisive force in everyday politics.

America's domestic situation also pushed for détente. The cycles of American politics converged with Reagan's wish to be recorded as a man of peace. Tired from half a decade of confrontational polemics and perceiving that Moscow yearned for a reprieve, Americans were ready to shift back from belligerence toward isolationism or some form of political idealism.[7] They and the president welcomed a chance to relax tensions with Moscow. Reagan could say that it was his bargaining from strength that reformed the evil empire and made its new leader a "friend."

Economic troubles reinforced these trends. The American GNP remained twice the size of any other single country's but had been outstripped by the Common Market. More important, the United States had also become the world's largest debtor. Inflation and unemployment were low, but confidence in the dollar and the stock market dropped sharply in 1987. In one domain after another—cars, electronics, soybeans—American hegemony had declined or evaporated. Whether or not defense spending played the main or only a supporting role, curtailing military expenditures and reorienting research efforts into civilian technology might ameliorate present problems and generate future opportunities. Détente made limits on defense spending more palatable. And many American capitalists perked up at the prospect of penetrating the immense Soviet market.

The World System

The international milieu was also favorable to détente. Other NATO and Warsaw Pact governments and peoples welcomed the INF and other signs that their grass would not be crushed by the stomping of elephants (or, as Shulman called them, dinosaurs). Whereas China in the late 1970s urged the West not to be taken in by Soviet blandishments, Beijing in the late 1980s was itself exploring détente with Moscow while attempting to hold on to a shaky entente with the West.

Moscow's Third World clients except for Vietnam and Cuba were unstable. None showed any deep affection for Soviet citizens or attachment to Moscow's leadership of the progressive forces. Because of its clients' willful or inept policies the USSR might be drawn onto a collision course with the United States. The Kremlin seemed to conclude that it should cultivate bourgeois governments in the Third World such as those of India or Latin America rather than the socialist-in-name regimes of "socialist orientation." If the West would not turn these countries *against* the USSR, the Kremlin appeared ready to pull back.

Washington was satisfied to show that Soviet power could be driven back or undermined in Kabul and elsewhere. But other American interventions—military, diplomatic, "covert"—failed in Lebanon, Iran, Nicaragua, El Salvador, and Panama. Washington could point only to one clear success: Grenada, though Reagan also claimed some credit for belated support of democracy in the Philippines and South Korea. Meanwhile, Israel was becoming an increasingly truculent and trouble-some partner, and Egypt loomed as an ever more fragile client. In short, there were few obstacles to détente arising from America's ties with the developing world; rather, there was an increasing interest in both Washington and Moscow to foster accommodations that might reduce tensions for all parties—for example, in Angola-Namibia-South Africa.

Soviet-American détente did not depend on a shared threat from a rising third party. Still, both superpowers feared catalytic war brought on by their bold clients in the Middle East. Therefore both Moscow and Washington were tending to favor accommodation in the region, though disagreeing on the proper role for Moscow in the peace process. The superpowers seemed also to fear the spillover effects of the Persian Gulf war and made some effort to terminate it—the Kremlin tiptoeing so as not to alienate either Iran or Iraq. Moscow began to normalize relations not only with Israel but with the Gulf sheikdoms.

The Kremlin and White House continued efforts to stop nuclear proliferation. And after Chernobyl the USSR proposed various ways to strengthen the IAEA's regulatory as well as antiproliferation efforts.

These trends in world affairs helped détente—and were helped by it—but they seem not to have been necessary or sufficient conditions for it. Conversely, experience showed that disturbances in the world system could kill détente and put the superpowers on a renewed collision course.

The evolution of international institutions has had contradictory but marginal effects on Soviet-U.S. relations to date. Whereas Soviet diplo-mats once performed as "Mr. Nyet" in response to pro-Western majorities at the United Nations (a style now condemned by Gorbachev[8]), in recent decades the United States has distrusted and often opposed the Third World consensus in the United Nations and its Specialized Agencies—Washington casting many more vetoes than the USSR.[9] The Reagan administration distanced itself from the International Court of Justice just as the USSR was calling for more use of the world court. The Reagan-Gorbachev détente was little affected by the strengths or weaknesses of international organization.

Bilateral Issues

The tsars at times aligned with Berlin and Vienna and, later, with Paris and London, but the USSR has never enjoyed such a special relationship with a major power except for 1939–45 and an unsatisfying honeymoon with China in the mid-1950s. The Soviet Union has found itself in the uncomfortable role of wanting to compete against the United States while demanding the prerogatives of equality or even hinting at a desire for duopoly.

Whereas Brezhnev in the early 1970s hoped to import Western technology to modernize Soviet technology *without* opening Soviet society to the winds of change, Gorbachev has wanted to shake things up within the Soviet Union and to push the country into the "contradictory but integral" world of the late twentieth century. This approach helped trade and détente to reinforce each other.

Both sides have been interested in pursuing their own visions of low politics: the Soviets accenting scientific exchanges and space ventures; the Americans, exchanges of information and people—even thousands of high school students. The Americans have agreed to be more open with their technology, and the Soviets have consented to frank analysis of human rights in both countries.

Domestic and international forces converged in the bilateral issues dividing and joining the superpowers. The INF, START, and other arms control negotiations focused on weapons, but they also reflected the economic and political pressures on each government. If substantial progress could be made in arms control, it promised some relief from the human and material costs of arms buildups and occasional confrontations; buttressed by a broader relaxation of tensions, arms control could lead to a world in which the threat of military force played a lesser role.

From 1899 through the 1980s the Kremlin's arms control policies were shaped first by strategic-military considerations: Russia's rulers sought to weaken or neutralize their foes' present or future advantages while strengthening Russia's special assets. Only when confronted with a fait accompli of NATO's INF deployment did Soviet negotiators return to the table and make a deal. The P2 missile in particular seems to have worried Kremlin planners and induced them to sacrifice many more missiles and warheads than the West to eliminate America's ground-based INF.

But strategic-military determinism was not the complete explanation of Soviet concessions on arms control. Paradoxes abound: superpower arsenals are more lethal than ever, but according to the new thinking, they play a declining role in world affairs. Soviet strategic parity with the United

States, Gorbachev says, does not guarantee peace; force levels, he says, should be reduced—to some extent even unilaterally. Having achieved Soviet superiority in some domains, Gorbachev offers asymmetrical cuts to spur negotiations. Faced with small but significant nuclear arsenals in Britain, France, and China, Gorbachev says Moscow can ignore them for the time being and proceed with Soviet-American arms reductions, even though the USSR's relative position vis-à-vis potential adversaries is weakened. The Soviet leaders seem worried about their technological inferiority, but they open their military installations for outside scrutiny—not merely the required INF sites but the radar and laser installations, which Westerners then judged as relatively primitive.

Is Moscow, then, driven by some form of economic determinism, bending to arms control and détente as preconditions for modernizing the Soviet economy? This explanation comes close to Gorbachev's own words: that the character of Soviet foreign policy is dictated by the need to restructure the economy. Nothing so diminishes ambition as limited capability. The Kremlin's ambitions to exert a powerful influence in the world arena and play the role of superpower are subverted by the weaknesses of its material base.

The cynical explanations based on strategic-military and economic determinism do not capture the complexity of the situation. There is also an idealistic side to Gorbachev's worldview that we have no right to ignore. His new thinking says to place human needs above class, nation, or race; discard stereotypes; and learn from each other. The details of his program in effect apply the concept of value creation to world affairs. It is a visionary worldview but one rooted in enlightened self-interest.

Thus the détente of the late 1980s seemed to have a stronger foundation than did its predecessors. Interests had converged; useful lessons had been learned; expectations had become more realistic.[10] There was reason to hope that it might be continued and expanded into the 1990s, but experience had often shown that détente is a fragile blossom, vulnerable to chilling winds from either country or the global arena.

Three broad futures were possible: (1) reversion to cold war and confrontation; (2) continued moderation of East-West tensions and their gradual transformation into a more cooperative relationship; or (3) movement toward a system of complex interdependence. The likelihood of each alternative future would hinge on the interaction of three broad factors: those endogenous to the Soviet system, those arising from the world system, and those specifically related to Soviet-American relations.

[329]

Renewed Cold War and Confrontation

Détente is French for "trigger." In the Middle Ages détente was the bolt of the crossbow; when pulled, it released tension. This led to the second meaning of *détente*—the relaxation of political tensions. The Russian term *razriadka* also means the discharge of tensions, electric or political. In French or in Russian, the release achieved by détente is a momentary effect. So it has been in recent history.

Détente is not robust. Because both sides are still wary and hostile, the process of détente cannot endure developments that make one or both sides believe they must act either to win or to prevent zero-sum outcomes.

It is difficult to maintain Soviet-U.S. relations in a delicate equilibrium juggling competition and cooperation. It is easier for uneasy rivals to lapse into renewed cold war competition than to transform their relationship so that cooperation prevails over conflict.

Previous détentes have wilted because of blows from many directions, many of them unanticipated and unsought by either party. The 1955 Spirit of Geneva, for example, wilted as Eisenhower was incapacitated by a heart attack, leaving John Foster Dulles to face off against his fellow hawk, V. M. Molotov, at the Geneva Foreign Ministers Meeting; by the realization that the Kremlin was arming Egypt and moving actively to displace the West in the Third World; and by the Polish and Hungarian events of late 1956, which occurred simultaneously with the Suez war and Russian threats against Egypt's invaders. All these external complications multiplied the objective difficulties to reaching accords on arms control, divided Germany, East-West trade, and other exchange programs.[11]

The détente initiated in the late 1980s could also collapse because of developments within each country, the world system, and in bilateral relations.

Domestic Politics and Economics

Both superpowers experience cycles in their domestic lives that affect their foreign relations. In the United States there is an alternation between expansion (usually under Democrats) and consolidation (under Republicans) and foreign policies of liberation/belligerency and isolation/détente. The USSR, for its part, seems to alternate between militancy and moderation, usually but not always in tandem at home and abroad—each beat usually lasting four to six years. Thus 1917–21: war communism; 1922–27: NEP; 1928–33: war scare and industrialization; 1934–39: collective security, 1939–41: militancy and nonaggression (a phase interrupted "early" by Hitler); 1941–46: grand alliance; 1947–52: cold war; 1953–58: thaw; 1958–62: Berlin and Cuba; 1963–67: Spirit of Moscow and Glassboro; 1968–70: Czechoslovakia (a second two-year period); 1971–75: "détente"; 1976–84: renewed cold war (with a brief respite for SALT II); 1985–?: renewed détente.

It is by no means certain that such cycles have existed in the past or that they will exist in the future. If they are real, their causes are multiple and poorly understood—as is their duration. Some observers see very long cycles in Western civilization, as long as forty or fifty years; some believe that America's cycles correspond roughly to the two terms American presidents may serve; Soviet cycles seem to last four to six years, though much shorter and longer periods have also occurred. Granted that cycles are difficult to analyze and understand, there is sufficient evidence of their reality to warrant great caution about the duration of any détente.

It appears that Democratic expansionism and liberation/belligerency under Kennedy overlapped in the early 1960s with Soviet militancy under Khrushchev. The usual pattern of Republican moderation emerged in the late Reagan years and overlapped with a new wave of Soviet moderation/ conciliation. The two sides, of course, can be out of phase—one bent on détente, the other on expansion. Perhaps Gorbachev's policies will break with the pattern of the past, but if precedent holds, Moscow may well turn left once more in the early 1990s.

Gorbachev's perestroika risks chaos without reward. If it fails and he falls, the movement toward better relations with the United States will likely collapse. Thoroughgoing reforms and an unprecedented openness are probably needed to bring new life to the Soviet system. Before the reforms yield material results, there will be a time of troubles: declining production as managers and workers try to adjust to new ways; ethnic revolts as long-repressed minorities make use of the new freedoms; weakened political discipline as the "blank spots" of Party history are filled in and all the idols are smashed—even Lenin.

There is a strong chance that the USSR will continue its economic slide relative to other technologically advanced nations; that it will lack parity to cooperate with America and other countries in nonmilitary endeavors; that its decline will lead to the fall of the perestroika team and/ or push the Kremlin to drop "interdependence/mutual security" and revert to one of the hard-line approaches adopted after earlier periods of moderation, as in 1928–33, 1947–53, or 1976/79–84.

In consequence of internal troubles the USSR may again act like a cornered Bear, standing aside as other nations flourish in a deepening network of global interdependence and perhaps lashing out with its remaining asset—brute strength.[12] The Soviet leaders may again want a foreign bogey to justify their ham-handed oppression and "explain" Russia's low living standards; they may even want foreign adventures—perhaps another Angola or Ethiopia—to show that communism still thrives and grows.

America's internal development could aggravate these trends. If Russia seems to betray détente—as in the late 1970s—a conservative backlash may rise in America. And if the United States fails to meet the new challenges from Europe and the Pacific Rim, or if revolution shakes Central America, Americans may scapegoat Russia and Soviet communism. Frustrated by their own imperial decline, Americans might want to reactivate the element of power in which they still hold some aces: high-tech wonder weapons and power projection from aircraft carriers and overseas bases such as Subic Bay and Diego Garcia. They might also call on allies to shape up or stand alone—all of which would require a target: the still threatening Soviet evil empire.

Domestic pressures of these kinds need not assert themselves tomorrow to break the movement toward moderating East-West tensions. They could lie low for some years and then hit with greater force as the evidence mounts that perestroika is not saving Soviet communism and that America's imperial and economic decline has not been arrested. These pressures may coast and then rise with other forces to generate another cycle of belligerency supplanting one of inward-looking consolidation.

The World System

Unforeseen developments in the Third World and Eastern Europe have derailed earlier détentes and could do so again. Soviet support for its Arab clients helped to unsettle East-West relations in 1955 and during the Arab-Israeli wars of 1967 and 1973. Soviet leaders have sometimes thought that the West should accept loss of its imperial influence as an inevitable trend of history, but Washington, Paris, and London saw things differently. Indeed, they often deny that the Kremlin has any legitimate role to play in the Third World. This dialectic has kept the pot boiling, as Moscow has little motive to endorse settlements denying Soviet participation.

Eastern Europe presents the greatest threat to continued moderation of tensions. The more Soviet-Western relations improve, the greater the likelihood that Eastern Europeans may jump at the chance for freedom.

Their hopes will be fanned by liberalization within the USSR, by Gorbachev's ostensible aversion to "command" and coercion, by European arms reductions, and by more East-West trade. Hoping that the Kremlin will not or cannot crush them again militarily, one or more Eastern European peoples may overthrow their own Communist leaders, or native Communists may declare their nonalignment or independence from Moscow. Whether or not Washington encourages such movements, the Kremlin might decide that maintenance of communism in Eastern Europe has greater priority than good relations with the West. It may hope too that as in 1968–71, détente can be quickly restored after a not-too-bloody use of force in its sphere—the Socialist Commonwealth.

If ethnic unrest rises in the USSR or if rival political "fronts" or "associations" are tolerated there, such developments would also encourage Eastern European separatism.

Perhaps the USSR will acquiesce in the defection of one or more Eastern European regimes. In some respects they have become a burden to Moscow. If Russia turns deeply inward and does not feel threatened by the West, perhaps it would permit an "Austrian" model in Eastern Europe. Indeed, one political-military exercise at Boston University suggested that if Soviet internal problems become acute simultaneously with Eastern European drives for independence, the Kremlin might concentrate on restoring order within the USSR even if this meant losses abroad.[13]

But affairs might not work out to please the rebels. Especially if things go poorly in Soviet domestic reforms, the Kremlin could not afford much laxity toward Eastern European upstarts. The Bear in an angry fit may move hard and fast, as in 1956, rather than watching and waiting, as in 1980–82. Whichever country seemed to be in the independence vanguard would be the first crushed—a sobering lesson to the others.

The Kremlin would be the more likely to act decisively because of past experience: four times the West sat still when Moscow asserted its hegemony in Eastern Europe and, after a year or two of mutual denunciation, resumed movement toward trade and détente. If Gorbachev's regime proved to be just as barbaric as its predecessors, however, this lesson would surely set limits as to how far the West would cooperate with the USSR.

Many other possible trends in the global system could worsen Soviet-U.S. relations. If a more intense and protracted war is waged between U.S.-backed insurgents and Soviet-backed regimes in Africa, the superpowers' stakes in the outcome might rise, complicating their bilateral relations. If more Third World countries opt for free-market economies and closer ties with the West, this could heighten Soviet inversion and defiance. If China or Japan become more of a military threat to Russia and still enjoy U.S.

[333]

support, ties between Moscow and Washington would suffer. If China somehow realigns with the USSR, that would sound alarms in Tokyo, Washington, and elsewhere about the need to unite against communism.

If international institutions are not strengthened or lack credibility in either Moscow or Washington, they will not be able to interpose and maintain the peace before the superpowers embark on a collision course.

If the USSR fails to adapt to the world of international commerce and trade or is spurned by GATT and the International Monetary Fund, this could contribute to Soviet inversion or even to Kremlin policies aimed at sabotaging West-West and West-South relations.

Bilateral Relations

Previous détentes have been harmed also by developments in bilateral relations. Examples are the aborted U-2 mission in 1960 and Khrushchev's response, and the refusal of Congress after SALT I to approve trade liberalization unless Moscow officially promised to relax emigration barriers.

Bilateral relations could collapse over implementation of the INF or other arms accords. As disarmament measures become more extensive, verification might become more difficult, generating incentives to cheat and suspicions of noncompliance. Such feelings may become sharper if either side "compensates" for agreed arms limitations by arms buildups in other spheres.

Obstacles to a START accord or general force reductions in Europe might be so strong that momentum toward arms control is broken. If this occurs, the achievements of INF may appear trivial and the dangers of force modernization loom as threatening. Should either side achieve a break-through in strategic defenses or battlefield lasers, it might be tempted to bully, or the other side might become more defiant, perhaps striking preemptively before the foe can exert its new leverage.

Trade and joint ventures may disappoint both sides, leaving a wake of frustration and unpaid debts rather than a growing material base of cooperation. Even if progress is moderately good in the economic realm, it might not suffice to muffle the heavy cannons of high politics.

Scientific and other exchanges could also prove disappointing. If the Soviet Union falls behind in the STR, Americans will see little point in one-sided exchanges. If swaps of high school students subvert traditional values, they might be discontinued. Even if exchange programs prove mutually useful, they may fall victim to high politics, as happened after Afghanistan.

[334]

A thousand and one factors could disrupt the best efforts of rivals to reach an armistice and promote common interests. Governments are organized to defend sovereignty, not to deplete or share it. Anarchy, Hobbes and others have taught, is the true state of nature. Attempts to build a social contract—especially between armed rival camps—might prove futile.

Transcending East-West Conflict

To prevent détente from reverting to confrontation, the relationship must be transformed so that the struggle for power is supplanted by a growing web of shared activities in which both sides find meaning and reward. Momentum toward improved relations must be maintained in both high and low politics.

Domestic Politics and Economics

The sine qua non for moderation is that the architects of perestroika remain in power and that their interests are served by expanding East-West cooperation. If the Gorbachev team were ousted, momentum toward improving East-West relations would be broken and difficult to restore.

The cycles of American politics appeared to be shifting from "enrich oneself" conservatism to new forms of idealism in the late 1980s toward curiosity and even a naive goodwill toward the Gorbachev experiment, buttressed by a desire to moderate military spending and cut budget deficits. But idealist internationalism could be cut short by a swing back toward anger and frustration over continued decline of America's global influence. "Contradictions" among Europe, Japan, and the United States could push America toward its own version of "defiant inversion."

To be sure, isolationism could moderate Soviet-U.S. relations. America might turn its anger on its erstwhile allies while quietly agreeing with Russia to curtail wasteful competition for empire and military supremacy. But another possible response would be to avoid facing the deepest causes for America's industrial and technological decline and to scapegoat Soviet communism, thus rationalizing another arms buildup to spur the economy. The White House might divert attention from domestic woes by a foreign confrontation to rally all around the flag.

Thus domestic weaknesses must be managed skillfully if each

[335]

country is to avoid the temptation to flay out at its old adversary in desperation over waning world influence. Moderating East-West tensions would have to reap domestic benefits in both the USSR and America if the processes of transformation were to continue.

The World System

All sides—the Eastern Europeans, the USSR, and the West—must deal with the problem of divided Europe with great caution and skill. The division is unnatural and has been breaking down for years. Eastern Europeans should move slowly so as to avoid provoking Soviet intervention; Westerners should show interest in Eastern Europe but avoid encouragement of revolutionary forces there; and the Kremlin should treat its imperial legacy in Eastern Europe as a Stalinist mistake that sooner or later needs to be rectified. The ideal solution would be for Eastern Europe and the USSR gradually to increase their cooperation with Western Europe. The 1988 agreement by the EEC and CMEA authorizing "bilateral" trade accords between the two organizations was a step in this direction. An "Austrian" solution could point the way.

Moderation of East-West tensions presupposes resolution of regional conflicts that have pitted Soviet and U.S.-backed forces throughout the Third World. Such confrontations need not all wind down simultaneously, but progress in ending each conflict would make it easier to perpetuate and extend improvement in American-Soviet relations.

Superpower stakes are higher in the Middle East than in most parts of the Third World. If a Middle Eastern client of either superpower is endangered, its patron will be pressed to come to the rescue. The most hopeful outcome would be that the superpowers encourage a broad settlement acceptable to the many conflicting parties in the region. Otherwise the United States will feel compelled to stand by Israel and Moscow will feel reluctant to leave the field.

Given the pressures for the old politics to continue, it is important to strengthen the peacekeeping and peacemaking functions of the United Nations. If international organization becomes more effective, leading to "recognized patterns of practice around which expectations converge,"[14] this could reduce the compulsions of the great powers to intervene in local conflicts. Many positive trends were under way in the late 1980s, including changes in Soviet policy and various proposals by Gorbachev for collective security and peacemaking.

Continued moderation of Soviet-U.S. relations also assumes that

Moscow's relations with Tokyo and Beijing remain on an even keel. If either of America's major Asian partners were threatened by the USSR— or if they became an active threat to Soviet interests—the United States would be pressured to back them up. Were there a reversal of alignments, similar pressures could fall on the Kremlin. If China or Japan became a threat to both superpowers, of course, that could drive Moscow and Washington to closer collaboration.

If superpower relations are to avoid the rollercoaster rides of previous decades, each must feel that it has little to gain by a forward advance. From Washington's standpoint this means that the U.S. alliance system must retain its ability and willingness to deter and contain Soviet expansion.

Just as important—perhaps more important—would be shared experiences in East-West-South cooperation. To make the world system stable and prosperous the superpowers should seek to supplant zero-sum striving—by themselves and others—with cooperative actions that benefit the First, Second, and Third Worlds. These actions could be in many spheres: helping to resolve regional conflicts, as in southern Africa; reducing infant mortality through programs to check dehydration; slowing fossil fuel consumption and cultivating alternative energy supplies; establishing seed banks and aquaculture farms.[15] East, West, and South could look for the kinds of three-sided cooperation existing in the 1970s when Iranian gas was piped to the USSR through lines built with European capital and technology and reimbursed by Soviet gas delivered to Europe.

Bilateral Issues

Ultimately the improvement of Soviet-U.S. relations hinges on controlling or diminishing the zero-sum rivalry of high politics and expanding the psychic and material rewards of low politics. Progress in each domain will reinforce and pave the way for greater movement in the other.

It is vital to sustain the movement toward arms control of the late 1980s. Arms control issues can inflame as well as modulate East-West tensions. Disputes over who won the most and compliance disputes could easily interrupt the movement toward arms control established in the late 1980s.

A wide range of measures are available to build on the negotiations of the late 1980s:

[337]

(1)   Exercise self-restraint, avoiding provocative behavior and threatening deployments; freeze or cut military spending.
(2)   Carry out the INF Treaty and its verification procedures.
(3)   Ratify the threshold test ban and peaceful explosions treaty; regulate or stop all nuclear tests.
(4)   Develop further confidence-building procedures to reduce fears of surprise attack in Europe.
(5)   Make the Nuclear Risk Reduction Centers and other mechanisms for communication and data exchange useful to both sides.
(6)   Tighten the nonproliferation regime with significant rewards and sanctions.
(7)   Reaffirm traditional ABM restraints.

More difficult but still feasible would be the following:

(8)   Avoid weapons modernization that mocks the INF Treaty.
(9)   Agree on a data base and move toward conventional force structures adequate for self-protection but inadequate for offense.
(10) Prepare for a worldwide elimination of chemical and biological weapon stockpiles.
(11) Proceed to cut Soviet and U.S. strategic arsenals by one-half and engage other nuclear weapons states in a plan for overall reductions.

Large-scale cuts in strategic and other arsenals should be negotiable if both sides are disposed to compromise. So long as Moscow and Washington feel compelled to make worst-case assumptions about the other, however, troublesome questions will impede arms control. As East-West trust increases, worries about loopholes, asymmetries, and breakthroughs might recede.

Both sides should avoid making arms controls more difficult—for example, by proliferating cruise missiles. Valid uses can be conceived for such weapons—especially with conventional warheads—but the long-term problems they portend outweigh their near-term utility. Such deployments also go against the spirit of the INF and other accords of the late 1980s. Given the opportunities of the new détente, the Pentagon and its Soviet counterpart should not conduct business as usual, deploying whatever technology can produce and money procure. Instead, each should study how to promote its country's security without adding to the other's insecurity. Self-restraint is needed until mutual restraint becomes negotiable.

High politics will probably benefit from positive experiences in trade, scientific, and cultural exchange. But contacts can lead to misunderstanding and contempt as well as to understanding and affection. In low politics as in high, seeking too much and going too fast could rekindle rather than relax tensions. Still, the Soviet system in the late 1980s absorbed more shocks and endured more uncertainty than would have seemed possible only a decade earlier.

Toward "Complex Interdependence"

An optimal response to global problems would be for Moscow and Washington to go beyond moderating their conflicts to building a relationship of "complex interdependence." This would require the emergence of three characteristics. First, multiple channels connect Soviet and American societies—interstate, transgovernmental, and transnational. They include not only formal foreign office connections but informal ties between governmental elites and working relationships between nongovernmental elites in banking, commerce, and science. Second, the agenda of interstate relationships consists of multiple issues not arranged in a clear or consistent hierarchy. Third, military force and its threat play a declining role in the policies of both countries—at least toward each other.[16]

In contrast to the more familiar world of power politics, the actors linked in complex interdependence do not pursue military security as their dominant goal. Instead, goals vary by issue area. The emergence of transgovernmental politics makes goals difficult to define; transnational actors increasingly pursue their own aims. Actors still bargain and make trade-offs among issues, but power resources specific to issue areas will be most relevant. International regimes and organizations help to set agendas and induce coalition-formation.[17]

It will surely take many years (if ever) for Soviet-U.S. relations to approach the kind of complex interdependence characterizing Canada and the United States. Even between these two neighbors, however, there is little political integration.[18] Loyalties are still national. There are virtually no common institutions such as link EEC members. There is some but not much coordination of policies—Canadians often balking at U.S. military activities. What does link the countries are similar political, economic and cultural institutions and even a common language, long-established habits of cooperation (including those of two world wars), a disposition toward conciliation, and a pattern of extensive trade and cross-border

[339]

investment—buttressed now by the 1988 treaty to reduce drastically tariffs and other impediments to mutual economic penetration. This situation has evolved out of cold and hot war. For much of the nineteenth century there lurked distrust and fear. Despite the vaunted disarmament treaty for the Great Lakes, each side kept additional warships nearby. As experience showed that neither side contemplated aggression, the border became truly disarmed. Still, Ottawa resolved to purchase a nuclear-powered submarine fleet to keep its northern passage free of U.S. and other submarines, only to drop the idea in 1989 as too expensive.

What forces, then, could transform the Soviet-U.S. relationship from diffidence to complex interdependence?

Domestic Politics and Economics

Convergence of the two countries' economic and political systems is not likely, nor is it necessary or sufficient for them to cooperate in a system of complex interdependence. Convergence is unlikely because of profound differences in the way each society has been formed and operates. Russian life has been formed by fiat from above; American, by forces rising from below. Even in the late 1980s perestroika and *demokratizatsiia* were initiated and guided from the Kremlin. Although market forces come to play a greater role in Soviet economic life, the CPSU will attempt to maintain state ownership of the means of production; even if the U.S. government does more to promote industrial competitiveness, most American factories and land will remain privately owned. Each society will adapt and evolve while resisting fundamental or revolutionary change. Parallel evolution of Russia and America is more likely than deep political-economic convergence.[19]

Democracy is probably not a precondition for complex interdependence. Indeed, democracy has its own dangers, illustrated by the frequent competition between America's two major parties to show which is the more patriotic and anti-Communist. If a Russian Patriots' Party gained power, it might well move to close off the country from Western influences, launch pogroms against Jews and other minorities, and possibly expand abroad to purify others from Western or Asiatic vandalism.

Still, the quality of domestic life certainly has some affect on a country's external behavior. Can a society at war with itself cooperate harmoniously with others? Perhaps despotism could coexist in a cold peace with another society, but it could not tolerate the varied contacts needed for complex interdependence. Indeed, a model for such relationships was sketched by Immanuel Kant in his essay *On Perpetual Peace*. He argued that national particularism can best be overcome by the growth of representative government, commerce, a common culture, and international law. Where "the consent of the citizenry is required . . . to determine whether there will be war," the citizens will hesitate before entering "so risky a game." A despotic ruler, conversely, can blithely declare war and leave it to his diplomats to justify the action. The *"spirit of trade*," Kant added, "cannot coexist with war." And although language and religion divide peoples, gradual progress toward agreement on common principles will be conducive to peace. As community prevails, "a transgression in *one* place in the world is felt *everywhere*. . . ." Because free governments will not tolerate any government over them, they will have to accommodate themselves to an enlarged body of international law that "will finally include all the people of the earth."[20]

The power of Kant's vision is suggested by the fact that in the almost two hundred years since he wrote, there has been virtually no war between liberal republics.[21] There is little prospect that the USSR will become a liberal republic in this century. But Gorbachev has pushed for more freedom—political, economic, cultural—to invigorate Soviet life. Within the Party, as in the soviets, he wants choice: free, multicandidate elections. It is conceivable that the CPSU may some day permit other parties or fronts to put forward candidates. Such moves were under way in Hungary, Poland, and the Baltic in the late 1980s, though they could easily be wiped out by a conservative counterrevolution. Indeed, Andrei Sakharov and others questioned whether the election system worked out in 1988–89 was not a sham.[22]

The CPSU will endeavor to guide Soviet democracy with a heavy hand, but glasnost' and other forces at work in the USSR are producing a more participative and mobile personality, one with rising empathy—the ability to evaluate distant objects and to incorporate distant values in oneself.[23] These trends reflect and contribute to a more cosmopolitan upbringing and education, greater attention to the media, the growth of "middle-class," urban values, greater personal freedom, and a greater capacity and desire for self-rule. Such a trend could be seen both within and outside the huge meeting hall where the CPSU Conference convened in 1988. Rank-and-file delegates as well as more distant TV viewers commented, "I thought I'd never experience such a thing in my lifetime." Though some disliked seeing the dirty linen in public, the experience whetted the appetite of many Soviet citizens for more of the same.

If the CPSU monopoly on privileged information and decision making is broken, if views other than the ruling Politburo's come to shape

[341]

state action, the result should be a less aggressive stance in foreign affairs. As more Soviet budget data are released, pressure will mount to cut defense spending.

Americans have learned to fear powerful dictators, seeing in each the image of Hitler. If the USSR is not ruled by a dictator, if the ruling Party itself provides a choice for the Soviet people, this would probably reduce American apprehensions. Even though most Soviet factories remain publicly owned, the less anticapitalist zeal in Russia, the less anti-Communist ardor in America.

If both countries move closer to Kant's ideal republic—consent of all the governed, a spirit of trade, a deeper participation in world culture, more dedication to law—this would also enhance the conditions needed for complex interdependence.

To reach and maintain complex interdependence it is essential that each society hold together and function so it contributes to and gains from ties with the other side. If perestroika does not halt the USSR's economic decline, nativist fears of foreign influences may revive. Economic collapse could evoke policy extremes such as autarky or aggression. The temptation to lash out at foreign devils may increase. The new rulers might be tempted to play their last trump—military power.

Convergence of values is more likely than of political and economic systems. Even before glasnost', urbanization and education were tilting the values of Soviet citizens (at least those living in the western and northern regions) toward those of contemporary Westerners. The new openness to outside influences and freedom from internal repression have stimulated the embrace of religion, rock music, political pluralism, avant-garde art, technological fetishism, and "enrichissez-vous" individualism and materialism. Even pacifism, ecologism, and national self-determination are asserting themselves openly from Riga to Erevan. The white three-fourths of the Soviet population must learn to coexist with a rising tide of Muslim and other minority values just as white Americans have had to adjust to assertions of black, Hispanic, red and now Asian power.

If such trends continue, the two societies may feel that what binds them is more important than what divides them. The experience of sharing and benefiting from interdependence should reduce the nativist tendencies toward xenophobia, black-and-white images of others, and dogmatism.

The ultimate attitudinal change conducive to peaceful participation in complex interdependence would be based on a paradigm similar to that suggested in Gorbachev's new thinking and in the notion of value-creating. It would place the values of humanity above those of nation, race, class, or creed; assert our collective responsibility to manage the biosphere in ways that enhance rather than destroy life; act on the understanding that the security of each depends on the security of all; and limit military force to last resort self-defense. It would see all life—local, national, transnational—as an enterprise for creating, not claiming, values. Mutual aid rather than mutually assured destruction would be the underlying principle.[24]

It would be an achievement to have leaders of all countries espouse these principles, but sermons will not suffice.[25] They must become driving forces within each country before they can be easily adopted on a world scale. New modes of upbringing, education, and interaction are needed, as well as new myths that inculcate devotion to humanity rather than to *mein Volk*.[26]

Still, complex interdependence does not require complete ethnic or class harmony within the USSR and United States. Russians may find it easier to solve problems with Americans than with Estonians, with whom they have shared an uncomfortable intimacy for centuries, one in which the larger party often abused the smaller creating wounds difficult to erase. And the U.S. president may find it easier to work with the general secretary to resolve civil strife in Angola than to deal with the grievances of Native Americans or black Muslims. International peace need not await total domestic harmony.

The World System

Many other Great Power reconciliations in the past have been spurred by a common enemy. The USSR and America once joined forces against Nazism, but no such threat looms in the foreseeable future. Concern over a rogue Third World government or terrorism does not equate to a shared danger from the Third Reich. But environmental threats are nearly palpable; they can be pushed off today's agenda, but they must surely be faced tomorrow.

Soviet and U.S. cooperation in complex interdependence is possible whether the world system is bipolar, multipolar, supranational, or even "unit-veto" (in which many nations exercise a nuclear threat).[27] What is important is that the role of military force recede—at least between the USSR and the United States—and that their societies link up through many channels and create values together. It is conceivable that this situation could develop in the context of a bipolar condominium: the superpowers cooperate and use sufficient force to keep others in line. It is less feasible

[343]

in a situation in which one country acquires unipolar dominion over all rivals—an unlikely development in any case.

The most feasible scenario for movement toward complex inter-dependence is that the USSR joins what is now the "trilateral world" of North America, Europe, and Japan. Nothing in the cards predicts a diminution of European or Japanese material power or, alternatively, a significant increase in their will for military power. Increasingly the trilateral bloc understands its responsibility for and vulnerability to the Third World. Accordingly, North-South ties deepen. If over time the USSR joins the North, then East-West tensions should decline while ties of shared experience and value creation mount. This trend demands evolution rather than revolution in Eastern Europe. It requires that the USSR relinquish its hold on the Warsaw Pact–CMEA countries and permit them to join the free world of postindustrial democracies.

Even if East-West relations shift toward complex interdependence, anarchy may increase in other parts of the global arena: South-North, South-South, or East-East. The growth of economic and ecological interdependence gives no clear guidelines for foreign policy. As military assets become less usable for many disputed issues, neither Moscow nor Washington will exercise the kind of hegemony that London enjoyed in the nineteenth century.[28]

Developments in the Third World and the Pacific Rim are more problematic than in Europe and North America. Will a resurgent China, Japan, India, or Pakistan disrupt the global trend toward cooperation amid diversity? If China retains its nuclear arsenal, will not India or Japan eventually insist on parity? And will not Pakistan or Taiwan some day do the same? So long as Israeli-Arab tensions fester and Israel maintains some kind of nuclear threat, will not one of its neighbors eventually acquire a "Muslim" bomb? Such prospects could stimulate cooperation between Moscow and Washington, but they could also break its back, magnifying Soviet-U.S. tensions just as the Indochina wars added to Chinese-Soviet differences from the 1960s through the 1980s.

Such problems could be better dealt with by a strengthened United Nations in which all centers of power found representation—from Buenos Aires and Brasilia to New Delhi and Tokyo. The more each country feels a stake in the global system of peaceful settlement and collective security, the less it would be tempted to claim its narrow goals in defiance of the majority.

Not every local dispute need disrupt Soviet-U.S. cooperation. Even in the 1980s the Iran-Iraqi war raged on, threatening some interests of each superpower but barely casting a shadow over the Gorbachev-Reagan meetings and accords. Ideally the superpowers would combine forces to prevent or quickly settle such disputes, but if that is impossible, they should deal with them in ways that promise no one-sided gain for either Moscow or Washington. The price of unilateralism in the Persian Gulf was paid twice by America's navy: first when the frigate *Stark* was hit by Iraqi missiles in 1987, and second when U.S. radars mistook an Iranian passenger plane for an attacking F-14.

A network of global economic security would be even more difficult to create, but a sense of movement in that direction would help to ameliorate East-West-South tensions. The USSR must, as Gorbachev and his advisers suggest, join GATT, make the ruble convertible, and take part in the IMF and other institutions of world commerce. Instead of carping at Western economic policies in the Third World, the Soviets should join the West in cooperative ventures aimed at creating values for East, West, and South. The most promising vehicles for such cooperation are probably the Specialized Agencies and Regional Commissions of the United Nations.

Despite much fanfare about joining in world trade, the USSR will have to overcome many self-imposed as well as external barriers. The country has little capital to invest overseas. Its "multinational" enterprises have been small and basically limited to trading rather than to production. They have operated under the cloud of ideological enmity toward international monopolies. Because the CMEA economies have not been export-driven in a manner similar to Japan and Korea, there has been little imperative to export manufactured goods in return for raw materials. Communist conservatism and risk-averse Soviet managers will be tempted to stick with familiar ways rather than wager their success in highly competitive world markets.[29]

Perestroika might break this pattern because it encourages individual Soviet ministries, firms, and other institutions to deal directly with counterparts abroad. Thus a Soviet factory manager told the 1988 Party Conference of his new freedoms:

> Comrades. . . if you'd told me five years ago that I could sign a piece of paper and one of my people could go abroad, if I'd dreamed that I were a general director and that I could make deals—Bulgaria, or North Korea, Hungary— I would have believed it impossible.
>
> I just got good news from the director of my foreign trade subsidiary. . . . He just got back from West Germany. He sold nine assembly lines to West Germany and Switzerland. He brought back three million green dollars. Of course, this is just peanuts for Comrade [Vladimir] Kamenstev [director of the new Ministry of Foreign Economic Relations]. But if he told me that half of this were mine—aaaaaahhhhhh. . . .[30]

Bilateral Issues

Complex interdependence requires extensive Soviet-U.S. inter-action in many spheres. Probably the goal should be that each economic-social system function relatively well on its own aided by a roughly balanced mutual dependence. Deep symmetrical interdependence might be the ideal; if this model is not attainable, there might be less friction if neither side becomes highly dependent on the other (witness the problems caused by one-sided dependencies in Canadian-U.S. relations).[31]

Since the late 1950s there has been a broad movement toward the establishment of informal as well as formal ties between Russia and America. Since 1986–87 this movement has increased, promising to create many formal and informal ties between governmental and nongovern-mental elites as well as ordinary citizens. Thus the joint statement issued after the Moscow summit, May 29–June 2, 1988, declared both govern-ments' intention to "intensify" bilateral ties in "transportation science and technology; maritime search and rescue; operational coordination between Soviet and U.S. radionavigation systems in the Northern Pacific and Bering Sea; and mutual fisheries relations." Gorbachev and Reagan welcomed a new accord on civilian nuclear reactor safety under the bilateral agreement on Peaceful Uses of Atomic Energy. They instructed their representatives to press ahead to achieve accords on maritime shipping, the Soviet-U.S. maritime boundary, basic scientific research, and emergency pollution clean-up in the Bering and Chukchi seas. They welcomed the start of bilateral discussions on ways to combat narcotic trafficking and consultations on the law of the sea and other areas of mutual interest in the field of law.

A rough content analysis of the long joint statement shows just over four full newspaper columns given to high politics, mostly arms control with a paragraph on regional issues such as the Horn of Africa and Afghanistan, four columns to cultural and scientific exchanges, and one paragraph to human rights and one to trade—the hardest nuts to crack.[32] Thus high and low politics got roughly equal treatment in the com-muniqué. Except for INF and Afghanistan, however, high politics in the statement was mostly aspiration; in culture and science, however, much fruitful progress had already been made and much more was likely. The projects approved in both domains would produce many contacts for years between officials and other citizens of both countries.

Use of multiple channels is encouraged by proliferation of communi-cation technologies with increasing speed and declining cost. "Space bridge" television programs permit Supreme Soviet deputies and U.S. congressmen to debate and rock audiences to see each other as they share the same music experiences. Some of these communications are artificially rigged and superficial, but the trend is toward greater depth.[33]

The multiplicity of goals and difficulty in arranging them hierarchically reflects the long-term development of the welfare state. Modern governments take responsibility for their citizens' welfare and security in a broad sense, not merely their military security.

In a setting of complex interdependence, when the USSR and United States disagree on some issue, bargaining will still take place, but with armaments kept far to the rear. Between Ottawa and Washington the threat of coercive power against each other's government is minimal, but the Canadian navy often uses force against errant U.S. fishermen. As the Canadian-U.S. case also shows, each side will exploit aspects of economic interdependence and transnational actors to gain bargaining leverage.[34]

What if a Soviet businessman could sell three million or three hundred million "green dollars" worth of goods in the United States? And what if an American did the same in Russia, being paid in some convertible currency? U.S. businessmen are certainly anxious to work out such deals in the USSR, but Soviet laws regarding joint ventures and other aspects of private enterprise remained vague and contradictory in the 1980s.[35]

Trade does not guarantee peace, for Germany was Russia's biggest trading partner in 1914 and again in 1941. Indeed, trade imbalances can lead to friction and customs wars such as between America and its Japanese and European partners.

Trade between Russia and America has always been low relative to each country's GNP and relative to its trade with other countries. Détente and moderation of tensions should lead to an expansion of Soviet-U.S. trade, but it may never reach high levels because the USSR has little to sell to the United States except petroleum. It is not clear that trade would increase a great deal if CoCom reduced barriers to high-tech exports or if Washington granted Soviet goods most-favored-nations treatment. Even if the Soviet economy modernizes and quality levels increase, the Kremlin may find its natural trading partners elsewhere. The better prospect for material ties is through joint ventures in which Americans and American firms work directly with their Soviet counterparts.

It is the STR—the scientific and technological revolution—that summons the complementary strengths of both societies: (a) to preserve and enhance our common habitat and its biosphere; (b) to create cheap, clean, and abundant energy; (c) to feed, house, and care for a much-expanded world population living on dwindling space; and (d) to explore the mysteries inside the earth and of outer space together. The Americans

[347]

lead in computers and many other essential tools; Soviets bring valuable assets to such work too, such as strength in pure mathematics. Many but not all Americans taking part in East-West studies in recent decades report that they gained as well as contributed.[36] As the USSR liberalizes and becomes more computerized, the quality of Soviet contributions is likely to rise.

The STR also provides a vehicle by which the USSR and Eastern Europe can simply join the efforts already uniting North America, Europe, Japan, and—albeit on a lesser scale—China, India, Israel, and some South American countries. Good science is open and international, thriving on constructive cross-fertilization. Secrets are hard to maintain in this milieu. Military security issues will become less inhibiting if the major countries share a complex interdependence.

Could the USSR "tolerate the neutrality" of Hungary, Poland, and other East-Central European states? Scholars at IMEMO answered yes in March 1989. Soviet civilian specialists on strategic affairs argued that there is no threat to the USSR from the West; that even a united Germany would not gravitate toward militarism because its prosperity and influence lie in exploiting the STR and international trade; that Eastern Europe has become a liability for the USSR and should do whatever necessary to become viable; and that the nuclear arsenals of France and Britain are maintained more for prestige reasons than because of fear or hostility toward the USSR. Low arms expenditures have benefited Japan and, to a lesser degree, Germany; Soviet analysts want their country to move in that direction. The Kremlin's achievement of parity with the United States has helped to devalue the utility of nuclear arms, but other countries have gained from this process—not the Soviet Union (or the United States).[37]

The drive of the Baltic countries for self-determination could lead to a conservative backlash—even to Soviet military rule in Tallinn, Riga, and Vilnius. But political and economic autonomy for the Baltic states could also create a transmission belt linking Russia to what Gorbachev says is its "European home." If Eastern European states and even Russia's border republics were allowed to become nonaligned, demilitarized, pluralistic market economies, they could ease Russia's struggle to share in the dynamism of the First World.

What about that ultimate guarantee of security and insecurity—deterrence? The place of military force has declined in superpower relations because of risks of escalation and the difficulty of conceiving a winning strategy. Nor have Moscow and Washington had great success in applying their mass and high tech in contests against smaller, more primitive peoples. These trends may continue, though they could be modified by the appeal of muscular strikes against rogue nations or terrorists.

In 1972 both countries had agreed to forswear strategic defenses and live hostage to each other's restraint. But both sides have also recognized that deterrence can fail and so have sought other steps—technical and political—to reduce the danger of deliberate or inadvertent attack.

Despite the cosmopolitanizing and peaceful tendencies posited in the scenario for Soviet-U.S. complex interdependence, it seems unrealistic to advocate absolute nuclear disarmament even for A.D. 2000 or 2020. Neither superpower would be advised to eliminate all nuclear arms. They should reduce but not eliminate their arsenals, keeping them at a sufficiently high level so that cheating from any quarter would convey no serious advantage to a potential aggressor. Perhaps Britain or France would feel sufficiently comfortable with its American connection to dispose of its arms altogether. If so, this would create a positive example for India and other threshold powers. But if Europe becomes more united, America might withdraw from the Continent, adding to incentives to maintain a European deterrent.

An example of the kind of reductions that might provide deterrence at lower but still stable levels of destructive power might be, for the United States and USSR, a dyad of 1,000 missiles with one warhead; a force one-third to one-half this size for China and for Britain and France (or Europe). The aim of such an arrangement would aim to leave all parties better off and no party worse off than it would be absent the pact.

The size and composition of the nuclear umbrella, however, is crucial. Each party must feel that it possesses an invulnerable deterrent capable of dissuading attack from any quarter or quarters. Soviet scholars at IMEMO in March 1989 suggested that the USSR and United States could get by with a force of 200 to 400 invulnerable weapons. (A Soviet general running for the Congress of People's Deputies proposed 50–70![38]) They downplayed the dangers of cheating so long as the remaining weapons are truly invulnerable; they minimized any problem for the USSR in having to live with a smaller number of weapons than its combined adversaries.

Movement to a minimum deterrent, of course, requires some assurance that nuclear weapons are not spreading to additional countries. Soviet specialists are quite aware of the special dangers posed by a Khomeini or Quaddafi armed with some kind of mass destruction terror weapon. This is one reason that they push for treaties to ban chemical and bacteriological weapons with extensive and intensive international verification procedures.

Whereas Americans tend to think that the safest place for a minimum deterrent is at sea (in submarines), Soviet specialists worry that sub-marines present great uncertainties: communication links could be severed or berzerk commanders could launch without authorization. Better to station the umbrella in mobile land-based missiles, or at ICBM sites protected by ABM defenses, or in airplanes. Given that no one can foresee the drift of technology or politics, perhaps the ultimate guarantee should consist of a strategic dyad or even a triad.[39]

Assuming that East-West-South cooperation becomes strong and stable, some Soviet scholars contemplate transferring the nuclear umbrella from individual nations to the United Nations. This idea probably strikes most Western analysts as impracticable because it makes excessive demands on international trust. After all, many states (including the USSR and India) have difficulty maintaining "international" peace even within their own borders. Still, that serious scholars consider such scenarios indicates the extent to which they believe military force has lost its meaning in world affairs.[40]

Means must be found to meet the security needs of India and other threshold countries other than resorting to the anarchy of further nuclear proliferation. Ultimately countries such as India and Pakistan must be persuaded that their domestic needs as well as their external security do not require nuclear weaponry. The answers to such problems are more likely to be found in regional arrangements than in external assurances. Still, Great Power disarmament might provide a useful example. Strengthened international institutions and security mechanisms should also be explored. The superpowers have already done a great deal to uphold the nonproliferation regime. Continuing and strengthening this regime will reinforce their perceptions of a shared interdependence.

To progress from détente through moderated tensions toward complex interdependence, the United States and USSR must progress on many fronts, capitalizing on each opportunity that emerges and avoiding the pitfalls and detours that lead back toward cold war and confrontation. They can utilize GRIT and tit-for-tat strategies to promote détente and moderated tensions; to move beyond that stage to transform their relationship will take an unprecedented steadiness and scope of vision, one broadly shared within each society and passed on from one generation to another. Cooperation in areas of high and low political saliency will take them toward strategic and functional interdependence.

Is such transformation possible? An analogous change overtook Europe in less than two generations. The European revolution had to overcome a legacy of hate and bloodshed that is absent in American-Soviet relations. Europe's transformation was aided by a widely shared fear of

[350]

Soviet Communist dominion and by a need for postwar reconstruction. Even though both pressures have receded, European unification continues. The threat of nuclear or ecological catastrophe facing the United States and USSR is more pressing (but less apparent) than the problems that faced Europe in the late 1940s. Still, today's world problematique—from ozone depletion to drought—makes headlines from New Delhi to Cape Town. Chernobyl has made Soviet citizens especially wary of nuclear power; but they are joined by increasing numbers of Ohioans and other Americans worried about nuclear pollution in their own backyards.

Global problems—hunger and many others—bring us back to immediate security issues. The famines threatening Africa and other parts of the world are among the problems too complex to be solved by any one country. More attention to such issues could take the superpowers' attentions away from potential space wars and back to earth, where the challenges of feeding, housing, and educating the globe's billions demand a synthesis of the best insights from Novosibirsk to Palo Alto to Ibadan and Hyderabad, and where none of us stands immune to the quirks of nature which, combined with those of man, can suddenly transform abundance to shortfall.

The value-creating approach to hard decisions helps to bridge the gap between political realism and utopianism. It suggests how narrow self-interest might be enhanced through mutual gain strategies with others. The approach is no panacea and very difficult to apply in practice. But it offers a more useful takeoff point than the zero-sum assumptions of Communist dogmatists and Western "realists" or the "everybody wins" school of optimistic idealists.

Notes

1. *War and Peace*, Epilogue, pt. 2.
2. Marshall D. Shulman, "The Superpowers: Dance of the Dinosaurs," *Foreign Affairs* 66, no. 3 (1987/88): 494–515.
3. See the recent upsurge of writings on the decline of empires by Mancur Olson and others; for some recent works, see Paul Kennedy, "Can the US Remain Number One?" *New York Review of Books* 36, no. 4 (March 16, 1989): 36–42; for a critique of "The Persistent Myth of Lost Hegemony," see Susan Strange in *International Organization* 41, no. 4 (Autumn 1987): 551–74; also Walter C. Clemens, Jr., "The Superpowers and the Third World: Aborted Ideals and Wasted Assets," in C. W. Kegley and P. J. McGowan, eds., *Sage International Yearbooks in Foreign Policy Studies*, Vol. VII: *Foreign Policy: USA-USSR* (Beverly Hills, CA: Sage Publications, 1982), 111–35.
4. See chapter 7 in this volume.
5. See Mikhail S. Gorbachev, *Perestroika: New Thinking for Our Country and the World* (New York: Harper & Row, 1987); less upbeat is Zbigniew Brzezinski, *The Grand*

Failure: The Birth and Death of Communism in the Twentieth Century (New York: Charles Scribners, 1989).

6. See "Gorbachev's Economic Program: Problems Emerge," Report by the Central Intelligence Agency and the Defense Intelligence Agency to the Subcommittee on National Security Economics, Joint Economic Committee, U.S. Congress, April 13, 1988, tables 1 and 3. Trade with the developed countries declined in 1985–87 relative to the previous three years; see table 8. The conclusions of Soviet economist Leonid I. Abalkin were no less dismal than those of the CIA-DIA report. He told the 1988 Party Conference that despite some positive shifts in the Soviet economy, the first two years of perestroika had achieved "no radical breakthrough" and the economy "still remains in a stage of stagnation." National income in 1986–87 had grown at a slower pace than during the stagnation years. Targets for resource savings were not met; indeed, this index performed worse than during the stagnation years. The gap between Soviet science and technology and world levels was continuing to expand, assuming "ominous proportions." Soviet decision makers were continuing to err in favoring quantity over quality, Abalkin charged.

Health Minister Yevgeny I. Chazov outlined the calamitous state of the country's public health record but noted some improvement in the last two years. For excerpts from these and other statements at the conference, see *The New York Times*, July 1, 1988, p. A6.

7. See Arthur M. Schlesinger, Jr., *The Cycles of American History* (Boston: Houghton Mifflin, 1986). For further analysis, see Joshua S. Goldstein, "Kondratieff Waves as War Cycles," *International Studies Quarterly* 29, no. 4 (December 1985): 441–44, and other references in his bibliography.

8. For Gorbachev on "Mr. Nyet," see chapter 7 in this book.

9. In 1976–79 the USSR cast two vetoes; the United States, nine; 1980–85 the USSR, four; the United States, twenty-five; in 1986–88, the USSR, none; the United States, thirteen. Tallies from Kevin J. Dunn, "Has Soviet Voting Practice Changed since Gorbachev?" (Boston University term paper, 1988).

10. For a systematic effort to learn from the past, see Alexander L. George, Philip J. Farley, and Alexander Dallin, eds., *U.S.-Soviet Security Cooperation: Achievements, Failures, Lessons* (New York: Oxford University Press, 1988); also Joseph S. Nye, Jr., "Nuclear Learning and U.S.-Soviet Security Regimes," *International Organization* XIL, no. 3 (Summer 1987): 371–402.

11. See Richard W. Stevenson, *The Rise and Fall of Détente* (Urbana: University of Illinois Press, 1985); Lincoln P. Bloomfield, Walter C. Clemens, Jr., and Franklyn Griffiths, *Khrushchev and the Arms Race* (Cambridge: MIT Press, 1966).

12. For more detailed consideration, see Kurt M. Campbell, "Prospects and Consequences of Soviet Decline," in Joseph S. Nye, Jr., Graham T. Allison, and Albert Carnesale, eds., *Fateful Visions: Avoiding Nuclear Catastophe* (Cambridge, MA: Ballinger, 1988), 153–70; Henry S. Rowen and Charles Wolf, Jr., eds., *The Future of the Soviet Empire* (New York: St. Martin's, 1988).

13. Walter C. Clemens, Jr., "Games Sovietologists Play," *Teaching Political Science* 3, no. 2 (January 1976): 140–60; idem, "An Austrian Solution for Eastern Europe," *The New York Times*, July 10, 1989, p. A18.

14. Oran R. Young, "International Regimes: Problems of Concept Formation," *World Politics* 32, no. 3 (April 1980): 331–56.

15. See the yearly *State of the World* reports by Lester R. Brown et al. of the Worldwatch Institute in Washington, D.C. (1988 and 1989 editions published in New York: W. W. Norton).

16. Robert O. Keohane and Joseph S. Nye, Jr., *Power and Interdependence* (Boston: Little, Brown, 1977), 24–25; also their review essay, "*Power and Interdependence* Revisited," *International Organization* 41, no. 4 (Autumn 1987): 725–53.

17. Keohane and Nye, *Power and Interdependence*, p. 37.

18. Ibid., p. 210; see also Sean M. Lynn-Jones and Stephen R. Rock, "From Confrontation to Cooperation," in Nye et al., *Fateful Visions*, pp. 111–32 at 126.

19. Zbigniew Brzezinski and Samuel P. Huntington, *Political Power: USA/USSR* (New York: Viking, 1964).

20. Immanuel Kant, *Perpetual Peace and Other Essays* (Indianapolis: Hackett, 1983), 107–43; emphases in the original. Kant praises "republics" but condemns "democracies." He treats all "democracy" as "pure democracy" in which there is no check on the ruler; hence democracy is another form of despotism.

21. See editors' "Conclusion" in *Fateful Visions*, pp. 215–16.

22. See "An Interview with Andrei Sakharov," *The New York Review of Books*, 36, no. 3 (March 2, 1989): 6, 7.

23. See Daniel Lerner, *The Passing of Traditional Society* (New York: Free Press, 1958), 47 ff.

24. On mutual aid versus the "survival of the fittest," see Petr Kropotkin, *Mutual Aid* (London, 1902).

25. On this argument by Pavel Simonov, see chapter 7.

26. The difficulty in countering simplistic chauvinism is illustrated in Andrei A. Gromyko's account of how his own "patriotism" began to be formed at birth. See his *Pamiatnoe*, 2 vols. (Moscow: Politizdat, 1988), I: 31–35. Anti-Americanism also began early. Gromyko's father used to explain how "America is richer than others . . . because Americans take with their own hands the wealth that belongs to others. Theodore Roosevelt was a crafty president"—to which a neighbor added: "Crafty and intelligent." Ibid., I: 17.

27. See Morton A. Kaplan, *System and Process in International Politics* (New York: John Wiley, 1957), 50–51.

28. See Aaron L. Friedberg, *The Weary Titan: Britain and the Experience of Relative Decline* (Princeton, NJ: Princeton University Press, 1988); also Keohane and Nye, *Power and Interdependence*, pp. 229, 242.

29. Geoffrey Hamilton, "Conclusions," in his edited work, *Red Multinationals or Red Herrings?* (New York: St. Martin's, 1986), 192–93; a more positive appraisal is Carl H. McMillan, *Multinationals from the Second World: Growth of Foreign Investment by Soviet and East European Enterprises* (New York: St. Martin's, 1987).

30. From statement by Vladimir P. Kabaidze, general director of the Ivanovo Machine Building Works, in *The New York Times*, June 30, 1988, p. A30.

31. Keohane and Nye, *Power and Interdependence*, p. 210.

32. Both governments also pledged support for intensified exchanges in culture and science including "Environmental Protection, Medical Science and Public Health, Artificial Heart Research and Development, Agriculture, and Studies of the World Ocean." They welcomed the beginning of work on "a conceptual design of an International Thermonuclear Experimental Reactor (ITER)" under IAEA auspices; the imminent institutionalization of the COSPAS/SAR-SAT space-based, life-saving global search and rescue system; and the WHO/UNICEF program to reduce preventable childhood death.

Reagan and Gorbachev endorsed bilateral and multilateral cooperation with respect to environmental protection including conservation of stratospheric ozone and a possible global warming trend. They agreed to expand civil space cooperation by exchanging flight opportunities for scientific instruments and exchanging results of independent national studies of future unmanned solar missions. They welcomed cooperation in the Arctic and Antarctic. They endorsed joint ventures, expanded trade, and expanded relations between Aeroflot and Pan American Airlines. Text of Joint Statement in Supplement to *Moscow News*, no. 24 (1988): 1–4; also in *Pravda*, June 2, 1988.

33. For periodic updates on Soviet-U.S. exchanges, see *Surviving Together* (Washington, DC: Friends Committee on National Legislation and the Institute for Soviet-American Relations, 1983–   ).

34. Keohane and Nye, *Power and Interdependence*, p. 225.

35. For a listing of 155 joint Soviet-foreign ventures, see *Interflo*, October 1988 and January 1989; the text of a Council of Ministers Resolution "On Further Developing the Foreign Economic Activity of State, Cooperative, and Other Public Enterprises, Associations and Organizations" is quoted in the January 1989 *Interflo*, taken from *Ekonomicheskaia gazeta*, no. 52 (December 1988) and *Izvestiia*, December 10, 1988.

36. On the views of U.S. participants in IIASA, see letters on file at the American

[353]

Academy of Arts and Sciences, Cambridge, Massachusetts; for a partial summary, see chapter 6. For an analysis of several earlier surveys, see Walter C. Clemens, Jr., *The USSR and Global Interdependence* (Washington, DC: American Enterprise Institute, 1978), 88–99.

37. This complaint is in N. Dolgopolova and A. Kokoshin, "Chemu uchat sud'by velikikh derzhav?" *Kommunist*, no. 17 (November 1988): 115–21 at 120–21. *Kommunist* article cited in the introduction to this volume, note 1.

38. Lt. General Dmitrii Volkogonov in *Novoe vremia*, no. 6 (February 3, 1989), 23.

39. Eliminating all stationary land-based missiles would remove a major source of vulnerability and end arguments about needing ABM defenses to shield land-based missiles.

40. See Walter C. Clemens, Jr., "Inside Gorbachev's Think Tank, World Monitor 2, no. 8 (August 1989): 28–36.

12

Managing Soviet-U.S. Relations:
Challenges and Choices

Can Russia Change? Can the Soviet Union Endure?

More than one hundred fifty years ago Pushkin sketched the bright future awaiting Russia but hinted that it might take five hundred years to accomplish. After Tatanya had been jilted by Eugene Onegin, she and her family rode by horse-drawn sleigh from their country estate to Moscow. Contrasting Russia's future with its early nineteenth-century reality, Pushkin exclaimed:

> When we expand further our frontiers
>   to beneficent enlightenment,
> In time (calculated by philosophic tables
>   about five hundred years),
> Our roads will surely change beyond measure:
> Paved highways uniting Russia
>   will intersect at this point and that.
> Iron bridges will stride forward
>   across waters in a wide arc.
> We shall part mountains, under water dig
>   daring tunnels,
> And the christened world will establish
>   a tavern at each station along the road.

For now our roads are bad;
    forgotten bridges decay.
At road stations the bedbugs and fleas
    don't stop biting for a minute.
No taverns. In a cold log hut
    pompous but meager,
    there hangs a price-list for show,
    tempting the appetite in vain,
While the rural Cyclopes
    repairs with a Russian hammer
    the light carriage made in Europe,
Blessing the ruts
    and ditches of the native land. [1]

The country has changed a great deal since 1830–31, when Pushkin wrote *Eugene Onegin*, but material Russia is closer to the rutted roads and menus "for show" of Pushkin's time than to his futuristic vision. There are continuities as well as striking changes linking and contrasting old and contemporary Russia. The country still lags the West (and now Japan) economically but has become—at least for a time—a military superpower. Nourished by Communist dreams as well as Russian cosmicism and titanism,[2] Soviet rulers no less than Alexander I and Nicholas II put forward grand plans for peace and harmony. Unlike the tsars, today's "new thinkers" claim to see little role for armed force in their external policies and offer to reduce some arms in which they are strong if their opponents reciprocate.

Civilizations rise and fall based on their ability to cope with challenges.[3] Tsarist absolutism—despite the efforts of many reformers from Peter the Great through Count Witte—did not adapt well to the challenges of modernization, the process by which societies are transformed under the impact of the Scientific-Technological Revolution (STR). This is a holistic process in which public and private institutions mobilize advances in science and technology to coordinate and control resources and individuals, gaining more power from inanimate sources. Both Russia and Japan started modernizing later than the West, but Russia has proved less adept than Japan, as suggested by Port Arthur, by the outcome of World War I, and now by Japan's economic-technological ascent and Soviet stagnation.[4]

Stalin complained that Russia had been beaten by others; he wanted to modernize so this would not recur. His methods proved useful for extensive industrialization, but they failed to produce qualitative changes that would tap the country's potential in the "technetronic age." Russia beat Germany and Japan in 1945, but not because the USSR surpassed them in modernization. By 1975 both countries were far ahead of Soviet society in living standards, democracy, and mastery of the STR.

Both Soviet and tsarist Russia have experienced great difficulty in shedding the institutions of command and control—and habits of obedience—that had some value in premodern times, but they cannot optimally energize a modern society. Soviet communism combined elements of old Russia with Western organizational forms and technology—inspired by a strand of Western thought (Marxism)—to struggle with the challenges of the early twentieth century. Lenin and Stalin reestablished a new empire on the ruins of the tsarist. The new regime promised to become a universal state with a universal religion. Even before Stalin's death it had stalled; by Brezhnev's passing it had clearly lost its dynamism; and under Gorbachev it is pulled and pummeled by internal and external threats. Can it survive? Can it adapt? Can it live in harmony with the rest of humanity? Or will it go down fighting?

Soviet civilization stands apart but in some ways belongs to Western and modern industrial civilization. Some problems facing Soviet communism are unique, but many are global in character. Gorbachev's Russia, like that of Peter the Great and Nicholas II, faces the perennial question of how to adapt to and keep up with modern technology and the social organizations that sustain and reflect this technology. Like the tsars, Gorbachev must also ask how, while adapting to challenges of modernization, to maintain traditional national values and the legitimacy of Communist ideology and institutions. How to preserve social order and centralized authority while promoting reform and unleashing the energies of a repressed people? Like the tsars, Gorbachev also faces the problems arising from a multinational empire in which the dominant group makes up only half the population and most of the other peoples prefer their own language and culture to Russian.

Compounding these challenges, Gorbachev's regime encounters global problems that directly or indirectly affect Soviet interests. What to do with the immense power for destruction or construction arising from nuclear and other modern technologies? What to do about the enormous gap between Third World living standards and those of the First and Second Worlds—a gap destined to multiply along with the rising populations and declining greenbelts of Africa, Asia, and Latin America. And how to reverse the planet's environmental decline—another threat to security—while rallying economic growth?

All these contradictions come together in the central question of this book: How to maintain security in a world that, Gorbachev says, is increasingly interdependent and when global problems require global

[357]

solutions? The same problem faces the United States and other governments. How can they retain sovereign control over their own fates while becoming more deeply enmeshed in transnational and international processes and organizations?

Soviet Dilemmas

The Soviet leadership faces at least fifteen issues on which it is likely to feel "damned if we do, damned if we don't." Originating in domestic problems, these issues quickly spill over to shape Russia's place in the world.

(1) Unless the USSR's technology and economy are modernized, the Soviet state could cease to be a major actor on the world stage and the Communist party could lose its authority. But to modernize may require injections of freedom, pluralism, and openness that cast a spotlight on the historical and current shortcomings of Soviet communism and create demands for alternative approaches that leave Marxist-Leninism on the ash heap of history.

(2) Unless market forces within the USSR are permitted to operate much more freely, the centralized command system will repress the forces of innovation, thrift, and hard work. But even the most liberal Eastern European systems—Yugoslavia and Hungary—have choked on Stalinist residues.[5] To go beyond these Eastern European experiments, however, could mean eroding the socialist model and the raison d'être for Communist rule.

(3) For perestroika to succeed, the Soviet system must be transformed. If the system is deeply altered, however, production and living standards will decline for some time until the new ways are mastered. Resultant unrest among the public and elites threatened by change could unseat the reformers and halt perestroika.

(4) Unless all manner of societal grievances are aired, they will fester and appropriate remedies will not be found. Permitting frank discussion of such grievances, however, may aggravate them, at least for a while. Baltic nationalists, for example, demand not only a full accounting of wartime deportations but a halt to contemporary Russification. Full documentation on the crimes of the 1940s, if made available, may well intensify resentment toward Moscow and Russian emigrants to the Baltic; incomplete documentation, however, will produce still other demands.[6]

[358]

(5) Unless the USSR's national minorities gain greater autonomy, interethnic cooperation within the country will suffer. Allowing greater autonomy, however, could also stimulate centrifugal forces—Central Asians gravitating toward Mecca and Balts toward Europe—generating a Great Russian backlash as well as demands for smaller groups within the Russian republic such as Jews, Volga Germans, and Crimean Tatars.[7]

(6) Unless Eastern Europeans experience greater freedom, their economic situation will suffer and their Communist leaderships will lose legitimacy. If Moscow loosens the reins on Eastern Europe, however, the Poles and others will gravitate westward and may try to defect altogether.

(7) If Moscow uses force to keep the Soviet nationalities and Eastern Europeans in line, this will contradict the new principles at home and undermine improved relations with the West and China. But unless force can be used or threatened against errant nationalists, the Soviet empire may well disintegrate.[8]

(8) Improvement of relations with Japan and China might require boundary revisions. A territorial concession to one neighbor will strengthen revisionist demands from Romania or other European neighbors as well as from Soviet republics (for example, Armenia vs. Azerbaijan) and Eastern European countries with claims against each other (such as Hungary and Romania).

(9) Unless perestroika succeeds, the Soviet military will increasingly be deprived of high-tech weapons similar to those in the American arsenal. The glasnost' that accompanies perestroika, however, may undercut the Soviet martial spirit and support for a substantial military establishment.[9]

(10) Unless the arms race can be contained, the USSR might not match the quality of Western arms and the Americans might score a breakthrough. To achieve significant arms limitations, however, requires permitting international on-site inspection of Soviet installations, exposing weaknesses as well as strengths and subverting the "vigilance" of the Soviet people.

(11) Unless nuclear arms are eliminated, Soviet and all civilization may perish in a nuclear war. If nuclear disarmament occurs, however, America's edge in "smart weapons" and exotic technologies might become more meaningful and China's capacity for mass mobilization could threaten Russia's empty spaces.

(12) Unless Moscow and Washington stop their zero-sum competition for the Third World, Soviet-American collaboration in other spheres will suffer. If Soviet military might is withdrawn from the Third World, however, most countries there will gravitate toward Western models, markets, and patrons.

(13) Unless Soviet economic institutions are liberalized and empowered to operate freely with transnational corporations and Western-dominated institutions such as the IMF, the USSR will not become a full-fledged participant in world economics and trade. Liberalizing foreign trade and opening the USSR to joint ventures, however, surrenders the controls by which the Soviet system has been shielded from foreign penetration. Without these defenses and with a convertible ruble, can Soviet-style socialism endure? Does not the USSR need a kind of "infant industries" protection while it seeks to catch up?

(14) Unless the USSR reduces its military advantages in East Central Europe, détente and arms control will stall. If Soviet troops are cut, however, Eastern Europe may be emboldened to seek autonomy or even independence; if détente proceeds "too far," American forces might withdraw from Europe, leaving a strong Germany that could again threaten Eastern Europe and the USSR.

(15) Unless the USSR conciliates with the West, the cold war will resume and grind on. But if the Soviet system relaxes its vigilance, domestic instability could increase, tempting the West to abuse a range of Soviet vulnerabilities.

Reviewing these dilemmas, some Soviet leaders and planners might prefer the known problems of the old ways to the uncertain gains and risks generated by the new ways of thinking and acting.

American Dilemmas

A different but related set of difficult choices confronts the United States:

(1) Should America want Gorbachev's reforms to fail or succeed? Without perestroika and glasnost', the USSR might slide back toward totalitarian dictatorship, not optimal for unleashing the country's energies but a system quite dangerous in decline. A wounded or cornered Bear could prove quite unpredictable.

If Gorbachev's reforms succeed, however, the USSR could become a more serious competitor economically, politically, and militarily. Greater mastery of the STR would make the Soviet Union more powerful; whether it uses this power aggressively is for a generation beyond Gorbachev to decide. A growing Bear might wish to apply its strength.

(2) Should the United States help Gorbachev and his reforms or "kick Russia while it's down"? If the West eases trade barriers and welcomes the

USSR into GATT and world commerce, the Soviet system might mellow and join humanity in a mutually rewarding partnership. But if the Soviet Union becomes a more active participant in world commerce and trade, it could subvert their institutions and practices from within and, in the long run, strengthen all aspects of Soviet power.

(3) If Washington keeps up military-political-economic pressures, either Russia will "convert" to capitalist democracy or perestroika will fail and Gorbachev fall. His successors will follow less innovative policies, but a resentful Kremlin might feel that it has a score to settle with America.

(4) With glasnost' the "captive nations"—the Soviet national minorities and Eastern Europeans—are more likely to revolt, thus weakening the Soviet empire. But if this occurs, American moral leadership is again tested; confrontation replaces détente in superpower relations; and the Kremlin is likely to use force against its subjects and perhaps outsiders as well.

(5) Gorbachev's smiles tend to reduce tensions and improve Soviet relations with Western Europe, China, and Japan as well as with the United States. This makes for a more tranquil world—at least for a time—and facilitates cooperation on various global problems of both high and low politics. But such conditions also subvert the West's willingness to invest in defense and maintain an alliance for containment, deterrence, and flexible response. If the Bear again threatens, will the free world be ready?

(6) What is the optimal blend of sticks and carrots? How can the West bargain from strength and make concessions at the same time? Does not the experience of the 1980s show that the Kremlin conciliates only when confronted with overwhelming force? If negotiating from strength evokes internal reform, withdrawal from Afghanistan, and asymmetrical INF cuts, should not the West keep up the pressure rather than ease up? But how then to adjust the pressure to avoid creating a cornered Bear syndrome?

(7) Unless both sides put a cap on military R&D, the arms volcano will steam on, costly and threatening some day to erupt. If America agrees to freeze military technology, however, we ignore a basic lesson of history: that humans will produce and then wield the most deadly weapons they can and surrender one of our major advantages vis-à-vis all competitors. We even diminish the chance of refining beam or other weapons that might destroy military targets with little collateral damage, thereby strengthening deterrence as well as defense.

(8) "Mutual security" and "lowest possible levels of arms for sufficiency" might sound good, but all recorded history shows that Hitlers, Pol Pots, and Quaddafis arise and threaten all within reach. It also shows

[361]

that governments do not keep bargains longer than their interests dictate. The USSR has shown a strong tendency to violate the spirit of arms accords and to exploit every ambiguity even though this undermines the stability arms control should promote. The more we disarm, the more trust we place in bilateral or multilateral accords, the greater the chance that some day our adversaries will radically exploit our vulnerabilities.

(9) Maintaining extended deterrence forces is expensive, but if we move toward nuclear disarmament, this neutralizes U.S. leadership in the one domain where America stands head and shoulders above the Japanese and Europeans: the size and quality of our nuclear arsenal. Radical arms reductions emasculate the mystique of American power, weaken the dynamism of research and development, and leave the United States increasingly vulnerable to unpredictable developments around the globe.

(10) Unless we can strengthen UN peacekeeping machinery, we are likely to be sucked into confrontations with the Soviet Union in the Third World. But how can we place confidence in a body controlled by an irresponsible bloc of otherwise powerless states—often voting in league with the USSR?

(11) How should the United States balance its commitments with its resources and problems? A major part of America's resources have been directed toward containing Soviet communism. But serious threats to America's way of life come now from environmental and economic problems, from commercial and trading challenges from other nations and blocs, from the spread of mass destruction weapons to a variety of Third World states and organizations, and from a decline in the work ethic and spiritual élan. This is a full plate of problems. How should we organize our energies to cope with them?

Unless Americans reverse the trends of recent decades, their power and influence will continue to decline relative to other states. Have our allies grown so strong and our erstwhile foes so tame that there is no need for an alliance leader? If so, the United States could devote more resources to its own spiritual, economic, and environmental revival.

(12) Americans find themselves with Soviets in a kind of prisoner's dilemma: if our side cooperates and the other prisoner reciprocates, we both can escape from our present entrapment; but if we cooperate and he defects, we suffer and he wins the prize; if he should trust us and we do not reciprocate, we win and he loses. Given that neither of us can trust the other, is it not smartest to guard against the other's defection and still have some chance for the big prize? The rub is that if both sides "defect," we remain trapped where we have been for decades: on the treadmill of arms race and cold war. The way to minimize loss and maximize gain is to spurn common cause and do what seems best for ourselves.

[362]

Joint Dilemmas

Posing survival questions as though the USSR and United States were both prisoners of circumstances—victims of fate without any opportunity to learn and communicate or create mutually useful safeguards—leads to blind alley paralysis. If both sides see their problem in egotistical terms as a *prisoner's* dilemma, narrow rationality tells them to avoid cooperation and to defect even though neither wins if both follow this course. If they see their situation rather as a shared *prisoner's* dilemma—a situation in which both can gain only if they cooperate— enlightened self-interest dictates cooperation.

In real life the players can talk and plan together; they can learn from past experiences; they can construct safeguards to ensure that if one side cheats, the consequences for the other will not be catastrophic and the defector will gain no serious advantage. Because there are endless rounds to their game played across many dimensions and through many channels, no one play is likely to be decisive. Rather, the game goes on so that small gains from cooperation accumulate, overshadowing the one big prize or punishment posited in a single PD encounter. Myopia might say "defect now" or when the other side lets down its guard; far-sighted rationality replies, "No, stay with the cooperative course that both parties win, gaining ever more as they put aside fear."

A different set of questions now becomes salient for both sides.

(1) What is the optimal way to enhance security and protect our respective ways of life—endless zero-sum competition or cooperation for mutual gain?

(2) What poses the greater threat to our security—the malevolent capability of the other side or our inability to contain our escalating capabilities for mutual destruction and those of third parties?

(3) Is the greater threat from the other's weapons or from the rising tides of economic and environmental problems that engulf each nation and the global habitat?

(4) If all this seems too naive, is it not a fact that both the USSR and the United States have suffered more than they have gained from arms racing, from military interventions abroad, from covert actions? Has not Moscow's most successful operation in the Third World been not Ethiopia or Angola, but India, which Soviet leaders treated with much respect and little bullying, helping over time to create a strong partner in mutually useful interdependence? Has not America's most successful foreign policy been the Marshall Plan, an exercise in mutual planning, contributions, and gains planned and implemented openly?[10] Do not the American failure in

[363]

Vietnam and Russia's in Afghanistan speak volumes about the dysfunctional costs of military intervention in the modern world?[11] Does not our brush with Armageddon in October 1962 tell us how fragile are the minds, hearts, and communications that endeavor to succeed at crisis management?

(5) Faced with extreme poverty and inequities at home and globally, faced with a greenhouse effect and depleted ozone shield, with global pollution of air, land, and water, with desiccation and rising populations, with pandemic disease, with military arsenals so powerful that even a partial use could bring on a nuclear winter, and with still other global problems, how can we jeopardize our survival and that of future generations by conducting traditional power politics?

(6) Are not such global problems sufficiently pressing to lead the Kremlin and White House to forge their swords (at least most of them) into plowshares? Are the USSR and United States split by a larger and deeper enmity than that which separated Germany from the rest of Western Europe after the world war? Has there been a millennium or more of Russian-American blood-letting in which the relatives of today's living killed one another? Do Russia and America have territorial disputes such as Alsace-Lorraine? No? Then what prevents them from transcending their conflicts as the European community did within a single decade?

What prevents Russia and America from moving in the same directions as America has with Japan and with China, despite their mutual blood-letting in the last half century, a phenomenon completely unknown in Russian-U.S. relations?

Granted that the world is "contradictory but integral and interdependent," what to do about it? Two basic approaches exist: to claim for oneself whatever one can take, or to create and share values with partners.[12] The first approach—the zero-sum or value-claiming orientation—underlies the struggle for power among rival nations: seize whatever values are available even if (or especially if) this hurts other claimants. Value claiming, history suggests, can produce short-term gains—at least for some segments of the claiming society—but tends to backfire in the longer run.[13]

Rather than focusing on claiming values for themselves, the superpowers would be better advised to coordinate efforts to create values of use to themselves and all humanity. Rather than dividing a limited pie, they should produce an ever bigger and more nutritious one.

Like the actors in PD, the superpowers are interdependent—strategically and in other ways. Interdependence was a fact of life noted by Karl Marx even in 1848. But it is an even more assertive and widespread reality at the end of the twentieth century. Governments may yearn for autarky, but as Shakhnazarov has noted, pursuit of this option will ensure that a nation falls ever further behind in the realms of science, wealth, and culture.[14]

What, then, should the superpowers do about their interdependence—their capacity to help or hurt each other? If they distrust and disdain each other, each will opt for a strategy that minimizes losses from the other's self-seeking and maximizes its own potential gain. Ironically, however, when both act in this way following what seems to be self-interest, both suffer. In the PD game, each must serve a jail term; in real life, each may be condemned to another round of arms racing or confrontation. The other option—instead of narrow pursuit of self-interest—is to coordinate policies with the other player. In the game the reward is freedom. In world politics it could mean an end to self-inflicted punishments and the opening of a new era in which mutual gain replaced mutual and assured destruction.

Present realities offer both challenges and opportunities. If they are not to follow the fate of the dinosaurs, today's superpowers must learn how to convert their fragile détente into a process that moves steadily toward reducing tensions and building cooperative ties, avoiding the many impulses to lurch back toward cold or even hot war. The previous chapter showed how domestic, global, and bilateral developments in Soviet-U.S. relations permit the two sides to move toward a partnership based on complex interdependence—one in which the two societies are linked on many levels, governmental and nongovernmental, in which the agenda of interstate relationships has no clear or consistent hierarchy, and in which military force plays a declining role. In such a relationship they can both focus on creating instead of claiming values.

Such a transformation could—but need not—threaten others. Indeed, the easiest and most rewarding way to achieve it would be for the USSR and East Central Europe to join the network of complex interdependence gradually encompassing North America, Western Europe, and Japan. This transformation toward mutually enriching interdependence should be open to all countries, each participating in whatever way its capacities permit.

There is a profound truth in the song lyrics, "We are all in the same boat," sung by a Soviet as well as other diplomats at Ambassador Arthur Hartman's Thanksgiving dinner at Spasso House in 1985. Still, recognizing our mutual vulnerability, we can choose to push with or against each other.

Russia can and must change; so must others.

[365]

Notes

1. Alexander Pushkin, *Eugene Onegin*, author's translation.
2. On Russian "cosmicism," see chapter 7 in this volume.
3. Arnold J. Toynbee, *A Study of History*, abridged 2-vol. ed. (New York: Oxford University Press, 1946).
4. There are five requirements for latecomers to modernization: (1) the ability to borrow extensively from abroad without losing the sense of national identity and the capacity to adapt foreign institutions to domestic ends; (2) the conversion of premodern patterns of coordination and control from their original purpose of preserving a predominately rural and agrarian society to that of fostering rapid change; (3) the adoption of policies to accelerate the growth of the traditional economy as a basis for modern economic growth; (4) rural-urban migration at a rate commensurate with development of political and economic capacities; and (5) rapid spread of primary education and provision of technical and advanced education. See Cyril E. Black et al., *The Modernization of Japan and Russia: A Comparative Study* (New York: Free Press, 1975), 3–4, 234.
5. For a case study, see Ronald H. Linden, "The Impact of Interdependence: Yugoslavia and International Change," *Comparative Politics* 18, no. 2 (January 1986): 211–34.
6. The impact of glasnost' and democratization on "inter-nationality" problems was noted by Gorbachev at the Party Conference on June 28, 1988, text in *Literaturnaia gazeta*, June 29, 1988, pp. 2–7 at 5. For this interaction in one republic, see Walter C. Clemens, Jr., "Estonia, A Place to Watch," *The National Interest*, no. 13 (Fall 1988): 85–92.
7. Rasma Karklins notes that "integration and conflict can exist side by side." *Ethnic Relations in the USSR* (Boston: Unwin Hyman, 1986), 224. But it is difficult to overestimate the feelings unleashed by fears of cultural genocide. See V. V. Koroteeva and M. N. Mosesova, "Problemy natsional'nykh iazikov i ikh otrazhenie v obshchestvennom soznanie (po materialam pisem chitalei v tsentralnye gazety)," *Sovetskaia etnografiia*, no. 5 (September-October 1988): 4–14.
8. See Maya Latynski and S. Enders Wimbush, "The Mujahideen and the Russian Empire," *The National Interest*, no. 11 (Spring 1988): 30–42.
9. Thus while seeming to approve Gorbachev's reforms, General Aleksandr Lizichev, head of the armed forces Main Political Directorate, found it necessary in 1988 to rebut suggestions put forward in many Soviet publications that the USSR should implement unilateral military cuts, if only because the burden of defense lies heavier on the USSR than on the United States. Lizichev dismissed these arguments, saying: "People who propose unilateral disarmament can only be either naive or [persons] who are singing a foreign line." The USSR must maintain sufficient defense so "if some madman wants to attack us, he receives a worthy answer." Interview reported in *The Christian Science Monitor*, June 30, 1988, p. 14.
10. In two surveys conducted among Wilson Center Fellows in 1976–77 and in 1986–87, the Marshall Plan was ranked as the leading success of U.S. foreign policy since 1917; Vietnam, the greatest failure. See Walter C. Clemens, Jr., "America's Greatest Achievement in Foreign Affairs," *Christian Science Monitor*, June 4, 1987, p. 17.
11. Gorbachev's final report to the Party Conference on June 28, 1988, complained that the former regime's use of "command-administrative" modes of decision making by a small group not consulting collectively led to inadequate responses to the opportunities and problems in foreign affairs. He called instead for the "democratization of international relations."
12. Thus the USSR "gained" from unilateral extractions (valued at over $20 billion) from Eastern Europe for a decade after the world war, only to be faced by enormous political and military costs. Had the USSR instead created values with the Eastern Europeans along the lines of the Marshall Plan in the West (costing the United States just over $13 billion), Soviet and Eastern European interests and relations would have been placed on a much sounder footing. A similar pattern has bedeviled Moscow's relations with virtually all its

neighbors: exploitative Soviet policies have backfired and spawned deep long-term problems. America's experiments with manipulating other peoples—from Iran to Central America—have also tended to boomerang.

13. The distinction is elaborated in David A. Lax and James K. Sebenius, *The Manager as Negotiator: Bargaining for Cooperation and Competitive Gain* (New York: Free Press, 1986).

14. For Shakhnazarov's views, see chapter 7 in this book.

Glossary

ABM antiballistic missile (as in ABM defenses limited by 1972/74 accords)
ABM battle management radar a radar that provides information for ABM defenses
ASAT antisatellite weapon
ASEAN Association of Southeast Asian Nations
ATTU Atlantic to the Urals
Ballistic missile a missile that flies to its target on an elliptical path outside the atmosphere
CoCom Coordinating Committee on Multilateral Export Controls (from Western nations and Japan to Communist nations)
"Complex interdependence" model for international and transnational relations (analyzed in chapter 11)
Counterforce strike attack against military forces, especially strategic weapons and command centers
Countervalue strike attack against cities and industries
"Correlation of forces" Soviet conception much broader than the military balance of power on which some Westerners dwell; it entails economic, political, and other factors, including the trend of the class struggle
CPSU Communist Party of the Soviet Union
Cruise missile unmanned, self-propelled vehicle whose flight is sustained by aerodynamic lift over most of the flight path; flies like an airplane at low altitudes to its target
CSEC Conference on Security and Cooperation in Europe
CTBT comprehensive test ban treaty
Deterrence military strategy calculated to inhibit an attack through terror of retaliation (usually *ustrashenie* but sometimes *sderzhivanie* [containment or restraint] in Russian); "deterrence" tries to prevent an attack whereas "defense" seeks to protect against one
Early warning radar a radar to warn that a ballistic missile attack is under way and give preliminary tracking data
ECOMIN Ecology-Man-Interaction project
FBS forward-based systems, especially aircraft
GATT General Agreement on Tariffs and Trade
Glasnost' giving voice, expressing the truth, at least within currently accepted limits of CPSU tolerance
GLCM ground-launched cruise missile such as the Tomahawk deployed in 1983

[369]

Globalistika "globalistics," the Soviet rubric for interdisciplinary analysis of global problems, especially when rooted in Marxism-Leninism

"*Global problems*" Soviet term for problems too complex for one nation to solve alone

GNP gross national product

"*High politics*" security and sovereignty issues in world politics, akin to *die Grosse Politik*

ICBM land-based intercontinental ballistic missile (range over 5500 km)

ICJ International Court of Justice

IIASA International Institute for Applied Systems Analysis, Laxenburg, Austria, formed with U.S.-Soviet cooperation

IISS International Institute for Strategic Studies, London

IMEMO Institute of World Economics and International Relations of the USSR Academy of Sciences

Interdependence the condition of mutual vulnerability; a concept that many Soviet analysts before 1985 treated as a propaganda mask for Western neocolonialism

IRBM intermediate-range ballistic missile such as the Soviet BGM-109G (known in the West as the SS-20) and the U.S. Pershing 2

IRM intermediate-range missile, range 500–5500 km, possibly armed with a conventional or nuclear warhead

INF intermediate-range forces or the 1987 treaty to eliminate them

KGB Committee for State Security

"*Kto kovo?*" Leninist conception that politics is a zero-sum contest (spelled *kto kogo* but pronounced *kto kovo*)

"*Low politics*" economic, scientific, cultural, and other issues with comparatively low political saliency; issues that call for functional cooperation across national borders

LPAR large phased-array radar using an electronic scan antenna to track many items simultaneously; defined in the ABM Treaty as a phased array radar with a potential (the product of mean emitted power, in watts, an antenna area, in square meters) greater than 3 million

LRINF longer-range INF (1,000–5,000 km)

MEMO journal of IMEMO, *f.v.*

MIRV multiple independently targetable reentry vehicles

NATO North Atlantic Treaty Organization (formed in 1949)

NRDC Natural Resources Defense Council (private agency)

Paradigm conceptual model that bounds people's mental horizons until it is displaced by a new way of thinking that seems to permit them to think and act more effectively

Perestroika Gorbachev's evolving plan to restructure the economy and other aspects of Soviet life

P2 or Pershing 2 U.S. ballistic IRM deployed in 1983

PNET Peaceful Nuclear Explosions Treaty

Preemption striking first so as to emasculate the opponent's presumed intent and ability to attack; differs from preventive war, which is motivated by an unfavorable shift in the balance of power

[370]

Prisoner's dilemma (PD) game theory test of coordination versus defection; differs from a *prisoners'* dilemma in which both sides perceive their problems as common, requiring value-creating rather than value-claiming solutions

Realpolitik political realism, power politics

Regime a particular governmental system; also a set of rules, institutions, or expectations guiding international behavior

RSFSR Russian Soviet Federative Socialist Republic

SALT I and II strategic arms limitations talks and treaties (1972, 1979)

SAM surface-to-air missile

SDI Strategic Defense Initiative ("Star Wars")

SLBM submarine-launched ballistic missile

SLCM sea-launched cruise missile

SRINF shorter-range INF (500–1000 km)

SRAM short-range attack missile

SRM short-range missile, range under 500 km

SCSC Standing Consultative Commission of Soviet and U.S. representatives to monitor SALT accords

START strategic arms reduction talks (U.S. term for strategic arms negotiations in the 1980s)

STR "scientific-technological revolution" recognized by USSR since the late 1960s

Throw-weight maximum weight of nuclear warheads, decoys, reentry vehicles, and guidance systems that can be carried on the powered stages of a ballistic missile. The lengthy definition in Article II.7, Second Agreed Statement of SALT II, however, contains several ambiguities that need clarification

TTBT Threshold Test Ban Treaty

Value claiming acting or negotiating to obtain unilateral gains

Value creating acting or negotiating to generate joint gains

VNIISI All-Union Scientific Institute for Systems Research

V/STOL vertical/short takeoff and land aircraft

"World problematique" complex of interrelated issues studied by the Club of Rome

WTO Warsaw Treaty Organization (formed in 1955); also Warsaw Pact

Zero-sum politics belief or reality that one side wins what the other loses

About the Author

WALTER C. CLEMENS, JR. is professor of political science at Boston University and adjunct research fellow, Harvard Center for Science and International Affairs. This book is based upon thirty-five years of research and travel to the USSR. Clemens is the author of *The Arms Race and Sino-Soviet Relations, The Superpowers and Arms Control*, and *Outer Space and Arms Control*; and co-author of *Khrushchev and the Arms Race; World Perspectives on International Politics*; and *Toward a Strategy of Peace*. He has contributed frequently to the columns of the *Christian Science Monitor, The New York Times*, and *Wall Street Journal* as well as to scholarly journals.

The author is a member of the International Institute for Strategic Studies and has been president, International Studies Association, New England. He has lectured in many countries under auspices of the U.S. State Department and was Executive Officer, Arms Control and Disarmament Committee, White House Commission on International Cooperation Year. He has served as an interpreter for Soviet delegations to the United States and has been a frequent traveler to the USSR and Eastern Europe.

Index

Gorbachev, Mikhail S. *(continued)*
testing 209, 255, 268; nuclear war 174; peace 280; perestroika 170, 265, 269, 324–5, 331; *Pravda* article 191, 192; Reagan 70, 263, 265, 274; relations with West 189, 360; revolution 172; rise to power 136, 171, 279; socialsim 171, 173; Stalin 3; style 199–200; technology 186, 279, 360; Third World 171, 173, 176, 186; tit-for-tat 209; unemployment; United Nations 189–91, 193; Western support 198, 360; war 168; zero option 277
Gradual and reciprocal initiatives in tension reduction (GRIT) 262, 350
Great Britain 62, 102, 153, 295; arms control and disarmament 64, 349; INF treaty 307; Middle East 291; nuclear arsenal 209, 329, 348
Grechko, Andrei 111
Greenberg, Daniel 150
Greenhouse effect 364
Greenland 235
Green Revolution 126
Grenada 7, 38, 45, 327
Ground Launched Reconnaissance Drones 305
Gromyko, Anatolii A. 170
Gromyko, Andrei A. 23, 85, 87; China; chemical weapons 296; presidency 170, 201, Reagan 108–9
Guevara, Ché 11
Guinea 46
Gvishiani, Dzherman M. 38, 147–53, 157, 179

Hague Conferences (1899, 1907) 62, 63, 64
Haig, Alexander 267
Hardin, Garrett 133
Hartman, Arthur 137, 365
Helsinki Final Act 296–7; Soviet compliance 271, 288; trade 297
Helsinki process 47, 78, 81, 122
High politics xx, 49, 346; Cold War 147; limited collaboration 121; relation to low politics 157, 159–60, 337–9
Hitler, Adolf 102, 331, 342, 361; *see also* Stalin
Holy Alliance 60, 61
Honecker, Erich 45, 272
Hong Kong 41
Hoover, Herbert 124
Human rights 168, 232, 328, 346
Hungary: economy 358; uprising xxiv, 10, 46, 79, 330, 341; Soviet intervention 106, 222, 312, 348, 359, 373

Hercules Plant 217
Hypersonic boost glide vehicle 306

ICJ 190, 191, 311, 327
ICBM 239, 289, 299–302; accuracy 77, 82, 86; balance 78; testing 103
IIASA 129, 147–9, 152–6, 159
IISS 230, 234, 308
Iklé, Fred 188
IMEMO 129; chemical weapons 270; Europe security 232, 273, 348; global problems; INF treaty 259; nuclear weapons 312, 349; socialism 180; Soviet defense 259, 269–70
Imperial Academy of Sciences 145
Imperialism 24
India: domestic problems 350; nuclear weapons 105, 273, 344; Pakistan 44; partnership with Soviet Union 7–8, 12, 20, 25, 43, 44, 48, 79, 105, 183, 326, 363; STR 348; Tamils 183; Indirect advance 48, 106
Indonesia 12, 37
INF Treaty 214–21, 246, 273, 276, 302, 308; asymmetrical cuts 211–17, 259–60, 276; compensation 218, 254, 307, 334; double zero 214–16; economy 220–1, 266, 328; enlightened self-interest 277; Euromissiles 216, 219–21, 278, 297, 304, 305, 338; European response 217, 220, 272; future 183, 254, 255, 261; NATO 70, 220–21; negotiations 231, 276, 361; new thinking 199, 220, 259; verification xxii, xxiii, 307–9, 354; zero option 215, 277; *see also* Arms control and disarmament; LRINF; Pershing 2; SRINF
Information technology 186
The Influence of Sea Power 63
Inozemstev, N. 149
Institute for U.S.A. and Canadian Studies 192, 193
International Atomic Energy Agency 124, 190, 235, 269–70, 327
International Congress on Logic, Methodology and the Philosophy of Science 193
International Labor Organization 125
International Monetary Fund (IMF) 245–6, 334, 345, 360
Interparliamentary Union 64
Inversion 47–8, 109, 136, 143, 324
Interconnectedness 30, 34, 35, 80, 115, 168
Interdependence: future of 329, 364–5; Gorbachev xvii, 172, 179, 184, 187; independence 182; mutual security 122, 331, 324; Soviet criticism 125, 134; *see also* complex interdependence
Iran 46; Soviet Union 5, 21, 36, 327; U.S. 327